11-19

THE AMERICAN CANON

The American Canon

LITERARY GENIUS FROM EMERSON TO PYNCHON

★ ★ ★ ★ ★ ★ ★ ★ ★ ★ ★ ★ ★

Harold Bloom

Edited by David Mikics

THE LIBRARY OF AMERICA

THE AMERICAN CANON
Introduction, headnotes, and volume compilation copyright © 2019 by
Literary Classics of the United States, Inc., New York, N.Y.
All rights reserved.

Published in the United States by Library of America.
Visit our website at www.loa.org.

Some of the material in this volume is reprinted with the permission of holders
of copyright and publishing rights. See acknowledgments on page 425.

Distributed to the trade in the United States by Penguin Random House Inc.
and in Canada by Penguin Random House Canada Ltd.

Library of Congress Control Number: 2019944549
ISBN 978–1–59853–640–9

1 3 5 7 9 10 8 6 4 2

Printed in the United States of America

Contents

Preface

READERS WHO ASSOCIATE Harold Bloom's name with Romantic poetry, the plays of William Shakespeare, and the Western canon may be surprised by the extent of his writings on American authors. His reflections on our national literature, written over fifty years, have until now been widely scattered, much of it unknown even to his most devoted readers. This book brings these writings together. It includes a number of introductions Bloom wrote for his anthologies of critical essays on various American authors, but I also excerpt from the following books (a few of them long out of print): *The Ringers in the Tower* (1971), *Figures of Capable Imagination* (1976), *Wallace Stevens: The Poems of Our Climate* (1976), *Poetics of Influence* (1988), *How to Read and Why* (2000), *Genius* (2002), and *The Daemon Knows* (2015).

Bloom has defined a canon of American writers, and this book respects his definition. He has long argued for a visionary tradition of American writing that can inspire every reader. The forefather of that tradition is Ralph Waldo Emerson, the first writer represented here. The selections are chronological by the authors' birth dates, beginning with Emerson, born in 1803, and ending with Thomas Pynchon, born in 1937. I have chosen to represent the figures about whom Bloom has made his strongest, most memorable arguments, and have omitted some well-known figures toward whom he has displayed mixed feelings in his criticism. Bloom is our most appreciative and wide-ranging critic of the American canon, and this book is intended to inspire readers to revisit the works discussed. Readers are encouraged to skip around and follow their own interests and impulses, but this book will also reward reading from beginning to end.

The pieces included here have been selected, arranged, and edited to make a single coherent work. This inevitably entailed ironing out small inconsistencies, cutting or updating dated references, and making other small changes; in the very few instances where something more substantive seemed desirable, I have consulted with Bloom and worked with him to come up with new wording.

Introduction

IN 1933 T. S. Eliot, lecturing at the University of Virginia, railed against a modern world "worm-eaten with liberalism." Eliot, who was from St. Louis, Missouri, had become a British subject six years earlier. Already the most influential critic of the twentieth century, he yearned for an orthodoxy that would impose moral law on a nation made homogeneous in "race" and manners, an impossible goal in America. In his Virginia talks, Eliot dabbled in anti-Semitism: "Reasons of race and religion combine to make any large number of free-thinking Jews undesirable," he proclaimed.

Many miles north of Virginia, also in 1933, a three-year-old Jewish toddler named Harold Bloom was learning to read Yiddish in his mother's kitchen in the East Bronx. Several years later, at age seven or eight, he would discover in the Melrose branch of the Bronx Public Library an American poet named Hart Crane, who burned with the heretical romantic flame that Eliot detested. That same year Bloom read *Moby-Dick* and exulted with Melville's doom-eager Ahab. (Meanwhile, oceans away, the Germans and Japanese were setting fire to the globe.) In high school he plunged into Faulkner's cauldron of Gothic torments and marveled at how the southern master raised shlock to the status of high art. In college at Cornell, Bloom studied with M. H. Abrams, who had begun to rehabilitate the Romantic poets against the wishes of Eliot. But when Bloom arrived at Yale graduate school, he entered a den of Eliotic orthodoxy. The lions of New Criticism glowered at the Yiddish-speaking proletarian from the Bronx.

"When I was a child, my ear had been ravished by Eliot's poetry, but his criticism—literary and cultural—dismayed me," Bloom later wrote. At Yale in the 1950s, Eliot's judgments were largely sacrosanct. He had deemed the Romantics dangerous eccentrics, Emerson and Whitman bad influences. Bloom was ready to fight back. By the 1980s, when I arrived at Yale grad school, Bloom's new anti-Eliot canon had won out: it included the central American Romantics Emerson, Whitman, Dickinson, Melville, Faulkner,

Stevens, and Bishop. Bloom had single-handedly made a revolution in literary taste, and American writers were basic to his vision.

Bloom likes to speak about the "daemon," the intimate yet alien spirit that makes literature a sublime influence on us. When we read one of Dickinson's cryptic, diamond-sharp lyrics, when we chase after Faulkner's nightmare-harried Joe Christmas or scale that "harp and altar, of the fury fused," Hart Crane's Brooklyn Bridge, we glimpse these authors' daemons. We grasp at least fitfully what makes their brilliance so true, so overwhelming. There are as many daemons as there are individuals, but exposing yourself to the radiance of Bloom's American masters will strike any genuine reader with the force of revelation.

Bloom defines the daemon as the inspiring power that appears whenever we write or read a work of true imagination, but also, following Yeats, as an aspect of personal destiny that both "delivers and deceives." The daemon is the highest and deepest force within the self, yet is somehow not of the self. It "runs a scale from divinity to guilt," Bloom writes, and so impels nightmares as well as creative joy. The daemon also runs between writers in the form of literary influence, the main and abiding preoccupation of Bloom's critical writing.

Bloom wrote his most famous book, *The Anxiety of Influence*, in a few days following a personal crisis in the summer of 1967. The book is dense, compact, and marked by a homemade jargon, but it shines with Bloom's new discovery: that writers, when they create new work, misread their precursors. In order to become who they are—to be original—they must deny their literary ancestors' true significance. The insight is a Freudian one, as Bloom knew: earlier authors are like the parents that their children must falsify and rebel against. So Melville, who announced in a letter, "I do not oscillate in Emerson's rainbow," turned the Sage of Concord into a mere confidence man, and Henry James slighted Hawthorne, whom he called simple and unsophisticated, unlike James himself.

Bloom is not always loyal to his anxiety-of-influence theory. He often suggests that authors have a clear-eyed, rather than distorted, view of their precursors. So Dickinson, Bloom persuasively says, answers Emerson's tough hopefulness with her iron-sealed guarantees about the permanence of loss. Writerly strength requires a far-reaching awareness of the literary parent's presence in you: so Stevens is finely conscious of Emerson and Whitman, Cormac McCarthy of Melville and Faulkner. Writers tend to either swerve away from their precursor, establishing their difference (Bloom calls this *clinamen*), or else complete that precursor, giving a fuller, possibly more drastic vision (the Bloomian term is *tessera*).

The primary American writer for Bloom, the most influential of them all, is Emerson. The inescapable American Romantic thinker. Emerson is the apostle of the self that, no matter how severe the blows of fate it suffers, returns to its own light and recovers its strength. The pessimistic angel with whom Emerson competes for Bloom's soul is Sigmund Freud, the twentieth century's far darker believer in fundamentally ironic lives: We do not—we cannot—know the truth about what we're doing, Freud insists. Whether we are daring or cautious in our loves, these loves cannot sufficiently transform us. Every bout of eros leads us back to the parents whom we first struggled with, and who always win the battle.

Emerson, again, is the Ur-precursor for American writers—so Bloom declares. All later authors must take him into account, whether they battle for or against his credo. Emerson's enemies, like the poet and critic Yvor Winters, charge that the Sage of Concord endorses "impulse as if it were conscience." Bloom's Emerson, by contrast, is a thoughtful quester after illumination who sounds by turns sweet, civilized, and barbaric. The impatient Emerson thirsts for an original relation to the universe, as distinct from a view of the universe, whole or partial. Emerson is a solitary: his moments of transport separate him from other people. Such aloofness is the ground of American imagination, Bloom argues, and our greatest authors know this. We feel we are only truly ourselves when alone with the universe—or the abyss.

Bloom knows that the American will to go it alone has damaged our politics and social life. In a memorable formulation, Bloom once wrote that "Emerson bet the American house (as it were) on self-reliance." "Contemporary America is too dangerous to be laughed away," he continues, "and I turn to its most powerful writers in order to see if we remain coherent enough for imaginative comprehension." Individualism, he also argues, "is more than ever the only hope for our imaginative lives." Literary greatness speaks to the private self and cannot be adjudicated by those who, following the herd, choose books for reasons other than their aesthetic power.

Isolation is really inner freedom, our writers tell us. "The American religion of self-reliance carries with it the burden that no American feels wholly free until she is truly alone," Bloom remarks. Our poets tend to be lone dreamers: Whitman, Dickinson, Eliot, Crane, Bishop, Ashbery, and more. Whitman, Bloom points out, for all his encomia of the mingling crowd, flees from its embrace, refusing to be known by others. Our novelists too cherish the solitary, strongly imaginative hero or heroine: Dreiser's Carrie, Cather's Ántonia, Fitzgerald's Gatsby, Hawthorne's Hester, James's Isabel Archer. Huck Finn's loneliness is a wild freedom, but he suffers from it too.

Bloom is a personal and passionate reader who prizes the face-to-face. For him reading resembles falling in love: the author who chooses you turns you inside out, making the world look utterly new and strange. Bloom explains that he read Whitman with new intensity in 1965, during his time of crisis. "Walt, more than any other poet, pulls you close to him," Bloom comments. Bloom needs the direct encounter with an author, and no author is more direct than Whitman: he expertly shows how Whitman's evasiveness fuses with his immediacy.

Whitman is a healer, and his soothing, puzzling incantations help us through our dark nights. Facing Whitman's poetry, Bloom asks, "How to convert my ravishment by this into knowledge?" One way ravishment becomes knowledge is by giving us a sharp sense of limits, and the primary human limit is death. Bloom cites Whitman's lines about the grass that springs from buried flesh in "Song of Myself": "This grass is very dark to be from the white heads of old mothers, / Darker than the colorless beards of old men, / Dark to come from under the faint red roofs of mouths." Then he marvelously notes that this is "a passage Hemingway must have pondered, since his characteristic voice—evenly weighted, usually precise, emotionally deferred—is both anticipated and surpassed by it." Whitman is the larger spirit because, unlike Hemingway, he sees that there is something beyond death and fate: the daemonic self's freedom, which for him feels like a cure.

Melville, unlike the compassionate Whitman, is a thundering prophet, and "Prophets do not heal; they exacerbate," as Bloom rightly says. The ardent Ahab stands for the side of American power that sees truth in vast ruin. He fathers the lethal, thrilling heroes of Faulkner and Cormac McCarthy. There is real danger in such taste for destruction, and Bloom knows it. Yet he insists that the daemon instructs, rather than merely filling us with Ahab's mad passion to strike at the gods. These days Melville's Pequod seems a microcosm of twenty-first century America, with its discordant voices crisscrossing throughout Ishmael's encyclopedic voyage.

Bloom traces a lineage of independent heroic women in American letters, from Hester Prynne to Isabel Archer to Faulkner's Lena Grove. Cather, Wharton, and Dreiser too produced superb heroines in their fiction. Standing against patriarchal threats, these women exhibit a quiet, stubborn power. Hawthorne's Hester clinging to her scarlet A is "our truest feminist," Bloom remarks, a rebel against Puritan patriarchy. Lena Grove in Faulkner's *Light in August* moves us because, oddly serene, she stands apart from the turbulent actions that surround her. "There are in Faulkner uncanny moments of listening," Bloom writes, "as if his narrative art sought a still center, where racial and personal violence, and the agonies of copulation and dying, could never intrude."

The contemplative "still center" that Bloom ascribes to Faulkner is a powerful factor in James, Hawthorne, and, among later novelists, Willa Cather and Ursula Le Guin. Le Guin describes a "solitude without privacy," Bloom notes. Stringently devoted to the communal, she still enshrines the sole self. In *The Left Hand of Darkness*, which describes an ambisexual, androgynous society, Le Guin redefines intimacy, liberating it from Oedipal fears. Her alien characters are nonerotic questers, moved by knowledge rather than sex. This utopian dream is American too, especially these days, when information technology charts our longings, promising to tell us who we are. Cather, who long precedes the reign of cybertech, inhabits a different world, the wide empty prairies of the Midwest. For her, self-knowledge is the haunting perception of lost beauty, embodied in Ántonia and Mrs. Forrester of *A Lost Lady*. Cather's pure, clear artistry makes her, for Bloom, one of the handful of great modern American novelists.

At the opposite pole from Cather's dead-sure composure stands Hart Crane, who was, like Faulkner, a sublime raider of the inarticulate. Dead before his thirty-fourth year, Crane had an absolute, unerring drive to consummation in both life and art. His poems are an orchestrated ecstasy, so rich and intense that they can both bewilder and intoxicate readers. Bloom has been fascinated by Crane's dense, hypnotic lines for more than seventy years now. For Bloom, in a sense, Crane will always be *the* poet.

But Bloom has devoted far more pages to Wallace Stevens than he has to Crane. In his life, Stevens was everything the reckless Crane was not: a cautious Hartford burgher, vice president of an insurance company. Stevens writes poems of visionary desire coupled with scholarly playfulness and a sense of how the extraordinary springs up within the everyday. For Stevens, the sublime returns at unexpected times, often subtly or in the sharp accents of the restless mind. Stevens's great lyric "The Poems of Our

Climate" puts it best: "The imperfect is our paradise. / Note that, in this bitterness, delight, / Since the imperfect is so hot in us, / Lies in flawed words and stubborn sounds."

Though he treasures Stevens's lucid, composed energy, Bloom also loves the hard-bitten extremist Nathanael West, whom he calls a "rhetorician of the abyss," a born nihilist who suffers "the messianic longing for redemption, through sin if necessary." West's humor "has no liberating element whatsoever," Bloom acknowledges. Like the scandalous Jewish Gnostic Jacob Frank, Bloom says, West launches a cry of outrage against the created world.

Bloom also relishes authors who, unlike West, pose imaginative extremism against a quieter yielding to beauty. Consider Eudora Welty's Lorenzo Dow in her incandescent story "A Still Moment." Dow, a preacher speeding along the Natchez Trace, hungers for souls as he rides headlong to his next revival meeting. But then, Bloom remarks, Dow gets distracted by beauty, "remains haunted by a vision greater than he can account for, and yet can never deny": the snowy white heron he glimpses at the story's end.

There are surprises in store for the reader in Bloom's criticism. He writes that Dickinson "in scores of her strongest poems compels us to confront the part that gender plays in her poetic identity." He is finely attuned to authors' readings of themselves. Bloom sees Hemingway's matchless story "The Snows of Kilimanjaro" as a summing up of the author's self-criticism: "If you love too much, and demand too much, then you . . . will wear it all out." Similarly, Nabokov in "The Vane Sisters" reflects on the limits of his own aesthete's skepticism. In Bloom's hands the message of Carson McCullers becomes a piercing irony: "We, as readers, also would rather love than be loved, a preference that, in the aesthetic register, becomes the defense of reading more intensely lest we ourselves be read, whether by ourselves or by others."

Poe is Bloom's bête noire, but nonetheless a central American mythmaker. "Emerson, for better and for worse, was and is the mind of America," Bloom comments,

> but Poe was and is our hysteria, our uncanny unanimity in our repressions. . . . Emerson exalted freedom, which he and Thoreau usefully called "wildness." No one in Poe is or can be free or wild. . . . To begin is to be free, god-like and Emersonian-

Adamic, or Jeffersonian. But for a writer to be free is bewildering and even maddening. What American writers and their exegetes half-unknowingly love in Poe is his more-than-Freudian oppressive and curiously original sense and sensation of overdetermination. . . . No one in a Poe story was ever young. As D. H. Lawrence once angrily observed, everyone in Poe is a vampire—Poe himself in particular.

Bloom concludes that Poe's weakness and despair, contending against Emerson's life-giving power, left their mark on American letters, especially the haunted writers of the South. And there is perhaps a kinship between the depressed Poe and those playwrights, like O'Neill and Albee, who describe what Bloom calls the "nightmare realities" of the American family. To these writers we can add Theodore Dreiser, since "Dreiser, like Poe," Bloom argues, is a harsh determinist who "tap[s] into our common nightmares."

In a different key than Dreiser, Ralph Ellison exemplifies for Bloom both Emersonian wildness (in the narrator of *Invisible Man*) and an apocalyptic paranoia presaging Thomas Pynchon (in the novel's character of Ras the Destroyer). Bloom's favorite personage in *Invisible Man* is Rinehart, a con man and shape-shifter. "Rine the rascal" is a slippery player who dwells in chaos, predicting the entropy-laden universe of Pynchon.

Among recent American novelists, Bloom most values Pynchon, DeLillo, McCarthy, and Roth. He seems particularly moved by Roth's rebellious creativity, so passionate in its scorn for all that is wholesome and acceptable, including mainstream Judaism. Yet Roth, too, is unalterably Jewish. Being a Jew, a fact so hard to describe, so hidden and so crucial, becomes for Bloom an emblem of the lonely self, brooding powerfully over its status as wanderer and outcast, and warring against all conventions, all the false promises that society makes.

Bloom loves McCarthy's *Blood Meridian* more than any other contemporary novel. He confesses that he failed to read it on his first two attempts, appalled by the book's relentless descriptions of carnage. Judge Holden, who survives the book's scalping expedition, is McCarthy's immortal god of war, a stupendously dedicated killer. Bloom compares the Judge, a gigantic albino without eyebrows, to Moby Dick rather than Ahab: he is a permanent enigma. *Blood Meridian*, like the works of Homer and Shakespeare, has a "morally ambiguous greatness," Bloom says, and in that respect it resembles America's conquest of the West, with all its terrifying slaughters.

American intellectuals have always had an uneasy relationship with the ferocious visionary enthusiasm that their countrymen and -women so often display. The American thirst for awakened, God-endorsed selfhood frequently strikes the intellectual as both reckless and naively romantic. Thirty years ago Bloom wrote *The American Religion*, a canny, spirited account of what he called our "post-Christian" sects. All of them, Bloom argued, insist on the self's direct knowledge of God, from Mormons to Pentecostals to Christian Scientists. Bloom was surprised by these believers' fierce certainty that God and the true self were one and the same. Jesus, they often said, knew and loved each of them personally, and even "falling in love was affirming Christ's love for each of them," Bloom wrote more recently. "In such a labyrinth of idealizations I get lost," he added, "lacking the thread that might lead to an escape." For Bloom, Jewish skeptical wisdom demands that we rein in such American zeal, our country's never-ending thirst to be loved by God. If there is chosenness, it must be conditional.

Bloom, a lifelong man of the left, laments the dire politics that often results from the American taste for unfettered, God-approved selfhood: self-absorbed greed, worship of power, the cult of masculine regeneration through violence. Yet he also genuinely admires his heretical enthusiasts, since they have their hands on the daemonic live wire. The wonder at an alien God runs in Bloom's veins as surely as in those of a snake handler from the Florida panhandle. Homgrown religious oddballs appeal to him as they did to Flannery O'Connor, whom he greatly admires. The daemon rides roughshod and splendid when a writer like O'Connor can turn raw American spiritual struggle into art and when a critic like Bloom can bring together the country's literature with its strange yearning for a God who validates selfhood.

We need more of Bloom's daemonic eagerness. Identity politics, censorious and condescending, not readerly passion, rules the day in many classrooms. The academy all too often produces criticism that lacks personal vision and directness, an injustice to both readers and books. At the opposite end of the spectrum, the American religion that exalts God in the lone self too frequently offers passionate vision untempered by sufficient critical skill. Making great art out of vision means testing and criticizing, not merely yielding to Dionysus. Bloom pursues the superior visions, the ones that depend on thought rather than raw instinct, and that's why we cherish his writing.

"Poems, novels, stories, plays matter only if we matter," Bloom writes. We ought to think about books the same way we think about ourselves. Why do books mean so much, why do they have the force to astound and cure, denounce and explain, condemn and save us? If we are curious enough about these questions, we might unlock the daemon, the inspiring secret that Bloom has been on the track of since he was a child lashed by Hart Crane's sublime words. His criticism opens us up the way Crane opened up the eight-year-old Bloom, by showing why some books matter to us like life and death. He is still our most inspirational critic, still the man who can enlighten us by telling us to read as if our lives depended on it: because, he insists, they do.

THE AMERICAN CANON

Ralph Waldo Emerson
(1803–1882)

E MERSON IS an experiential critic and essayist, and not a Transcendental philosopher. He is the mind of our climate, the principal source of the American difference in poetry, criticism, and pragmatic postphilosophy. That is a less obvious truth, and it also needs restating, now and always. Emerson, by no means the greatest American writer, perhaps more an interior orator than a writer, is the inescapable theorist of all subsequent American writing. From his moment to ours, American authors either are in his tradition, or else in a counter-tradition originating in opposition to him. This continues even in a time when he is not much read, such as the period from 1945 to 1965 or so. But since then, Emerson has returned, burying his undertakers. "The essays of Emerson," T. S. Eliot remarked, "are already an encumbrance," one of those judicial observations that governed the literary academy during the Age of Eliot, but that now have faded into an antique charm.

Other judicial critics, including Yvor Winters and Allen Tate, sensibly blamed Emerson for everything they disliked in American literature and even to some extent in American life. Robert Penn Warren culminated the counter-traditional polemic of Eliot and Tate in his lively sequence "Homage to Emerson, On a Night Flight to New York." Reading Emerson's essays in the "pressurized gloom" of the airliner, Warren sees the glowing page declare: "There is / No sin. Not even error." Only at a transcendental altitude can Warren's heart be abstract enough to accept the Sage of Concord, "for / At 38,000 feet Emerson / Is dead right." At ground level, Emerson "had forgiven God everything" because "Emerson thought that significance shines through everything."

Sin, error, time, history, a God external to the self, the visiting of the crimes of the fathers upon the sons: these are the topoi of the literary cosmos of Eliot and his southern followers, and these were precisely of no interest whatsoever to Ralph Waldo Emerson. Of Emerson I am moved to say what Borges said of Oscar Wilde: he was always right. But he himself always says it better:

> That is always best which gives me to myself. The sublime is excited
> in me by the great stoical doctrine, obey thyself. That which shows
> God in me, fortifies me. That which shows God out of me, makes
> me a wart and wen. There is no longer a necessary reason for my
> being.

One might say that the Bible, Shakespeare, and Freud show us as caught
in a psychic conflict, in which we need to be everything in ourselves while
we go on fearing that we are nothing in ourselves. Emerson dismisses the
fear and insists upon the necessity of the single self achieving a total autonomy, of becoming a cosmos without first ingesting either nature or other
selves. He wishes to give us to ourselves, although these days supposedly
he preaches to the converted, since it is the fashion to assert that we live in
a culture of narcissism, of which our President is the indubitable epitome.
Emerson, in this time of Trump, should be cited upon the limitations of all
American politics whatsoever:

> We might as wisely reprove the east wind, or the frost, as a political
> party, whose members, for the most part, could give no account
> of their position, but stand for the defense of those interests in
> which they find themselves. . . . A party is perpetually corrupted
> by personality. Whilst we absolve the association from dishonesty,
> we cannot extend the same charity to their leaders. They reap the
> rewards of the docility and zeal of the masses which they direct. . . .
> Of the two great parties, which, at this hour, almost share the nation
> between them, I should say, that, one has the best cause, and the
> other contains the best men. The philosopher, the poet, or the reli-
> gious man, will, of course, wish to cast his vote with the democrat,
> for free trade, for wide suffrage, for the abolition of legal cruelties
> in the penal code, and for facilitating in every manner the access
> of the young and the poor to the sources of wealth and power. But
> he can rarely accept the persons whom the so-called popular party
> propose to him as representatives of these liberalities.

Emerson writes of the Democrats and of the Whigs (precursors of our
modern Republicans) in the early 1840s, when he still believes that Daniel Webster (foremost of "the best men") will never come to advocate the
worst cause of the slaveholders. Though his politics have been categorized

as "transcendental anarchism," Emerson was at once a believer in pure power and a prophet of the moral law, an apparent self-contradiction that provoked Yvor Winters in an earlier time and A. Bartlett Giamatti more recently. Yet this wise inconsistency led Emerson to welcome Whitman in poetry for the same reasons he had hailed Daniel Webster in politics, until Webster's Seventh of March speech in 1850 moved Emerson to the most violent rhetoric of his life. John Jay Chapman, in a great essay on Emerson, remarked that, in his polemic against Webster, Emerson "is savage, destructive, personal, bent on death." Certainly no other American politician has been so memorably denounced in public as Webster was by Emerson:

> Mr. Webster, perhaps, is only following the laws of his blood and constitution. I suppose his pledges were not quite natural to him. He is a man who lives by his memory; a man of the past, not a man of faith and of hope. All the drops of his blood have eyes that look downward, and his finely developed understanding only works truly and with all its force when it stands for animal good; that is, for property.

"All the drops of his blood have eyes that look downward": that bitter figuration has outlived every phrase Webster himself ventured. Many modern historians defend Webster for his part in the Compromise of 1850, by which California was admitted as a free state while the North pledged to honor the Fugitive Slave Law. This defense maintains that Webster helped preserve the Union for another decade, while strengthening the ideology of Union that culminated in Lincoln. But Emerson, who had given Webster every chance, was driven out of his study and into moral prophecy by Webster's support of the Fugitive Slave Law:

> We are glad at last to get a clear case, one on which no shadow of doubt can hang. This is not meddling with other people's affairs: this is hindering other people from meddling with us. This is not going crusading into Virginia and Georgia after slaves, who it is alleged, are very comfortable where they are:—that amiable argument falls to the ground: but this is befriending in our own State, on our own farms, a man who has taken the risk of being shot or burned alive, or cast into the sea, or starved to death, or suffocated

in a wooden box, to get away from his driver: and this man who has run the gauntlet of a thousand miles for his freedom, the statute says, you men of Massachusetts shall hunt, and catch, and send back again to the dog-hutch he fled from. And this filthy enactment was made in the nineteenth century, by people who could read and write. I will not obey it, by God.

As late as 1843, Emerson's love of Webster as incarnate Power had prevailed: "He is no saint, but the wild olive wood, ungrafted yet by grace." After Webster's defense of the Fugitive Slave Law, even Emerson's decorum was abandoned: "The word *liberty* in the mouth of Mr. Webster sounds like the word *love* in the mouth of a courtesan." I suspect that Emerson's deep fury, so uncharacteristic of him, resulted partly from the violation of his own cheerfully amoral dialectics of power. The extraordinary essay on "Power" in *The Conduct of Life* appears at first to worship mere force or drive as such, but the Emersonian cunning always locates power in the place of crossing over, in the moment of transition:

> In history, the great moment is, when the savage is just ceasing to be a savage, with all his hairy Pelasgic strength directed on his opening sense of beauty;—and you have Pericles and Phidias,— not yet passed over into the Corinthian civility. Everything good in nature and the world is in that moment of transition, when the swarthy juices still flow plentifully from nature, but their astringency or acridity is got out by ethics and humanity.

A decade or so before, in perhaps his central essay, "Self-Reliance," Emerson had formulated the same dialectic of power, but with even more exuberance:

> Life only avails, not the having lived. Power ceases in the instant of repose; it resides in the moment of transition from a past to a new state, in the shooting of a gulf, in the darting to an aim. This one fact the world hates, that the soul *becomes*; for that for ever degrades the past, turns all riches to poverty, all reputation to shame, confounds the saint with the rogue, shoves Jesus and Judas equally aside. Why, then, do we prate of self-reliance? Inasmuch as the soul is present, there will be power not confident but agent.

To talk of reliance is a poor external way of speaking. Speak rather of that which relies, because it works and is.

Magnificent, but surely even the Webster of 1850 retained his Pelasgic strength, surely even *that* Webster works and is? Emerson's cool answer would have been that Webster had failed the crossing. I think Emerson remains *the* American theoretician of power—be it political, literary, spiritual, economic—because he took the risk of exalting transition for its own sake. Admittedly, I am happier when the consequence is Whitman's "Crossing Brooklyn Ferry" than when the Emersonian product is the first Henry Ford, but Emerson is canny enough to prophesy both disciples. There is a great chill at the center of his cosmos, which remains ours, both the chill and the cosmos:

> But Nature is no sentimentalist,—does not cosset or pamper us. We must see that the world is rough and surly, and will not mind drowning a man or a woman; but swallows your ship like a grain of dust. The cold, inconsiderate of persons, tingles your blood, benumbs your feet, freezes a man like an apple.

This is from the sublime essay "Fate," which leads off *The Conduct of Life* and culminates in the outrageous question: "Why should we fear to be crushed by savage elements, we who are made up of the same elements?" Elsewhere in "Fate," Emerson observes: "The way of Providence is a little rude," while in "Power" he restates the law of Compensation as "nothing is got for nothing." Emerson is no sentimentalist, and it is something of a puzzle how he ever got to be regarded as anything other than a rather frightening theoretician of life or of letters. But then, his personality also remains a puzzle. He was the true American charismatic and founded the actual American religion, which is Protestant without being Christian. Was the man one with the essayist, or was only the wisdom uncanny in our inescapable sage?

A biography of Emerson is necessarily somewhat redundant at best, because Emerson, like Montaigne, is almost always his own subject, though hardly in Montaigne's own mode. Emerson would not have said: "I am myself the matter of my book," yet Emerson on "History" is more Emerson than history. Though he is almost never overtly autobiographical, his best lesson nevertheless is that all true subjectivity is a difficult achievement, while supposed objectivity is merely the failure of having become an amalgam of other selves and their opinions. Though his is in the oral tradition, his true genre was no more the lecture than it had been the sermon, and certainly not the essay, though that is his only formal achievement, besides a double handful of strong poems. His journals are his authentic work and seem to me poorly represented by all available selections. Perhaps the journals simply ought not to be condensed, because Emerson's reader needs to be immersed in their flow and ebb, their own experience of the influx of insight followed by the perpetual falling back into skepticism. They move endlessly between a possible ecstasy and a probable shrewdness, while knowing always that neither daemonic intensity nor worldly irony by itself can constitute wisdom.

The essential Emerson begins to emerge in the journals in the autumn of 1830, when he was twenty-seven, with his first entry on Self-Reliance, in which he refuses to be "a secondary man" imitating any other being. A year later (October 27, 1831) we hear the birth of Emerson's reader's Sublime, the notion that what moves us in the eloquence, written or oral, of another, must be what is oldest in oneself, which is not part of the Creation, and indeed is God in oneself:

> Were you ever instructed by a wise and eloquent man? Remember then, were not the words that made your blood run cold, that brought the blood to your cheeks, that made you tremble or delighted you,—did they not sound to you as old as yourself? Was it not truth that you knew before, or do you ever expect to be moved from the pulpit or from man by anything but plain truth? Never. It is God in you that responds to God without, or affirms his own words trembling on the lips of another.

On October 28, 1832, Emerson's resignation from the Unitarian ministry was accepted (very reluctantly) by the Second Church, Boston. The supposed issue was the proper way of celebrating the Lord's Supper, but the underlying issue, at least for Emerson himself, was celebrating the self as God. Stephen Whicher, in his superb *Emerson: An Organic Anthology* (with David Mikics's *The Annotated Emerson*, the two best one-volume Emerson collections), gathered together the relevant notebook texts of October 1832. We find Emerson, sustained by daemonic influx, asserting:

"It is light. You don't get a candle to see the sun rise," where clearly Jesus is the candle and Emerson is the sunrise (prophetic, like so much else in early Emerson, of Nietzsche's *Zarathustra*). The most outrageous instance of an inrush of God in Emerson is the notorious and still much derided Transparent Eyeball passage in *Nature* (1836), which is based upon a journal entry of March 19, 1835. But I give the final text from *Nature*:

> Crossing a bare common, in snow puddles, at twilight, under a clouded sky, without having in my thoughts any occurrence of special good fortune, I have enjoyed a perfect exhilaration. I am glad to the brink of fear. . . . There I feel that nothing can befall me in life,—no disgrace, no calamity, (leaving me my eyes,) which nature cannot repair. Standing on the bare ground,—my head bathed by the blithe air, and uplifted into infinite space,—all mean egotism vanishes. I become a transparent eyeball; I am nothing; I see all; the currents of the Universal Being circulate through me; I am part or particle of God.

Nature, in this passage as in the title of the little book, *Nature*, is rather perversely the wrong word, since Emerson does not mean "nature" in any accepted sense whatsoever. He means Man, and not a natural man or fallen Adam, but original man or unfallen Adam, which is to say America, in the transcendental sense, just as Blake's Albion is the unfallen form of Man. Emerson's primal Man, to whom Emerson is joined in this epiphany, is all eye, seeing earliest, precisely as though no European, and no ancient Greek or Hebrew, had seen before him. There is a personal pathos as well, which Emerson's contemporary readers could not have known. Emerson feared blindness more than death, although his family was tubercular and frequently died young. But there had been an episode of hysterical blindness during his college years, and its memory, however repressed, hovers throughout his work. Freud's difficult "frontier concept" of the bodily ego, which is formed partly by introjective fantasies, suggests that thinking can be associated with any of the senses or areas of the body. Emerson's fantastic introjection of the transparent eyeball as bodily ego seems to make thinking and seeing the same activity, one that culminated in self-deification.

Emerson's power as a kind of interior orator stems from this self-deification. Nothing is got for nothing, and perhaps the largest pragmatic consequence of being "part or particle of God" is that your need for other people necessarily is somewhat diminished. The transparent eyeball passage itself goes on to manifest an estrangement from the immediacy of other selves:

> The name of the nearest friend sounds then foreign and accidental: to be brothers, to be acquaintances, master or servant, is then a trifle and a disturbance.

This passage must have hurt Emerson himself, hardly a person for whom "to be brothers" ever was "a trifle and a disturbance." The early death of his brother Charles, just four months before *Nature* was published in 1836, was one of his three terrible losses, the others being the death of Ellen Tucker, his first wife, in 1831, after little more than a year of marriage, and the death of his first born child, Waldo, in January 1842, when the boy was only five years old. Emerson psychically was preternaturally strong, but it is difficult to interpret the famous passage in his great essay "Experience," where he writes of Waldo's death:

> An innavigable sea washes with silent waves between us and the things we aim at and converse with. Grief too will make us idealists. In the death of my son, now more than two years ago, I seem to have lost a beautiful estate—no more. I cannot get it nearer to me. If tomorrow I should be informed of the bankruptcy of my principal debtors, the loss of my property would be a great inconvenience to me, perhaps, for many years; but it would leave me as it found me,—neither better nor worse. So is it with this calamity; it does not touch me; something which I fancied was a part of me, which could not be torn away without tearing me nor enlarged without enriching me, falls off from me and leaves no scar.

Perhaps Emerson should have written an essay entitled "The Economic Problem of Grief," but perhaps most of his essays carry that as a hidden subtitle. The enigma of grief in Emerson, after all, may be the secret cause of his strength, of his refusal to mourn for the past. Self-reliance, the American religion he founded, converts solitude into a firm stance against history, including personal history. That there is no history, only biography, is the Emersonian insistence, which may be why a valid biography of Emerson appears to be impossible. Emerson knows only biography, a knowledge that makes personal history redundant. What then is the biographer of Emerson to do?

Where someone lives so massively *from within*, he cannot be caught by chroniclers of events, public and private. Unfortunately, Emerson's encounters with others—whether his brothers, wives, children, or Transcendental and other literary colleagues, are little more revelatory of his inner life than are his encounters with events, whether it be the death of Waldo or the Civil War. With the partial exception of Robert Richardson's useful and eloquent *Emerson: The Wind on Fire*, a biography of Emerson becomes as baffling as a biography of Nietzsche, though the two lives have nothing in common, except of course for ideas. Nietzsche acknowledged Emerson, with affection and enthusiasm, but he probably did not realize how fully Emerson had anticipated him, particularly in unsettling the status of the self while proclaiming simultaneously a greater overself to come.

The critic of Emerson is little better off than the biographer, since Emerson, again like Nietzsche and remarkably also akin to Freud, anticipates his critics and does their work for them. Emerson resembles his own hero, Montaigne, in that you cannot combat him without being contaminated by him. T. S. Eliot, ruefully contemplating Pascal's hopeless agon with Montaigne, observed that fighting Montaigne was like throwing a hand grenade into a fog. Emerson, because he appropriated America, is more like a climate than an atmosphere, however misty. Attempting to write the order of the variable winds in the Emersonian climate is a hopeless task, and the best critics of Emerson, from John Jay Chapman and O. W. Firkins through Stephen Whicher to Barbara Packer and Richard Poirier, wisely decline to list his ideas of order. You track him best, as writer and as person, by learning the principle proclaimed everywhere in him: that which you can get from another is never instruction, but always provocation.

But what is provocation, in the life of the spirit? Emerson insisted that he called you forth only to your self, and not to any cause whatsoever. The will to power, in Emerson as afterwards in Nietzsche, is reactive rather than active, receptive rather than rapacious, which is to say that it is a will to interpretation. Emerson teaches interpretation, but not in any of the European modes fashionable either in his day or in our own, modes currently touching their nadir in a younger rabblement celebrating itself as having repudiated the very idea of an individual reader or an individual critic. Group criticism, like group sex, is not a new idea, but seems to revive whenever a sense of resentment dominates the aspiring clerisy. With resentment comes guilt, as though societal oppressions are caused by how we read, and so we get those academic covens akin to what Emerson, in his 1838 *Journal*, called "philanthropic meetings and holy hurrahs," for which read now "Posthumanist literary groups" and "postcolonial theory circles":

> As far as I notice what passes in philanthropic meetings and holy hurrahs there is very little depth of interest. The speakers warm each other's skin and lubricate each other's tongue, and the words flow and the superlatives thicken and the lips quiver and the eyes moisten, and an observer new to such scenes would say, Here was true fire; the assembly were all ready to be martyred, and the effect of such a spirit on the community would be irresistible; but they separate and go to the shop, to a dance, to bed, and an hour afterwards they care so little for the matter that on slightest temptation each one would disclaim the meeting.

Emerson, according to A. Bartlett Giamatti, "was as sweet as barbed wire," a judgment achieved independently by John Updike. Yes, and doubtless Emerson gave our politics its particular view of power, as Giamatti laments, but a country deserves its sages, and we deserve Emerson. He has the peculiar dialectical gift of being precursor for both the perpetual New Left of student non-students and the perpetual New Right of preacher non-preachers. The American Religion of Self-Reliance is a superb *literary* religion, but its political, economic, and social consequences, whether manifested Left or Right, have now helped place us in a country where literary satire of politics is impossible, since the real thing is far more outrageous than even a satirist of genius could invent. Nathanael West presumably was parodying Calvin Coolidge in *A Cool Million*'s Shagpoke Whipple, but is this Shagpoke Whipple or President Trump speaking?

> America is the land of opportunity. She takes care of the honest and industrious and never fails them as long as they are both. This is not a matter of opinion, it is one of faith. On the day that Americans stop believing it, on that day will America be lost.

Emerson unfortunately believed in Necessity, including "the offence of superiority in persons," and he was capable of writing passages such as the following one in "Self-Reliance":

> Then again, do not tell me, as a good man did today, of my obligation to put all poor men in good situations. Are they *my* poor? I tell thee, thou foolish philanthropist, that I grudge the dollar, the dime, the cent I give to such men as do not belong to me and to whom I do not belong. There is a class of persons to whom by all spiritual affinity I am bought and sold; for them I will go to prison if need be; but your miscellaneous popular charities; the education at college of fools; the building of meeting-houses to the vain end to which many now stand; alms to sots; and the thousand-fold Relief Societies;—though I confess with shame I sometimes succumb and give the dollar, it is a wicked dollar, which by and by I shall have the manhood to withhold.

True, Emerson meant by his "class of persons" men such as Henry Thoreau and Jones Very and the Reverend William Ellery Channing, which is not exactly Shagpoke Whipple, Donald Trump, and Mark Zuckerberg, but Self-Reliance translated out of the inner life and into the marketplace is difficult to distinguish from our current religion of selfishness. Shrewd Yankee that he was, Emerson would have shrugged off his various and dubious paternities. His spiritual elitism could only be misunderstood, but he did not care much about being misread or misused. Though he has been so oddly called "the philosopher of democracy" by so many who wished to claim him for the Left, the political Emerson remains best expressed in one famous and remarkable sentence by John Jay Chapman: "If a soul be taken and crushed by democracy till it utter a cry, that cry will be Emerson."

I return with some relief to Emerson as literary prophet, where Emerson's effect, *pace* Yvor Winters, seems to me again dialectical but in the end both benign and inevitable. Emerson's influence, from his day until ours, has helped to account for what I would call the American difference in literature, not only in our poetry and criticism, but even in our novels and stories—ironic since Emerson was at best uneasy about novels. What is truly surprising about this influence is its depth, extent, and persistence, despite many concealments and even more evasions. Emerson does a lot more to explain most American writers than any of our writers; even Whitman or Thoreau or Dickinson or Hawthorne or Melville serves to explain *him*. The important question to ask is not "How?" but "Why?" Scholarship keeps showing the "how" (though there is a great deal more to be shown), but it ought to be a function of criticism to get at that scarcely explored "why."

Emerson was controversial in his own earlier years and then became all but universally accepted (except, of course, in the South) during his later years. This ascendancy faded during the Age of Literary Modernism (circa 1915–45) and virtually vanished, as I remarked earlier, in the hey-day of academic New Criticism or Age of Eliot (circa 1945–65). Despite the humanistic protests of Giamatti and the churchwardenly mewings of John Updike, recent decades have witnessed an Emerson revival, and I prophesy that he, rather than Marx or Heidegger, will be the guiding spirit of our imaginative literature and our criticism for some time to come. In that prophecy, "Emerson" stands not only for the theoretical stance and wisdom of the historical Ralph Waldo, but for Nietzsche, Walter Pater, and Oscar Wilde, and much of Freud as well, since Emerson's elitist vision of the higher individual is so consonant with theirs. Individualism, whatever damages its American ruggedness continues to inflict on our politics and social economy, is more than ever the only hope for our imaginative lives. Emerson, who knew that the only literary and critical method was oneself, is again a necessary resource in a time beginning to weary of Gallic scientism in what are still called the Humanities.

Lewis Mumford, in *The Golden Day* (1926), still is the best guide as to *why* Emerson was and is the central influence upon American letters: "With most of the resources of the past at his command, Emerson achieved nakedness." Wisely seeing that Emerson was a Darwinian before Darwin, a Freudian before Freud, because he possessed "a complete vision," Mumford was able to make the classic formulation as to Emerson's strength: "The past for Emerson was neither a prescription nor a burden: it was rather an esthetic experience." As a poem already written, the past was not a force for Emerson; it had lost power, because power for him resided only at the crossing, at the actual moment of transition.

The dangers of this repression of the past's force are evident enough, in American life as in its literature. In our political economy, we get the force of secondary repetition; Trump as Coolidge out-Shagpoking Nathanael West's Whipple. We receive also the rhythm of ebb and flow that makes all our greater writers into crisis-poets. Each of them echoes, however involuntarily, Emerson's formula for discontinuity in his weird, irrealistic essay "Circles":

> Our moods do not believe in each other. Today I am full of thoughts and can write what I please. I see no reason why I should not have the same thought, the same power of expression, tomorrow. What I write, whilst I write it, seems the most natural thing in the world; but yesterday I saw a dreary vacuity in this direction in which now I see so much; and a month hence, I doubt not, I shall wonder who he was that wrote so many continuous pages. Alas for this infirm faith, this will not strenuous, this vast ebb of a vast flow! I am God in nature; I am a weed by the wall.

From God to weed and then back again; it is the cycle of Whitman from "Song of Myself" to "As I Ebb'd with the Ocean of Life," and of Emerson's and Whitman's descendants ever since. Place everything upon the nakedness of the American self, and you open every imaginative possibility from self-deification to absolute nihilism. But Emerson knew this, and he saw no alternative for us if we were to avoid the predicament of arriving too late in the cultural history of the West. Nothing is got for nothing; Emerson is not less correct now than he was 185 years ago. On November 21, 1834, he wrote in his journal: "When we have lost our God of tradition and ceased from our God of rhetoric then may God fire the heart with his presence." Our God of tradition, then and now, is as dead as Emerson and Nietzsche declared him to be. He belongs, in life, to the political clerics and the clerical politicians and, in letters, to the secondary men and women. Our God of rhetoric belongs to the academies. That leaves the American imagination free as always to open itself to the third God of Emerson's prayer.

On Christmas Day, 1846, Emerson's *Poems* appeared. The poet was forty-three and had published much of his most characteristic prose; *Nature* in 1836, and the two series of *Essays* in 1841 and 1844. Like so many American poets, Emerson was a late starter; few of his important poems precede his thirtieth year, and most were written after he turned forty. The few early exceptions would include "The River" (1827) and some extraordinary chants of self-recognition in the 1831 *Journals*, which resemble certain sermons of Meister Eckhart in their dangerously intense realization that the soul's substance is uncreated, and their conclusion that the soul alone is the Law. By 1832, the *Journals* show a dialectical recoil: "It is awful to look into the mind of man and see how free we are. . . . inside, the terrible freedom!" Throughout Emerson's great period (1832–41, with a sudden but brief resurgence in 1846) there is a dialectic or interplay between the assertion of imagination's autonomy, and a shrewd skepticism of any phenomenon reaching too far into the unconditioned. This rhythm appears again in the Emersonian Whitman in his great years (1855–60), in Dickinson throughout her life, and in every Emersonian poet we have enjoyed since (Cummings, Hart Crane, Roethke) except for poets who stem from the later, resigned Emerson (*The Conduct of Life*, particularly the essay "Fate"), including Robinson and Frost. The relation of Stevens to Emerson, early and late, is too complex for summary, being hidden, perhaps partly an unconscious one, and will receive some consideration further on.

The notable poems in Emerson's first volume are "The Sphinx" (probably 1840), "Uriel" (1845), "Hamatreya" (1845–46), "The Humble-Bee" (1837), "Woodnotes" (1840–41), "Monadnoc" (1845), "Ode: Inscribed To William H. Channing" (1846), "Forerunners" (date unknown), "Merlin" (1846), "Bacchus" (1846), "Saadi" (1842), and "Threnody" (1842–43). From late in 1845 and almost all through 1846, Emerson seems to have revived in himself something of his earlier Transcendental fury. Stephen Whicher dated 1841 as the end of Emerson's "Period of challenge" and the start of his long "Period of acquiescence," a useful enough categorizing if we grant the year 1846 as an exception. The year's prelude is in "Uriel," a late response to the furor following the Divinity School Address and Frost's candidate for the best American poem. The poem turns on Uriel's "sentiment divine":

> "Line in nature is not found;
> Unit and universe are round;
> In vain produced, all rays return;
> Evil will bless, and ice will burn."

The poem is deliberately and successfully comic in a unique mode; indeed, the positive magic of poetic influence (as exalted by Borges) appears to be at work; and at moments Frost is writing the poem, even as Yeats writes certain passages in "The Witch of Atlas," or Stevens in "The Recluse," or Dickinson in Emerson's "The Humble-Bee." But "Uriel" (again like some Frost) is very dark in its comedy and records the inner cost of angelic defiance:

> A sad self-knowledge, withering, fell
> On the beauty of Uriel;
> In heaven once eminent, the god
> Withdrew, that hour, into his cloud;
> Whether doomed to long gyration
> In the sea of generation,
> Or by knowledge grown too bright
> To hit the nerve of feebler sight.

Line in human nature is not to be found either, least of all in Emerson's spiral of a spirit. The Eternal Return is perpetual in the single soul, and Emerson anticipates the doctrines of Yeats as well as Nietzsche. Self-knowledge withers because it teaches the terrible truths of the grand essay "Circles"; Uriel too is only a proud ephemeral whose revelation must be superseded. Emerson's wisdom, by limiting the self's discourse, gives the poem firm outline; Uriel sings out when possessed but then gyres into a cloudy silence.

"Monadnoc," a powerful ramble of a poem, now absurdly undervalued, shows the same discretion, allowing much everyday lumber to ballast the ascents to vision. Its direct modern descendant, Stevens's "Chocorua to Its Neighbor," suffers from refusing similar ballast; it is a purer but not a better poem. Monadnoc expects to disappear in the mightier chant of the Major Man it awaits, a god no longer in ruins. Chocorua celebrates only the shadow of the Major Man but already begins to disappear in that celebration:

> Upon my top he breathed the pointed dark.
> He was not man yet he was nothing else.
> If in the mind, he vanished, taking there
> The mind's own limits, like a tragic thing
> Without existence, existing everywhere.

This is painfully said, but since the mind is the mountain's, Chocorua himself is being skeptically raised to sublimity, where limits vanish.

Monadnoc is a sturdier Titan, and sees a form, not a shadow, of centrality. In Emerson's poem, we find the shadow, in the mountain:

> Thou seest, O watchman tall,
> Our towns and races grow and fall,
> And imagest the stable good
> For which we all our lifetime grope,
> In shifting form the formless mind,
> And though the substance us elude,
> We in thee the shadow find.

Probably Emerson was not aware he echoed the "Intimations" Ode here, as in so many other places:

> thou Eye among the blind,
> That, deaf and silent, read'st the eternal deep,
> Haunted for ever by the eternal mind,—
> Mighty Prophet! Seer blest!
> On whom those truths do rest,
> Which we are toiling all our lives to find,
> In darkness lost, the darkness of the grave;

Wordsworth addresses the Child, Emerson Monadnoc, but the Other is the same; Monadnoc is a "Mute orator," sending "conviction without phrase" to "succor and remede / The shortness of our days," promising "long morrow" to those of "mortal youth." The Child, though silent, prophesies the same good news.

Thoreau, throughout his use of the "Ode" in his *Journal*, emphasizes a music within, remembering that "there was a time when the beauty and the music were all within . . . When you were an organ of which the world was but one poor broken pipe." Wordsworth turns to a music in the later time, but emphasizes the lost glory as a light, something seen. What for Wordsworth is a movement from the despotic eye to the liberating ear becomes in Thoreau a double loss, involving both senses. Emerson, from 1831 on a more consistent Wordsworthian than the more drastic (and even more American) Thoreau, wavers more cunningly from the "Ode." Monadnoc takes the Child's place, for the stone Titan is free of the tragic rhythm by which the Child is father of the Man. In this *tessera*, Wordsworthian Nature is perhaps overhumanized, and Monadnoc becomes a Transcendentalist rather too benign, less a flaw in the poem than it might be, since the whole work demands so generous a suspension of our skepticism.

Skepticism, the powerful undersong in Emerson's dialectic, returns in "Hamatreya," as awesome a rebuff to a naturalistic humanism as Yeats's great sonnet "Meru" in the "Supernatural Songs," and proceeding from much the same sources as "Meru." "Hamatreya" is the necessary prelude to what is most difficult yet inviting in Emerson's two supreme poems, "Merlin" and "Bacchus." Because of the dominance of certain pseudo-critical shibboleths for several decades, there is a certain fashion still to deprecate all of Emerson's poetry, with the single exception of "Days." F. O. Matthiessen pioneered in grudgingly accepting "Days" as the one Emerson poem that seemed readable by Eliotic standards. I suspect the poem passed because Emerson condemns himself in it, though only for not being Emersonian enough. "Days," in Emerson's canon, is a miniature of his later retreat into the acceptance of Necessity. Necessity speaks as the Earth-Song in "Hamatreya," is defied by the Dionysiac spirit of the poet in "Bacchus," but then subsumes that spirit in "Merlin." The three poems together evidence Emerson's major venture into his own cosmos in the *Poems* of 1846, and are the furthest reach of his imagination beyond his Wordsworthian heritage, since the *May-Day* volume and later work largely return to the Wordsworthianism of "Monadnoc" and "Woodnotes."

The passage copied from the *Vishnu Purana* into his 1845 *Journal* by Emerson has one crucial sentence: "Earth laughs, as if smiling with autumnal flowers to behold her kings unable to effect the subjugation of themselves." In "Hamatreya," this laughter is darkened, for this is a Mortality Ode:

> Earth laughs in flowers, to see her boastful boys
> Earth-proud, proud of the earth which is not theirs;
> Who steer the plough, but cannot steer their feet
> Clear of the grave.

The Earth-Song ends in the spirit of Stevens's "Madame La Fleurie," provoking an extraordinary quatrain that presents Emerson's savage *tessera* to the conclusion of Wordsworth's "Ode":

> When I heard the Earth-song
> I was no longer brave;
> My avarice cooled
> Like lust in the chill of the grave.

The forsaken courage here is Wordsworth's Stoic comfort at the "Ode"'s close. "Thoughts that do often lie too deep for tears," prompted by a flower that *blows*, that still lives, become only "avarice," unsuited to our deep poverty, when we hear the earth's true song in its laughing flowers. Since Emerson is to American Romanticism what Wordsworth is to the British or parent version, a defining and separating element in later American poetry begins to show itself here. Emerson had more cause, always, to fear an imminent mortality than Wordsworth did (though in fact both poets lived to be quite old), but he shared with Wordsworth a healthy realism toward natural dangers. I cannot think of another major American writer who is so little credulous in regard to preternatural phenomena as Emerson, who had no patience for superstition, even when manifested as folklore. As an admirer of Sir Thomas Browne, Emerson might have been expected to be at least a touch Yeatsian in this region, but every journal reference to the occult is strongly disparaging. Wordsworth too is reluctant, even when he approaches the form of romance. The largest aspect of the super-natural, the life-after-death, so pervasive in romance traditions as well as folk superstitions, makes no thematic appeal to Emerson or Wordsworth, neither of whom could imagine a life apart from the natural. Wordsworth's "immortality," as many critics have noted, is less Platonic or Christian than it is primordial, personal, almost literal, resembling most closely the child's undivided consciousness, not yet sundered to the self-realization of mortality. But Emerson, though he longed for this and loved the "Ode" as much as any poem, could not as a poet accept this "immortality" either. Robert C. Pollock, in his fine study of Emerson's "Single Vision," shows how much that vision emphasizes man's "continual self-recovery." Wordsworth's vision declined to offer so much, for his temperament was harsher and his experience less exuberant. But Pollock is writing of the earlier Emerson, whose last major expression is in "Bacchus," not the Emerson who is partly inaugurated by "Merlin," the essay "Experience," and the essay on Montaigne in *Representative Men*. "Hamatreya" is another prelude to this Emerson, who speaks his whole mind in the great essay "Fate":

But Fate against Fate is only parrying and defence: there are also the noble creative forces. The revelation of Thought takes man out of servitude into freedom. We rightly say of ourselves, we were born and afterward we were born again, and many times. We have successive experiences so important that the new forgets the old, and hence the mythology of the seven or the nine heavens. The day of days, the great day of the feast of life, is that in which the inward eye opens to the Unity in things, to the omnipresence of law:—see that what is must be and ought to be, or is the best. This beatitude dips from on high down on us and we see. It is not in us so much as we are in it. If the air come to our lungs, we breathe and live; if not, we die. If the light come to our eyes, we see; else not. And if truth come to our mind we suddenly expand to its dimensions, as if we grew to worlds. We are as lawgivers; we speak for Nature; we prophesy and divine.

This insight throws us on the party and interest of the Universe, against all and sundry; against ourselves as much as others. A man speaking from insight affirms of himself what is true of the mind: seeing its immortality, he says, I am immortal; seeing its invincibility, he says, I am strong. It is not in us, but we are in it. It is of the maker, not of what is made. All things are touched and changed by it. This uses and is not used. It distances those who share it from those who share it not.

Wordsworth, with his extraordinary precision in measuring the spirit's weather, said of his "spots of time" that they gave knowledge of to what extent and how the mind held mastery over outward sense. In the passage above, the spirit's weather is perpetual cyclone, and the mind's mastery is beyond extent or means. This is more than very American; for glory and loss, it is as central a passage as American literature gives, more so even than the splendid and much-maligned "transparent eyeball" passage in *Nature*, which is to the earlier Emerson what being thrown "on the party and interest of the Universe . . . against ourselves" is to the later. Though the Stevens of *Ideas of Order* mocks the first Emerson (see "Sailing After Lunch": "To expunge all people and be a pupil / Of the gorgeous wheel and so to give / That slight transcendence to the dirty sail, / By light . . ."), the greater Stevens of *The Auroras of Autumn* reaches the resolution of "Fate," precisely attaining the late Emersonian balance (or rather oscillation) between Fate and Freedom. The anxiety of influence abided in Stevens, who continued to satirize his American ancestor (as in the Mr. Homburg of "Looking Across the Fields and Watching the Birds Fly," whose enterprise is "To think away the grass, the trees, the clouds, / Not to transform them into other things"). Burrowing away somewhere in Stevens's imagination were memories of reading *The Conduct of Life* (where the essay "Illusions" contains "The Rock" in embryo) and *Letters and Social Aims* (where the long, meandering "Poetry and Imagination" holds more of Stevens's poetics than Valéry or Santayana does). I instance Stevens in relation to "Fate," but the essay touches, directly or dialectically, a company of American poets that includes also Whitman, Dickinson, Melville, Frederick Goddard Tuckerman, Robinson, Frost, Jeffers, Aiken, Crane, Roethke, and Ammons, none of whom would have completed the self's circle without it, or at least without modifying into a somewhat different self. That this influence was neither as benevolent as a confirmed Emersonian would have it (see H. H. Waggoner's *American Poets*) nor as destructive as Yvor Winters insisted (*In Defense of Reason*) need not surprise anyone who has reflected upon the long course of Wordsworth's influence upon British poets (or Milton's, before that).

The central passage of "Fate" exhilarates and dismays, as it should; Emerson's notion of "Fate" is Indian enough to be at last unassimilable by him or by us. A *Journal* entry contrasts the Greek "Fate" as "private theatricals" in contrast to India, where "it is the dread reality, it is the cropping-out in our planted gardens of the core of the world: it is the abysmal Force, untameable and immense." This Force inspires a shaman rather than a humanizing poet, an augurer not a prophet, the poet of "Merlin" but not of the misnamed and sublime "Bacchus." Force is irrational, but the inspiration of Bacchus, though more than rational, is the "later reason" of Stevens's "Notes," or more historically the Idealist Reason that Coleridge and Wordsworth took (though only in part) from assorted Germans. With the contrast between "Bacchus" and "Merlin," we can attempt to clarify two allied strains in Emerson (they cannot be regarded only as early and late, *Nature* and "Self-Reliance" against *The Conduct of Life*, because traces of each can be found from youth through age). Clarification must begin with the 1846 *Journal*, where something of the complexity of Emerson's last great year can be recovered.

In his disgust with the politics of Polk and Webster, in the year of our aggression against Mexico, Emerson consciously turned to the Muse, but with a skeptical reserve: "The life which we seek is expansion; the actual life even of the genius or the saint is obstructive." But, in some mysterious passages, as in the one that is the greatest of his prophecies of the Central Man (from the *Journal*, April 1846), the reserve vanishes. Here is another, premonitory of Nietzsche's Overman, of Whitman's Self, and (much diminished) of Stevens's Major Man (particularly in the second and third paragraphs, with which compare "Notes toward a Supreme Fiction," part I, sections IX–X):

> He lurks, he hides,—he who is success, reality, joy, power, that which constitutes Heaven, which reconciles impossibilities, atones for shortcomings, expiates sins, or makes them virtues, buries in oblivion the crowded historical Past, sinks religions, philosophies, nations, persons to legends; reverses the scale of opinion, of fame; reduces sciences to opinion, and makes the thought of the moment the key to the universe and the egg of history to come. . . .
>
> This is he that shall come, or if he come not, nothing comes; he that disappears on the instant that we go to celebrate him. If we go to burn those that blame our celebration, he appears in them.
>
> Hoe and spade; sword and pen; cities, pictures, gardens, laws, bibles, are prized only because they were means he sometimes used: so with astronomy, arithmetic, caste, feudalism. We kiss with devotion these hems of his garment. They crumble to ashes on our lips.

This is not Christ, but rather an Orphic god-poet, such a divinity as Emerson assumed Hafiz to have celebrated. This is also not the Force or Necessity apotheosized by shamans and bards. Is Emerson constant in distinguishing the three: Christ, Central Man, Ananke? As a poet, yes; in prose, not always, for there (despite the fallacious assumptions of Winters) he refuses to "label and ticket, one thing, or two," as he rightly charges the mystic with doing. The 1846 *Journal* frequently approximates Blake, not least when it attacks the mystic, like Swedenborg, as being a Devil turned Angel: "The mystic, who beholds the flux, yet becomes pragmatist on some one particular of faith, and, what is the mischief, seeks to accredit this new jail because it was builded by him who has demolished so many jails." Fearing even an antinomian or visionary dogmatism, the mature Emerson refuses distinctions where we, as his ephebes, badly want and need them. Uriel, like Nature, hates lines, knowing that all new generation comes when matter rolls itself into balls. In the midst of the 1846 *Journal*, there is a great antithetical prayer: "O Bacchus, make them drunk, drive them mad, this multitude of vagabonds, hungry for eloquence, hungry for poetry." The great poem "Bacchus," to me Emerson's finest, comes in answer to this prayer. I wish here only to look at its marvelous close:

> Let wine repair what this undid;
> And where the infection slid,
> A dazzling memory revive;
> Refresh the faded tints,
> Recut the aged prints,
> And write my old adventures with the pen
> Which on the first day drew,
> Upon the tablets blue,
> The dancing Pleiads and eternal men.

Stevens's "Large Red Man Reading" aloud "the great blue tabulae" gives to earth-returning ghosts "the outlines of being and its expressings, the syllables of its law," a characteristic reduction of the greater Emersonian dream. Emerson's poem goes as far as apocalyptic poetry can go, but the impulse for refreshing and recutting was stronger even than "Bacchus" and gave Emerson "Merlin," scarcely a lesser poem, but a dangerous and divided work. "Bacchus" asks for more than Wordsworth did, for a renovation as absolute as Blake's vision sought. The poetic faculty is to free man from his own ruins and restore him as the being Blake called Tharmas, instinctual innocence triumphantly at home in his own place. Stevens, at his most hopeful, asserted that the poem refreshes life so that we share, but only for a moment, the First Idea, which belonged to Tharmas. Like Wordsworth, Stevens yields to a version of the Reality Principle. Blake and Emerson do not, but Emerson departs from Blakean affinities when, in his extraordinary impatience, most fatedly American of qualities, he seeks terms with his Reality Principle only by subsuming it, as he does in "Merlin." Not "Bacchus" but "Merlin" seems to me the archetypal American poem that our best poets keep writing, once they have passed through their crises of individuation, have found their true limit, and then fail to accept any limit as their own. The American Muse is a daemon of disorder, whose whispered counsel in the dark is: "evade and multiply." Young and old at once, bewilderingly from their start, the great among our poets seek to become each a process rather than a person, Nemesis rather than accident, as though it could be open to any imagination to be enthroned where only a handful have ever come.

If a single American has incarnated our daemon, it is Emerson, not our greatest writer but merely our only inescapable one, to be found always where Whitman asked to be sought, under our boot-soles, effused and drifted all through our lives and our literature, just as he is to be found on every page, almost in every line, of Whitman. Denied or scorned, he turns up again in every opponent, however orthodox, classical, conservative, or even just southern. Why he stands so much at the center may always be a mystery, but who else can stand in his place? Nineteenth-century American culture is the Age of Emerson, and what we undergo now seems more than ever his. A good part of what has been urged against him, even by very negative critics like James Truslow Adams and Winters, is true, but this appears to mean mostly that Emerson did subsume something inevitable in the national process, that he joined himself forever to the American version of what Stevens called "fatal Ananke . . . the final god."

"Merlin," a text in which to read both the American Sublime and the American poetic disaster, was finished in the summer of 1846 but had its origins in the *Journal* of 1845, in a strong doggerel:

I go discontented thro' the world
Because I cannot strike
The harp to please my tyrannous ear:
Gentle touches are not wanted,
These the yielding gods had granted.
It shall not tinkle a guitar,
But strokes of fate
Chiming with the ample winds,
With the pulse of human blood,
With the voice of mighty men,
With the din of city arts,
With the cannonade of war,
With the footsteps of the brave
And the sayings of the wise,
Chiming with the forest's tone

When they buffet boughs in the windy wood,
Chiming with the gasp and moan
Of the ice-imprisoned flood.
I will not read a pretty tale
To pretty people in a nice saloon
Borrowed from their expectation,
But I will sing aloud and free
From the heart of the world.

It is almost the universal motto of the American poet, from Whitman down to the transformation of W. S. Merwin into the nearly impersonal bard of *The Lice* and *The Carrier of Ladders*. From the "gentle touches" of *Green With Beasts* ("the gaiety of three winds is a game of green / Shining, of grey-and-gold play in the holly-bush"), Merwin went on to Emersonian "strokes of fate" ("We are the echo of the future / On the door it says what to do to survive / But we were not born to survive / Only to live"), and Merwin is probably the representative poet of my own generation. Learned accomplishment will not suffice where the Muse herself masks as Necessity; if Emerson was aware that this was a masking, he failed to show it, an imaginative failure, fine as the finished "Merlin" is:

Thy trivial harp will never please
Or fill my craving ear;
Its chords should ring as blows the breeze,
Free, peremptory, clear.
. . . .
The kingly bard
Must smite the chords rudely and hard,
As with hammer or with mace;
That they may render back
Artful thunder, which conveys
Secrets of the solar track,
Sparks of the supersolar blaze.
Merlin's blows are strokes of fate.

"Artful thunder" is cousin to "fearful symmetry," reversing the parodistic awe of an argument from apparent design but still mockingly urging us to yield to an other-than-human splendor and terror. Power is "Merlin"'s subject, "strokes of fate" as the essay "Fate" defines them: "Why should we fear to be crushed by savage elements, we who are made up of the same elements?" We are ourselves strokes of fate, on this view, and most ourselves in Merlin the Bard, whose "mighty line / Extremes of nature reconciled." The dangers, social and solipsistic, of so amazingly unconditioned a bardic vision crowd upon us in the poem's second part, with great eloquence:

> Perfect-paired as eagle's wings,
> Justice is the rhyme of things;
> Trade and counting use
> The self-same tuneful muse;
> And Nemesis,
> Who with even matches odd,
> Who athwart space redresses
> The partial wrong,
> Fills the just period,
> And finishes the song.

No reader of Emerson ought to brood on these lines without juxtaposing them to the magnificent and famous *Journal* entry of April 1842, in which Emerson gave his fullest dialectic of Nemesis, which "Merlin" seems to slight:

> In short, there ought to be no such thing as Fate. As long as we use this word, it is a sign of our impotence and that we are not yet ourselves. There is now a sublime revelation in each of us which makes us so strangely aware and certain of our riches that although I have never since I was born for so much as one moment expressed the truth, and although I have never heard the expression of it from any other, I know that the whole is here,—the wealth of the Universe is for me, everything is explicable and practicable for me. And yet whilst I adore this ineffable life which is at my heart, it will not condescend to gossip with me, it will not announce to me any particulars of science, it will not enter into the details of my biography, and say to me why I have a son and daughters born to me, or why my son dies in his sixth year of joy. Herein, then, I have this latent omniscience coexistent with omni-ignorance. Moreover, whilst this Deity glows at the heart, and by his unlimited presen-

timents gives me all Power, I know that tomorrow will be as this day, I am a dwarf, and I remain a dwarf. That is to say, I believe in Fate. As long as I am weak, I shall talk of Fate; whenever the God fills me with his fulness, I shall see the disappearance of Fate.

I am *Defeated* all the time; yet to Victory I am born.

But Merlin, who can no more be defeated than Nemesis can be thwarted, becomes one with the spirit that "finishes the song." There is nothing like this unity with the serpent Ananke before Emerson in American poetry (or in English) but all too much after. Before Emerson, we can take Bryant and Poe as representative of the possibilities for Romantic poetry in America, and see in both of them a capable reservation that Emerson abolished in himself. Bryant's "The Poet" is very late (1863) but presents a stance firmly established by more than fifty years of composing good poetry. "Make thyself a part / Of the great tumult," Bryant tells the poet, but the same poem severely contrasts the organized violence within the mind and the unorganized violence of nature:

> A blast that whirls the dust
>   Along the howling street and dies away;
> But feelings of calm power and mighty sweep,
> Like currents journeying through the windless deep.

Poe, despite his celebrated and angelic ambitions for the poet, follows Shelley and Byron in emphasizing the pragmatic sorrows of Prometheanism, even as Bryant follows Cowper and Wordsworth in a Stoic awareness of the mind's separation from its desired natural context. "Israfel" remains a poem of real excellence because in it the mind is overwhelmed by auguries of division, between the angelic bard and his wistfully defiant imitator below, who is reduced to doubting his divine precursor's powers where they are to be brought down into nature: "He might not sing so wildly well / A mortal melody." Bryant and Poe are both of them closer to English Romantic consciousness than the Emerson of "Merlin" and "Fate," who thus again prophesied what Wright Morris calls "the territory ahead," the drastic American Romanticism of heroic imaginative failure, or perhaps a kind of success we have not yet learned to apprehend. For the doctrine of "Merlin" is dangerous in that it tempts our poets to a shamanism they neither altogether want nor properly can sustain.

Nathaniel Hawthorne

(1804–1864)

IF THE MYTHIC BEING "Walt Whitman" is our closest representation of the American "Adam early in the morning," then Hawthorne's Hester Prynne, besieged heroine of *The Scarlet Letter*, is still more the fictive American Eve, a worthy rival to Milton's rather English Eve in *Paradise Lost*. Hester luminously stands out against the darkening backgrounds of Hawthorne's vision of Puritan repression. Critics have remarked that Hester's tragedy was to have existed too early in American social history, a judgment I reject. Feminism and our enlightened sexual politics might not have saved the vitalistic, high-spirited Hester from the dilemma of never finding a man worthy of her sexual power and her self-reliance. The Satanic Chillingworth and the pathetic Dimmesdale would have been archaic objects for Henry James's Isabel Archer in *The Portrait of a Lady*, but the sublime Isabel, heiress of all the ages, marries the dreadful Osmond, fortune-hunter, snob, and parody of a Paterian aesthete. I meditate upon the thousands of young women I have taught. How many of them—brilliant, beautiful, absolutely free to choose—have emulated Hester Prynne and Isabel! Shakespeare teaches us that most remarkable women have to marry down: Rosalind, Portia, Beatrice, Imogen, quite aside from Lady Macbeth in what I fear is the happiest marriage in all the plays. Both Hawthorne and his reluctant disciple, Henry James, emulate the Shakespearean model.

I do not dispute the general judgment that James was, is, and perhaps always will be the most eminent of American novelists. Hawthorne, like his friend Melville, and like Faulkner in more recent time, composed romances rather than Balzacian novels. James's comments upon Hawthorne generally display (if I may reappropriate the phrase) the anxiety of influence. One could demonstrate that *The Wings of the Dove* is a strong creative misreading of Hawthorne's *The Marble Faun*, just as Isabel Archer is a beguiling misprision of the superb Hester Prynne.

Aside from his two major novels, Hawthorne matters for his tales, the best of which seem to me superior to those of Melville, Mark Twain, James, Faulkner, Fitzgerald, and Hemingway. His masterpieces in this genre are extraordinarily diverse, from a historical story like "My Kinsman, Major Molineux" to fantasies like "Young Goodman Brown" and the uncanny "Wakefield" and "Feathertop." A flawless artist, Hawthorne provoked Henry James to a defensive condescension, manifested by James also in regard to George Eliot's *Middlemarch* and to much of Dickens. A marvelous critic where he felt unthreatened, as on Balzac and Turgenev, James could be rendered uneasy by genius closer to home. His most outrageous display was his review of Whitman's *Drum-Taps*, which he disowned later on, after Whitman had become the favorite poet of the James family.

Hawthorne, despite popular misconceptions, was no more a Puritan than was *his* favorite poet, Edmund Spenser. Any sensitive reader of Hawthorne would be wise to approach him without preconceptions. Emerson's "stairway of surprise" is about the only appropriate location for Hawthorne's fiction. Haunted by American history, Hawthorne nevertheless was a prophetic writer, hoping (like his Hester Prynne) for a new relation between women and men that may never transpire.

Of the four principal figures in *The Scarlet Letter*, Pearl is at once the most surprising and the largest intimation of Hawthorne's farthest imaginings. There is no indication that Hawthorne shared his friend Melville's deep interest in ancient Gnosticism, though esoteric heresies were clearly part of Hawthorne's abiding concern with witchcraft. The Gnostic *Gospel of Thomas* contains a remarkable mythic narrative, "The Hymn of the Pearl," that juxtaposes illuminatingly with the uncanny daughter of Hester Prynne and the Reverend Mr. Dimmesdale. In Gnostic symbolism, the pearl is identical with the spark or *pneuma* that is the ontological self of the adept who shares in the Gnosis, in the true knowing that surmounts mere faith. The pearl particularly represents what is best and oldest in the adept, because creation is the work of a mere demiurge, while the best part of us, that which is capable of knowing, was never made, but is one with the original Abyss, the Foremother and Forefather who is the true or alien God. When Hawthorne's Pearl passionately insists she was not made by God, we hear again the most ancient and challenging of all Western heresies:

> The old minister seated himself in an arm-chair, and made an effort
> to draw Pearl betwixt his knees. But the child, unaccustomed to

the touch or familiarity of any but her mother, escaped through the open window and stood on the upper step, looking like a wild, tropical bird, of rich plumage, ready to take flight into the upper air. Mr. Wilson, not a little astonished at this outbreak,—for he was a grandfatherly sort of personage, and usually a vast favorite with children,—essayed, however, to proceed with the examination.

"Pearl," said he, with great solemnity, "thou must take heed to instruction, that so, in due season, thou mayest wear in thy bosom the pearl of great price. Canst thou tell me, my child, who made thee?"

Now Pearl knew well enough who made her; for Hester Prynne, the daughter of a pious home, very soon after her talk with the child about her Heavenly Father, had begun to inform her of those truths which the human spirit, at whatever stage of immaturity, imbibes with such eager interest. Pearl, therefore, so large were the attainments of her three years' lifetime, could have borne a fair examination in the New England Primer, or the first column of the Westminster Catechism, although unacquainted with the outward form of either of those celebrated works. But that perversity, which all children have more or less of, and of which little Pearl had a tenfold portion, now, at the most inopportune moment, took thorough possession of her, and closed her lips, or impelled her to speak words amiss. After putting her finger in her mouth, with many ungracious refusals to answer good Mr. Wilson's question, the child finally announced that she had not been made at all, but had been plucked by her mother off the bush of wild roses, that grew by the prison-door.

That Pearl, elf-child, is the romance's prime knower no reader would doubt. The subtlest relation in Hawthorne's sinuously ambiguous romance is not that between Chillingworth and Dimmesdale, let alone the inadequate ghost of the love between Hester and Dimmesdale. It is the ambivalent and persuasive mother-daughter complex in which Hester is saved both from suicidal despair and from the potential of becoming the prophetess of a feminist religion only by the extraordinary return in her daughter of everything she herself has repressed. I will venture the speculation that both Hester and Pearl are intense representations of two very different aspects of Emersonianism, Hester being a prime instance of Emerson's American religion of Self-Reliance, while Pearl emerges from a deeper stratum of

Emerson, from the Orphism and Gnosticism that mark the sage's first anar-chic influx of power and knowledge, when he celebrated his own version of what he called, following the Swedenborgians, the terrible freedom or newness. Emerson, Hawthorne's Concord walking companion, is generally judged by scholars and critics to be antithetical to Hawthorne. I doubt that judgment, since manifestly Hawthorne does not prefer the pathetic Dimmesdale and the mock-Satanic Chillingworth to the self-reliant Hester and the daemonic Pearl. Henry James, like T. S. Eliot, considered Emer-son to be deficient in a sense of sin, a sense obsessive in Dimmesdale and Chillingworth, alien to Pearl, and highly dialectical in Hester.

In the Gnostic mode of Pearl, the young Emerson indeed affirmed: "My heart did never counsel me to sin. . . . / I never taught it what it teaches me." This is the adept of Orphic mysteries who also wrote: "It is God in you that responds to God without, or affirms his own words trembling on the lips of another," words that "sound to you as old as yourself." The direct precursor to *The Scarlet Letter*'s Pearl is a famous moment in Emerson's "Self-Reliance," an essay surely known to Hawthorne:

> I remember an answer which when quite young I was prompted to make to a valued adviser who was wont to importune me with the dear old doctrines of the church. On my saying, "What have I to do with the sacredness of traditions, if I live wholly from within?" my friend suggested,—"But these impulses may be from below, not from above." I replied, "They do not seem to me to be such; but if I am the Devil's child, I will live then from the Devil."

Call this Pearl's implicit credo, since her positive declaration is "I have no Heavenly Father!" Even as Pearl embodies Emerson's most anar-chic, antinomian strain, Hester incarnates the central impulse of "Self-Reliance." This is the emphasis of chapter 13 of the romance "Another View of Hester," which eloquently tells us: "The scarlet letter had not done its office." In effect, Hawthorne presents her as Emerson's American pre-cursor and as the forerunner also of movements still working themselves through among us.

Only the emanation of Pearl from the spiritual world has saved Hester from the martyrdom of a prophetess, which is Hawthorne's most cunning irony, since without Pearl his romance would have been transformed into a tragedy. That may be our loss aesthetically, since every reader of *The*

Scarlet Letter comes to feel a great regret at Hester's unfulfilled potential. Something in us wants her to be a greater heretic even than Anne Hutchinson. Certainly we sense an unwritten book in her, a story that Hawthorne did not choose to write. But what he has written marks the true beginning of American prose fiction, the absolute point of origin from which we can trace the sequence that goes from Melville and James to Faulkner and Pynchon and that domesticates great narrative art in America.

"Wakefield" frightens me because wife and home constitute my reality in old age. Several students came to see me here today, and a close friend who is a trainer came by to supervise my exercise. Otherwise, I have been alone when my wife went forth on errands or to meet a friend. Hawthorne had perhaps the happiest marriage of any major American writer, if not indeed of the great writers of all ages and nations. He met Sophia Peabody in 1837, when he was thirty-three, and married her five years later. Until he died—sadly, at fifty-nine—they had twenty-seven years of unbroken harmony together. "Wakefield" and its nincompoop protagonist are absolutely antithetical to Hawthorne's superb married existence. Is that a pathway to meaning here?

"Wakefield" is an allegorical fiction only in Angus Fletcher's sense of a compulsive syndrome. Wretched Wakefield, then, would be a kind of daemon for whom there is no freedom of choice. Obsessed by the idea of taking clandestine lodgings a block away from his own house, Wakefield is out of control, a possessed nonentity. Weirdly, he has no goal except staying not too far from home. He is the polar opposite of the artist-thinkers in Hawthorne's stories "The Artist of the Beautiful," "The Prophetic Pictures," "Drowne's Wooden Image," "Chippings with a Chisel." They, however brokenly, are purposeful without purpose, but Wakefield does not exist in the realm of purpose.

Why is this tale so powerful? Its reverberation is out of proportion with its slight, offhand tonality. None of us would wish to lunch with the Wakefields; we do not even care to speculate how Mrs. Wakefield received him after his two-decade jape. I think we are troubled because so few among us can be so perfectly married as Hawthorne and his Sophia. Haunted each by her or his own daemon, how can we know that a compulsion will not suddenly detach us from home and companion?

There is another deep opening beneath that one. Women and men in their eighties are not given to unexpected passions or violent elopements. Only a master of the grotesque—Carson McCullers or Flannery O'Connor—would seek such images. Dying and death have more to do with the effect of "Wakefield" upon all of us and on aged readers in particular. Mrs. Wakefield lives as a widow after her husband's daemonic withdrawal, and her presumed two-decade bereavement seems unlikely to be redressed by his rain-drenched reentry. Each time I reread and teach "Wakefield," I limp through our large New England shingle house (late nineteenth-century) and try to envision it occupied only by my wife. I stare at the innumerable bookcases and murmur the Stevensian tag from "The Auroras of Autumn": "The house will crumble and the books will burn."

For reasons I cannot comprehend, "Rappaccini's Daughter," a tale that gives me nightmares, haunts my days also. I take no pleasure from rereading it, yet even Hawthorne is rarely this powerful. It is as though his unmediated daemon composed this allegory of the heart in Shakespeare's sense of "heart": total consciousness of Hamlet's sort.

Image generates action in Hawthorne: the power of an icon determines event and character. He sees and then points, and we follow as though we are fixed, divided, and determined by a cosmic vision not our own. Each time I turn to this erotic tale, I am enthralled by Beatrice and appalled by her father, her lover, and the envious Baglioni, whose remedy actually murders her. What was Hawthorne trying to do for himself, as man and romancer, by writing "Rappaccini's Daughter"?

With the exceptions of Nina Baym and a few more recent scholars, most criticism of Hawthorne seems to me wrong. He is an American High Romantic, akin to Emerson, Melville, and Whitman, and not at all a neo-orthodox ancestor of T. S. Eliot. He celebrates the sexual vitality of women as a potentially saving force, tragically curtailed by male inadequacy and societal restraint. "Rappaccini's Daughter" is a frightening parable of a paternal will converting that vitality into poison. Dr. Rappaccini's madness is a daemonization of the male dread of female sexual power and expresses Hawthorne's subtle despair at the prolongation of patriarchal society. Of all Hawthorne, this story is closest to William Blake, whom the author of *The Scarlet Letter* could not have read.

Edgar Allan Poe

(1809–1849)

V ALÉRY, IN A LETTER to Gide, asserted that "Poe is the only impeccable writer. He was never mistaken." If this judgment startles an
American reader, it is less remarkable than Baudelaire's habit of making
his morning prayers to God and to Edgar Poe. If we add the devotion of
Mallarmé to what he called his master Poe's "severe ideas," then we have
some sense of the scandal of what might be called "French Poe," perhaps as
much a Gallic mystification as "French Freud." French Poe is less bizarre
than French Freud, but more puzzling, because its literary authority ought
to be overwhelming and yet vanishes utterly when confronted by what Poe
actually wrote. Here is the second stanza of the impeccable writer's celebrated lyric, "For Annie":

> Sadly, I know
>   I am shorn of my strength,
> And no muscle I move
>   As I lie at full length—
> But no matter!—I feel
>   I am better at length.

Though of a badness not to be believed, this is by no means unrepresen-
tative of Poe's verse. Aldous Huxley charitably supposed that Baudelaire,
Mallarmé, and Valéry simply had no ear for English and so just could not
hear Poe's palpable vulgarity. Nothing even in Poe's verse is so wickedly
funny as Huxley's parody in which a grand Miltonic touchstone is trans-
muted into the mode of Poe's "Ulalume." First Milton, in *Paradise Lost*,
IV, 268–72:

> Not that fair field
> of Enna, where Proserpine gathering flowers
> Her self a fairer flower by gloomy Dis

Was gathered, which cost Ceres all that pain
To seek her through the world;

Next, Huxley's Poe:

It was noon in the fair field of Enna,
    When Proserpina gathering flowers—
    Herself the most fragrant of flowers,
Was gathered away to Gehenna
    By the Prince of Plutonian powers;
Was borne down the windings of Brenner
    To the gloom of his amorous bowers—
Down the tortuous highway of Brenner
    To the God's agapemonous bowers.

What then did Baudelaire hear, what music of thought, when he read the actual Poe of "Ulalume"?

Here once, through an alley Titanic,
    Of cypress, I roamed with my Soul—
    Of cypress, with Psyche, my Soul.
These were days when my heart was volcanic
    As the scoriac rivers that roll—
    As the lavas that restlessly roll
Their sulphurous currents down Yaanek,
    In the ultimate climes of the Pole—
That groan as they roll down Mount Yaanek,
    In the realms of the boreal Pole.

If this were Edward Lear, poet of "The Dong with the Luminous Nose" or "The Jumblies," one might not question Baudelaire and the other apostles of French Poe. But the hard-driven Poe did not set out to write nonsense verse. His desire was to be the American Coleridge or Byron or Shelley, and his poetry, at its rare best, echoes those High Romantic forerunners with some grace and a certain plangent urgency. Yet even "The City in the Sea" is a touch too close to Byron's "Darkness," while "Israfel" weakly revises Shelley's "To a Skylark." Nineteenth-century American poetry is considerably better than it is generally acknowledged to be. There are no other figures comparable to Whitman and Dickinson, but at least the following are clearly preferable to Poe, taking them chronologically: Bryant, Emerson, Longfellow, Whittier, Jones Very, Thoreau, Melville, Henry Timrod, and Frederick Goddard Tuckerman. Poe scrambles for twelfth place with Sidney Lanier; if this judgment seems harsh, or too arithmetical, it is prompted by the continued French overevaluation of Poe as lyricist. No reader who cares deeply for the best poetry written in English can care greatly for Poe's verse. Huxley's accusation of vulgarity and bad taste is just: "To the most sensitive and high-souled man in the world we should find it hard to forgive, shall we say, the wearing of a diamond ring on every finger. Poe does the equivalent of this in his poetry; we notice the solecism and shudder."

Whatever his early ambitions, Poe wrote relatively little verse; there are scarcely a hundred pages of it in the remarkable edition of his complete writings, in two substantial volumes, published by the Library of America. The bulk of his work is in tale-telling and criticism, with the exception of the problematic *Eureka: A Prose Poem*, a hundred-page cosmology that I take to be Poe's answer to Emerson's Transcendental manifesto, *Nature*. Certainly *Eureka* is more of a literary achievement than Poe's verse, while the popularity and influence of the shorter tales have been and remain immense. Whether either *Eureka* or the famous stories can survive authentic criticism is not clear, but nothing could remove the stories from the canon anyway. They are a permanent element in Western literary culture, even though they are best read when we are very young. Poe's criticism has mixed repute but in fact has never been made fully available until the Library of America edition.

Poe's survival raises perpetually the issue as to whether literary merit and canonical status necessarily go together. I can think of no other American writer, down to this moment, at once so inevitable and so dubious. Mark Twain cataloged Fenimore Cooper's literary offenses, but all that he exuberantly listed are minor compared to Poe's. Allen Tate, proclaiming Poe "our cousin" in 1949, at the centenary of Poe's death, remarked: "He has several styles, and it is not possible to damn them all at once." Uncritical admirers of Poe should be asked to read his stories aloud (but only to themselves!). The association between the acting style of Vincent Price and the styles of Poe is alas not gratuitous, and indeed is an instance of deep crying out unto deep. Lest I be considered unfair by those devoted to Poe, I hasten to quote him at his strongest as a storyteller. Here is the opening paragraph of "William Wilson," a tale admired by Dostoevsky and still central to the great Western topos of the double:

> Let me call myself, for the present, William Wilson. The fair page lying before me need not be sullied with my real appellation. This has already been too much an object for the scorn—for the horror—for the detestation of my race. To the utter-most regions of the globe have not indignant winds bruited its unparalleled infamy? Oh, outcast of all outcasts most abandoned!—to the earth art thou not forever dead? to its honors, to its flowers, to its golden aspirations?—and a cloud, dense, dismal, and limitless, does it not hang eternally between thy hopes and heaven?

This rhetoric, including the rhetorical questions, is British Gothic rather than German Gothic, Ossian or Monk Lewis rather than Tieck or E. T. A. Hoffmann. Its palpable squalors require no commentary. The critical question surely must be: How does "William Wilson" survive its bad writing? Poe's awful diction, whether here or in "The Fall of the House of Usher" or "The Purloined Letter," seems to demand the decent masking of a competent French translation. The tale somehow is stronger than its telling, which is to say that Poe's actual text does not matter. What survives, despite Poe's writing, are the psychological dynamics and mythic reverberations of his stories about William Wilson and Roderick Usher. Poe can only gain by a good translation, and he scarcely loses if each reader fully retells the stories to another. C. S. Lewis, defending the fantasies of George MacDonald, formulated a curious principle that seems to me more applicable to Poe than to MacDonald:

> The texture of his writing as a whole is undistinguished, at times fumbling. . . . But this does not quite dispose of him even for the literary critic. What he does best is fantasy—fantasy that hovers between the allegorical and the mythopoeic. And this, in my opinion, he does better than any man. The critical problem with which we are confronted is whether this art—the art of mythmaking—is a species of the literary art. The objection to so classifying it is that the Myth does not essentially exist in words at all. We all agree that the story of Balder is a great myth, a thing of inexhaustible

value. But of whose version—whose words—are we thinking when we say this?

Lewis replies that he is not thinking of anyone's words, but of a particular pattern of events. Of course that means Lewis is thinking of his own words. He goes so far as to remember:

> . . . when I first heard the story of Kafka's *Castle* related in conversation and afterwards read the book for myself. The reading added nothing. I had already received the myth, which was all that mattered.

Clearly mistaken about Kafka, Lewis was certainly correct about MacDonald's *Lilith*, and I think the insight is valid for Poe's stories. Myths matter because we prefer them in our own words, and so Poe's diction scarcely distracts us from our retelling, to ourselves, his bizarre myths. There is a dreadful universalism pervading Poe's weird tales. The Freudian reductions of Marie Bonaparte pioneered at converting Poe's universalism into the psychoanalytical universalism, but Poe is himself so reductive that the Freudian translations are in his case merely redundant. Poe authentically frightens children, and the fright can be a kind of trauma. I remember reading Poe's tales and Bram Stoker's *Dracula*, each for the first time, when I was about ten. *Dracula* I shrugged off (at least until I confronted Bela Lugosi murmuring: "I never drink—wine!"), but Poe induced nasty and repetitious nightmares that linger even now. Myth may be only what the Polish aphorist Stanisław Lec once called it, "gossip grown old," but then Poe would have to be called a very vivid gossip, though not often a very eloquent one.

Critics, even good ones, admire Poe's stories for some of the oddest of reasons. Poe, a true southerner, abominated Emerson, plainly perceiving that Emerson (like Whitman, like Lincoln) was not a Christian, not a royalist, not a classicist. Self-Reliance, the Emersonian answer to Original Sin, does not exist in the Poe cosmos, where you necessarily start out damned, doomed, and dismal. But I think Poe detested Emerson for some of the same reasons Hawthorne and Melville more subtly resented him, reasons that persisted in Robert Penn Warren, and continue today in many current academic literary critics in our country. If you dislike

Emerson, you probably will like Poe. Emerson fathered pragmatism; Poe fathered precisely nothing, which is the way he would have wanted it. Yvor Winters accused Poe of obscurantism, but that truthful indictment no more damages Poe than do tastelessness and tone-deafness. Emerson, for better and for worse, was and is the mind of America, but Poe was and is our hysteria, our uncanny unanimity in our repressions. I certainly do not intend to mean by this that Poe was deeper than Emerson in any way whatsoever. Emerson cheerfully and consciously threw out the past. Critics tend to share Poe's easy historicism; perhaps without knowing it, they are gratified that every Poe story is, in too clear a sense, over even as it begins. We don't have to wait for Madeline Usher and the house to fall in upon poor Roderick; they have fallen in upon him already, before the narrator comes upon the place. Emerson exalted freedom, which he and Thoreau usefully called "wildness." No one in Poe is or can be free or wild, and some academic admirers of Poe truly like everything and everyone to be in bondage to a universal past. To begin is to be free, god-like and Emersonian-Adamic, or Jeffersonian. But for a writer to be free is bewildering and even maddening. What American writers and their exegetes half-unknowingly love in Poe is his more-than-Freudian oppressive and curiously original sense and sensation of overdetermination. Walter Pater once remarked that museums depressed him because they made him doubt that anyone had ever once been young. No one in a Poe story was ever young. As D. H. Lawrence once angrily observed, everyone in Poe is a vampire—Poe himself in particular.

Among Poe's tales, the near-exception to what I have been saying is the longest and most ambitious, *The Narrative of Arthur Gordon Pym of Nantucket*, just as the best of Poe's poems is the long prose poem *Eureka*. Alas, even these works are somewhat overvalued, if only because Poe's critics understandably become excessively eager to see him vindicated. *Pym* is readable, but *Eureka* is extravagantly repetitious. Auden was quite taken with *Eureka*, but he could remember very little of it in conversation, and one can doubt that he read it through, at least in English. Poe's most advanced critic is John T. Irwin, in his book *American Hieroglyphics*. Irwin rightly centers upon *Pym*, while defending *Eureka* as an "aesthetic cosmology" addressed to what in each of us Freud called the "bodily ego." Irwin is too shrewd to assert that Poe's performance in *Eureka* fulfills Poe's extraordinary intentions:

What the poem *Eureka*, at once pre-Socratic and post-Newtonian, asserts is the truth of the feeling, the bodily intuition, that the diverse objects which the mind discovers in contemplating external nature form a unity, that they are all parts of one body which, if not infinite, is so gigantic as to be beyond both the spatial and temporal limits of human perception. In *Eureka*, then, Poe presents us with the paradox of a "unified" macrocosmic body that is without a totalizing image—an alogical, intuitive belief whose "truth" rests upon Poe's sense that cosmologies and myths of origin are forms of internal geography that, under the guise of mapping the physical universe, map the universe of desire.

Irwin might be writing of Blake, or of other visionaries who have sought to map total forms of desire. What Irwin catches, by implication, is Poe's troubling anticipation of what is most difficult in Freud, the "frontier concepts" between mind and body, such as the bodily ego, the non-repressive defense of introjection, and above all, the drives or instincts. Poe, not just in *Eureka* and in *Pym*, but throughout his tales and even in some of his verse, is peculiarly close to the Freudian speculation upon the bodily ego. Freud, in *The Ego and the Id* (1923), resorted to the uncanny language of E. T. A. Hoffmann (and of Poe) in describing this difficult notion:

> The ego is first and foremost a bodily ego; it is not merely a surface entity, but is itself the projection of a surface. If we wish to find an anatomical analogy for it we can best identify it with the "cortical homunculus" of the anatomists, which stands on its head in the cortex, sticks up its heels, faces backwards and, as we know, has its speech-area on the left-hand side.

A footnote in the English translation of 1927, authorized by Freud but never added to the German editions, elucidates the first sentence of this description in a way analogous to the crucial metaphor in Poe that concludes *The Narrative of Arthur Gordon Pym*:

> I.e. the ego is ultimately derived from bodily sensations, chiefly from those springing from the surface of the body, . . . besides, as we have seen above, representing the superficies of the mental apparatus.

A considerable part of Poe's mythological power emanates from his own difficult sense that the ego is always a bodily ego. The characters of Poe's tales live out nearly every conceivable fantasy of introjection and identification, seeking to assuage their melancholia by psychically devouring the lost objects of their affections. D. H. Lawrence, in his *Studies in Classic American Literature* (1923), moralized powerfully against Poe, condemning him for "the will-to-love and the will-to-consciousness, asserted against death itself. The pride of human conceit in KNOWLEDGE." It is illuminating that Lawrence attacked Poe in much the same spirit as he attacked Freud, who is interpreted in *Psychoanalysis and the Unconscious* (1921) as somehow urging us to violate the taboo against incest. The interpretation is as extravagant as Lawrence's thesis that Poe urges vampirism upon us, but there remains something suggestive in Lawrence's violence against both Freud and Poe. Each placed the elitist individual in jeopardy, Lawrence implied, by hinting at the primacy of fantasy not just in the sexual life proper, but in the bodily ego's constitution of itself through acts of incorporation and identification.

The cosmology of *Eureka* and the narrative of *Pym* alike circle around fantasies of incorporation. *Eureka's* subtitle is "An Essay on the Material and Spiritual Universe," and what Poe calls its "general proposition" is heightened by italics: "*In the Original Unity of the First Thing lies the Secondary Cause of All Things, with the Germ of their Inevitable Annihilation.*" Freud, in *his* cosmology, *Beyond the Pleasure Principle* (1920), posited that the inorganic had preceded the organic, and also that it was the tendency of all things to return to their original state. Consequently, the aim of all life was death. The death drive, which became crucial for Freud's later dualisms, is nevertheless pure mythology, since Freud's only evidence for it was the repetition compulsion, and it is an extravagant leap from repetition to death. This reliance upon one's own mythology may have prompted Freud's audacity when, in the *New Introductory Lectures*, he admitted that the theory of drives was, so to speak, his own mythology, drives being not only magnificent conceptions but particularly sublime in their indefiniteness. I wish I could assert that *Eureka* has some of the speculative force of *Beyond the Pleasure Principle* or even of Freud's disciple Ferenczi's startling *Thalassa: A Theory of Genitality*, but *Eureka* does badly enough when compared to Emerson's *Nature*, which itself has only a few passages worthy of what Emerson wrote afterwards. And yet Valéry in one sense was justified in his praise for *Eureka*. For certain intellectuals,

Eureka performs a mythological function akin to what Poe's tales continue to do for hosts of readers. *Eureka* is unevenly written, badly repetitious, and sometimes opaque in its abstractness, but like the tales it seems not to have been composed by a particular individual. The universalism of a common nightmare informs it. If the tales lose little, or even gain, when we retell them to others in our own words, *Eureka* gains by Valéry's observations, or by the summaries of modern critics like John Irwin or Daniel Hoffman. Translation even into his own language always benefits Poe.

I haven't the space, or the desire, to summarize *Eureka*, and no summary is likely to do anything besides deadening both my readers and myself. Certainly Poe was never more passionately sincere than in composing *Eureka*, of which he affirmed: "*What I here propound is true.*" But these are the closing sentences of *Eureka*:

> Think that the sense of individual identity will be gradually merged in the general consciousness—that Man, for example, ceasing imperceptibly to feel himself Man, will at length attain that awfully triumphant epoch when he shall recognize his existence as that of Jehovah. In the meantime bear in mind that all is Life-Life-Life within Life—the less within the greater, and all within the Spirit Divine.

To this, Poe appends a "Note":

> The pain of the consideration that we shall lose our individual identity, ceases at once when we further reflect that the process, as above described, is, neither more nor less than that of the absorption, by each individual intelligence of all other intelligences (that is, of the Universe) into its own. That God may be all in all, *each* must become God.

Allen Tate, not unsympathetic to his cousin, Mr. Poe, remarked of Poe's extinction in *Eureka* that "there is a lurid sublimity in the spectacle of his taking God along with him into a grave which is not smaller than the universe." If we read closely, Poe's trope is "absorption," and we are where we always are in Poe, amid ultimate fantasies of introjection in which the bodily ego and the cosmos become indistinguishable. That makes Poe the most cannibalistic of authors, and seems less a function of his "angelic" theological imagination than of his mechanisms of defense. Again, I suspect this judgment hardly weakens Poe, since his strength is no more cognitive than it is stylistic. Poe's mythology, like the mythology of psychoanalysis that we cannot yet bear to acknowledge as primarily a mythology, is peculiarly appropriate to any modernism, whether you want to call it early, high, or postmodernism. The definitive judgment belongs here to T. W. Adorno, certainly the most authentic theoretician of all modernisms, in his last book, *Aesthetic Theory*. Writing on "reconciliation and mimetic adaptation to death," Adorno blends the insights of Jewish negative theology and psychoanalysis:

> Whether negativity is the barrier or the truth of art is not for art to decide. Art works are negative *per se* because they are subject to the law of objectification; that is, they kill what they objectify, tearing it away from its context of immediacy and real life. They survive because they bring death. This is particularly true of modern art, where we notice a general mimetic abandonment to reification, which is the principle of death. Illusion in art is the attempt to escape from this principle. Baudelaire marks a watershed, in that art after him seeks to discard illusion without resigning itself to being a thing among things. The harbingers of modernism, Poe and Baudelaire, were the first technocrats of art.

Baudelaire was more than a technocrat of art, as Adorno knew, but Poe would be only that except for his mythmaking gift. C. S. Lewis may have been right when he insisted that such a gift could exist even apart from other literary endowments. Blake and Freud are inescapable mythmakers who were also cognitively and stylistically powerful. Poe is a great fantasist whose thoughts were commonplace and whose metaphors were dead. Fantasy, mythologically considered, combines the stances of Narcissus and Prometheus, which are ideologically antithetical to one another, but figuratively quite compatible. Poe is at once the Narcissus and the Prometheus of his nation. If that is right, then he is inescapable, even though his tales contrast weakly with Hawthorne's, his poems scarcely bear reading, and his speculative discourses fade away in juxtaposition to Emerson's, his despised Northern rival.

To define Poe's mythopoeic inevitability more closely, I turn to his story "Ligeia" and to the end of *Pym*. Ligeia, a tall, dark, slender transcendentalist, dies murmuring a protest against the feeble human will, which cannot keep us forever alive. Her distraught and nameless widower, the narrator, endeavors to comfort himself, first with opium, and then with a second bride, "the fair-haired and blue-eyed Lady Rowena Trevanian, of Tremaine." Unfortunately, he has little use for this replacement, and so she sickens rapidly and dies. Recurrently, the corpse revivifies, only to die yet again and again. At last, the cerements are stripped away, and the narrator confronts the undead Ligeia, attired in the death-draperies of her now evaporated successor.

As a parable of the vampiric will, this works well enough. The learned Ligeia presumably has completed her training in the will during her absence, or perhaps merely owes death a substitute, the insufficiently transcendental Rowena. What is mythopoeically more impressive is the ambiguous question of the narrator's will. Poe's own life, like Walt Whitman's, is an American mythology, and what all of us generally remember about it is that Poe married his first cousin, Virginia Clemm, before she turned fourteen. She died a little more than ten years later, having been a semi-invalid for most of that time. Poe himself died less than three years after her, when he was just forty. "Ligeia," regarded by Poe as his best tale, was written a bit more than a year into the marriage. The later Freud implicitly speculates that there are no accidents; we die because we will to die, our character being also our fate. In Poe's myth also, ethos is the daemon, and the daemon is our destiny. The year after Virginia died, Poe proposed marriage to the widowed poet Sarah Helen Whitman. Biographers tell us that the lady's doubts were caused by rumors of Poe's bad character, but perhaps Mrs. Whitman had read "Ligeia"! In any event, this marriage did not take place, nor did Poe survive to marry another widow, his childhood sweetheart Elmira Shelton (née Royster). Perhaps she too might have read "Ligeia" and forborne.

The narrator of "Ligeia" has a singularly bad memory, or else a very curious relationship to his own will, since he begins by telling us that he married Ligeia without ever having troubled to learn her family name. Her name itself is legend, or romance, and that was enough. As the story's second paragraph hints, the lady was an opium dream with the footfall of a shadow. The implication may be that there never was such a lady, or even that if you wish to incarnate your reveries, then you must immolate your consubstantial Rowena. What is a touch alarming, to the narrator, is the intensity of Ligeia's passion for him, which was manifested, however, only by glances and voice so long as the ideal lady lived. Perhaps this baffled intensity is what kills Ligeia, through a kind of narcissistic dialectic, since she is dominated not by the will of her lust but by the lust of her will. She wills her infinite passion toward the necessarily inadequate narrator and when (by implication) he fails her, she turns the passion of her will against dying and at last against death. Her dreadful poem "The Conqueror Worm" prophesies her cyclic return from death: "Through a circle that ever returneth in / To the self-same spot." But when she does return, the spot is hardly the same. Poor Rowena only becomes even slightly interesting to her narrator-husband when she sickens unto death, and her body is wholly usurped by the revived Ligeia. And yet the wretched narrator is a touch different, if only because his narcissism is finally out of balance with his first wife's grisly Prometheanism. There are no final declarations of Ligeia's passion as the story concludes. The triumph of her will is complete, but we know that the narrator's will has not blended itself into Ligeia's. His renewed obsession with her eyes testifies to a continued sense of her daemonic power over him, but his final words hint at what the story's opening confirms: she will not be back for long—and remains "my lost love."

The conclusion of *Pym* has been brilliantly analyzed by John Irwin, and so I want to glance only briefly at what is certainly Poe's most effective closure:

> And now we rushed into the embraces of the cataract, where a chasm threw itself open to receive us. But there arose in our pathway a shrouded human figure, very far larger in its proportions than any dweller among men. And the hue of the skin of the figure was of the perfect whiteness of the snow.

Irwin demonstrates Poe's reliance here upon the Romantic topos of the Alpine White Shadow, the magnified projection of the observer himself. The chasm Pym enters is the familiar Romantic Abyss, not a part of the natural world but belonging to eternity, before the creation. Reflected in that abyss, Pym beholds his own shrouded form, perfect in the whiteness of the natural context. Presumably, this is the original bodily ego, the Gnostic self before the fall into creation. As at the close of *Eureka*, Poe brings Alpha and Omega together in an apocalyptic circle. I suggest we read Pym's, which is to say Poe's, white shadow as the American triumph of the will, as illusory as Ligeia's usurpation of Rowena's corpse.

Poe teaches us, through Pym and Ligeia, that as Americans we are both subject and object of our own quests. Emerson, in Americanizing the European sense of the abyss, kept the self and the abyss separate as facts: "There may be two or three or four steps, according to the genius of each, but for every seeing soul there are two absorbing facts—I and the Abyss." Poe, seeking to avoid Emersonianism, ends with only one fact, and it is more a wish than a fact: "I will to be the Abyss." This metaphysical despair has appealed to the Southern American literary tradition and to its Northern followers. The appeal cannot be refuted, because it is myth, and Poe backed the myth with his life as well as his work. If the Northern or Emersonian myth of our literary culture culminates in the beautiful image of Walt Whitman as wound-dresser, moving as a mothering father through the Civil War Washington, D.C., hospitals, then the Southern or counter-myth achieves its perfect stasis at its start, with Poe's snow-white shadow shrouding the chasm down which the boat of the soul is about to plunge. Poe's genius was for negativity and opposition, and the affirmative force of Emersonian America gave him the impetus his daemonic will required.

It would be a relief to say that Poe's achievement as a critic is not mythological, but the splendid, almost complete edition of his essays, reviews, and marginalia testifies otherwise. It shows Poe indeed to have been Adorno's "technocrat of art." Auden defended Poe's criticism by contrasting the subjects Baudelaire was granted—Delacroix, Constantin Guys, Wagner—with the books Poe was given to review, such as *The Christian Florist*, *The History of Texas*, and *Poetical Remains of the Late Lucretia Maria Davidson*. The answer to Auden is that Poe also wrote about Bryant, Byron, Coleridge, Dickens, Hawthorne, Washington Irving, Longfellow, Shelley, and Tennyson, a nonet providing scope enough for any authentic critical consciousness. Nothing that Poe had to say about these poets and storytellers is in any way memorable or at all an aid to reading them. There are no critical insights, no original perceptions, no accurate or illuminating juxtapositions or historical placements. Here is Poe on Tennyson, from his *Marginalia*, which generally surpasses his other criticism:

> Why do some persons fatigue themselves in attempts to unravel such phantasy-pieces as the "Lady of Shalott"? . . . If the author

did not deliberately propose to himself a suggestive indefinite-ness of meaning, with the view of bringing about a definiteness of vague and therefore of spiritual effect—this, at least, arose from the silent analytical promptings of that poetic genius which, in its supreme development, embodies all orders of intellectual capacity.

I take this as being representative of Poe's criticism, because it is uninter-estingly just plain *wrong* about "The Lady of Shalott." No other poem, even by the great word-painter Tennyson, is deliberately so definite in meaning and effect. Everything vague precisely is excluded in this perhaps most Pre-Raphaelite of all poems, where each detail contributes to an impres-sion that might be called hard-edged phantasmagoria. If we take as the three possibilities of nineteenth-century practical criticism the sequence of Arnold, Pater, and Wilde, we find Poe useless in all three modes: Arnold's seeing the object as in itself it really is, Pater's seeing accurately one's own impression of the object, and the divine Oscar's sublime seeing of the object as in itself it really is not. If "The Lady of Shalott" is the object, then Poe does not see anything: the poem as in itself it is, one's impression of the poem as that is, or best of all the Wildean sense of what is missing or excluded from the poem. Poe's descriptive terms are "indefinitiveness" and "vague," but Tennyson's poem is just the reverse:

> She left the web, she left the loom,
> She made three paces through the room,
> She saw the water-lily bloom,
> She saw the helmet and the plume,
>   She looked down to Camelot.
> Out flew the web and floated wide;
> The mirror cracked from side to side;
> "The curse is come upon me," cried
>   The Lady of Shalott.

No, Poe as practical critic is a true match for most of his contemporary subjects, such as S. Anna Lewis, author of *The Child of the Sea and Other Poems* (1848). Of her lyric "The Forsaken," Poe wrote: "We have read this little poem more than twenty times and always with increasing admiration. *It is inexpressibly beautiful*" (Poe's italics). I quote only the first of its six stanzas:

It hath been said—for all who die
   there is a tear;
Some pining, bleeding heart to sigh
   O'er every bier:
But in that hour of pain and dread
   Who will draw near
Around my humble couch and shed
   One farewell tear?

Well, but there is Poe as theoretician, Valéry has told us. Acute self-consciousness in Poe was strongly misread by Valéry as the inauguration and development of severe and skeptical ideas. Presumably, this is the Poe of three famous essays: "The Philosophy of Composition," "The Rationale of Verse," and "The Poetic Principle." Having just reread these pieces, I have no possibility of understanding a letter of Valéry to Mallarmé which prizes the theories of Poe as being "so profound and so insidiously learned." Certainly we prize the theories of Valéry for just those qualities, and so I have come full circle to where I began, with the mystery of French Poe. Valéry may be said to have read Poe in the critical modes of both Pater and Wilde. He saw his impression of Poe clearly, and he saw Poe's essays as in themselves they really were not. Admirable, and so Valéry brought to culmination the critical myth that is French Poe."

Hart Crane's vision of Poe, in "The Tunnel" section of *The Bridge*, tells us again why the mythopoeic Poe is inescapable for American literary mythology. Poe's nightmare projections and introjections suggest the New York city subway as the new underground, where Coleridge's "deep Romantic chasm" has been internalized into "the chasms of the brain."

Whose head is swinging from the swollen strap?
Whose body smokes along the bitten rails,
Bursts from a smoldering bundle far behind
In back forks of the chasms of the brain—
Puffs from a riven stump far out behind
In interborough fissures of the mind . . . ?

Whatever his actual failures as poet and critic, whatever the gap between style and idea in his tales, Poe is central to the American canon, both for us and for the rest of the world. Hawthorne implicitly and Melville explicitly made far more powerful critics of the Emersonian national hope, but they were by no means wholly negative in regard to Emerson and his pragmatic vision of American Self-Reliance. Poe was savage in denouncing minor transcendentalists like Bronson Alcott and William Ellery Channing, but his explicit rejection of Emerson confined itself to the untruthful observation that Emerson was indistinguishable from Thomas Carlyle. Poe should have survived to read Carlyle's insane and amazing pamphlet on "The Nigger Question," which he would have adored. Mythologically, Poe is necessary because all of his work is a hymn to negativity. Emerson was a great theoretician of literature as of life, a good practical critic (when he wanted to be, which was not often), a very good poet (sometimes), and always a major aphorist and essayist. Poe, on a line-by-line or sentence-by-sentence basis, is hardly a worthy opponent. But looking in the French way, as T. S. Eliot recommended: "we see a mass of unique shape and impressive size to which the eye constantly returns." Eliot was probably right, in mythopoeic terms.

Henry David Thoreau
(1817–1862)

ALL OF US, however idiosyncratic, begin by living in a generation that overdetermines more of our stances and judgments than we can hope to know, until we are far along in the revisionary processes that can bring us to a Second Birth. I myself read *Walden* while I was very young, and "Civil Disobedience" and "Life without Principle" soon afterwards. But I read little or no Emerson until I was an undergraduate and achieved only a limited awareness of him then. I began to read Emerson obsessively just before the middle of the journey, when in crisis, and have never stopped reading him since. More even than Freud, Emerson helped change my mind about most things, in life and in literature, myself included. Going back to Thoreau, when one has been steeped in Emerson for more than twenty years, is a curious experience. A distinguished American philosopher, my contemporary, has written that he underwent the reverse process, coming to Emerson only after a profound knowing of Thoreau, and has confessed that Emerson seemed to him at first a "second-rate Thoreau." I am not tempted to call Thoreau a second-rate Emerson, because Thoreau, at his rare best, was a strong writer, and he revised Emerson with passion and with cunning. But Emerson was for Thoreau even more massively what he was for Walt Whitman and all Americans of sensibility ever since: the metaphor of "the father," the pragmatic image of the ego ideal, the inescapable precursor, the literary hero, the mind of the United States of America.

My own literary generation had to recover Emerson, because we came after the critics formed by the example and ideology of T. S. Eliot, who had proclaimed that "the essays of Emerson are already an encumbrance." I can recall conversations about Emerson with R. P. Blackmur, who informed me that Emerson was of no relevance, except insofar as he represented an extreme example for America of the unsupported and catastrophic Protestant sensibility, which had ruined the Latin culture of Europe. Allen Tate more succinctly told me that Emerson simply was the devil, a judgment amplified in my single conversation with the vigorous Yvor Winters. In

many years of friendship with Robert Penn Warren, my only disputes with
that great poet concerned Emerson. As these were the critical minds that
dominated American letters from 1945 to 1965 (except for Lionel Trilling,
who was silent on Emerson), it is no surprise that Emerson vanished in that
era. From 1965 through the present, Emerson has returned, as he always
must and will, because he is the pragmatic origin of our literary culture.
Walt Whitman and Emily Dickinson, Robert Frost and Wallace Stevens,
Hart Crane, Elizabeth Bishop, and John Ashbery have written the poems
of our climate, but Emerson was and is that climate.

How does Thoreau now read in our recovered sense of the Emersonian
climate? Is the question itself unfair? Rereading *Walden* and the major
essays, I confess to an experience different in degree, but not in kind,
from a fresh encounter with Thoreau's verse. As a poet, Thoreau is in the
shadow of Wordsworth, toward whom his apotropaic gestures are sadly
weak. In prose, conceptually and rhetorically, Thoreau strongly seeks to
evade Emerson, wherever he cannot revise him directly. But this endless
agon, unlike Whitman's, or the subtler subversion of Emerson by Dickinson
and by Henry James, is won by the image of the father. Rereading Thoreau,
either I hear Emerson overtly, or more darkly I detect him in what Stevens
called "the hum of thoughts evaded in the mind."

During that 1945–65 heyday of what then was called "the New Criticism," only *Walden*, among all of Thoreau's works, was exempt from cen-
sure. I have never understood the New Critical tolerance for *Walden*,
except as a grudging bit of cultural patriotism, or perhaps as a kind of ultimate act of revenge against Emerson, the prophet who organized support
for John Brown, cast out Daniel Webster because of the Fugitive Slave Act,
and burned himself into a premature senility by his fierce contempt for the
South and its culture throughout the Civil War. Thoreau, no less an enthu-
siast for John Brown, and equally apocalyptic against the South, somehow escaped the wrath of Tate, Warren, and their cohorts. This may have
something to do with the myth of Thoreau as a kind of American Mahatma
Gandhi, a Tolstoyan hermit practicing native arts and crafts out in the
woods. Homespun and reputedly naive, such a fellow may have seemed
harmless enough, unlike the slyly wicked Sage of Concord, Ralph Waldo
Lucifer, impediment to the United States somehow acquiring a Southern
and Latin culture.

Thoreau's crucial swerve away from Emerson was to treat natural objects
as books, and books as chunks of nature, thus evading all literary tradition,

Emerson's writings not excepted. Unfortunately, Thoreau was not really an oppositional or dialectical thinker, like Emerson, though certainly an oppositional personality, as the sane and sacred Emerson was not. Being also something of a prig and an elitist, again unlike Emerson, Thoreau could not always manage Emerson's insouciant praxis of building up a kind of Longinian discourse by quoting amply without citation. Self-consciousness kept breaking in, as it rarely does with Emerson, unless Emerson wills it thus. But, if you cannot achieve freedom in quotation, if you cannot convert the riches of others to your own use without a darkening of consciousness, then what can it mean to demand that books and natural objects interchange their attributes? *Walden*, for all its incessant power, is frequently uneasy because of an unspoken presence, or a perpetual absence that might as well be a presence, and that emerges in Thoreau's *Journal*:

> Emerson does not consider things in respect to their essential utility, but an important partial and relative one, as works of art perhaps. His probes pass one side of their center of gravity. His exaggeration is of a part, not of the whole.

This is, of course, to find the fault that is not there, and qualifies only as a weak misreading of Emerson. Indeed, it is to attribute to Emerson what is actually Thoreau's revision of Emerson, since it is Thoreau who considers things as books, not Emerson, for whom a fact was an epiphany of God, God being merely what was oldest in oneself, that which went back before the Creation-Fall. Emerson, like the considerably less genial Carlyle, was a kind of Gnostic, but the rebel Thoreau remained a Wordsworthian, reading nature for evidences of a continuity in the ontological self that nature simply could not provide.

Thoreau on "Reading" in *Walden* is therefore chargeable with a certain bad faith, as here in a meditation where Emerson, the Plato of Concord, is not less than everywhere, present by absence, and perhaps even more absent by repressed presence:

> I aspire to be acquainted with wiser men than this our Concord soil has produced, whose names are hardly known here. Or shall I hear the name of Plato and never read his book? As if Plato were my townsman and I never saw him,—my next neighbor and I never heard him speak or attended to the wisdom of his words. But how

actually is it? His Dialogues, which contain what was immortal in him, lie on the next shelf, and yet I never read them. We are underbred and low-lived and illiterate; and in this respect I confess I do not make any very broad distinction between the illiterateness of my townsman who cannot read at all, and the illiterateness of him who has learned to read only what is for children and feeble intellects. We should be as good as the worthies of antiquity, but partly by first knowing how good they were. We are a race of titmen, and soar but little higher in our intellectual flights than the columns of the daily paper.

It is not all books that are as dull as their readers. There are probably words addressed to our condition exactly, which, if we could really hear and understand, would be more salutary than the morning or the spring to our lives, and possibly put a new aspect on the face of things for us. How many a man has dated a new era in his life from the reading of a book. The book exists for us perchance which will explain our miracles and reveal new ones. The at present unutterable things we may find somewhere uttered. These same questions that disturb and puzzle and confound us have in their turn occurred to all the wise men; not one has been omitted; and each has answered them, according to his ability, by his words and his life. Moreover, with wisdom we shall learn liberality. The solitary hired man on a farm in the outskirts of Concord, who has had his second birth and peculiar religious experience, and is driven as he believes into silent gravity and exclusiveness by his faith, may think it is not true; but Zoroaster, thousands of years ago, travelled the same road and had the same experience; but he, being wise, knew it to be universal, and treated his neighbors accordingly, and is even said to have invented and established worship among men. Let him humbly commune with Zoroaster then, and, through the liberalizing influence of all the worthies, with Jesus Christ himself, and let "our church" go by the board.

The wisest man our Concord soil has produced need not be named, particularly since he vied only with Thoreau as a devoted reader of Plato. The second paragraph I have quoted rewrites the "Divinity School Address," but with the characteristic Thoreauvian swerve toward the authority of books, rather than away from them in the Emersonian manner. The reader or student, according to Emerson, is to consider herself or himself the text, and all received texts only as commentaries upon the scholar of one candle, as the title-essay of *Society and Solitude* prophesies Wallace Stevens in naming that single one for whom all books are written. It may be the greatest literary sorrow of Thoreau that he could assert his independence from Emerson only by falling back upon the authority of texts, however recondite or far from the normative the text might be.

One can read Thoreau's continued bondage in *Walden's* greatest triumph, its preternaturally eloquent "Conclusion":

> The life in us is like the water in the river. It may rise this year higher than man has ever known it, and flood the parched uplands; even this may be the eventful year, which will drown out all our muskrats. It was not always dry land where we dwell. I see far inland the banks which the stream anciently washed, before science began to record its freshets. Every one has heard the story which has gone the rounds of New England, of a strong and beautiful bug which came out of the dry leaf of an old table of apple-tree wood, which had stood in a farmer's kitchen for sixty years, first in Connecticut, and afterwards in Massachusetts,—from an egg deposited in the living tree many years earlier still, as appeared by counting the annual layers beyond it; which was heard gnawing out for several weeks, hatched perchance by the heat of an urn. Who does not feel his faith in a resurrection and immortality strengthened by hearing of this? Who knows what beautiful and winged life, whose egg has been buried for ages under many concentric layers of woodenness in the dead dry life of society, deposited at first in the alburnum of the green and living tree, which has been gradually converted into the semblance of its well-seasoned tomb,—heard perchance gnawing out now for years by the astonished family of man, as they sat round the festive board,—may unexpectedly come forth from amidst society's most trivial and handselled furniture, to enjoy its perfect summer life at last!
>
> I do not say that John or Jonathan will realize all this; but such is the character of that morrow which mere lapse of time can never make to dawn. The light which puts out our eyes is darkness to us. Only that day dawns to which we are awake. There is more day to dawn. The sun is but a morning star.

The first of these paragraphs echoes, perhaps unknowingly, several crucial metaphors in the opening pages of Emerson's strongest single essay, "Experience," but more emphatically Thoreau subverts Emerson's emphasis upon a Transcendental impulse that cannot be repressed, even if one sets out deliberately to perform the experiment of "Experience," which is to follow empirical principles until they land one in an intolerable, more than skeptical, even nihilistic entrapment. Emerson, already more than Nietzschean in "Experience," is repudiated in and by the desperately energetic, indeed apocalyptic Transcendentalism of the end of *Walden*, an end that refuses Emersonian (and Nietzschean) dialectical irony. But the beautiful, brief final paragraph of *Walden* brings back Emerson anyway, with an unmistakable if doubtless involuntary allusion to the rhapsodic conclusion of *Nature*, where, however, the attentive reader always will hear (or overhear) some acute Emersonian ironies. "Try to live as though it were morning" was Nietzsche's great admonition to us, if we were to become Overmen, free of the superego. Nietzsche was never more Emersonian than in this, as he well knew. But when Thoreau eloquently cries out: "The sun is but a morning star," he is not echoing but trying to controvert Emerson's sardonic observation that you don't get a candle in order to see the sun rise. There may indeed be a sun beyond the sun, as Blake, D. H. Lawrence, and other heroic vitalists have insisted, but Thoreau was too canny, perhaps too New England, to be a vitalist. *Walden* rings out mightily as it ends, but it peals another man's music, a man whom Thoreau could neither accept nor forget.

Walt Whitman

(1819–1892)

A S POET and as person, Walt Whitman remains large and evasive. We cannot know, even now, much that he desired us not to know, despite the best efforts of many devoted and scholarly biographers. The relation between his life and his poetry is far more uncertain than most of his readers believe it to be. Yet Whitman is so important to us, so crucial to an American mythology, so absolutely central to our literary culture, that we need to go on trying to bring his life and his work together. Our need might have delighted Whitman, and might have troubled him also. Like his master, Emerson, Whitman prophesied an American religion that is post-Christian, but while Emerson dared to suggest that the Crucifixion was a defeat and that Americans demand victory, Whitman dared further and suggested that he himself had satisfied the demand. Here is Emerson in his *Journal* in April 1842:

> The history of Christ is the best document of the power of character which we have. A youth who owed nothing to fortune and who was "hanged at Tyburn"—by the pure quality of his nature has shed this epic splendor around the facts of his death which has transfigured every particular into a grand universal symbol for the eyes of all mankind ever since.
>
> He did well. This great Defeat is hitherto the highest fact we have. But he that shall come shall do better. The mind requires a far higher exhibition of character, one which shall make itself good to the senses as well as to the soul; a success to the senses as well as to the soul. This was a great Defeat; we demand Victory.

This grand journal entry concludes, magnificently: "I am *Defeated* all the time; yet to Victory I am born." And here is Whitman, "he that shall come," doing better:

That I could forget the mockers and insults!
That I could forget the trickling tears and the blows of the
    bludgeons and hammers!
That I could look with a separate look on my own crucifixion
    and bloody crowning.
I remember now,
I resume the overstaid fraction,
The grave of rock multiplies what has been confided to it,
    or to any graves,
Corpses rise, gashes heal, fastenings roll from me.

I troop forth replenish'd with supreme power, . . .

This is Walt Whitman "singing and chanting the things that are part of him, / The worlds that were and will be, death and day," in the words of his involuntary heir, Wallace Stevens. But which Walt Whitman is it? His central poem is what he finally entitled "Song of Myself," rather than, say, "Song of My Soul." But which self? There are two in the poem, besides his soul, and the true difficulties of reading Whitman begin (or ought to begin) with his unnervingly original psychic cartography, which resists assimilation to the Freudian maps of the mind. Freud's later system divides us into the "I" or ego, the "above-I" or superego, and the "it" or id. Whitman divided himself (or recognized himself as divided) into "my self," "my soul," and the "real Me" or "Me myself," where the self is a kind of ego, the soul not quite a superego, and the "real Me" not at all an id. Or to use a vocabulary known to Whitman, and still known to us, the self is personality, the soul is character, and again the "real Me" is a mystery. Lest these difficulties seem merely my own, and not truly Whitman's, I turn to the text of "Song of Myself." Here is Walt Whitman, "My self," the persona or mask, the personality of the poet:

Walt Whitman, a kosmos, of Manhattan the son,
Turbulent, fleshy, sensual, eating, drinking and breeding,
No sentimentalist, no stander above men and women or apart
    from them,
No more modest than immodest.

This is Walt Whitman, one of the roughs, an American, but hardly Walter Whitman, Jr., whose true personality, "real Me" or "Me myself," is presented in the passage I love best in the poem:

These come to me days and nights and go from me again,
But they are not the Me myself.

Apart from the pulling and hauling stands what I am,
Stands amused, complacent, compassionating, idle, unitary,
Looks down, is erect, or bends an arm on an impalpable certain
    rest,
Looking with side-curved head curious what will come next,
Both in and out of the game and watching and wondering at it.

This "Me myself" is not exactly "hankering, gross, mystical, nude," nor
quite "turbulent, fleshy, sensual, eating, drinking and breeding." Graceful
and apart, cunningly balanced, charming beyond measure, this curious
"real Me" is boy-like and girl-like, very American yet not one of the roughs,
provocative, at one with itself. Whatever the Whitmanian soul may be, this
"Me myself" evidently can have no equal relationship with it. When the
Whitmanian "I" addresses the soul, we hear a warning:

I believe in you my soul, the other I am must not abase itself
    to you,
And you must not be abased to the other.

The "I" here is the "Myself" of "Song of Myself," poetic personality,
robust and rough. "The other I am" is the "Me myself," in and out of the
game, and clearly not suited for embraces with the soul. Whitman's wariness, his fear of abasement, whether of his soul or of his true, inner personality, one to the other, remains the enigma of his poetry, as of his life, and
accounts for his intricate evasions both as poet and as person.

Whitman's critics thus commence with a formidable disadvantage as they
attempt to receive and comprehend his work. The largest puzzle about the
continuing reception of Whitman's poetry is the still prevalent notion that
we ought to take him at his word, whether about his self (or selves) or about
his art. No other poet insists so vehemently and so continuously that he
will tell us all, and tell us all without artifice, and yet tells us so little, and
so cunningly. Except for Dickinson (the only American poet comparable to
him in magnitude), there is no other nineteenth-century poet as difficult
and hermetic as Whitman; not Blake, not Browning, not Mallarmé. Only
an elite can read Whitman, despite the poet's insistence that he wrote for
the people, for "powerful uneducated persons," as his "By Blue Ontario's

Shore" proclaims. His more accurate "Poets to Come" is closer to his readers' experience of him:

> I am a man who, sauntering along without fully stopping, turns
>   a casual look upon you and then averts his face.

Whitman was surely too sly to deceive himself, or at least both of his
selves, on this matter of his actual poetic evasiveness and esotericism.
Humanly, he had much to evade, in order to keep going, in order to start
writing and then to keep writing. His biographers cannot give us a clear
image of his childhood, which was certainly rather miserable. His numerous siblings had mostly melancholy life histories. Madness, retardation,
marriage to a prostitute, depressiveness, and hypochondria figure among
their fates. The extraordinary obsession with health and cleanliness that
oddly marks Whitman's poetry had a poignant origin in his early circumstances. Of his uneasy relationship with his father we know a little, though
not much. But we know nothing really of his mother and how he felt toward
her. Perhaps the most crucial fact about Whitman's psyche we know well
enough; he needed, quite early, to become the true father of all his siblings,
and perhaps of his mother also. Certainly he fathered and mothered as
many of his siblings as he could, even as he so beautifully became a surrogate father and mother for thousands of wounded and sick soldiers, Union
and Confederate, white and black, in the hospitals of Washington, D.C.,
throughout the Civil War.

The extraordinary and truthful image of Whitman that haunts our
country; the vision of the compassionate, unpaid, volunteer wound-dresser
comforting young men in pain and soothing the dying, is the climax of
Paul Zweig's book on how the man Walter Whitman, Jr., became the poet
Walt Whitman. This vision informs the finest pages of Zweig's uneven but
moving study; I cannot recall any previous Whitman biographer or critic
so vividly and humanely portraying Whitman's hospital service. Searching for the authentic Whitman, as Zweig shows, is a hopeless quest; our
greatest poet will always be our most evasive and perhaps our most self-
contradictory. Whitman, at his greatest, has overwhelming pathos as a poet;
equal I think to anything in the language. The *Drum-Taps* poem called
"The Wound-Dresser" is far from Whitman at his astonishing best, and
yet its concluding lines carry the persuasive force of his poetic and human
images for once unified:

Returning, resuming, I thread my way through the hospitals,
The hurt and wounded I pacify with soothing hand,
I sit by the restless all the dark night, some are so young,
Some suffer so much, I recall the experience sweet and sad,
(Many a soldier's loving arms about this neck have cross'd and
    rested,
Many a soldier's kiss dwells on these bearded lips.)

Zweig is admirably sensitive in exploring the ambiguities in Whitman's hospital intensities, and more admirable still in his restraint at not voicing how much all of us are touched by Whitman's pragmatic saintliness during those years of service. I cannot think of a Western writer of anything like Whitman's achievement who ever gave himself or herself up so directly to meeting the agonized needs of the most desperate. There are a handful of American poets comparable to Whitman in stature: Emily Dickinson, certainly, Wallace Stevens and Robert Frost perhaps, and maybe one or two others. Our image of them, or of our greatest novelists, or even of Whitman's master, Emerson, can move us sometimes, but not as the image of the wound-dresser Whitman must move us. Like the Lincoln whom he celebrated and lamented, Whitman is American legend, a figure who has a kind of religious aura even for secular intellectuals. If Emerson founded the American literary religion, Whitman alone permanently holds the place most emblematic of the life of the spirit in America.

These religious terms are not Zweig's, yet his book's enterprise usefully traces the winding paths that led Whitman on to his apotheosis as healer and comforter. Whitman's psychosexuality, labyrinthine in its perplexities, may have been the central drive that bewildered the poet into those ways, but it was not the solitary, overwhelming determinant that many readers judge it to have been. Zweig refreshingly is not one of these overdetermined readers. He surmises that Whitman might have experienced little actual homosexual intercourse. I suspect none, though Whitman evidently was intensely in love with some unnamed man in 1859, and rather differently in love again with Peter Doyle about five years later. Zweig accurately observes that "few poets have written as erotically as Whitman, while having so little to say about sex. For the most part, his erotic poetry is intransitive, self-delighting." Indeed, it is precisely autoerotic rather more than it is homoerotic; Whitman overtly celebrates masturbation, and his most authentic sexual passion is always for himself. One would hardly know this from reading many of Whitman's critics, but one certainly knows it by closely reading Whitman's major poems. Here is part of a crucial crisis-passage from "Song of Myself," resolved through successful masturbation:

> I merely stir, press, feel with my fingers, and am happy,
> To touch my person to some one else's is about as much as I can
>   stand.
>
> Is this then a touch? quivering me to a new identity,
> Flames and ether making a rush for my veins,
> Treacherous tip of me reaching and crowding to help them,
> My flesh and blood playing out lightning to strike what is hardly
>   different from myself,
> . . . .
> I went myself first to the headland, my own hands carried me
>   there.
> You villain touch! what are you doing? my breath is tight in its
>   throat,
> Unclench your floodgates, you are too much for me.
>
> Blind loving wrestling touch, sheath'd hooded sharp-tooth'd
>   touch!
> Did it make you ache so, leaving me?
> Parting track'd by arriving, perpetual payment of perpetual loan,
> Rich showering rain, and recompense richer afterward.
> Sprouts take and accumulate, stand by the curb prolific and vital,
> Landscapes projected masculine, full-sized and golden.

I take it that this celebratory mode of masturbation, whether read metaphorically or literally, remains the genuine scandal of Whitman's poetry. This may indeed be one of the kernel passages in Whitman, expanded and elaborated as it is from an early notebook passage that invented the remarkable trope of "I went myself first to the headland," the headland being the psychic place of *extravagance*, of wandering beyond limits, from which you cannot scramble back to the shore, place of the father, and from which you may topple over into the sea, identical with night, death, and the fierce old mother. "My own hands carried me there," as they fail to carry Whitman in "When Lilacs Last in the Dooryard Bloom'd":

O great star disappear'd—O the black murk that hides the star!
O cruel hands that hold me powerless—O helpless soul of me!

These are Whitman's own hands, pragmatically cruel because they cannot hold him potently, disabled as he is by a return of repressed guilt. Lincoln's death has set going memories of filial guilt, the guilt that the mortal
sickness of Walter Whitman, Sr., should have liberated his son into the full
blood of creativity that ensued in the 1855 first edition of *Leaves of Grass*
(the father died a week after the book's publication). What Whitman's
poetry does not express are any reservations about autoeroticism, which
more than sadomasochism remains the last Western taboo. It is a peculiar
paradox that Whitman, who proclaims his love for all men, women, and
children, should have been profoundly solipsistic, narcissistic, and self-
delighting, but that paradox returns us to the Whitmanian self or rather
selves, the cosmological persona as opposed to the daemonic "real Me."

The most vivid manifestation of the "real Me" in Whitman comes in the
shattering "Sea-Drift" poem, "As I Ebb'd with the Ocean of Life":

O baffled, balk'd bent to the very earth,
Oppress'd with myself that I have dared to open my mouth,
Aware now that amid all that blab whose echoes recoil upon me
    I have not once had the least idea who or what I am,
But that before all my arrogant poems the real Me stands yet
    untouch'd, untold, altogether unreach'd,
Withdrawn far, mocking me with mock-congratulatory signs
    and bows,
With peals of distant ironical laughter at every word I have written,
Pointing in silence to these songs, and then to the sand beneath.
I perceive I have not really understood any thing, not a single object,
    and that no man ever can,
Nature here in sight of the sea taking advantage of me to dart
    upon me and sting me,
Because I have dared to open my mouth to sing at all.

It is Walt Whitman, Kosmos, American, rough, who is mocked here by
his real self, a self that knows itself to be a mystery, because it is neither
mother, nor father, nor child; neither quite female nor quite male; neither

voice nor voicelessness. Whitman's "real Me" is what is best and oldest in him, and like the faculty Emerson called "Spontaneity," it is no part of the creation, meaning both nature's creation and Whitman's verbal cosmos. It is like a surviving fragment of the original Abyss preceding nature, not Adamic but pre-Adamic. This "real Me" is thus also presexual and so plays no role either in the homoerotic "Calamus" poems or in the dubiously heterosexual "Children of Adam" group. Yet it seems to me pervasive in the six long or longer poems that indisputably are Whitman's masterpieces: "The Sleepers," "Song of Myself," "Crossing Brooklyn Ferry," "As I Ebb'd with the Ocean of Life," "Out of the Cradle Endlessly Rocking," and "When Lilacs Last in the Dooryard Bloom'd." Though only the last of these is overtly an elegy, all six are in covert ways elegies for the "real Me," for that "Me myself" that Whitman could not hope to celebrate as a poet and could not hope to fulfill as a sexual being. This "real Me" is not a spirit that denies, but rather one that always remains out of reach, an autistic spirit. In English Romantic poetry and in later nineteenth-century prose romance, there is the parallel being that Shelley called "the Spirit of Solitude," the daemon or shadow of the self-destructive young Poet who is the hero of Shelley's *Alastor*. But Whitman's very American "real Me" is quite unlike a Shelleyan or Blakean Spectre. It does not quest or desire, and it does not want to be wanted.

Though Zweig hints that Whitman has been a bad influence on other writers, I suspect that a larger view of influence would reverse this implicit judgment. Whitman has been an inescapable influence not only for most significant American poets after him (Frost, indebted directly to Emerson, is the largest exception) but also for the most gifted writers of narrative fiction. This influence transcends matters of form and has everything to do with the Whitmanian split between the persona of the rough Walt and the ontological truth of the "real Me." Poets as diverse as Wallace Stevens and T. S. Eliot have in common perhaps only their hidden, partly unconscious reliance upon Whitman as prime precursor. Hemingway's acknowledged debt to *Huckleberry Finn* is real enough, but the deeper legacy came from Whitman. The Hemingway protagonist, split between an empirical self of stoic courage and a "real Me" endlessly evasive of others while finding its freedom only in an inner perfection of loneliness, is directly descended from the dual Whitman of "Song of Myself." American elegiac writing since Whitman (and how surprisingly much of it *is* covertly elegiac) generally revises Whitman's elegies for the self. *The Waste Land* is "When Lilacs Last in the Dooryard Bloom'd" rewritten, and Stevens's "The Rock" is not less Whitmanian than Hart Crane's *The Bridge*.

Zweig's book belongs to the biographical criticism of Whitman by such scholars as Bliss Perry, Gay Wilson Allen, Joseph Jay Rubin, Justin Kaplan, and others whose works are all part of a useful tradition that illuminates the Americanism of Whitman and yet cannot do enough with Whitman's many paradoxes. Of these, I judge the most crucial to be expressed by this question: How did someone of Whitman's extraordinarily idiosyncratic nature become so absolutely central to nearly all subsequent American literary high culture? This centrality evidently cannot ebb among us, as can be seen in the poems of John Ashbery in his splendid book *A Wave*. Whitman's powerful yet unstable identities were his own inheritance from the Orphic Emerson, who proclaimed the central man or poet-to-come as necessarily metamorphic, Bacchic and yet original, and above all American and not British or European in his cultural vistas. This prescription was and is dangerous, because it asks for pragmatism and yet affirms impossible hopes. The rough Whitman is democratic, "real Me" an elitist, but both selves are equally Emersonian.

Politically, Whitman was a Free Soil Democrat who rebelled against the betrayal by the New York Democratic Party of its Jacksonian tradition, but Zweig rightly emphasizes the survival of Emersonian "Prudence" in Whitman, which caused him to oppose labor unions. I suspect that Whitman's politics paralleled his sexual morality; the rough Walt homoerotic and radical, the "real Me" autoerotic and individualistically elitist. The true importance of this split emerges neither in Whitman's sexuality nor in his politics, but in the delicacy and beauty of his strongest poems. Under the cover of an apparent rebellion against traditional literary form, they extend the poetic tradition without violating it. Whitman's elegies for the self have much in common with Tennyson's but are even subtler, more difficult triumphs of High Romanticism. Here I dissent wholly from Zweig, who ends his book with a judgment I find both wrong and puzzling:

> *Leaves of Grass* was launched on a collision course with its age. Whitman's work assaulted the institution of literature and language itself and, in so doing, laid the groundwork for the anti-cultural ambition of modernist writing. He is the ancestor not only of

Henry Miller and Allen Ginsberg but of Kafka, Beckett, André
Breton, Borges—of all who have made of their writing an attack
on the act of writing and on culture itself.

To associate the subtle artistry, delicate and evasive, of Whitman's greatest poems with Miller and Ginsberg, rather than with Hemingway and Stevens and Eliot, is already an error. To say that Kafka, Beckett, and Borges
attack, by their writing, the act of writing and culture is to mistake their
assault upon certain interpretive conventions for a war against literary culture. But the gravest misdirection here is to inform readers that Whitman
truly attacked the institutions of language and literature. Whitman's "real
Me" has more to do with the composition of the great poems than the
rough Walt ever did. "Lilacs," which Zweig does not discuss, is as profoundly traditional an elegy as *In Memoriam* or *Adonais*. Indeed, "Lilacs"
echoes Tennyson, while "As I Ebb'd" echoes Shelley and "Crossing Brooklyn Ferry" invokes *King Lear.* Zweig is taken in by the prose Whitman who
insists he will not employ allusiveness, but the poet Whitman knew better
and is brilliantly allusive, as every strong poet is compelled to be, echoing
his precursors and rivals but so stationing the echoes as to triumph with
and in some sense over them.

Zweig's study is an honorable and useful account of Whitman's poetic
emergence, but it shares in some of the severe limitations of nearly all
Whitman criticism so far published. More than most of the biographical
critics, Zweig keeps alert to Whitman's duality, and I am grateful to him for
his eloquent representations of the poet's war years. Yet Whitman's subtle
greatness as a poet seems to me not fully confronted, here or elsewhere.
The poetry of the "real Me," intricate and forlorn, is addressed to the "real
Me" of the American reader. That it reached what was oldest and best in
Eliot and Stevens is testified to by their finest poetry, in contradistinc-
tion to their prose remarks upon Whitman. Paradoxically, Whitman's best
critic remains not an American but D. H. Lawrence, who lamented that
"the Americans are not worthy of their Whitman." Lawrence believed that
Whitman had gone further, in actual living expression, than any other poet.
The belief was extravagant, certainly, but again the Whitmanian poems of
Lawrence's superb final phase show us what Lawrence meant. I give the
last word here though not to Lawrence but to Emerson, who wrote the first
words about Whitman in his celebrated 1855 letter to the poet, words that
remain true nearly 165 years further on in our literary culture:

I am not blind to the worth of the wonderful gift of *Leaves of Grass*. I find it the most extraordinary piece of wit and wisdom that America has yet contributed.

What we call "Song of Myself," in the form first read and acclaimed by Emerson, was a single text of 1,362 lines, without section divisions. A reader now needs to revive Emerson's shock of recognition when beholding the opening lines:

> I celebrate myself,
> And what I assume you shall assume,
> For every atom belonging to me as good belongs to you.
>
> I loafe and invite my soul,
> I lean and loafe at my ease . . . . observing a spear of summer
>   grass.

As an epic opening, this was unique. To "celebrate" is to launch a festivity, proclaim a hero, rejoice in a Eucharist, display praise. All this for "myself"? To "assume" is to take upon oneself, as in a rule, to put on a garment, to feign, to avoid self-justification, above all to receive another person into association. You—the reader, whoever she is—is so received by Walt Whitman. His credentials are a Lucretian-Epicurean universality, shared atoms, and his insouciance: a loafer, a leaner, at ease, observing what is most worth beholding, a spear of summer grass.

A "loafer" was even more a term of reproach in 1855 than it is today. Walt is idle and unitary, at leisure to address us. His prophetic word is anti-apocalyptic: "But I do not talk of the beginning or the end." Inception is perpetual; perfection is now and in America.

Authority in classical terms meant augmenting the foundations. Walt's authority, his call, is different. It is daemonic and emanates from his "Me myself," which he defines by indirection:

> Apart from the pulling and hauling stands what I am,
> Stands amused, complacent, compassionating, idle, unitary,
> Looks down, is erect, bends an arm on an impalpable certain rest,

Looks with its sidecurved head curious what will come next,
Both in and out of the game, and watching and wondering at it.

Backward I see in my own days where I sweated through fog
   with linguists and contenders,
I have no mockings or arguments . . . . I witness and wait.

I believe in you my soul . . . . the other I am must not abase
   itself to you,
And you must not be abased to the other.

Loafe with me on the grass . . . . loose the stop from your throat,
Not words, not music or rhyme I want . . . . not custom or lecture,
   not even the best,
Only the lull I like, the hum of your valved voice.

The "real Me" or "Me myself" is an androgyne, whereas the persona Walt
is male and the soul female, her images being night, death, the mother, and
the sea. An authentic difficulty for the reader arrives with the questions of
abasement between the soul and "the other I am." To abase is to degrade
in rank or to lessen in esteem. Why inevitably do the soul and the daemon,
Whitman's genius, tend to degrade each other?

The revelation making possible the breakthrough that is *Leaves of Grass*
1855 was neither mystical nor psychosexual. It was the invention of the
mask "Walt Whitman, an American, one of the roughs, a kosmos," who
could not reconcile his soul and his true self and so took up the middle
ground between them.

I recall conversations with Gershom Scholem in Jerusalem and New
Haven, during which he discoursed upon his conviction that Whitman was
"an intuitive Kabbalist." When I reminded the sage that Whitman knew
nothing about Kabbalah, he observed the palpably Hermetic elements that
present the poet as an Adam-God hybrid, like the Adam Kadmon of Kabbalah. As usual, Scholem was right: Whitman had derived, from reading
George Sand, a rough notion of the Hermetic Corpus. The rest was the
work of the daemon, who is excluded from the highly metaphoric embrace
between Walt and his soul:

I mind how we lay in June, such a transparent summer morning;
You settled your head athwart my hips and gently turned over
    upon me,
And parted the shirt from my bosom-bone, and plunged your
    tongue to my barestript heart,
And reached till you felt my beard, and reached till you held
    my feet.

Literal-minded scholars can read this as though "my barestript heart" is the Whitmanian phallus. That is reductive and neglects what might be termed the inspired gymnosophistry that calls forth the epic's first grand epiphany, a testimony in the mode of the Quaker meetings the boy Whitman attended with his father, a follower of Elias Hicks. It seems to me a little inadequate that this Hicksite spiritual declaration be provoked by an exuberant act of fellatio:

Swiftly arose and spread around me the peace and joy and
    knowledge that pass all the art and argument of the earth;
And I know that the hand of God is the elderhand of my own,
And I know that the spirit of God is the eldest brother of my own,
And that all the men ever born are also my brothers . . . . and the
    women my sisters and lovers,
And that a kelson of the creation is love;
And limitless are leaves stiff or drooping in the fields,
And brown ants in the little wells beneath them,
And mossy scabs of the wormfence, and heaped stones, and elder
    and mullen and pokeweed.

Chant this aloud to others and yourself, for it is one of the glories of Whitman. The three final lines, extending his love to what most of us regard as the bottom of creation's scale, are unique to the greatest celebrant of the American Sublime.

The stunning fantasia on the grass follows, but I turn to the title *Leaves of Grass* before proceeding to that poetic triumph, since Whitman's title is in itself a difficult poem. Kenneth Burke and John Hollander taught me how to read Whitman's perpetual title. Burke found it too rich for any single conclusion, while Hollander pondered the rich ambiguities of the title's "of." Wallace Stevens attempted to subsume Shelley and Whitman in his poem "The Rock," in what he named "the fiction of the leaves." That trope passes from Homer and Pindar through Virgil and Dante on to Edmund Spenser, Milton, and Shelley, before Whitman fuses it with Second Isaiah 40:6–8:

> The voice said, Cry. And he said, What shall I cry? All flesh
> *is* grass, and all the goodliness thereof *is* as the flower of
> the field:
> The grass withereth, the flower fadeth: because the spirit of the
> Lord bloweth upon it: surely the people *is* grass.
> The grass withereth, the flower fadeth: but the word of our
> God shall stand for ever.

In March 1842, Whitman attended Emerson's lecture on "Nature and the Powers of the Poet" in New York City and heard the sage remark: "All things are symbols. We say of man that he is grass." Leaves are pages in a book and, due to Shelley's "Ode to the West Wind," also words quickening a new birth.

One offers multiple conjectures as to what the trope "leaves of grass" might be made to mean. In the Homeric fiction of the leaves, each stands for a single mortal life falling away. Isaiah's metaphor is transposed by Whitman, who invests more heavily in grass-as-flesh than in leaf-as-mortal span. His title is not *Grass of Leaves*, because that "of" means both "concerning" and "consisting of."

We tend to call Whitman's descriptive lists "catalogs"; Emerson jokingly called them "inventories." Rhetorically, they are synecdoches: part-for-whole substitutions that tend to become antithetical completions, Whitman's most characteristic trope. Walt puts the world together again with images of voice, his "tallies":

> The blab of the pave . . . . the tires of carts and sluff of bootsoles
> and talk of the promenaders,
> The heavy omnibus, the driver with his interrogating thumb,
> the clank of the shod horses on the granite floor,
> The carnival of sleighs, the clinking and shouted jokes and pelts
> of snowballs;
> The hurrahs for popular favorites . . . . the fury of roused mobs,
> The flap of the curtained litter—the sick man inside, borne
> to the hospital,

The meeting of enemies, the sudden oath, the blows and fall,
The excited crowd—the policeman with his star quickly working
    his passage to the centre of the crowd;
The impassive stones that receive and return so many echoes,
The souls moving along . . . . are they invisible while the least
    atom of the stones is visible?
What groans of overfed or half-starved who fall on the flags
    sunstruck or in fits,
What exclamations of women taken suddenly, who hurry home
    and give birth to babes,
What living and buried speech is always vibrating here . . . .
    what howls restrained by decorum,
Arrests of criminals, slights, adulterous offers made, acceptances,
    rejections with convex lips,
I mind them or the resonance of them . . . . I come again and
    again.

Wonderful as this is, how does he accomplish it? Partly by the dominance of the auditory over the visual: blab, sluff of bootsoles, talk, clank,
shouted jokes, hurrahs, mob fury, flap of litter, sudden oath, echoed groans,
exclamations, vibrating speech, howls, erotic offers made, accepted and
rejected, resonances of a metropolitan litany. Whitman tallies voices and
not urban visions, unless and until he can render them a little hard to see.
    Vision returns in the extraordinary lunar parable of twenty-eight young
men swimming together while they are spied on by a twenty-eight-year-old
virginal woman:

Twenty-eight young men bathe by the shore,
Twenty-eight young men, and all so friendly,
Twenty-eight years of womanly life, and all so lonesome.

She owns the fine house by the rise of the bank,
She hides handsome and richly drest aft the blinds of the window.

Which of the young men does she like the best?
Ah the homeliest of them is beautiful to her.

Where are you off to, lady? for I see you,
You splash in the water there, yet stay stock still in your room.

Dancing and laughing along the beach came the twenty-ninth bather,
The rest did not see her, but she saw them and loved them.

The beards of the young men glistened with wet, it ran from
   their long hair,
Little streams passed all over their bodies.

An unseen hand also passed over their bodies,
It descended tremblingly from their temples and ribs.

The young men float on their backs, their white bellies swell
   to the sun . . . . they do not ask who seizes fast to them,

They do not know who puffs and declines with pendant and
   bending arch,
They do not think whom they souse with spray.

In one sense, "she" is the moon, yet that only starts an appreciation of this
splendor. I am puzzled here again by the redundancies of a current school
of homoerotic scholars, who urge a reading in which the young woman
fades away to be replaced by the poetic speaker himself, rendering matters
politically correct. Nothing in the text justifies the argument of the generally astute Michael Moon: "The nature of the exchange that takes place
midway in the passage might be interpreted as the speaker's appropriation
of the woman's position for his own. Leaving her standing at her window, he
passes from one of its sides to the other on the energy of her desire." Why,
then, is she in the poem as Whitman composed it? What happens to the
wonderful pathos of her unacted desires, a quality in which Whitman here
resembles the "Mariana" lyric of Tennyson? Remove the young woman as
twenty-ninth bather and you mar the poem.

Like all great poets, Whitman is omnisexual in most of his strongest
work. In this aspect he needs to be read as we read Shakespeare's sonnets,
except that he lacked both the Fair Youth and the Dark Lady. Keep in mind
always his declarations that he is "maternal as well as paternal, a child as
well as a man" and "I am the poet of the woman the same as the man." I
again recall provoking resentment by dubbing the American bard "a male
lesbian," much as Shakespeare was when writing the sonnets.

Two hundred and forty lines farther on and Walt himself becomes one
with the twenty-ninth bather:

> You sea! I resign myself to you also . . . . I guess what you mean,
> I behold from the beach your crooked inviting fingers,
> I believe you refuse to go back without feeling of me;
> We must have a turn together . . . . I undress . . . . hurry me out
>   of sight of the land,
> Cushion me soft . . . . rock me in billowy drowse,
> Dash me with amorous wet . . . . I can repay you.
>
> Sea of stretched ground-swells!
> Sea breathing broad and convulsive breaths!
> Sea of the brine of life! Sea of unshovelled and always-ready
>   graves!
> Howler and scooper of storms! Capricious and dainty sea!
> I am integral with you . . . . I too am of one phase and of all phases.

He is the moonlike woman of the nonexistent twenty-ninth phase and
also the twenty-eight male bathers of the lunar cycle. Wallace Stevens parodies Walt in "Notes toward a Supreme Fiction" as the Canon Aspirin's sister, who attires her twenty-eight children—the days. As always in Stevens,
the Whitman parody is uneasily wrought, since the poet of "Notes" identified the evening sun with his intimidating precursor. Whitman's principal
power fascinated Stevens and Hart Crane, as it should us, whenever the
voice that is great within Walt rises up:

> Through me many long dumb voices,
> Voices of the interminable generations of slaves,
> Voices of prostitutes and of deformed persons,
> Voices of the diseased and despairing, and of thieves and dwarfs,
> Voices of cycles of preparation and accretion,
> And of the threads that connect the stars—and of wombs,
>   and of the fatherstuff,
> And of the rights of them the others are down upon,
> Of the trivial and flat and foolish and despised,
> Of fog in the air and beetles rolling balls of dung.

Through me forbidden voices,
Voices of sexes and lusts . . . . voices veiled, and I remove
     the veil,
Voices indecent by me clarified and transfigured.

These lines hammer me like those utterances of Macbeth's that break
into him from some higher realm of eloquence. What shall we make of the
uncanny voices in Whitman?

For Walt, they were a sublimity larger than location. "It is not every day,"
Stevens remarked, "that the world arranges itself into a poem." Whitman
wanted that daily transformation, even though he could not bring it about.
No man, no woman, can live in a continuous secular epiphany, though it is
the enabling fiction that made possible "Song of Myself."

At moments, Whitman is so strong that we do not desire to argue the
fiction:

The heaved challenge from the east that moment over my head,
The mocking taunt, See then whether you shall be master!

Dazzling and tremendous how quick the sunrise would kill me,
If I could not now and always send sunrise out of me.

We also ascend dazzling and tremendous as the sun,
We found our own my soul in the calm and cool of the daybreak.

My voice goes after what my eyes cannot reach,
With the twirl of my tongue I encompass worlds and volumes
     of worlds.

This is the American Sublime properly in place, centering upon the
image of voices, the tally, "the twirl of my tongue" that can encompass
volumes of worlds, "keeping tally with the meaning of all things."

The cost of this confirmation is steep and results in two severe crises,
the first autoerotic:

Mine is no callous shell,
I have instant conductors all over me whether I pass or stop,
They seize every object and lead it harmlessly through me.

I merely stir, press, feel with my fingers, and am happy,
To touch my person to someone else's is about as much as I
    can stand.

Is this then a touch? . . . . quivering me to a new identity,
Flames and ether making a rush for my veins,
Treacherous tip of me reaching and crowding to help them,
My flesh and blood playing out lightning, to strike what is hardly
    different from myself,
On all sides prurient provokers stiffening my limbs,
Straining the udder of my heart for its withheld drip,
Behaving licentious toward me, taking no denial,
Depriving me of my best as for a purpose,
Unbuttoning my clothes and holding me by the bare waist,
Deluding my confusion with the calm of the sunlight and
    pasture fields,
Immodestly sliding the fellow-senses away,
They bribed to swap off with touch, and go and graze at the
    edges of me,
No consideration, no regard for my draining strength or
    my anger,
Fetching the rest of the herd around to enjoy them awhile,
Then all uniting to stand on a headland and worry me.

The sentries desert every other part of me,
They have left me helpless to a red marauder,
They all come to the headland to witness and assist against me.

I am given up by traitors;
I talk wildly . . . . I have lost my wits . . . . I and nobody else am
    the greatest traitor,
I went myself first to the headland . . . . my own hands carried
    me there.

   Whitman's notebooks indicate that the starting point for his emergence
as the persona Walt Whitman was "I went myself first to the headland."
This extravagance, or wandering beyond limits, places you upon a promon-
tory from which you cannot scramble back unaided.

Overtly autoerotic and at moments grotesque, the poetic power of this obscures the unresolved conflict between Whitman's mask or persona—the rough "Myself" of what became the poem's title—and his daemon or "real Me," an interior paramour or muse. Like its major descendants—T. S. Eliot's *The Waste Land*, Hart Crane's *The Bridge*, Wallace Stevens's "Notes toward a Supreme Fiction," William Carlos Williams's *Paterson*, Conrad Aiken's *The Kid*, A. R. Ammons's *Sphere*, John Ashbery's *A Wave*—"Song of Myself" is an internalized quest-romance, whose antecedents include the long English Romantic tradition of falling in love with the poet's failure. That tradition goes from Wordsworth's *The Excursion* and Coleridge's nightmare "Rime of the Ancient Mariner" on through Shelley's *Alastor* and Keats's *Endymion* to Browning's ruined questers and the daemonic defeats of poets by their antithetical muse in Yeats.

The professed program of "Song of Myself" is American democracy, just as Hart Crane's *The Bridge* wants to affirm American imaginative potential against *The Waste Land*. Yet the actual drama of Whitman's and Crane's brief epics has little relevance to myths of America. Walt's authentic drive is self-integration, which he discovers he can never achieve, while Hart's search is for a bridal fulfillment that could never accommodate his uncompromising nature. Both great poets lived and died without ever finding an answering voice. Whitman's eros, like his verbs, remained intransitive; Crane created a new rhetoric of negations and made himself the most difficult American poet of true eminence down to our own day, in a different sense from Whitman, rhetorical rather than misleadingly direct.

There is no question here of self-deception: Both "Song of Myself" and *The Bridge* know and intimate the irreconcilable rift betwixt daemon and project. Whitman is not tormented by this, as he had a blessed calm in his nature. Crane, a Pilgrim of the Absolute, like Shelley and Byron, knows only what Melville had Ishmael call "the tornadoed Atlantic of my being."

Though "Song of Myself" will end in earliness and strength, this freedom results from voluntary disintegration: "I effuse my flesh in eddies, and drift it in lacy jags." *The Bridge's* much more violent coming/spent is Crane's Orphic *sparagmos*, or rending apart by the Dionysian women.

Whitman's deeper crisis in "Song of Myself" results from an anxiety of lost identity:

> I become any presence or truth of humanity here,
> And see myself in prison shaped like another man,
> And feel the dull unintermitted pain.

For me the keepers of convicts shoulder their carbines and
    keep watch,
It is I let out in the morning and barred at night.

Not a mutineer walks handcuffed to the jail, but I am handcuffed
    to him and walk by his side,
I am less the jolly one there, and more the silent one with sweat
    on my twitching lips.

Not a youngster is taken for larceny, but I go up too and am tried
    and sentenced.

Not a cholera patient lies at the last gasp, but I also lie at the
    last gasp,
My face is ash-colored, my sinews gnarl . . . . away from me
    people retreat.

Askers embody themselves in me, and I am embodied in them,
I project my hat and sit shamefaced and beg.

I rise extatic through all, and sweep with the true gravitation,
The whirling and whirling is elemental within me.

Somehow I have been stunned. Stand back!
Give me a little time beyond my cuffed head and slumbers
    and dreams and gaping,
I discover myself on a verge of the usual mistake.

That I could forget the mockers and insults!
That I could forget the trickling tears and the blows of the
    bludgeons and hammers!
That I could look with a separate look on my own crucifixion
    and bloody crowning!

I remember . . . . I resume the overstaid fraction,
The grave of rock multiplies what has been confided to it . . . .
    or to any graves,
The corpses rise . . . . the gashes heal . . . . the fastenings
    roll away.

Quaker by upbringing, Whitman could never bear seeing himself as an asker or beggar. Overextended in this great passage, he becomes a crucified redeemer—Walt, not Jesus—and then is resurrected. His new life will sustain him for the rest of the poem.

So rich are the next three hundred lines that I must keep myself to the observation that Whitman justifies his resurrected vaunt: "I troop forth replenished with supreme power." That plenty of the world and of the self achieves a magnificence in the poem's closing passage:

> The past and present wilt . . . . I have filled them and emptied
>   them,
> And proceed to fill my next fold of the future.
>
> Listener up there! Here you . . . . what have you to confide to me?
> Look in my face while I snuff the sidle of evening,
> Talk honestly, for no one else hears you, and I stay only
>   a minute longer.
>
> Do I contradict myself?
> Very well then . . . . I contradict myself;
> I am large . . . . I contain multitudes.
>
> I concentrate toward them that are nigh . . . . I wait on the
>   door-slab.
>
> Who has done his day's work and will soonest be through with
>   his supper?
> Who wishes to walk with me?
>
> Will you speak before I am gone? Will you prove already
>   too late?
>
> The spotted hawk swoops by and accuses me . . . . he complains
>   of my gab and my loitering.
>
> I too am not a bit tamed . . . I too am untranslatable,
> I sound my barbaric yawp over the roofs of the world.

The last scud of day holds back for me,
It flings my likeness after the rest and true as any on the
    shadowed wilds,
It coaxes me to the vapor and the dusk.

I depart as air . . . . I shake my white locks at the runaway sun,
I effuse my flesh in eddies and drift it in lacy jags.

I bequeath myself to the dirt to grow from the grass I love,
If you want me again look for me under your bootsoles.

You will hardly know who I am or what I mean,
But I shall be good health to you nevertheless,
And filter and fibre your blood.

Failing to fetch me at first keep encouraged,
Missing me one place search another,
I stop some where waiting for you.

Poets like Stevens and Crane, readers like myself, are invited to a formidable agon by the American bard at his most urgent: "Will you speak
before I am gone? Will you prove already too late?" Containing multitudes
yet self-contained, Walt touches apotheosis as a redeemer, inviting us to
accompany him on the road to Emmaus, anticipating *The Waste Land*'s
neo-Christian "What the Thunder Said."

The promise of good health rings with special force for me, going from
one illness or accident to another in my old age. Yet any among us, young
or old, hale or faltering, respond to Walt Whitman's generosity:

I stop some where waiting for you.

Of the five major poems flanking "Song of Myself," what we now call "As
I Ebb'd with the Ocean of Life," seems to me, now, grander even than
"A Word Out of the Sea," "Crossing Brooklyn Ferry," "The Sleepers," and
the "Lilacs" elegy for Lincoln. This original is stronger than the smoother
version Whitman came to favor and is a worthy answer to Shelley's "Ode
to the West Wind," its covert agonist. Shelley's tropes—the dirge of the
dying year, the dead leaves, each like a little corpse, the blare of the

cloud-trumpets of prophecy, the poet lying in drifts at the feet of the gods of the storm—are appropriated by Whitman forty years after the English revolutionary poet addressed the elements.

"Elemental drifts!," the first line of "As I Ebb'd," is a worthy title, and I will employ it here. "Impress," in the second line, takes every range of meaning in the word, and "As I ebbed with an ebb of the ocean of life" repeats "an ebb" for a more Whitmanian rhythm than the shorter, later version. By changing to "Held by this electric self out of the pride of which I utter poems," Whitman lost much of the powerful pathos of "Alone, held by the eternal self of me that threatens to get the better of me, and stifle me," with its hint that the eternal self is the real Me or Me myself, and not the fiction of rough Walt the American. The restored contrast vivifies the Jobean spirit that trails in the lines underfoot, the accusing daemon that haunts the lines of the poem and in the sand.

Stand back from "Elemental Drifts!" and you can behold a more original design than in "A Word Out of the Sea." The metaphors stem from Western tradition, as mediated by Shelley's *Adonais*, a fierce ode to "the breath whose might I have invoked in song," but their patterning is more daemonic than ever before. Musing in an autumnal twilight, the beach-walker encounters his dusky daemon, the other self or personal genius who has come only to mock him. Hart Crane's "Passage" in *White Buildings* and Stevens's masterwork, "The Auroras of Autumn," inherit Whitman's scenario, as does Eliot's "The Dry Salvages."

The "thought of likeness" may be old, as reflected by Joyce's Stephen Dedalus recalling Jakob Boehme's "signatures of all things I am here to read." Whitman employs it with radical newness since his signatures, the types he seeks, are purely daemonic, agencies for reproving his own failures in freedom. Beckett's motto—"Fail better!"—catches Walt's spirit, bowed certainly though unbroken:

> As I wend the shores I know not,
> As I listen to the dirge, the voices of men and women
>   wrecked,
> As I inhale the impalpable breezes that set in upon me,
> As the ocean so mysteriously rolls toward me closer and closer,
> At once I find, the least thing that belongs to me, or that I see
>   or touch, I know not;
> I, too, but signify, at the utmost, a little washed-up drift,

A few sands and dead leaves to gather,
Gather, and merge myself as part of the sands and drift.

—"As I Ebb'd" (1860)

The 1867 revision omits "At once I find, the least thing that belongs to me, or that I see or touch, I know not." This canceled line in itself falters, an instance of what the late Yvor Winters called "the fallacy of imitative form," his name for loose, sprawling poetry—which is how he regarded Whitman's work in general. My personal relations with Winters were cordial; I shared his delight in Edwin Arlington Robinson and admired his early friendship with Hart Crane. But on Crane, Whitman, Emerson, and Stevens, we had to cease discussion, as each aggrieved the other. An admirable critic in other respects, Winters had no use for what Crane called "the logic of metaphor," tropological thinking, without which Shakespeare is inconceivable.

Self-revision in Whitman generally retreats from his own rhetoric of colors and forms into ineffective gestures of Tennysonian emulation. But the superb struggle between the 1860 and 1867 versions, both of which follow, does show both gain and loss in revision:

O baffled, balked,
Bent to the very earth, here preceding what follows,
Oppressed with myself that I have dared to open my mouth,
Aware now, that, amid all the blab whose echoes recoil upon me,
    I have not once had the least idea who or what I am,
But that before all my insolent poems the real Me still stands
    untouched, untold, altogether unreached,
Withdrawn far, mocking me with mock-congratulatory signs
    and bows,
With peals of distant ironical laughter at every word I have
    written or shall write,
Striking me with insults till I fall helpless upon the sand.

O I perceive I have not understood anything—not a single
    object—and that no man ever can.

I perceive Nature here, in sight of the sea, is taking advantage
    of me, to dart upon me, and sting me,

Because I was assuming so much,
And because I have dared to open my mouth to sing at all.

(1860)

O baffled, balk'd, bent to the very earth,
Oppress'd with myself that I have dared to open my mouth,
Aware now that amid all that blab whose echoes recoil upon me
    I have not once had the least idea who or what I am,
But that before all my arrogant poems the real Me stands yet
    untouch'd, untold, altogether unreach'd,
Withdrawn far, mocking me with mock-congratulatory signs
    and bows,
With peals of distant ironical laughter at every word I have
    written,
Pointing in silence to these songs, and then to the sand beneath.

I perceive I have not really understood any thing, not a single
    object, and that no man ever can,
Nature here in sight of the sea taking advantage of me to dart
    upon me and sting me,
Because I have dared to open my mouth to sing at all.

(1867)

"Striking me with insults till I fall helpless upon the sand" is far less effective than the high art of "Pointing in silence to these songs, and then to the sand beneath." In a brilliant afterthought, the beach-walker confronts waves and daemon with a copy of *Leaves of Grass* in his hand (presumably the second edition, 1856), again equating poetic lines and windrows (in either spelling). In the other significant change, Whitman cuts "Because I was assuming so much," which is a loss because it undoes the superb confidence manifested in "Song of Myself": "And what I assume you shall assume."

Walt's most direct confrontation with his daemon (real Me, or Me myself) yields the bitter self-parody of "mock-congratulatory signs and bows." And yet this yields also an exquisite pathos almost Shakespearean:

You oceans both! You tangible land! Nature!
Be not too rough with me—I submit—I close with you,
These little shreds shall, indeed, stand for all.

Was Walt right to eliminate the following three lines from the later versions?

> For I fear I shall become crazed, if I cannot emulate it,
>   and utter myself as well as it.
>
> Sea-raff! Crook-tongued waves!
> O, I will yet sing, some day, what you have said to me.

True, they break the beautifully subdued mood of the reconciliation with the father. But his desperate need of continuing to compose poetry has its own poignance, less in dignity perhaps but more in urgency. How infrequently Walt entertains the thought of madness!

For me the high point of all Whitman comes in one tercet:

> I throw myself upon your breast, my father,
> I cling to you so that you cannot unloose me,
> I hold you so firm, till you answer me something.

I think back to carrying my younger son in my arms, when he was just past a year in age. He held me so tightly that I hardly knew how to set him down safely or transfer him to another person's grasp. I could not bear to detach him by mere force and became abashed whenever it became necessary.

There is great pathos when Whitman writes: "Touch me with your lips, as I touch those I love." It is worth recalling here that, except in his apotheosis as wound-dresser and comforter of the maimed and dying soldiers, Walt's eros was intransitive: "To touch my body to someone else's is about as much as I can bear."

"Elemental Drifts!" concludes familiarly for the reader with what will become essentially the text of "As I Ebb'd with the Ocean of Life," beginning with "Ebb, ocean of life, (the flow will return,)" and ending with "Whoever you are—we too lie in drifts at your feet."

Shelley's "Ode to the West Wind" haunted Whitman and Wallace Stevens alike. The "little corpses" return to Shelley's dead leaves, "each like a corpse within its grave," and "that blare of the cloud-trumpets" recalls Shelley's "the trumpet of a prophecy." Both Whitman and Shelley were Lucretian materialists, and Whitman invokes the Epicurean gods at the close: "You, up there, walking or sitting, / Whoever you are."

Against that divine indifference, Shelley offers a secular apocalypse, as he leaps from the advent of autumn to "If Winter comes, can Spring be far behind?" Whitman places a more modest hope in a marvelous modulation from "Up just as much out of fathomless workings" through "Just as much for us" on to "Just as much, whence we come."

The tragedy of a dialectical eros plays itself out in the forty-five "Calamus" poems of the 1860 *Leaves of Grass*. Whitman learned again that only an intransitive eros could accommodate his daemon, which celebrated contact but could not bear it. The great artist of the intransitive verb also avoided objects of his sexual drive; what evidence we have indicates that he carnally embraced himself only, and he walked the open road with only the thought of death and the knowledge of death as his close companions. "Calamus" should not be externalized any more than we read Shakespeare's sonnets for veracity.

Shakespeare's sonnets may have been the model for the twelve-poem manuscript "Live Oak, with Moss," which was the seedbed for "Calamus."

The great poem of the sequence is the renowned vision of a luxuriant live oak:

> I saw in Louisiana a live-oak growing,
> All alone stood it, and the moss hung down from the branches,
> Without any companion it grew there, glistening out joyous
>   leaves of dark green,
> And its look, rude, unbending, lusty, made me think of myself;
> But I wondered how it could utter joyous leaves, standing alone
>   there without its friend, its lover—For I knew I could not;
> And I plucked a twig with a certain number of leaves upon it,
>   and twined around it a little moss, and brought it away—
>   And I have placed it in sight in my room,
> It is not needed to remind me as of my friends, (for I believe
>   lately I think of little else than of them,)
> Yet it remains to me a curious token—I write these pieces,
>   and name them after it;
> For all that, and though the live-oak glistens there in Louisiana,
>   solitary in a wide flat space, uttering joyous leaves all its life,
>   without a friend, a lover, near—I know very well I could not.

The twig is another instance of Whitman's prime emblem of poetic voice, the "tally." Beautifully paced, this exquisite lyric meditation intimates an erotic self-sufficiency that Walt wants to deny but unpersuasively. Throughout "Calamus," Whitman is strongest when he asserts least:

Who is now reading this?

May-be one is now reading this who knows some wrong-doing
    of my past life,
Or may-be a stranger is reading this who has secretly loved me,
Or may-be one who meets all my grand assumptions and
    egotisms with derision,
Or may-be one who is puzzled at me.

As if I were not puzzled at myself!
Or as if I never deride myself! (O conscience-struck! O
    self-convicted!)
Or as if I do not secretly love strangers! (O tenderly, a long time,
    and never avow it;)
Or as if I did not see, perfectly well, interior in myself, the stuff
    of wrong-doing,
Or as if it could cease transpiring from me until it must cease.

Such disquietude abounds, whether between the lines or overt:

O love!
O dying—always dying!
O the burials of me, past and present!
O me, while I stride ahead, material, visible, imperious as ever!
O me, what I was for years, now dead, (I lament not—
    I am content;)
O to disengage myself from those corpses of me, which I turn
    and look at, where I cast them!
To pass on, (O living! always living!) and leave the corpses
    behind!

My late friend the poet Mark Strand, deeply affected by this, has composed several variations upon it. Allied to such darkness are the fading glimpses that doubt appearances:

That shadow, my likeness, that goes to and fro, seeking a
   livelihood, chattering, chaffering,
How often I find myself standing and looking at it where it flits,
How often I question and doubt whether that is really me;
But in these, and among my lovers, and carolling my songs,
O I never doubt whether that is really me.

Indirection, central to Whitman's poetics, attains a triumph in the two
final sections of "Calamus":

Here my last words, and the most baffling,
Here the frailest leaves of me, and yet my strongest-lasting,
Here I shade down and hide my thoughts—I do not expose
   them,
And yet they expose me more than all my other poems.

Full of life, sweet-blooded, compact, visible,
I, forty years old the Eighty-third Year of The States,
To one a century hence, or any number of centuries hence,
To you, yet unborn, these, seeking you.

When you read these, I, that was visible, am become invisible;
Now it is you, compact, visible, realizing my poems, seeking me,
Fancying how happy you were, if I could be with you, and
   become your lover;
Be it as if I were with you. Be not too certain but I am now with you.

Kenneth Burke enjoyed chanting the four lines of section 44 to
me—"Here my last words . . ."—as we clambered about the Battery in the
autumn of 1976, and he adored equally the envoi to "Calamus." Both brief
poems dazzle—in the diction of John Ashbery—as shields of a greeting,
protecting what is exposed. That is Whitman's art: to promise absolute self-
revelation and give us fresh gestures of evasion, hesitation, concealment.
Better thus, though Walt proclaimed: "I swear I dare not shirk any part
of myself." Stevens learned from Whitman "the intricate evasions of as."
So Walt's last words are the most baffling, his frailest leaves his strongest-
lasting, and his shaded, hidden thoughts expose him more than all his
other poems.

Leaves of Grass 1860 gave no offense with the homoerotic "Calamus" but was attacked for what became the "Children of Adam" grouping. Emerson had cautioned Whitman to avoid provocation, doubtless forgetting his own maxim that what is gained from others is never instruction but only provocation. Rereading Whitman's celebrations of love for a woman, I recant my earlier judgment that they are in any way poorer than the "Calamus" hymns to manly love. It is true that the 1860 texts tend to improve in later revisions, unlike "Calamus." Whitman agilely assumes the identity of the American Adam in "To the Garden the World":

> To the garden the world anew ascending,
> Potent mates, daughters, sons, preluding,
> The love, the life of their bodies, meaning and being,
> Curious here behold my resurrection after slumber,
> The revolving cycles in their wide sweep having brought me
>   again,
> Amorous, mature, all beautiful to me, all wondrous,
> My limbs and the quivering fire that ever plays through them,
>   for reasons, most wondrous,
> Existing I peer and penetrate still,
> Content with the present, content with the past,
> By my side or back of me Eve following,
> Or in front, and I following her just the same.

This strong prelude is almost worthy of "As Adam Early in the Morning," the famous postlude to "Children of Adam":

> As Adam early in the morning,
> Walking forth from the bower refresh'd with sleep,
> Behold me where I pass, hear my voice, approach,
> Touch me, touch the palm of your hand to my body as I pass,
> Be not afraid of my body.

This compressed epitome of Whitman's aesthetic eminence intimates Walt as Hermetic God-Man, Adam, and American Christ, and makes of us so many doubting Thomases. Subtly cadenced, the major Adamic song goes back to the 1855 *Leaves of Grass*, became "Poem of the Body" in 1856, and took its first line as title from 1867 onward: "I Sing the Body Electric." A remarkable performance, influential and exuberant, it nevertheless never finds me. I miss Whitman's sublimity whenever I work through its inventories. Far better is "Spontaneous Me," an ecstatic hymn of self-gratification, perhaps the true scandal of Whitman's work. Kenneth Burke loved reciting the poem, chuckling at its overtness. Though the poem celebrates both heterosexuality and homoeroticism, the only object of the drive is Walt himself:

> The young man that wakes deep at night, the hot hand seeking
>   to repress what would master him,
> The mystic amorous night, the strange half-welcome pangs,
>   visions, sweats,
> The pulse pounding through palms and trembling encircling
>   fingers, the young man all color'd, red, ashamed, angry;
> The souse upon me of my lover the sea, as I lie willing and
>   naked,
> The merriment of the twin babes that crawl over the grass in the
>   sun, the mother never turning her vigilant eyes from them,
> The walnut-trunk, the walnut-husks, and the ripening or ripen'd
>   long-round walnuts,
> The continence of vegetables, birds, animals,
> The consequent meanness of me should I skulk or find myself
>   indecent, while birds and animals never once skulk or find
>   themselves indecent,
> The great chastity of paternity, to match the great chastity of
>   maternity,
> The oath of procreation I have sworn, my Adamic and fresh
>   daughters,
> The greed that eats me day and night with hungry gnaw, till I
>   saturate what shall produce boys to fill my place when I am
>   through,
> The wholesome relief, repose, content,
> And this bunch pluck'd at random from myself,
> It has done its work—I toss it carelessly to fall where it may.

In its first appearance in *Leaves of Grass* 1856, this was called "Bunch Poem," a more effective title, much admired by Kenneth Burke in our

Whitmanian dialogues. He kindled my affection also for the splendid "Facing West from California's Shores" (the first line added in 1867):

Facing west from California's shores,
Inquiring, tireless, seeking what is yet unfound,
I, a child, very old, over waves, towards the house of maternity,
    the land of migrations, look afar,
Look off the shores of my Western sea, the circle almost circled;
For starting westward from Hindustan, from the vales of
    Kashmere,
From Asia, from the north, from the God, the sage, and the
    hero,
From the south, from the flowery peninsulas and the spice
    islands,
Long having wander'd since, round the earth having wander'd,
Now I face home again, very pleas'd and joyous,
(But where is what I started for so long ago?
And why is it yet unfound?)

Indic thought reached Whitman through back channels or by natural affinity. Emerson and Thoreau absorbed it through translations, unlike T. S. Eliot, a profound student of Sanskrit and Pali texts. Cleo Kearns links Eliot's Indic knowledge to Whitman's quest for a gnosis transcending the death of the self. The startling resemblances between "When Lilacs Last in the Dooryard Bloom'd" and *The Waste Land* are in part a matter of repressed influence but also suggest Indic sensibilities shared by the two poets in opening themselves to the thought and knowledge of death.

I leap ahead to the aesthetic puzzle presented to me by Whitman's ambitious poem of 1871, "Passage to India." Frequent rereadings make me unhappy: it seems unworthy of the poet who composed "Song of Myself," "The Sleepers," "Crossing Brooklyn Ferry," and the great threnodies "Out of the Cradle Endlessly Rocking," "As I Ebb'd with the Ocean of Life," and "Lilacs." And yet I cannot dismiss a poem whose progeny includes *Four Quartets*, *The Bridge*, D. H. Lawrence's "The Ship of Death," and E. M. Forster's *A Passage to India*.

Still, what are lovers of Whitman to do with "For what is the present after all but a growth out of the past?" Continuous affirmation wearies the reader and tempts her to long for a few saving touches of negation or of the comic, both of which abound in "Song of Myself," as does incremental redundancy. After 1865, we receive mostly redundancy unmitigated. There are still a few scattered epiphanies: "The Dalliance of the Eagles," "Warble for Lilac-Time," "A Noiseless Patient Spider," "Night on the Prairies," "The Last Invocation," "A Clear Midnight." Yet these are drowned out by banal sentiments and crunching platitudes, as in the "Song of the Universal":

> And thou America,
> For the scheme's culmination, its thought and its reality,
> For these (not for thyself) thou hast arrived.

> Thou too surroundest all,
> Embracing carrying welcoming all, thou too by pathways
>   broad and new,
> To the ideal tendest.

That is our great poet, perhaps our greatest American, in 1874. At just fifty-five, his extraordinary gift of 1855–65 has abandoned him. Wordsworth provides an illuminating parallel. Almost all his vital poetry emanates from his great decade of 1797–1807. The departure of Wordsworth's daemon remains mysterious, but it seems clear that by 1866 one too many young soldiers had died in Whitman's arms. The cost of absorbing such pain and suffering would have been too high for anyone, even for our nation's ministering angel.

Herman Melville
(1819–1891)

MATTHEW ARNOLD, who expressed exasperation with Whitman, took his own touchstones rather seriously. Mine are marks of pleasure, of delight in reading. I would not change a sentence of *Moby-Dick*. A chapter like 101, "The Decanter," devoted to beef and beer aboard whalers, manifests Ishmael's comic zest:

> The quantity of beer, too, is very large, 10,800 barrels. Now, as those polar fisheries could only be prosecuted in the short summer of that climate, so that the whole cruise of one of these Dutch whalemen, including the short voyage to and from the Spitzbergen sea, did not much exceed three months, say, and reckoning 30 men to each of their fleet of 180 sail, we have 5,400 Low Dutch seamen in all; therefore, I say, we have precisely two barrels of beer per man, for a twelve weeks' allowance, exclusive of his fair proportion of that 550 ankers of gin. Now, whether these gin and beer harpooners, so fuddled as one might fancy them to have been, were the right sort of men to stand up in a boat's head, and take good aim at flying whales; this would seem somewhat improbable. Yet they did aim at them, and hit them too. But this was very far North, be it remembered, where beer agrees well with the constitution; upon the Equator, in our southern fishery, beer would be apt to make the harpooner sleepy at the mast-head and boozy in his boat; and grievous loss might ensue to Nantucket and New Bedford.

Without such ballast, the metaphysics of the hunt might sink *Moby-Dick*. Ahab, daemonic in drive, is not too huge for his book because it contains the cosmos. Walt, benign daemon, is ballasted by the giant cavalcade that *Leaves of Grass* presents; a list alternating epiphanies and commodities transmutes into the story of the American self, glorying Adam early in the morning of a new world.

Are all Americans Ahabs? Some—then and now—surely strive not to be. Jewish, I would prefer to be Ishmael, but forever he is the progenitor of the Arabs. One of my students in a class discussion of *Moby-Dick* declared her choice to be Queequeg, with the White Whale in second place. She read aloud from chapter 133, "The Chase—First Day":

> A gentle joyousness—a mighty mildness of repose in swiftness, invested the gliding whale. Not the white bull Jupiter swimming away with ravished Europa clinging to his graceful horns; his lovely, leering eyes sideways intent upon the maid; with smooth bewitching fleetness, rippling straight for the nuptial bower in Crete; not Jove, not that great majesty Supreme! did surpass the glorified White Whale as he so divinely swam.
>
> On each soft side—coincident with the parted swell, that but once leaving him, then flowed so wide away—on each bright side, the whale shed off enticings. No wonder there had been some among the hunters who namelessly transported and allured by all this serenity, had ventured to assail it; but had fatally found that quietude but the vesture of tornadoes. Yet calm, enticing calm, oh, whale! thou glidest on, to all who for the first time eye thee, no matter how many in that same way thou may'st have bejuggled and destroyed before.

This marked erotic intensity fuses delicious Fayaway of *Typee* with the dangerous beauty of innocence in *Billy Budd*. Genders mingle and subdivide in a fluid dissolve of erotic imagination. Snowy androgyne, Moby Dick masks his/her "vesture of tornadoes" enticingly as a gliding calm. Harpooners and lancers are at once phallic and commercial in their fiery hunt.

It can be illuminating to read *Moby-Dick* as Melville's autobiography, just as the 1860 third edition of *Leaves of Grass* is Walt Whitman's. In 1855 and 1856, Whitman's self epiphanies are more like journal entries than a narrative. A crisis, perhaps homoerotic, in the winter of 1859–60, may have sparked Walt's movement toward a fuller story of the self.

Melville's masterwork was composed in a year and a half by a mariner who had just turned thirty, become a husband and father, and lived on borrowed money from in-laws and relatives. Even the creative wilderness of *Mardi and a Voyage Thither* (1849) could not prepare a reader, then and now, for the magnificence of *Moby-Dick*. Why the corposants electrified Herman Melville into this one absolute sublimity is probably unanswerable. I think of *As I Lay Dying*, McCarthy's *Blood Meridian*, Roth's *Sabbath's Theater*, and—on a smaller scale—West's *Miss Lonelyhearts* and Pynchon's *The Crying of Lot 49* as similar breakthroughs beyond the reach of art. The daemon knows how it is done.

Many readers now exalt the later novella *Billy Budd* to the eminence of *Moby-Dick*, but I regret my inability to agree. Like poor Billy himself, the little book relapses into inarticulateness. *The Confidence-Man*, also now admired, is a botch, though not a disaster like *Pierre*. I have a personal taste for the long poem *Clarel*, but its length is excessive and its metric inadequate. *The Piazza Tales* include the justly renowned "Bartleby, the Scrivener" and "Benito Cereno" and I admire both "The Bell-Tower" and "The Encantadas." What else? Of the poems, *Battle-Pieces* is dwarfed by *Drum-Taps*, but there are a scattering that remain memorable: "After the Pleasure Party," "The Maldive Shark," and "Shelley's Vision" among them. *Moby-Dick* rises up from the rest of Herman Melville, a snowy summit and Leviathan surrounded by minnows.

This phenomenon of one singular work scarcely is unique to the United States. Twain has a few hilarious sketches, like "Cannibalism in the Cars" and "Journalism in Tennessee," but only *The Adventures of Huckleberry Finn* has the special status of *Moby-Dick*, *Leaves of Grass* (1860), *Walden*, *The Scarlet Letter*, *The Portrait of a Lady*, *The Great Gatsby*.

I strongly urge readers of *Moby-Dick* to employ the Norton Critical Edition (revised 2017), ably edited by Hershel Parker, so as to provide a reliable text. Shrewdly, Melville divided his immense narrative into one hundred and thirty-five brief chapters. Teaching the great book in three two-hour discussions with a dozen brilliant students, I suggest they think of it as tripartite.

1. 1–49 "Loomings" through "The Hyena"
2. 50–87 "Ahab's Boat and Crew—Fedallah" through "The Grand Armada"
3. 88–135 "Schools and Schoolmasters" through "The Chase— Third Day" and "Epilogue."

Part 1 might be called "Ishmael," part 2, "Ahab," and part 3, "Moby Dick."

Few initial chapters haunt me as does "Loomings," with its uncanny onset:

> Call me Ishmael. Some years ago—never mind how long precisely—having little or no money in my purse, and nothing particular to interest me on shore, I thought I would sail about a little and see the watery part of the world. It is a way I have of driving off the spleen, and regulating the circulation. Whenever I find myself growing grim about the mouth; whenever it is a damp, drizzly November in my soul; whenever I find myself involuntarily pausing before coffin warehouses, and bringing up the rear of every funeral I meet; and especially whenever my hypos get such an upper hand of me, that it requires a strong moral principle to prevent me from deliberately stepping into the street, and methodically knocking people's hats off—then, I account it high time to get to sea as soon as I can. This is my substitute for pistol and ball. With a philosophical flourish Cato throws himself upon his sword; I quietly take to the ship. There is nothing surprising in this. If they but knew it, almost all men in their degree, some time or other, cherish very nearly the same feelings towards the ocean with me.

I write on a damp, drizzly November day in New Haven, at four in the afternoon, when the outside air reminds me (as it does rarely) that our dreary university town actually is a seaport. It startles me how little has changed when Ishmael sketches his playbill:

> *"Grand Contested Election for the Presidency of the*
> *United States."*
> "WHALING VOYAGE BY ONE ISHMAEL."
> "BLOODY BATTLE IN AFFGHANISTAN."

Casual, unhurried, paradoxically driven yet easygoing, Ishmael starts off upon a questless quest not at all his own. His loneliness ends with a New Bedford marriage to the harpooner Queequeg: the single figure in our literature almost as likable as Huck Finn and Nigger Jim. Chapter 110, "Queequeg in His Coffin," is an epitome of the heroic composure of Ishmael's comrade:

Leaning over in his hammock, Queequeg long regarded the coffin with an attentive eye. He then called for his harpoon, had the wooden stock drawn from it, and then had the iron part placed in the coffin along with one of the paddles of his boat. All by his own request, also, biscuits were then ranged round the sides within: a flask of fresh water was placed at the head, and a small bag of woody earth scraped up in the hold at the foot; and a piece of sail-cloth being rolled up for a pillow, Queequeg now entreated to be lifted into his final bed, that he might make trial of its comforts, if any it had. He lay without moving a few minutes, then told one to go to his bag and bring out his little god, Yojo. Then crossing his arms on his breast with Yojo between, he called for the coffin lid (hatch he called it) to be placed over him. The head part turned over with a leather hinge, and there lay Queequeg in his coffin with little but his composed countenance in view. "Rarmai" (it will do; it is easy), he murmured at last, and signed to be replaced in his hammock.

With dignity, yet statelier, the harpooner wills himself to live:

But now that he had apparently made every preparation for death; now that his coffin was proved a good fit, Queequeg suddenly rallied; soon there seemed no need of the carpenter's box; and thereupon, when some expressed their delighted surprise, he, in substance, said, that the cause of his sudden convalescence was this;—at a critical moment, he had just recalled a little duty ashore, which he was leaving undone; and therefore had changed his mind about dying: he could not die yet, he averred. They asked him, then, whether to live or die was a matter of his own sovereign will and pleasure. He answered, certainly. In a word, it was Queequeg's conceit, that if a man made up his mind to live, mere sickness could not kill him: nothing but a whale, or a gale, or some violent, ungovernable, unintelligent destroyer of that sort.

Queequeg is not a noble savage but the most civilized man aboard the *Pequod*: gracious, tradition-soaked, loving, spontaneous, responsible, and yet ultimately mysterious. We can read neither the hieroglyphs tattooed upon him nor the living hieroglyph he represents in himself. Why will he

not return to reclaim his Maori kingdom, of which he is legitimate successor: "ascending the pure and undefiled throne of thirty pagan Kings before
him"? Why does so grand a person adopt Ahab's ferocious quest as his own?
Queequeg, unlike Ishmael, has no quarrel (however loving) with existence.

The central mystery of *Moby-Dick* is also its daemonic glory: the reader
who is free of cant and creed will also be drawn into Ahab's quest to strike
through the mask of a cosmos that fell apart in its own creation. High
Romanticism's antithetical religion is a kind of purified Gnosticism. When I
teach the book, I ask my students to consider both the contrast and the con-
sonance between the sublime eloquences of Father Mapple and of Captain
Ahab. Is Mapple truly more Christian than the Gnostic lord of the *Pequod*?
Here is Father Mapple:

> He drooped and fell away from himself for a moment; then lifting
> his face to them again, showed a deep joy in his eyes, as he cried
> out with a heavenly enthusiasm,—"But oh! shipmates! on the star-
> board hand of every woe, there is a sure delight; and higher the
> top of that delight, than the bottom of the woe is deep. Is not the
> main-truck higher than the kelson is low? Delight is to him—a far,
> far upward, and inward delight—who against the proud gods and
> commodores of this earth, ever stands forth his own inexorable
> self. Delight is to him whose strong arms yet support him, when
> the ship of this base treacherous world has gone down beneath
> him. Delight is to him, who gives no quarter in the truth, and
> kills, burns, and destroys all sin though he pluck it out from under
> the robes of Senators and Judges. Delight,—top-gallant delight is
> to him, who acknowledges no law or lord, but the Lord his God,
> and is only a patriot to heaven. Delight is to him, whom all the
> waves of the billows of the seas of the boisterous mob can never
> shake from this sure Keel of the Ages. And eternal delight and
> deliciousness will be his, who coming to lay him down, can say
> with his final breath—O Father!—chiefly known to me by Thy
> rod—mortal or immortal, here I die. I have striven to be Thine,
> more than to be this world's, or mine own. Yet this is nothing; I
> leave eternity to Thee; for what is man that he should live out the
> lifetime of his God?"

And here is Ahab:

"Thou knowest not how came ye, hence callest thyself unbegotten;
certainly knowest not thy beginning, hence callest thyself unbegun.
I know that of me, which thou knowest not of thyself, oh, thou
omnipotent. There is some unsuffusing thing beyond thee, thou
clear spirit, to whom all thy eternity is but time, all thy creativeness
mechanical. Through thee, thy flaming self, my scorched eyes do
dimly see it. Oh, thou foundling fire, thou hermit immemorial, thou
too hast thy incommunicable riddle, thy unparticipated grief. Here
again with haughty agony, I read my sire. Leap! leap up, and lick the
sky! I leap with thee; I burn with thee; would fain be welded with
thee; defyingly I worship thee!"

Father Mapple's colors of rhetoric conceal a Melvillean, un-Christian
gnosis: "his own inexorable self." With subtle skepticism—"mortal or
immortal, here I die"—Mapple comes to rest upon "for what is man that
he should live out the lifetime of his God?" Is not that God also "mortal
or immortal"?

Mapple echoes equivocal Job, neither so patient nor so pious a sufferer
as orthodoxy wants him to be. Ahab, who shouts, "No! In thunder," to any
injunction to submit or yield, is not so much the anti-Job as Job emanci-
pated, set forth to hook and spear him. Moby Dick swims away, while Ahab
and all his crew, save Ishmael, are destroyed. Is Ahab vanquished? No. Like
Milton's Satan, what *is* else, provided one is not overcome, except by one's
own heart alone.

Melville's heroic protagonists are worthy of the book's dedication to
Nathaniel Hawthorne: Ahab, Queequeg, Starbuck, Stubb. Ishmael stands
apart: there is no confrontation or exchange between him and Ahab.
Instead, he *reads* Ahab, as we are compelled to read Hamlet. The Prince
of Denmark's darkness did not commence with the death of his father and
his mother's remarriage, and Ahab's sorrow preceded his dismemberment
by the White Whale. Ishmael—transcendentalist *and* skeptic (like Emerson himself), his alienation cured by comradeship with Queequeg—intuits
Ahab's Gnostic rebellion against the Leviathan, imposed upon us by God
through nature, and senses the metaphysics of Ahab's Prometheanism.

As the American Prometheus, Ahab need not steal fire from the gods.
Fire is his Zarathustran birthright from far back before the creation and
fall. But his right worship of that fire is defiance: "Who's over me?" A man
who would strike the sun if it insulted him is beyond good and evil. His

paradigm for Melville was Macbeth, a creative choice both brilliant and erring. Macbeth and Ahab share a sense of outrage, metaphysical yet personal. Very subtly, Shakespeare hints at a sexual failing in Macbeth. His enormous passion for Lady Macbeth is afflicted by his powerfully proleptic imagination: he arrives perpetually before the event, as it were. That appears to have been D. H. Lawrence's burden with his wife, Frieda, if we are to believe his disciple John Middleton Murry, though Murry is regarded by Aldous Huxley as a supposed Judas.

Ahab's castration by Moby Dick is rather less than an analogue, but the parallel with Macbeth is suggestive enough. These days we would try to convict Macbeth for crimes against humanity: he is prone to child murder. Ahab has no guilt whatsoever, even though his mad quest suborns and destroys his crew, who yield not only to his authority but to their own huntsman's instinct. If they are not culpable for seeking to spear Yahweh's King Leviathan, why, then, is Ahab? Even as a boy I apprehended, though remotely, that Ahab's drive was ontotheological, like Iago, whose Moby Dick was the war-god Othello, or Edmund, who wanted to coerce the gods into standing up for bastards.

Ahab's cousins are Don Quixote, Hamlet, Milton's Satan, Shelley's Prometheus: antithetical questers almost too large for their negative enterprises. As the American overreacher, Ahab has all the stigmata of a latecomer.

Ahab is Hamlet in the graveyard, with his carpenter playing the gravedigger. Queequeg's coffin, converted to a life buoy, will be Birnam Wood come to Dunsinane, presaging Ahab's doom and providing Ishmael with survival. Earlier, in chapter 37, a compendium of Shakespearean soliloquies are heard:

> What I've dared, I've willed, and what I've willed, I'll do! They think me mad—Starbuck does; but I'm demoniac, I am madness maddened! That wild madness that's only calm to comprehend itself! The prophecy was that I should be dismembered; and—Aye! I lost this leg. I now prophesy that I will dismember my dismemberer. Now, then, be the prophet and the fulfiller one. That's more than ye, ye great gods, ever were. I laugh and hoot at ye, ye cricket-players, ye pugilists, ye deaf Burkes and blinded Bendigoes! I will not say as schoolboys do to bullies,—Take some one of your own size; don't pommel *me*! No, ye've knocked me down, and I am up

again; but *ye* have run and hidden. Come forth from behind your cotton bags! I have no long gun to reach ye. Come, Ahab's compliments to ye; come and see if ye can swerve me. Swerve me? ye cannot swerve me, else ye swerve yourselves! man has ye there. Swerve me? The path to my fixed purpose is laid with iron rails, whereon my soul is grooved to run. Over unsounded gorges, through the rifled hearts of mountains, under torrents' beds, unerringly I rush! Naught's an obstacle, naught's an angle to the iron way!

In chapter 36, "The Quarter-Deck," Ahab's driving will and rhetoric have seduced the entire crew of his whaler to his dark quest. Knowingly daemonic, he harkens back to Elijah's prophecy in chapter 19, neatly dovetailed with the savage Elijah of First Kings, remorseless enemy of King Ahab, who is slain in battle "and the dogs licked up his blood."

Two daemonic powers, or agents (to adopt Angus Fletcher's term), meet head-on in Moby Dick and Captain Ahab. Daemonic agency *is* the hidden tradition of American literature, an assertion clearer regarding narrative (Poe, Melville, Hawthorne, Twain, James, Faulkner) than wisdom writing (Emerson, Thoreau) or poetry (Whitman, Dickinson, Frost, Stevens, Eliot, Hart Crane). In narrative, the protagonists are possessed by daemons, conquistadores somehow ordering a chaos of unruly other selves. Lyric and essayistic image-making becomes the mode of ordering the autobiographical self in ghostlier demarcations, keener sounds.

Moby-Dick is one major American variant upon the Homeric-Virgilian-Miltonic epic. The other, "Song of Myself," transumes the mode shared by Wordsworth, Carlyle, Tennyson, and Ruskin (in *Praeterita*): the growth of the poet-sage's mind. Miscalled modernism (Eliot, Pound, Lawrence, Joyce, Woolf) remains in these orbits, though Joyce bursts the vessels of inherited forms as energetically as Whitman and Melville had done.

The art of *Moby-Dick* marvelously balances encyclopedic catalog with a world of diverse personalities. My students find in the *Pequod*'s crew a prophecy of the newer America breaking upon us now, to the perplexity of the wretched theocrats, plutocrats, and aging moralists. Ishmael cheerfully converts from his dried-up Presbyterianism to his comrade Queequeg's South Sea island portable idol, while Ahab is a Quaker turned first to Manichaean Zoroastrian fire worship and then to Melvillean gnosis. Starbuck is a firm Quaker, Stubb and Flask godless New Englanders, while the magnificent Queequeg is joined by three highly disparate fellow harpooners:

Tashtego the Native American, Daggoo the African black, and Ahab's dae-mon, the Parsee Fedallah. And the crew, aside from Fedallah's underlings, comprises a gallery of the nations: from the Azores to the Isle of Man, a "deputation from all the isles of the sea, and all the ends of the earth, accompanying old Ahab in the *Pequod* to lay the world's grievances before that bar from which not very many of them ever come back."

"The world's grievances" are the Jobean burden of *Moby-Dick*, of so massive a heft that Melville's fighting motto transcends American hyper-bole: "Give me a condor's quill! Give me Vesuvius' crater for an inkstand! . . . To produce a mighty book, you must choose a mighty theme." That would be Davy Crockett's half horse/half alligator fustian, except that this one time Melville's achievement soars beyond even his astonishing ambitions. Whitman overtly intended *Leaves of Grass* to become the New Bible for Americans. Properly regarded, it is, particularly when read in conjunc-tion with Emerson, *Moby-Dick*, *Huckleberry Finn*, Emily Dickinson, *The Scarlet Letter*, *Walden*, *The Portrait of a Lady*, Robert Frost and Wallace Stevens, *As I Lay Dying*, and *The Bridge*. With *Leaves of Grass* 1860, *Moby-Dick* is at the center of this American heretical scripture, our wor-ship of the god within, which pragmatically means of the daemon who knows how it is done.

Emily Dickinson
(1830–1886)

EMILY DICKINSON rivals Walt Whitman, Wallace Stevens, Robert Frost, T. S. Eliot, and Hart Crane; these six are the major poets thus far engendered by the United States. Like the other five, Dickinson had an antithetical relation to Ralph Waldo Emerson. Emerson, neither transcendental optimist nor fatalistic pessimist, ultimately took his stand upon experience, thus fostering pragmatism. Dickinson too was a pragmatist before that American philosophy was formulated. No poet teaches more compellingly that the only differences that matter are those that make a difference. Dickinson differed from Emersonianism and differed from Calvinist Christianity. Yet she went to school with Emerson and with the poets he celebrated: Shakespeare, Milton, and Wordsworth, to whom she added Keats. Her spiritual attachments, like Emerson's, were to what she called "this loved Philology," that is, to poetry itself. The self, which is part or particle of God, is exalted by Emerson. Dickinson also had no positive use for a God external to the self. Self-reliance, both cognitive and spiritual, is as much her mode as it was Emerson's, though unlike Emerson she chose as her prime poetic subject the high cost of confirmation.

Dickinson is a very difficult poet; even her best critics tend to underestimate just how subtle and complex a body of work ensued from her immense cognitive originality. She thought through not less than everything for herself. Only Shakespeare, Milton, Blake, and Emerson can be judged to have made all things new as Dickinson did. Walt Whitman, the other major American poet of the nineteenth century, manifests an originality of vision comparable to Dickinson's, though his cognitive powers are not his primary endowment. Whitman perpetually surprises us by nuance, as Wallace Stevens was to do a century later. Dickinson mounts Emerson's "stairway of surprise," but with an intellectual difference:

> Surprise is like a thrilling – pungent –
> Upon a tasteless meat

> Alone – too acrid – but combined
> An edible delight.

Comic poet as she frequently is, Dickinson is unique in terming surprise a kind of acrid herb, not to be taken by itself. Her target rather genially is Emerson, from whom she had learned: "Tell all the truth but tell it slant." The Truth's superb surprise, as blinding as it is too acrid, requires mediation, a certain slant of light. Oxymoron, the rhetoric of seeming contradiction, was inherited by Dickinson from Keats, and Poem 320 (as numbered in the Franklin Edition), with its "Heavenly Hurt" and "imperial affliction," weaves Keats's kind of sensuous apprehension into the subtle reception of a New England light that signifies mortality. The "internal difference, / Where the Meanings, are" is wholly Dickinson's own realm. Clearly this is a difference that makes a considerable difference from Emerson, and from all other forerunners. Despair is a purely Dickinsonian seal, and ambiguously it can neither be instructed nor expounded by others.

Poem 320 is packed with enigmas. What takes place between the arrival and the departure of the slant of light? The listening landscape and the breathless shadows inaugurate the coming of the slant, and its going is a similitude for the distance we see on the faces of our dead. Death and the dead are Dickinson's obsessive subjects. Poem 479, "Because I could not stop for Death," is the most playful of her masterpieces in this area. Here Death comes courting, in a manner suitable for Miss Dickinson of Amherst, with Immortality serving as chaperone or duenna during the courting drive.

From the third stanza on, the journey has no precedents, and it parts from ordinary categories of space and time. Erotic despair is the authentic burden of "Because I could not stop for Death," and Death is a surrogate for a lover either renounced or lost to circumstances. The tone of this lyric is extraordinarily subtle, even for Dickinson. There is no panic or alarm in her apparent abduction by a demon lover. Death's civility remains impeccable; he is the finest gentleman in Amherst. Indeed, he receives no individual mention after the second stanza. The courtship remains enthralling; centuries feel shorter than a particular day. But how should the speaker's affect be described, even as she experiences being carried off? Dickinson's tonalities are never more uncanny. The reader, teased into imagination and into thought, is given the pleasure and the perplexity of unriddling this great lyric of loss.

It is not a rare quality for great poets to possess such cognitive strength that we are confronted by authentic intellectual difficulties when we read them. "Poems are made by fools like me," yes, and by Dante, Milton, Blake, and Shelley, but only God can make a tree, to reappropriate a rejoinder I remember making to W. H. Auden many years ago when he deprecated the possibilities of poetry as compared with the awful truths of Christian theology. But there are certainly very grand poets who are scarcely thinkers in the discursive modes. Tennyson and Whitman are instances of over-whelming elegiac artists who make us fitful when they argue, and the subtle rhetorical evasions of Wallace Stevens do not redeem his unfortunate essay "A Collect of Philosophy."

Of all poets writing in English in the nineteenth and twentieth centuries, I judge Emily Dickinson to present us with the most authentic cognitive difficulties. Vast and subtle intellect cannot in itself make a poet; the essential qualities are inventiveness, mastery of trope and craft, and that weird flair for intuiting significance through rhythm to which we can give no proper name. Dickinson has all these, as well as a mind so original and powerful that we scarcely have begun, even now, to catch up with her.

Originality at its strongest—in the Yahwist, Plato, Shakespeare, and Freud—usurps immense spaces of consciousness and language, and imposes contingencies upon all who come after. These contingencies work so as to conceal authentic difficulty through a misleading familiarity. Dickinson's strangeness, partly masked, still causes us to wonder at her, as we ought to wonder at Shakespeare or Freud. Like them, she has no single, overwhelming precursor whose existence can lessen her wildness for us. Her agon was waged with the whole of tradition, but particularly with the Bible and with Romanticism. As an agonist, she takes care to differ from any male model and places us upon warning:

> I cannot dance upon my Toes –
> No Man instructed me –
> But oftentimes, among my mind,
> A Glee possesseth me,
>
> . . . .
>
> Nor any know I know the Art
> I mention – easy – Here –
> Nor any Placard boast me –
> It's full as Opera –
> [381]

The mode is hardly Whitmanian in this lyric of 1862, but the vaunting is, and both gleeful arts respond to the Emersonian prophecy of American Self-Reliance. Each responds with a difference, but it is a perpetual trial to be a heretic whose only orthodoxy is Emersonianism or the exaltation of whim:

> If nature will not tell the tale
> Jehovah told to her
> Can human nature not survive
> Without a listener?
> [1776]

Emerson should have called his little first book, *Nature*, by its true title of "Man," but Dickinson in any case would have altered that title also. Alas, that Emerson was not given the chance to read the other Titan that he fostered. We would cherish his charmed reaction to:

> A Bomb upon the Ceiling
> Is an improving thing –
> It keeps the nerves progressive
> Conjecture flourishing –
> [1150]

Dickinson, after all, could have sent her poems to Emerson rather than to the nobly obtuse Higginson. We cannot envision Whitman addressing a copy of the first *Leaves of Grass* to a Higginson. There is little reason to suppose that mere diffidence prevented Miss Dickinson of Amherst from presenting her work to Mr. Emerson of Concord. In 1862, Emerson was still Emerson; his long decline dates from after the conclusion of the war. A private unfolding remained necessary for Dickinson, according to laws of the spirit and of poetic reason that we perpetually quest to surmise. Whereas Whitman masked his delicate, subtle, and hermetic art by developing the outward self of the rough Walt, Dickinson set herself free to invest her imaginative exuberance elsewhere. The heraldic drama of her reclusiveness became the cost of her confirmation as a poet more original even than Whitman, indeed more original than any poet of her century after (and except) Wordsworth. Like Wordsworth, she began anew upon a tabula rasa of poetry, to appropriate Hazlitt's remark about

Wordsworth. Whitman rethought the relation of the poet's self to his own vision, whereas Dickinson rethought the entire content of poetic vision. Wordsworth had done both, and done both more implicitly than these Americans could manage, but then Wordsworth had Coleridge as stimulus, while Whitman and Dickinson had the yet more startling and far wilder Emerson, who was and is the American difference personified. I cannot believe that even Dickinson would have written with so absolutely astonishing an audacity had Emerson not insisted that poets were as liberating gods:

> Because that you are going
> And never coming back
> And I, however absolute,
> May overlook your Track –
>
> Because that Death is final,
> However first it be,
> This instant be suspended
> Above Mortality –
>
> Significance that each has lived
> The other to detect
> Discovery not God himself
> Could now annihilate
>
> Eternity, Presumption
> The instant I perceive
> That you, who were Existence
> Yourself forgot to live –

These are the opening quatrains of poem 1314, dated by R. W. Franklin as about January 1874, but it must be later, if indeed the reference is to the dying either of Samuel Bowles (1878) or of Judge Otis Lord (1884), the two men Richard Sewall, Dickinson's principal biographer, considers to have been her authentic loves, if not in any conventional way her lovers. The poem closes with a conditional vision of God refunding to us finally our "confiscated Gods." Reversing the traditional pattern, Dickinson required and achieved male Muses, and her "confiscated Gods" plays darkly against

Emerson's "liberating gods." Of Emerson, whose crucial work (*Essays, The Conduct of Life, Society and Solitude*, the *Poems*) she had mastered, Dickinson spoke with the ambiguity we might expect. When Emerson lectured in Amherst in December 1857 and stayed next door with Dickinson's brother and sister-in-law, he was characterized by the poet: "as if he had come from where dreams are born." Presumably the Transcendental Emerson might have merited this, but it is curious when applied to the exalter of "Fate" and "Power" in *The Conduct of Life*, or to the dialectical pragmatist of "Experience" and "Circles," two essays that I think Dickinson had internalized. Later, writing to Higginson, she observed: "With the Kingdom of Heaven on his knee, could Mr. Emerson hesitate?" The question, whether open or rhetorical, is dangerous and wonderful, and provokes considerable rumination.

Yet her subtle ways with other male precursors are scarcely less provocative. Since Shelley had addressed *Epipsychidion* to Emilia Viviani, under the name of "Emily," Dickinson felt authorized to answer a poet who, like herself, favored the image of volcanoes. Only ten days or so before Judge Lord died, she composed a remarkable quatrain in his honor (and her own):

> Circumference thou Bride of Awe
> Possessing thou shalt be
> Possessed by every hallowed Knight
> That dares to covet thee
> [1636]

Sewall notes the interplay with some lines in *Epipsychidion*:

> Possessing and possessed by all that is
> Within that calm circumference of bliss,
> And by each other, till to love and live
> Be one:—
> [549–52]

Shelley's passage goes on to a kind of lovers' apocalypse:

> One hope within two wills, one will beneath
> Two overshadowing minds, one life, one death,
> One Heaven, one Hell, one immortality,

And one annihilation. . . .
[584–87]

In his essay "Circles," Emerson had insisted: "There is no outside, no inclosing wall, no circumference to us." The same essay declares: "The only sin is limitation." If that is so, then there remains the cost of confirmation, worked out by Dickinson in an extraordinary short poem that may be her critique of Emerson's denial of an outside:

I saw no Way – The Heavens were stitched
I felt the Columns close –
The Earth reversed her Hemispheres –
I touched the Universe –

And back it slid – and I alone
A Speck upon a Ball –
Went out upon Circumference –
Beyond the Dip of Bell –
[633]

"My Business is Circumference—" she famously wrote to Higginson, to whom, not less famously, she described herself as "the only Kangaroo among the Beauty." When she wrote, to another correspondent, that "the Bible dealt with the Centre, not with the Circumference—," she would have been aware that the terms were Emerson's, and that Emerson also dealt only with the Central, in the hope of the Central Man who would come. Clearly, "Circumference" is her trope for the Sublime, as consciousness and as achievement or performance. For Shelley, Circumference was a Spenserian cynosure, a Gardens of Adonis vision, while for Emerson it was no part of us, or only another challenge to be overcome by the Central, by the Self-Reliant, Man.

If the Bible's concern is Centre, not Circumference, it cannot be because the Bible does not quest for the Sublime. If Circumference or Dickinson is the bride of Awe or of the authority of Judge Lord, then Awe too somehow had to be detached from the Centre:

No man saw awe, nor to his house
Admitted he a man

Though by his awful residence
Has human nature been.

Not deeming of his dread abode
Till laboring to flee
A grasp on comprehension laid
Detained vitality.

Returning is a different route
The Spirit could not show
For breathing is the only work
To be enacted now.

"Am not consumed," old Moses wrote,
"Yet saw him face to face" –
That very physiognomy
I am convinced was this.
[1342]

This might be called an assimilation of Awe to Circumference, where "laboring to flee" and returning via "a different route" cease to be antithetical to one another. "Vitality" here is another trope for Circumference or the Dickinsonian Sublime. If, as I surmise, this undated poem is a kind of proleptic elegy for Judge Lord, then Dickinson identifies herself with "old Moses," and not for the first time in her work. Moses, denied entrance into Canaan, "wasn't fairly used –," she wrote, as though the exclusion were her fate also. In some sense, she chose this fate, and not just by extending her circumference to Bowles and to Lord, unlikely pragmatic choices. The spiritual choice was not to be post-Christian, as with Whitman or Emerson, but to become a sect of one, like Milton or Blake. Perhaps her crucial choice was to refuse the auction of her mind through publication. Character being fate, the Canaan she would not cross to was poetic recognition while she lived.

Dickinson is cognitively so endowed, and so original, that her only peers among poets writing in English might be Shakespeare, Milton, and Blake. Like them, she reconceptualizes very nearly every idea she considers, and more in the overt mode of Milton and of Blake than in Shakespeare's extraordinary and deftly misleading manner. Like Milton and the High Romantics, she excels at the difficult art of making herself prior to what genetically precedes her. Consider the remarkable Poem 319:

> Of Bronze – and Blaze –
> The North – Tonight –
> So adequate – it forms –
> So preconcerted with itself –
> So distant – to alarms –
> An Unconcern so sovereign
> To Universe, or me –
> Infects my simple spirit
> With Taints of Majesty –
> Till I take vaster attitudes –
> And strut upon my stem –
> Disdaining Men, and Oxygen,
> For Arrogance of them –
>
> My splendors, are Menagerie –
> But their Competeless Show
> Will entertain the Centuries
> When I, am long ago,
> An Island in dishonored Grass –
> Whom none but Beetles – know.

This overtly is "about" the northern lights but actually is mediated by Emerson's essay "The Poet" (1843):

> For it is not metres, but a metre-making argument, that makes a poem,—a thought so passionate and alive, that, like the spirit of a plant or an animal, it has an architecture of its own, and adorns nature with a new thing. The thought and the form are equal in order of time, but in the order of genesis the thought is prior to the form. The poet has a new thought: he has a whole new experience to unfold; he will tell us how it was with him, and all men will be the richer in his fortune. For, the experience of each new age requires a new confession, and the world seems always waiting for

its poet. I remember, when I was young, how much I was moved one morning by tidings that genius had appeared in a youth who sat near me at table. He had left his work, and gone rambling none knew whither, and had written hundreds of lines, but could not tell whether that which was in him was therein told: he could tell nothing but that all was changed,—man, beast, heaven, earth, and sea. How gladly we listened! how credulous! Society seemed to be compromised. We sat in the aurora of a sunrise which was to put out all the stars. Boston seemed to be at twice the distance it had the night before, or was much farther than that. Rome,—what was Rome? Plutarch and Shakespeare were in the yellow leaf, and Homer no more should be heard of. It is much to know that poetry has been written this very day, under this very roof, by your side. What! that wonderful spirit has not expired! these stony moments are still sparkling and animated! I had fancied that the oracles were all silent, and nature had spent her fires, and behold! all night, from every pore, these fine auroras have been streaming.

Emerson is frolicking here, and yet his thought is so passionate and alive, his meter-making argument so compelling, that his little fable of the youth has its darker side also. The image of the aurora begins here as dawn, indeed an apocalyptic sunrise that might dim all the stars for good, but by a marvelous crossing is transformed into the aurora borealis proper, streaming from every pore of the night. The northern lights therefore represent, for Emerson, a reversal of belatedness into earliness, executed here with superb irony, since the belatedness belongs to Shakespeare and Homer, and the earliness to "a youth who sat near me at table."

Dickinson, frequently deft at taking hints from Emerson and then swerving away from them (in a process ably studied by Joanne Feit Diehl), seems to have taken the hint with more than usual dialectical agility in "Of Bronze – and Blaze –." I no longer agree with Charles R. Anderson's strong commentary upon this poem, which interprets its teaching as being that "the mortal poet corrupts his true nature if he attempts to be divine" and that "the poet must remain earth-bound." That tends to negate Dickinson's subtler ironies, which dominate the poem. The North, meaning the night sky and the auroras streaming through it, is so adequate as to overwhelm what might seem adequate desire to Dickinson, and infects her "simple spirit" with sublime longings. Her own bronze and blaze becomes the rhetorical stance of her poetry, which rises to the heights ("vaster attitudes") in order to manifest a sovereign unconcern all her own. Certainly the crucial irony is in "And strut upon my stem," which is a negative or downward metamorphosis, but only of the natural woman, as it were, and not of the poet. To say that her splendors are Menagerie is indeed to admit that she is a performer, but the ancient Pindaric assertion of canonical renown and poetic survival follows with enormous authority. To be a "Competeless Show," able to entertain the centuries, indeed is to be preconcerted with oneself, to be distant to alarms, even to the prophecy of one's organic fate.

Why do we apprehend, beyond error, that "Of Bronze – and Blaze –" was written by a woman? In a way more singular and persuasive than any other woman poet has managed (at least since Sappho), Dickinson in scores of her strongest poems compels us to confront the part that gender plays in her poetic identity:

The Tint I cannot take – is best –
The Color too remote
That I could show it in Bazaar –
A Guinea at a sight –

The fine – impalpable Array –
That swaggers on the eye
Like Cleopatra's Company –
Repeated – in the sky –

The Moments of Dominion
That happen on the Soul
And leave it with a Discontent
Too exquisite – to tell –

The eager look – on Landscapes –
As if they just repressed
Some Secret – that was pushing
Like Chariots – in the Vest –

The Pleading of the Summer –
That other Prank – of Snow –

That Cushions Mystery with Tulle,
For fear the Squirrels – know.

Their Graspless manners – mock us –
Until the Cheated Eye
Shuts arrogantly – in the Grave
Another way – to see –
[696]

"Of Bronze – and Blaze –" does not quite name the auroras, which is
a typical procedure for Dickinson. "The Tint I cannot take – is best –"
goes further and avoids naming anything. American male theorists and
poets from Emerson and Whitman through Stevens and W. C. Williams are
programmatic in urging an unnaming upon us, and Stevens in particular
achieves some of his greatest effects in that mode:

This is nothing until in a single man contained,
Nothing until this named thing nameless is
And is destroyed. He opens the door of his house

On flames. The scholar of one candle sees
An Arctic effulgence flaring on the frame
Of everything he is. And he feels afraid.

This is the crisis of "The Auroras of Autumn," where "this named thing"
is the aurora borealis, which flames forth to frighten the poet or scholar of
one candle and so undoes his attempt to enact the program of unnaming.
But Dickinson, shrewdly exploiting her identity as woman poet, chooses
another way to see, a way that unnames without defiance or struggle. The
best tint is what she cannot take, too remote for showing, impalpable, too
exquisite to tell, secret, graspless. Such a tint seems unavailable to the eye of
the male poet, even to a Keats or a Shelley, even to Wordsworth's extraordinary mediation between the visual and the visionary. No woman poet since
Dickinson has had the power to teach us so urgently and intuitively that
women need not see as men see, need not will as men will, need not appropriate for themselves as men perhaps need to do. Freud, when he sadly
admitted that women were a mystery, echoed the bafflement of Milton, and

might have been echoing Blake. Only three men who wrote in English—Chaucer, Shakespeare, Samuel Richardson—seem able to convey the sense of a difference between women and men in a way comparable to the greatest women writers in the language, Jane Austen, George Eliot, Dickinson. If Austen is comparable to Chaucer as a craftsman in irony and George Eliot comparable to Richardson as a moral psychologist of the Protestant temperament, then Dickinson is quite comparable to some of the subtlest aspects of Shakespearean representation. Without Shakespeare, our sense of reality would be much diminished. Without Dickinson, our sense of reality might not be diminished, but we would know far less than we do about the sufferings and the satisfactions of a really isolated consciousness at its highest powers, particularly if it were the consciousness of a woman.

Who among the poets thinks through every question so probingly as Dickinson does?:

This Consciousness that is aware
Of Neighbors and the Sun
Will be the one aware of Death
And that itself alone

Is traversing the interval
Experience between
And most profound experiment
Appointed unto Men –

How adequate unto itself
It's properties shall be
Itself unto itself and None
Shall make discovery –

Adventure most unto itself
The Soul condemned to be –
Attended by a single Hound
It's own identity.
[817]

Consciousness ("conscience" in *Hamlet*) is her resource and her sublime agon with the limits of existence. She will not say with Hamlet: "Let be" or "Let it be." Poem 817 marches with a radical Protestant beat in rhythm of thought, proudly asserting her unsponsored freedom to be in the difficulty of what it is to be. No solipsist "aware / Of Neighbors and the Sun," her consciousness proudly calls out its autonomy. "Itself alone," "adequate unto itself," "Itself unto itself," "most unto itself" constitute a rugged litany of spiritual independence.

Death, her death, is an awareness, a most profound experiment, discovery, adventure, condemnation. The poem's surprise is its marvelous close: a shamanistic single Hound, the image of a doubled identity. Antony, bungling even his suicide, has not heard the music of his god or daemon Heracles abandoning him. Dickinson's daemon will attend her in the final experiment and implicitly marks the poet's shamanistic capacity for shape-shifting survival.

The Walt Whitman of "Song of Myself" declares his role and function as healing shaman. Close reading reveals Dickinson to be as uncanny:

> It was not Death, for I stood up,
> And all the Dead, lie down –
> It was not Night, for all the Bells
> Put out their Tongues, for Noon.
>
> It was not Frost, for on my Flesh
> I felt Siroccos – crawl –
> Nor Fire – for just my marble feet
> Could keep a Chancel, cool –
>
> And yet, it tasted, like them all,
> The Figures I have seen
> Set orderly, for Burial,
> Reminded me, of mine –
>
> As if my life were shaven,
> And fitted to a frame,
> And could not breathe without a key,
> And 'twas like Midnight, some –

When everything that ticked – has stopped –
And space stares – all around –
Or Grisly frosts – first Autumn morns,
Repeal the Beating Ground –

But, most, like Chaos – Stopless – cool –
Without a Chance, or spar –
Or even a Report of Land –
To justify – Despair.
[355]

Beneath the spooky clarity of this vision, darker speculations cluster. In teaching Dickinson I find that students emphasize their fascination with where in relation to what she depicts is the lyric's speaker *now*? The classical critic on this enigma remains Sharon Cameron in her *Lyric Time* where Kant is the ultimate model: the realities of space and of time are modes of perception rather than objects, and yet appearances in time have something permanent in them.

Still, archaic ecstasies and shamanistic dislocations are closer to the daemonic Dickinson, who dodges death while knowing the necessities of dying. Her temporal displacements exceed whatever norms lyric tradition manifests. Bells ring for high noon, and Dickinson *tastes* oxymoronic cold-and-heat and beholds herself as a standing cadaver:

As if my life were shaven,
And fitted to a frame,
And could not breathe without a key . . .

Time stops, space stares. The final quatrain challenges limits of poetic difficulty:

But, most, like Chaos – Stopless – cool –
Without a Chance, or spar –
Or even a Report of Land –
To justify – Despair.

"Justify" itself is tropological—despair does not convey the affect of this poem. "Chaos" is formless ocean; the poet's power of mind over that universe of death is firm enough to achieve Kant's sense of "something permanent," of images cohering into a fiction of duration. One of my students, answering her own query, regarded Dickinson's *now* as Emersonian Newness, opening into disclosures of the poem's own potential for survival.

Tone or stance is Dickinson's strength, as it is Whitman's, yet Walt— an American, one of the roughs—centers his poems upon himself, as the Amherst visionary would not. Always she is there: self-assertive, self-reliant, self-radiant. And yet Whitmanian advertisements-for-myself are antithetical to her experiment in renunciation. Like her only American poetic rival, she is joined to what Yeats in *Per Amica Silentia Lunae* called "the place of the daemon," but she enters it through another gate.

Shamans are not prophets, and Whitman composed poorly when he proclaimed futurity. The pathos of annihilation, Dickinson's truest conviction, is shared by her with Hamlet. Whitman at his darkest incarnates this truth. Dickinson, dark and light, teaches it incessantly, but she is masked by her diction, and most readers get this wrong. Immortality in Whitman is our survival in the memory of others. In Dickinson it is merely a metaphor, the duenna or chaperone who accompanies Death and the Maiden on their buggy ride.

Is there a more radical nihilist in American literature than Miss Dickinson of Amherst? Hamlet-like again, she thinks not too much but much too well and thinks her way to the truth. She possesses her art lest she perish of the truth, and her truth is annihilation: the rest is silence.

Mark Twain
(1835–1910)

M Y LATE FRIEND Robert Penn Warren, who loathed Emerson and
was indifferent to Whitman, considered nineteenth-century American imaginative literature to have achieved an apotheosis in Mark Twain,
with Melville and John Greenleaf Whittier also admitted to admiration.
Something of Warren's ferocity toward the protagonists of his own fiction caught its zeal from Twain's ambivalence toward most of his adult
creations.

In our weekly luncheons, before Warren went off to research at the Yale
library and I stumbled out to teach, he discoursed eagerly upon our national
literature. A quarter century his junior, I mostly listened and learned, dis-
senting only upon Emerson, whom at last we agreed never to discuss again.

Warren saw Mark Twain as the ultimate American nihilist, but that was
a bad eminence he also granted to the abhorred Emerson, champion of the
murderous John Brown. A secular Augustinian, Warren would not agree
with my seeing Twain as a secular American Gnostic, damning Yahweh as
the God of this hellish world.

I first met my late friend James Cox in the summer of 1969, when he
kindly gave me a copy of his splendid *Mark Twain: The Fate of Humor*
(1966). It remains for me the most illuminating of Twain studies, because it
argues that this parodistic humor subverts and unmasks all of the demands
made upon us by the censorious superego. Parody could not save Mark
Twain from himself, yet it opened his daemon to the great achievement of
The Adventures of Huckleberry Finn (1885), a work of the stature of *The
Scarlet Letter, Moby-Dick*, and *Leaves of Grass*.

If our literature has produced a single work of universal appeal, popular
and elitist, it must be the story of Huck Finn. There are only a few dissent-
ers: Jane Smiley, who insists she prefers *Uncle Tom's Cabin*, and a phalanx
of ecocritics who shrug Twain and Huck away as mere materialists who
entertained equivocal stances toward nature. I do not adhere to this school
but agree in a limited way: Huck's longed-for "freedom" is not natural.

Freedom for both Mark Twain and his daemon Huck Finn is the freedom of the storyteller, partly alienated from society and from nature.

I turn now to freshly reread *The Adventures of Huckleberry Finn*, centering upon Huck himself, whose character and personality reflect the lifelong act of renaming by which Samuel Langhorne Clemens became Mark Twain, at once scathing critic yet also embodiment of the Gilded Age, which he named. As a financial speculator, he came to resemble Jay Gould rather more than Huck Finn.

The great dragon guarding *The Adventures of Huckleberry Finn* cannot be slain: black slavery and all its consequences for the spirit of the fourteen-year-old Huck, who need never grow up. Toni Morrison, in an essay included in the Norton Critical Edition, has had what could be the last word here:

> Pleasant as this relationship is, suffused as it is by a lightness they both enjoy and a burden of responsibility both assume, it cannot continue. Knowing the relationship is discontinuous, doomed to separation, is (or used to be) typical of the experience of white/ black childhood friendships (mine included), and the cry of inevitable rupture is all the more anguished by being mute. Every reader knows that Jim will be dismissed without explanation at some point; that no enduring adult fraternity will emerge. Anticipating this loss may have led Twain to the over-the-top minstrelization of Jim.

This perhaps is founded on the assumption that *The Adventures of Huckleberry Finn* is a Balzacian novel or a Woolfian-Faulknerian blend, like the best earlier narratives of Morrison. However, Twain's masterpiece is Cervantine and belongs to the Quixotic order of play. Huck is as evasive as Walt Whitman: the goal of the book and its protagonist is a freedom whose single aim is storytelling pleasure.

T. S. Eliot, in an essay that magnified the Mississippi River into Huck's god, nevertheless observed usefully the high quality of Huck's awareness. The boy sees everything and everyone and avoids all judging. He decidedly is not a critic. Always interested, he nevertheless is remarkably disinterested. For a fourteen-year-old, Huck is uncanny in certain aspects of maturity and knowledge. But then he is not just Mark Twain's daemon; the storytelling genius of America is incarnate in him, and its principles are evade, escape, keep lying against time.

Huck's father is murderous, alcoholic, hateful. You have to flee from him; otherwise, you have to slay him before he kills you, and Huck has no interest in hurting anyone. Unlike in *The Adventures of Tom Sawyer*, the violence of Huck's book is incessant. With a Shakespearean detachment, Huck records much of what he sees and hears while saying little in response. But we learn over and again the pragmatic goodness of the boy. Nigger Jim says it best: "Dah you goes, de ole true Huck; de on'y white genlman dat ever kep' his promise to ole Jim."

Defining Huck's character is difficult, in part because he is not a quester striving to attain a goal. Cox sensibly emphasizes that Huck's journey is "a flight *from* tyranny, not a flight toward freedom." A survivor, virtually a refugee, the boy has become expert in the arts of evasion and dissimulation.

The freedom of consciousness enables the storyteller's liberty, and Huck gives us more than the narrative of his isolated self. Who else in Western prose fiction is as free of malice as Huck Finn? There are Cervantes's Mournful Knight and Sancho, Dickens's Samuel Pickwick, and Joyce's Poldy Bloom. Pap Finn calls him the Angel of Death when he attempts to butcher Huck, but that is an inversion of actuality.

Twain's one full-length masterwork is a comedy only because it concludes insouciantly. Of no genre, Twain's book of the daemon has been creatively misread by Sherwood Anderson and Hemingway, Fitzgerald and J. D. Salinger. To different degrees, they interpreted it as a parable of their own inception and as nostalgia for a lost American dream. Their Huck is not a shape-shifter. Twain's Huck *wants* to stay the same, yet his need to keep moving means he must change. It is as though his creator, Twain, wants him to emulate Benjamin Franklin and Henry Thoreau but cannot keep Huck away from Emersonianism. Contra Eliot, the river, though a refuge, is not Huck's god. There is a god within us, Emerson tells us. This god speaks when it will. Genius, daemon, god—they were the same to Huck, who used none of these names, and to Emerson, who did. The aesthetic wonder of Huck's book centers upon not the river but the life it makes possible for Jim and Huck.

Henry James
(1843–1916)

THE PORTRAIT OF A LADY, my favorite among all of Henry James's novels, originally appeared in 1880–81. James revised it extensively, more than a quarter century later, in 1908, for the definitive New York edition of *The Novels and Tales of Henry James*. Thirty-seven when he first sketched his portrait of Isabel Archer, James was sixty-five when he returned to it.

There are almost two Isabel Archers, so that the reader is well advised to choose a reprint carefully, the later version being preferable. No novelist— not even Cervantes or Austen or Proust—had James's vast consciousness. One would have to go back to Shakespeare to find, as Emily Dickinson phrased it, a larger demonstration that the brain is wider than the sky. Isabel Archer, always a heroine of consciousness, manifests a palpably expanded consciousness in the revision of 1908.

Why read *The Portrait of a Lady*? We ought to read for many purposes and to gain copious benefits, but the cultivation of an individual conscious- ness is certainly a prime purpose, and a major benefit, of deep reading. Zest and insight: these are the attributes of the solitary reader's conscious- ness that are most enhanced by reading. Social information, whether past or contemporary, seems to me a peripheral gain of reading, and political awareness an even more tenuous dividend.

As James revises *The Portrait of a Lady*, his near-identity with Isabel Archer is augmented. Since Isabel is James's most Shakespearean char- acter, her identity is placed in the reader's perspectives upon her. We are more guided by James in the revised version, so that it could be argued that Isabel was a richer, more enigmatic personality in 1881 than in 1908. Put another way, the most masterful of all American novelists seems to trust his readers less, and himself more, as his own perspectives upon Isabel changed.

Isabel, in 1881, is a victim of her drive for autonomy. By 1908, James converts her partial loss of autonomy, caused by her errors of judgment, into a gain in her consciousness. She *sees* much more, at the apparent cost of much of her freedom. To adopt one of our current modes, a feminist reader might be happier with the Isabel of 1881 than with the more Jamesian figure of 1908, whose prime concern is to stand beyond being deceived. Isabel's earlier attempt at *Self*-Reliance, brave but mistaken, is replaced by an emphasis upon the self's superior optics. Self-Reliance is Ralph Waldo Emerson's prime doctrine, and Isabel Archer is one of Emerson's children, as James, on some interior level, must have been aware. Since Henry James, Sr., never achieved independence from Emerson, his son's comments upon the Sage of Concord require wary reading:

> It is hardly too much, or too little, to say of Emerson's writings in general that they were not composed at all.

> But no one has had so steady and constant, and above all so natural, a vision of what we require and what we are capable of in the way of aspiration and independence.

> . . . the rarity of Emerson's genius, which has made him so, for the attentive peoples, the first, and the one really rare, American spirit in letters . . .

The first remark is absurdly condescending; read Emerson's essay "Experience" and you may not agree with Henry James. But the second excerpt is pure Isabel Archer: that is precisely her vision. Whether James really meant the third extract, I rather doubt; he preferred Hawthorne, Emerson's uneasy walking companion. The passionate Hester Prynne, in Hawthorne's *The Scarlet Letter*, seems to me even more an Emersonian heroine than does Isabel Archer, who flees passion, as did Henry James. Emerson was in love with both his wives, Ellen and Lidian; perhaps more passionately with Ellen, who died so young. James, not Emerson, is responsible for Isabel's repression of her sexual nature. Never much of a novel reader, Emerson read *The Scarlet Letter* but underesteemed it; and I doubt that he would have admired *The Portrait of a Lady*. Yet he would have recognized in the idealistic Isabel a true child, and would have deprecated the aestheticism that led her to choose for a husband the dreadful Gilbert Osmond, a parody both of Emerson and of Walter Pater, high priest of the Aesthetic Movement in England.

Reading *The Portrait of a Lady* for the first time, you may find it useful to realize that Isabel Archer is always mediated for you by the narrator, Henry James, and by her admirers—Ralph Touchett, Lord Warburton, and Caspar Goodwood (unforgivably outrageous name!). Of Isabel as a dramatic personality, in the Shakespearean sense, James is able to give us very little. We take her on faith, because James's skill at studying her consciousness is so elaborate and artful, and because she has so strong an effect upon everyone else in the novel, male or female, with the ironic exception of her husband, the poseur Osmond. For Osmond, she ought to be only a portrait or a statue; her largeness of soul offends his narrowness. The crucial enigma of the novel, as every reader recognizes, is why did she marry the tiresome Osmond, and even more, why does she return to him at the end?

Why do so many readers, women as well as men, fall in love with Isabel Archer? If you are an intense enough reader when you are still very young, your first love is likelier to be fictive than actual. Isabel Archer, famously termed by Henry James "the heiress of all the ages," attracts many among us because she is the archetype of all those young women, in fiction or in actuality, who are pragmatically doom-eager because they seek complete realization of their potential while maintaining an idealism that rejects selfishness. George Eliot's Dorothea Brooke in *Middlemarch* aspires bravely, but her transcendental yearnings do not have the element added by Isabel Archer's Emersonianism, which is to drive for inward freedom almost at any cost.

Since Isabel is Henry James's self-portrait as a lady, her consciousness has to be extraordinarily large, almost the rival of her creator's. This renders any reader's moral judgment of her character rather irrelevant. The novelist Graham Greene, a Jamesian disciple, insisted that James's moral passion in *The Portrait of a Lady* centers upon the idea of treachery, as exemplified by Madame Merle, who plots successfully to marry Isabel to Osmond so that he and Pansy, her daughter by Osmond, can enjoy Isabel's wealth. But Madame Merle, despite her deception, makes very little of a mark upon Isabel's capacious consciousness. Treachery obsessed Graham Greene, far more than it did Henry James.

Though *The Portrait of a Lady* is a kind of tragicomedy, few readers are going to be moved to laughter by the book. Despite the nasty vividness of Osmond and Madame Merle, and the different types splendidly exemplified by Isabel's admirers—Touchett, Warburton, Goodwood—James carefully sees to it that Isabel Archer is always at the center of our concern. It is indeed her portrait that matters; everyone else exists only in relation to her. The figure of Isabel means too much to James, and to the sensitive reader, for any comic perspective upon her to be adequate. Nor is irony allowed to dominate James's account of her odyssey of consciousness, though her situation is almost absurdly ironic. She took Osmond in the delusion that she was choosing—and granting—freedom. He knew everything worth knowing, she had thought, and in turn he would wish her to know all that could be known of life. Her terrible error might almost seem to be a cruelty toward her on James's part, but he suffers with her and for her, and her mistake is absolutely central for the book. "Error about life is necessary for life," Nietzsche remarked. Neither Henry James nor Isabel Archer is at all Nietzschean, but his adage illuminates Isabel's enormous blunder.

What is it that has blinded Isabel? Or, to ask that another way, why does James inflict such a catastrophe upon his own self-portrait as a woman? In James's revisions for the 1908 edition, Osmond is considerably darkened into authentic snobbishness, uselessness, and fakery, which makes Isabel's bad judgment all the more peculiar. James's first description of Gilbert Osmond is enough to warn the reader that Isabel's future husband is very bad news:

> He was a man of forty, with a high but well-shaped head, on which the hair, still dense, but prematurely grizzled, had been cropped close. He had a fine, narrow, extremely modelled and composed face, of which the only fault was just this effect of its running a trifle too much to points; an appearance to which the shape of the beard contributed not a little. This beard, cut in the manner of the portraits of the sixteenth century and surmounted by a fair moustache, of which the ends had a romantic upward flourish, gave its wearer a foreign, traditionary look and suggested that he was a gentleman who studied style. His conscious, curious eyes, however, eyes at once vague and penetrating, intelligent and hard, expressive of the observer as well as of the dreamer, would have assured you that he studied it only within well-chosen limits, and that in so far as he sought it he found it. You would have been much at a loss to determine his original clime and country; he had none of the superficial signs that usually render the answer to this question an insipidly easy one. If he had English blood in his veins it had probably received some French or Italian commixture; but he suggested,

fine gold coin as he was, no stamp nor emblem of the common mintage that provides for general circulation; he was the elegant complicated medal struck off for a special occasion. He had a light, lean, rather languid-looking figure, and was apparently neither tall nor short. He was dressed as a man who takes little other trouble about it than to have no vulgar things.

Osmond, an American permanently settled in Italy, "studied style" but "only within well-chosen limits, and . . . in so far as he sought it he found it." Wonderfully Jamesian, that tells the reader how narrow and dubious Osmond is. Contrast that to the novel's opening description of Isabel Archer:

> She had been looking all round her again—at the lawn, the great trees, the reedy, silvery Thames, the beautiful old house; and while engaged in this survey she had made room in it for her companions; a comprehensiveness of observation easily conceivable on the part of a young woman who was evidently both intelligent and excited. She had seated herself and had put away the little dog; her white hands, in her lap, were folded upon her black dress; her head was erect, her eye lighted, her flexible figure turned itself easily this way and that, in sympathy with the alertness with which she evidently caught impressions. Her impressions were numerous, and they were all reflected in a clear, still smile. "I've never seen anything so beautiful as this."

Isabel studies, not style, but people and places, and never within self-chosen limits. Intelligent and excited, knowingly beautiful, alert to her numerous impressions, amiably amused: it is no wonder that Ralph Touchett, Lord Warburton, and old Mr. Touchett have fallen in love with her at first sight, and that we will also, as we get to see her more clearly. The two initial descriptions in the 1908 edition are 170 pages apart, but the juxtaposition, though delayed, is direct and disconcerting. The sublime Isabel Archer—like the Shakespearean heroines Rosalind, Viola, Beatrice, Helena, and others—is compelled to marry down, but Ralph Touchett, Lord Warburton, and Caspar Goodwood are none of them potential disasters; Gilbert Osmond is a catastrophe. Each reader must judge for herself whether Henry James really makes Isabel's choice of Osmond persuasively inevitable. Much as I love James, Isabel, and *The Portrait of a Lady*, I have never been persuaded, and it seems to me the one flaw in an otherwise perfect novel. Isabel's blindness is necessary if the book is to work, but the more Jamesian Isabel of the 1908 revision simply seems too perceptive to be deceived by Osmond, particularly since James revises him into someone who quite definitely is *not* "the heir of all the ages."

James, subtlest of novelistic masters (excepting Proust), exerts all his art to make Isabel's misjudgment plausible. Osmond is, as he says, "convention itself," whose theoretic function is to liberate us from chaos, but whose pragmatic effect is to stifle Isabel's possibilities. His daughter, Pansy, is, for him, primarily a work of art to be sold, preferably to "a rich and noble husband." Osmond, a walking "gold coin," sees in Isabel not only her fortune (bequeathed to her by her kinspeople, the Touchetts) but also "material to work with," a portrait to be painted. But Isabel recognizes none of that until it is too late to save herself. Why? James gives us many hints, none definitive. There is Pansy, who awakens her maternal instincts (her boy, by Osmond, dies at six months, and James intimates that the sexual relation between Osmond and Isabel dies soon after). And there is Isabel's growing obsession to "choose" a form of life: Ralph Touchett is her kinsman and is ill; Lord Warburton represents English aristocracy, which her Americanness shuns; Caspar Goodwood, her early Albany suitor, is too possessive and passionate, too much in love with her. Like Henry James, Isabel wants to be loved, but not to be the object of another's overwhelming sexual passion.

James in addition ascribes Isabel's acceptance of Osmond, whose tastes are expensive but whose income is slight, to the girl's (she is still very young) generous idealism and to her guilt as to the Touchett inheritance. Is all this enough? I think not, as I've said already, but James is quite Shakespearean and perhaps realistic in regard to the mysteries of marital choice. Shakespeare married Anne Hathaway and then lived apart from her in London for twenty years, sending money to Stratford for her and the children, and going home as little as possible. James, homoerotic to the core, but not acting on it, expressed an extraordinary regard for the value and sanctity of heterosexual marriage, while dryly observing that he himself thought too little of life to venture upon the blessed state himself.

I find more soluble, though still enigmatic, why Isabel returns to Rome and Osmond at the end of the story. Again rejecting Goodwood, she nevertheless experiences (and fears) the force of his passion:

He glared at her a moment through the dusk, and the next instant she felt his arms about her and his lips on her own lips. His kiss was like white lightning, a flash that spread, and spread again, and stayed; and it was extraordinarily as if, while she took it, she felt each thing in his hard manhood that had least pleased her, each aggressive fact of his face, his figure, his presence, justified of its intense identity and made one with this act of possession. So had she heard of those wrecked and under water following a train of images before they sink. But when darkness returned she was free.

She is free to take "a very straight path" back to Rome and Osmond. That will keep her free of Goodwood, but life with Osmond can be at best only an armed truce. Is *that* to be the final fate of James's heiress of all the ages? James will not tell us, because his part in the story is over; he knows no more, and probably, at the close, Isabel does not know either. But what will become of her potential for greatness of spirit, for amplitude of consciousness, without which the book must sink? James has declined to give her alternatives to Osmond; Goodwood threatens her sense of autonomy, as somehow the wretched Osmond does not. But even in 1908, Isabel could have been her own alternative: divorce, and a financial settlement, would free her from Osmond. Perhaps that yet may happen, but James gives us no clues toward this. Osmond, however mean-spirited, is not so formidable as Isabel. She goes back, I surmise, to work through the consequences of her idealistic blunder, and thus assert a continuity in her own consciousness. That is quite Jamesian, though readers are not wrong to protest against it. *The Portrait of a Lady*, in its final form, demands close and sympathetic reading. We may not be satisfied by Isabel's choice, but her story tells us again one motive for why we read: to know better the consciousness too valuable for us to ignore.

The Wings of the Dove takes its beautiful title from Psalm 68:13, perhaps by way of Walter Pater, who in the fourth edition of *The Renaissance* added the first line as epigraph:

Though ye have lien among the pots, yet shall ye be as the
    wings of a dove
covered with silver, and her feathers with yellow gold.

I place *The Portrait of a Lady* first among James's novels, yet this later masterwork seems to me his most beautiful performance, outdoing even *The Golden Bowl*. *The Wings of the Dove* is even more fabulistic than its companions of 1902–4, *The Ambassadors* and *The Golden Bowl*. Walter Pater's positive influence on *The Wings of the Dove* remains underesteemed, perhaps because Jamesian scholars do not know and appreciate the sublime Walter, one of my critical heroes. Odious Osmond is a mock-Paterian; Henry James was a true aesthetic novelist and critic, no more ironic toward the aesthetic vision than Pater himself was.

Most literary modernism stemmed from Pater: Yeats, Joyce, Eliot, Pound, Woolf, Stevens, and Hart Crane, among others—and Henry James and Conrad as much as anyone else. What Pater called the privileged moment became the secularized epiphany of the modernists, sudden bursts of illumination against the gathering darkness. As a mode of narrative, that suits poetry and drama, prophecy and wisdom-writing, better than the Balzacian novel that Henry James affirmed he deserved to attain. Balzac's friends nicknamed him Vautrin, who was his daemon, and the furiously energetic seer of *The Human Comedy* indeed achieved an all but Shakespearean "complete representation" in prose fiction. That was part of the lesson of Balzac for Henry James, who shrewdly observed the Parisian master's command of the "conditions" that inform each and all of us. *The Wings of the Dove*, though, is not a very Balzacian performance—unlike *The Bostonians*—and the question of just who Milly Theale, Kate Croy, and Merton Densher *are* is not fully resolved. Since *The Wings of the Dove* ultimately is a fable, that may be an aesthetic advantage.

Milly is the transcendent being of the fable, the true daemon of love and loss, except that Kate and Densher also love and lose each other. Since Densher loves Milly only posthumously, as it were, his loss is doubled. I confess to finding him plainly inadequate to both his superb young women and always wonder at his all but universal appeal to everyone in the book. James loves Milly and Kate and seems oddly charmed by Densher.

When I have been away from *The Wings of the Dove* for a year or two, I think first about Kate Croy, because it is her book just as much as *The Portrait of a Lady* is Isabel Archer's. Milly Theale, famously founded on James's cousin Minny Temple, who also died tragically young, somehow does not quite inhabit the book. She surrounds it like an aura no matter how firmly James delineates her conditions and circumstances. Orphaned, wealthy, doomed, marked for victimization, she nevertheless triumphs over what ought to have obliterated her acute consciousness.

I recall amiable arguments with my late friend Dorothea Krook back in mid-1950s Cambridge, when she was developing her lectures that became *The Ordeal of Consciousness in Henry James* (1962). Her Milly was nothing but a victim and guilty also of spiritual pride, judgments I still find unacceptable. Like James's other American heroines, Milly is an Emersonian, a believer in self-reliance, aspiration, and the soul's sufficiency unto itself, as in a lyric by Emily Dickinson. A High Transcendentalist, Milly is too grand a figure to be categorized as anyone's victim.

Edith Wharton
(1862–1937)

EDITH WHARTON fiercely resented any designation of her as the female Henry James, and her regard for Proust's achievement was larger than her estimate of James's. Though Mrs. Wharton and Henry James were good (if uneasy) friends, she found the novels of his major phase unreadable, while he increasingly came to resent and even fear her "deranging and desolating, ravaging, burning and destroying energy . . . The angel of Devastation."

Mrs. Wharton's life force was extraordinary and augmented with each year, even when she aged. Her "All Souls'" contrasts wonderfully with a Jamesian ghost story like "The Jolly Corner," which is a parable of the unlived life, whereas Mrs. Wharton's story implies an orgiastic underlying reality always ready to break in upon the social surfaces of existence.

Edith Wharton's genius (it cannot be judged less) is vitalistic: she is a profoundly sexual writer, and her stories and novels subtly intimate an erotic realism that is stronger for being implicit. She had the great gift of writing her fictions as if she indeed had lived them, with more passion even than they overtly expressed.

After rereading virtually all of Wharton, I have to settle for *The Custom of the Country* as her best book and the disturbing Undine Spragg as her strongest character. Becky Sharp in *Vanity Fair* always makes me fall in love with her again, but you have to be coldly depraved to lose your soul to Undine. Wharton, a grand artist schooled despite herself by the master, Henry James, coolly appropriates Becky Sharp from Thackeray and then transforms her into the virulent Undine Spragg. This is as it should be; Thackeray was no menace. Though Henry James and Wharton became close, lifelong friends, she fought hard against all insinuations that he overinfluenced her books. R. W. B. Lewis, Wharton's distinguished biographer, also deprecates the influence, and yet it seems to me palpable. Wharton's drive toward satire, particularly of the artistic life, reads to me as a reaction-formation against James. It was only after the death of Henry James (1916) that Wharton's complex (and loving) defenses against his influence began to give way, so that her later work is her most Jamesian: *The Age of Innocence, Old New York, Hudson River Bracketed, A Backward Glance*. It seems to me a classic instance of the anxiety of influence, in which the strong will of the latecomer diverts her from her natural mode and makes her labor against the grain. Wharton's best fiction—*The House of Mirth, Ethan Frome, The Custom of the Country*, and the finest of her short stories—all benefit from the antithetical strain in them. Her vision is darker than that of James; after he was a memory, she was free to study the nostalgias.

The story of Undine Spragg, as created by Edith Wharton, has epic dimensions and thuggish protagonists, a contrast that keeps it lively. Undine is an unstoppable sexual force, almost occult in her destructive drive. She is a kind of troll or *huldre*, as her given name intimates, a descendant of Adam's first wife, Lilith. Fouqué's *Undine* (1811) tells the tale of a water-nymph turned loose among humans. Undine Spragg, however, boils up out of Kansas into New York City, where she marries the wealthy socialite and would-be artist Ralph Marvell. Later, she gives herself to Peter Van Degen for a two-month affair. After rejecting poor Marvell, inducing his suicide, Undine devours a French aristocrat, Raymond de Chelles, and then returns to her first, secret Kansan marriage with Elmer Moffatt, now a New York billionaire. That is the gist of Wharton's fable; Elaine Showalter sees Undine as the answer to Freud: "While Freud asks, 'What do women want?,' Wharton replies, 'What have you got?'"

As readers we follow Wharton in disliking Undine, but we become aware that Undine has an exasperating relationship to Edith Wharton. R. W. B. Lewis alarmingly suggests that Undine is what Wharton would have been without her more gracious and redeeming aspects:

> So imagined, we see in Undine Spragg how Edith somehow appeared to the view of the harried and aging Henry James: demanding, imperious, devastating, resolutely indifferent to the needs of others, something like an irresistible force of nature.

Undine then is Wharton's anti-genius, the enemy of the novelist's daemonic sympathy for otherness. Wharton of course was a snob, an anti-Semite, a racist: it went with her era and social class, and while unpleasant, it is not particularly virulent, as it is in the Anglo-Catholic moralist T. S. Eliot. Undine is certainly the most memorable character in Wharton, but is she a fully achieved representation of a personality? Thackeray's Becky Sharp is a person; Showalter accurately observes that Undine "lacks Becky's spirit, irreverence, and humor." Wharton, enthralled by a daemonic antiself to her own genius, is content to mythify Undine as a grand villain, a truly fatal woman.

R. W. B. Lewis, immensely sympathetic to Wharton, is content to describe her as "a writer of near genius." Like Iris Murdoch, Edith Wharton can be undervalued if you make demands upon her that belong more to the novel than to the romance. Can there be, on a high aesthetic level, romances of society? In romance, states of being and places that are visionary, however realistic they seem, substitute for the representation of character. Edith Wharton's Kansas, that is to say Undine Spragg's Kansas, is a purely visionary locale, like Oz. But are the New York City and the Paris in which Undine exercises her sexual powers not equally visionary?

Perhaps Wharton was only a near-genius, except in the best of her short stories, like the ghostly tale "All Souls'." If her literary achievement needs to be bolstered, in our current fashion, by gender concerns and sociological contexts, then it would fall short of the qualities of innovation and continual freshness that genius ought to encompass. I am not sure that her life story, as recounted by Lewis, is more than the history of a will, rather than of an imagination.

In her later years, Wharton confessed her strong admiration for the novels of Colette, who had conveyed a more accurate sense of female sexuality than Joyce and Lawrence had achieved. Except for a posthumous fragment like "Beatrice Palmato," Wharton's good manners had prevented her from anticipating Colette. Whether one reads *The Custom of the Country* as realistic novel or as romance myth, we are left with too cold a splendor in the depiction of Undine. Her sexual power is asserted but never truly demonstrated, by which I do not mean that we wish to behold her in full action. But consider Hawthorne's *The Scarlet Letter*, where Hester Prynne's sexual splendor is subtly and powerfully conveyed, by all the nuances of which a genius of romance is capable. Inhibition is not the issue; the grace of genius is.

A profound study of Edith Wharton's own nostalgias, *The Age of Innocence* (1920) achieved a large discerning audience immediately and has retained it since. For Wharton herself, the novel was a prelude to her autobiography, *A Backward Glance*, published fourteen years later and three years before her death. Wharton, who was fifty-seven in 1919 when *The Age of Innocence* was in most part composed, associated herself with both her protagonists, Newland Archer and Ellen Olenska. *The Age of Innocence* is a historical novel set in socially prominent Old New York of the early 1870s, a vanished world indeed when seen from a post–World War I perspective. Wrongly regarded by many critics as a novel derived from Henry James, *The Age of Innocence* is rather a deliberate complement to *The Portrait of a Lady*, seeking and finding a perspective that James was conscious of having excluded from his masterpiece. Wharton might well have called her novel *The Portrait of a Gentleman*, since Newland Archer's very name is an allusion to Isabel Archer, a far more attractive and fascinating character than Wharton's unheroic gentleman of Old New York.

Not that Newland is anything but a very decent and good man who will become a useful philanthropist and civic figure. Unfortunately, however, he has no insight whatsoever as to the differences between men and women, and his passion is of poor quality compared to Ellen's. R. W. B. Lewis regards *The Age of Innocence* as a minor masterpiece. Time so far has confirmed Lewis's judgment, but we now suffer through an age of ideology, and I am uncertain as to whether *The Age of Innocence* will be strong enough to endure. I have no doubts about Wharton's *The House of Mirth* and *The Custom of the Country*, but I wonder whether Newland Archer may yet sink his own book. The best historical novel of Old New York, *The Age of Innocence* retains great interest both as social history and as social anthropology. One is always startled by the farewell dinner of Ellen Olenska, where Newland realizes that he is attending "the tribal rally around a kinswoman about to be eliminated from the tribe." Wharton's own judgment, as narrator, sums up this tribal expulsion.

> It was the old New York way of taking life "without effusion of blood": the way of people who dreaded scandal more than disease, who placed decency above courage, and who considered that nothing was more ill-bred than "scenes," except the behavior of those who gave rise to them.

That seems a condemnation of Old New York, and yet it is not. Throughout the novel, Wharton acknowledges that Newland's world centers upon an idea of order, a convention that stifles passion and yet liberates from chaos. The old order at least was an order; Wharton was horrified at the post–World War I United States. Newland Archer is flawed in perception: of his world, of his wife, most of all of Ellen. And yet Wharton subtly makes it clear that even a more courageous and perceptive Newland would not have made a successful match with Ellen. Their relationship in time must have dissolved, with Newland returning to the only tribe that could sustain him. Henry James's Isabel Archer, returning to her dreadful husband Osmond, also accepts an idea of order, but one in which her renunciation has a transcendental element. Wharton, shrewder if less sublime than her friend James, gives us a more realistic yet a less consequential Archer.

Edith Wharton's three principal women characters—Lily Bart, Undine Spragg, Ellen Olenska—are remarkably varied, though Lily and Ellen both are motherless members of Old New York society, and Undine is an outsider who conquers and destroys that society, on her own egregious terms. Lily, though she struggles tenaciously, is finally too weak to survive the contradictions between her upbringing and her situation. It is Ellen, superbly self-reliant, who reconciles her heritage and her dilemmas, and who evokes our admiration. Lily dies of a sleeping-drug overdose; Undine, the American answer to Thackeray's Becky Sharp, holds on unpleasantly in our memory; while Ellen, who has affinities to Henry James's Isabel Archer in *The Portrait of a Lady*, declines Isabel's example, and flourishes (so far as we know) apart from the dying society of Old New York, in which Edith Wharton had been raised.

I once was outrageous enough to ask a group of students whom they would choose—either to love or to be—among Lily, Undine, and Ellen, and was startled by their consensus, which was Undine, since sensibly I had expected Ellen to be their answer. Since I knew that they also had read *Vanity Fair*, I protested that Becky Sharp was charming if unsettling, but that Undine frightened me. She did not dismay them, whereas Lily's ill luck depressed them, and Ellen they felt was rather too good to be true. Perhaps Wharton, a powerful ironist, would have appreciated their choice, but to an archaic Romantic like myself, it came as a considerable surprise, or as another instance of what my mentor, Frederick A. Pottle, had called "shifts of sensibility."

Undine, I protested lamely, was bad news, but they forgave her vulgarity (as Wharton could not) and one of them accurately indicated that the novel's famous conclusion was now seriously outdated:

"Oh, that reminds me—" instead of obeying her he unfolded the paper. "I brought it in to show you something. Jim Driscoll's been appointed Ambassador to England."

"Jim Driscoll—!" She caught up the paper and stared at the paragraph he pointed to. Jim Driscoll—that pitiful nonentity, with his stout mistrustful commonplace wife! It seemed extraordinary that the government should have hunted up such insignificant people. And immediately she had a great vague vision of the splendours they were going to—all the banquets and ceremonies and precedences . . .

"I shouldn't say she'd want to, with so few jewels—" She dropped the paper and turned to her husband. "If you had a spark of ambition, that's the kind of thing you'd try for. You could have got it just as easily as not!"

He laughed and thrust his thumbs in his waistcoat armholes with the gesture she disliked. "As it happens, it's about the one thing I couldn't."

"You couldn't? Why not?"

"Because you're divorced. They won't have divorced Ambassadresses."

"They won't? Why not, I'd like to know?"

"Well, I guess the court ladies are afraid there'd be too many pretty women in the Embassies," he answered jocularly.

She burst into an angry laugh, and the blood flamed up into her face. "I never heard of anything so insulting!" she cried, as if the rule had been invented to humiliate her.

There was a noise of motors backing and advancing in the court, and she heard the first voices on the stairs. She turned to give herself a last look in the glass, saw the blaze of rubies, the glitter of her hair, and remembered the brilliant names on her list.

But under all the dazzle a tiny black cloud remained. She had learned that there was something she could never get, something that neither beauty nor influence nor millions could ever buy for

her. She could never be an Ambassador's wife; and as she advanced
to welcome her first guests she said to herself that it was the one
part she was really made for.

In our current political climate, Undine could well be appointed an
ambassador and thus transcend being an Ambassador's wife. It is more than
a century since the publication of *The Custom of the Country*, and I have
met Undine many times, here and abroad, in the universities, the media,
and among diplomats. Wharton may have rendered Undine Spragg with
a vividness beyond authorial intention. One remembers Lily Bart for her
brave pathos, and Ellen Olenska for her decency and vitality. But Undine
Spragg is one of the great white sharks of literature: dangerous, distasteful,
and yet permanently valid as a representation of reality.

In 1911, two years before *The Custom of the Country* was published, Wharton brought out the short novel that seems her most American story, the
New England tragedy *Ethan Frome*. I would guess that it is now her most
widely read book, and it is likely to remain so. Certainly *Ethan Frome* is
Wharton's only fiction to have become part of the American mythology,
though it is hardly an early twentieth-century *Scarlet Letter*. Relentless
and stripped, *Ethan Frome* is tragedy not as Hawthorne wrote it, but in the
mode of pain and of a reductive moral sadism, akin perhaps to Robert Penn
Warren's harshness toward his protagonists, particularly in *World Enough
and Time*. The book's aesthetic fascination, for me, centers in Wharton's
audacity in touching the limits of a reader's capacity at absorbing really
extreme suffering when that suffering is bleak, intolerable, and in a clear
sense unnecessary. Wharton's astonishing authority here is to render such
pain with purity and economy, while making it seem inevitable, as much
in the nature of things and of psyches as in the social customs of its place
and time.

R. W. B. Lewis praises *Ethan Frome* as "a classic of the realistic genre";
doubtless it is, and yet literary "realism" is itself intensely metaphorical, as
Lewis keenly knows. *Ethan Frome* is so charged in its representation of
reality as to be frequently phantasmagoric in effect. Its terrible vividness
estranges it subtly from mere naturalism and makes its pain just bearable.
Presumably Edith Wharton would not have said: "Ethan Frome—that is
myself," and yet he is more his author than Undine Spragg was to be. Like

Wharton, Ethan has an immense capacity for suffering and an overwhelming sense of reality; indeed like Edith Wharton, he has too strong a sense
of what was to be the Freudian reality principle.

Though an exact contemporary of Freud, Edith Wharton showed no
interest in him, but she became an emphatic Nietzschean, and *Ethan Frome*
manifests both a Nietzschean perspectivism, and an ascetic intensity that
I suspect goes back to a reading of Schopenhauer, Nietzsche's precursor.
What fails in Ethan, and in his beloved Mattie, is precisely what Schopenhauer urged us to overcome: the Will to Live, though suicide was hardly a
Schopenhauerian solution. In her introduction to *Ethan Frome*, Wharton
states a narrative principle that sounds more like Balzac, Browning, or
James, but that actually reflects the Nietzsche of *The Genealogy of Morals*:

> Each of my chroniclers contributes to the narrative just so much
> as he or she is capable of understanding of what, to them, is a com-
> plicated and mysterious case; and only the narrator of the tale has
> scope enough to see it all, to resolve it back into simplicity, and to
> put it in its rightful place among his larger categories.

But does Wharton's narrator have scope enough to see all of the tale that
is *Ethan Frome*? Why is the narrator's view more than only another view,
and a simplifying one at that? Wharton's introduction memorably calls her
protagonists "these figures, my *granite outcroppings*; but half-emerged
from the soil, and scarcely more articulate." Yet her narrator (whatever her
intentions) lacks the imagination to empathize with granite outcroppings
who are also men and women:

> Though Harmon Gow developed the tale as far as his mental and
> moral reach permitted there were perceptible gaps between his
> facts, and I had the sense that the deeper meaning of the story was
> in the gaps. But one phrase stuck in my memory and served as the
> nucleus about which I grouped my subsequent inferences: "Guess
> he's been in Starkfield too many winters."
>
> Before my own time there was up I had learned to know what
> that meant. Yet I had come in the degenerate day of trolley, bicycle
> and rural delivery, when communication was easy between the
> scattered mountain villages, and the bigger towns in the valleys,
> such as Bettsbridge and Shadd's Falls, had libraries, theatres and

Y.M.C.A. halls to which the youth of the hills could descend for recreation. But when winter shut down on Starkfield, and the village lay under a sheet of snow perpetually renewed from the pale skies, I began to see what life there—or rather its negation—must have been in Ethan Frome's young manhood.

I had been sent up by my employers on a job connected with the big power-house at Corbury Junction, and a long-drawn carpenters' strike had so delayed the work that I found myself anchored at Starkfield—the nearest habitable spot—for the best part of the winter. I chafed at first, and then, under the hypnotising effect of routine, gradually began to find a grim satisfaction in the life. During the early part of my stay I had been struck by the contrast between the vitality of the climate and the deadness of the community. Day by day, after the December snows were over, a blazing blue sky poured down torrents of light and air on the white landscape, which gave them back in an intenser glitter. One would have supposed that such an atmosphere must quicken the emotions as well as the blood; but it seemed to produce no change except that of retarding still more the sluggish pulse of Starkfield. When I had been there a little longer, and had seen this phase of crystal clearness followed by long stretches of sunless cold; when the storms of February had pitched their white tents about the devoted village and the wild cavalry of March winds had charged down to their support; I began to understand why Starkfield emerged from its six months' siege like a starved garrison capitulating without quarter. Twenty years earlier the means of resistance must have been far fewer, and the enemy in command of almost all the lines of access between the beleaguered villages; and, considering these things, I felt the sinister force of Harmon's phrase: "Most of the smart ones get away." But if that were the case, how could any combination of obstacles have hindered the flight of a man like Ethan Frome?

The narrator's "mental and moral reach" is not in question, but his vision has acute limitations. Winter indeed is the cultural issue, but *Ethan Frome* is not exactly Ursula K. Le Guin's *The Left Hand of Darkness*. It is not a "combination of obstacles" that hindered the flight of Ethan Frome, but a terrible fatalism which is a crucial part of Edith Wharton's Emersonian heritage. Certainly the narrator is right to express the contrast between the winter sublimity of "a blazing blue sky poured down torrents of light and air on the white landscape, which gave them back in an intenser glitter" and the inability of the local population to give back more than sunken apathy. But Frome, as the narrator says on the novel's first page, is himself a ruined version of the American Sublime: "the most striking figure in Starkfield . . . his great height . . . the careless powerful look he had . . . something bleak and unapproachable in his face." Ethan Frome is an Ahab who lacks Moby Dick, self-lamed rather than wounded by the white whale, and by the whiteness of the whale. Not the whiteness of Starkfield but an inner whiteness or blankness has crippled Ethan Frome, perhaps the whiteness that goes through American tradition "from Edwards to Emerson" and on through Wharton to Wallace Stevens contemplating the beach world lit by the glare of the northern lights in "The Auroras of Autumn":

> Here, being visible is being white,
> Is being of the solid of white, the accomplishment
> Of an extremist in an exercise . . .
>
> The season changes. A cold wind chills the beach.
> The long lines of it grow longer, emptier,
> A darkness gathers though it does not fall
>
> And the whiteness grows less vivid on the wall.
> The man who is walking turns blankly on the sand.
> He observes how the north is always enlarging the change,
>
> With its frigid brilliances, its blue-red sweeps
> And gusts of great enkindlings, its polar green,
> The color of ice and fire and solitude.

That, though with a more sublime eloquence, is the visionary world of *Ethan Frome*, a world where the will is impotent, and tragedy is always circumstantial. The experiential puzzle of *Ethan Frome* is ultimately also its aesthetic strength: we do not question the joint decision of Ethan and Mattie to immolate themselves, even though it is pragmatically outrageous and psychologically quite impossible. But the novel's apparent realism is a mask for its actual fatalistic mode, and truly it is a northern romance, akin even to *Wuthering Heights*. A visionary ethos dominates Ethan and Mattie, and would have dominated Edith Wharton herself had she not battled against it with her powerful gift for social reductiveness. We can wonder whether even *The Age of Innocence*, with its Jamesian renunciations in the mode of *The Portrait of a Lady*, compensates us for what Wharton might have written, had she gone on with her own version of the American romance tradition of Hawthorne and Melville.

Edwin Arlington Robinson
(1869–1935)

THE BEST EMERSONIAN POETS are, by rationally universal agreement, Whitman and Dickinson, who found their own versions of a
dialectic between Bacchus and Merlin. I pass though to a smaller but still
powerful figure, to trace the vagaries of Nemesis in a later "first volume"
of our poetry. For the oscillation between poetic incarnation (Bacchus)
and the merging with Necessity (Merlin) is most evident and crucial in
each new poet's emergence and individuation. Emerson our father, more
than Whitman the American Moses, has become the presiding genius of
the American version of poetic influence, the anxiety of originality that he
hoped to dispel, but ironically fostered in a more virulent form than it has
taken elsewhere.

The Torrent and the Night Before (published late in 1896 by Robinson
himself) remains one of the best first volumes in our poetry. Three of its
shorter poems—"George Crabbe," "Luke Havergal," "The Clerks"—Robinson hardly surpassed, and three more—"Credo," "Walt Whitman" (which
Robinson unfortunately abandoned), and "The Children of the Night"
(reprinted as title-poem in his next volume)—are memorable work, all in
the earlier Emersonian mode that culminates in "Bacchus." The stronger
"Luke Havergal" stems from the darker Emersonianism of "Experience"
and "Fate," and has a relation to the singular principles of "Merlin." It
prophesies Robinson's finest later lyrics, such as "Eros Turannos" and "For
a Dead Lady," and suggests the affinity between Robinson and Frost that
is due to their common Emersonian tradition.

In Captain Craig (1902) Robinson published "The Sage," a direct hymn
of homage to Emerson, whose The Conduct of Life had moved him profoundly at a first reading in August 1899. Robinson had read the earlier
Emerson well before, but it is fascinating that he came to essays like "Fate"
and "Power" only after writing "Luke Havergal" and some similar poems,
for his deeper nature then discovered itself anew. He called "Luke Havergal" "a piece of deliberate degeneration," which I take to mean what an

early letter calls "sympathy for failure where fate has been abused and self demoralized." Browning, the other great influence upon Robinson, is obsessed with "deliberate degeneration" in this sense; Childe Roland's and Andrea del Sarto's failures are willful abuses of fate and demoralizations of self. "The Sage" praises Emerson's "fierce wisdom," emphasizes Asia's influence upon him, and hardly touches his dialectical optimism. This Emerson is "previsioned of the madness and the mean," fit seer for "the fiery night" of "Luke Havergal":

> But there, where western glooms are gathering,
> The dark will end the dark, if anything:
> God slays Himself with every leaf that flies,
> And hell is more than half of paradise.

These are the laws of Compensation, "or that nothing is got for nothing," as Emerson says in "Power." At the depth of Robinson is this Emersonian fatalism, as it is in Frost, and even in Henry James. "The world is mathematical," Emerson says, "and has no casualty in all its vast and flowing curve." Robinson, brooding on the end of "Power," confessed: "He really gets after one," and spoke of Emerson as walloping one "with a big New England shingle," the cudgel of Fate. But Robinson was walloped too well. Unlike Browning and Hardy, Robinson yielded too much to Necessity, and too rapidly assimilated himself to the tendency I have named Merlin. Circumstances and temperament share in Robinson's obsession with Nemesis, but poetic misprision is part of the story also, for Robinson's *tessera* in regard to Emerson relies on completing the sage's fatalism. From Emerson's categories of power and circumstance, Robinson fashions a more complete single category, in a personal idealism that is a "philosophy of desperation," as he feared it might be called. The persuasive desperation of "Luke Havergal" and "Eros Turannos" is his best expression of this nameless idealism that is also a fatalism, but "The Children of the Night," for all its obtrusive echoes of Tennyson and even Longfellow, shows more clearly what Robinson found to be a possible stance:

> It is the crimson, not the gray,
>   That charms the twilight of all time;
> It is the promise of the day
>   That makes the starry sky sublime;

It is the faith within the fear
  That holds us to the life we curse;—
So let us in ourselves revere
  The Self which is the Universe!

The bitter charm of this is that it qualifies so severely its too-hopeful and borrowed music. Even so early, Robinson has "completed" Emersonian Self-Reliance and made it his own by emphasizing its Stoic as against its Transcendental or Bacchic aspect. When, in "Credo," Robinson feels "the coming glory of the Light!", the light nevertheless emanates from unaware angels who wove "dead leaves to garlands where no roses are." It is not that Robinson believed, with Melville, that the invisible spheres were formed in fright, but he shrewdly suspected that the ultimate world, though existent, was nearly as destitute as this one. He is an Emersonian incapable of transport, an ascetic of the Transcendental spirit, contrary to an inspired saint like Jones Very or to the Emerson of "The Poet," but a contrary, not a negation, to use Blake's distinction. Not less gifted than Frost, he achieves so much less because he gave himself away to Necessity so soon in his poetic life. Frost's Job quotes "Uriel" to suggest that confusion is "the form of forms," the way all things return upon themselves, like rays:

Though I hold rays deteriorate to nothing,
First white, then red, then ultra red, then out.

This is cunning and deep in Frost, the conviction that "all things come round," even the mental confusions of God as He morally blunders. What we miss in Robinson is this quality of savagery, the strength that can end "Directive" by saying:

Here are your waters and your watering place.
Drink and be whole again beyond confusion.

To be beyond confusion is to be beyond the form of forms that is Fate's, and to be whole beyond Fate suggests an end to circlings, a resolution to all the Emersonian turnings that see unity, and yet behold divisions. Frost will play at being Merlin, many times, but his wariness saved him from Robinson's self-exhaustions.

There is a fine passage in "Captain Craig" where the talkative captain asks: "Is it better to be blinded by the lights, / Or by the shadows?" This supposes grandly that we are to be blinded in any case, but Robinson was not blinded by his shadows. Yet he was ill-served by American Romanticism. It demands the exuberance of a Whitman in his fury of poetic incarnation, lest the temptation to join Ananke come too soon and too urgently to be resisted. Robinson was nearly a great poet, and would have prospered more if he had been chosen by a less drastic tradition.

Theodore Dreiser
(1871–1945)

T HE PHRASE THAT HAUNTS Dreiser criticism is Lionel Trilling's "reality in America," implying as it does that *An American Tragedy* (1925) represents a rather drab projection of a dead-level naturalistic vision. Post-World War II novelistic reality in America extends rather widely, from Norman Mailer's not un-Dreiserian *The Executioner's Song* all the way to Thomas Pynchon's phantasmagoria in *The Crying of Lot 49*. Reality in America in the Age of Trump includes Trump's threats to jail his Democratic opponent in 2016, Russian interference in the election, and the President's Twitter tantrums. Not even Pynchon can rival such inventions, and at this time Dreiser is in danger of seeming drabber than ever.

Irving Howe, writing in the mid-1960s, at a time of rising social protest, praised *An American Tragedy* for its grasp of the realities of American institutions:

> Dreiser published *An American Tragedy* in 1925. By then he was fifty-four years old, an established writer with his own fixed and hard-won ways, who had written three first-rate novels: *Sister Carrie*, *Jennie Gerhardt* and *The Financier*. These books are crowded with exact observation—observation worked closely into the grain of narrative—about the customs and class structure of American society in the phase of early finance capitalism. No other novelist has absorbed into his work as much knowledge as Dreiser had about American institutions: the mechanisms of business, the stifling rhythms of the factory, the inner hierarchy of a large hotel, the chicaneries of city politics, the status arrangements of rulers and ruled. For the most part Dreiser's characters are defined through their relationships to these institutions. They writhe and suffer to win a foothold in the slippery social world or to break out of the limits of established social norms. They exhaust themselves to gain success, they destroy themselves in acts of impulsive deviancy.

But whatever their individual lot, they all act out the drama of determinism—which, in Dreiser's handling, is not at all the sort of listless fatality that hostile critics would make it seem, but is rather a fierce struggle by human beings to discover the harsh limits of what is possible to them and thereby perhaps to enlarge those limits by an inch or two. That mostly they fail is Dreiser's tribute to reality.

That is rugged and sincere criticism, yet it repeats Dreiser's own tendency to identify reality with existent institutions, and to assume that reality is entirely social in its nature. "The harsh limits of what is possible" meant to Heraclitus (and Freud) a reminder that character is fate. Tragedy in America aesthetically can manifest the American difference, but that difference is hardly a naive social determinism. If *An American Tragedy* indeed is a tragedy, it requires something more than Howe asserts for Dreiser. Clyde Griffiths would have to have something in him that cannot be defined entirely through his relationships to social institutions. Howe, knowing that poor Clyde is rather puny, insists that Dreiser "nevertheless manages to make the consequences of Clyde's mediocrity, if not the mediocrity itself, seem tragic." Like Dreiser, Howe is a master of pathos, but the tragic cannot be a matter of pathos alone. It demands ethos (and Clyde has no character) and at least a touch of logos (and Clyde has no mind to speak of). I think we must defend *An American Tragedy* as a masterpiece of pathos alone, and I suggest we think of the book as *An American Suffering* or *An American Passion*. It then will require much less defense, and Dreiser's aesthetic permanence would not be questioned by critics who believe that the aesthetic is, after all, at least partly a matter of perception and of cognition.

Robert Penn Warren's homage to Dreiser shrewdly sought to defend *An American Tragedy* as a "root tragedy," naturalistic with the proverbial vengeance, "grounded in the essential human condition." Since Warren is a dualist who rejects transcendence, his view of Clyde is Cartesian: "A mechanism with a consciousness." It would seem that "root tragedy" is strong pathos, which returns us to the Passion of Clyde as Dreiser's true subject. That *An American Tragedy* has an authentic aesthetic dignity I do not doubt; rereading it is both a depressing and an engrossing experience. But I am persuaded that the critical defense of Dreiser, like that of Eugene O'Neill and indeed most serious American drama, depends upon restoring a sense of the aesthetics of suffering, which means of a sharing without transcendence or redemption.

In tragedy, the protagonist joins a beyond, which is a sharing with some sense of the Sublime. What Hart Crane nobly called "the visionary company of love" chooses its members, generally at very great cost. Clyde joins nothing, and would never have been capable of joining himself to anything, which is to repeat, in another range, Philip Fisher's insight as to Clyde's "defective membership" in any realm whatsoever. Pathos is universal, but it does not provide membership. That is the one certain principle of Dreiser's vision, maintaining itself into the moment before dying:

> And then in the dark of this midwinter morning—the final moment—with the guards coming, first to slit his right trouser leg for the metal plate and then going to draw the curtains before the cells: "It is time, I fear. Courage, my son." It was the Reverend McMillan—now accompanied by the Reverend Gibson, who, seeing the prison guards approaching, was then addressing Clyde.
>
> And Clyde now getting up from his cot, on which, beside the Reverend McMillan, he had been listening to the reading of John, 14, 15, 16: "Let not your heart be troubled. Ye believe in God—believe also in me." And then the final walk with the Reverend McMillan on his right hand and the Reverend Gibson on his left—the guards front and rear. But with, instead of the customary prayers, the Reverend McMillan announcing: "Humble yourselves under the mighty hand of God that He may exalt you in due time. Cast all your care upon Him for He careth for you. Be at peace. Wise and righteous are His ways, who hath called us into His eternal glory by Christ Jesus, after that we have suffered a little. I am the way, the truth and the life—no man cometh unto the Father but by me."
>
> But various voices—as Clyde entered the first door to cross to the chair room, calling: "Good-by, Clyde." And Clyde, with enough earthly thought and strength to reply: "Good-by, all." But his voice sounding so strange and weak, even to himself, so far distant as though it emanated from another being walking alongside of him, and not from himself. And his feet were walking, but automatically, it seemed. And he was conscious of that familiar shuffle—shuffle—as they pushed him on and on toward that door. Now it was

here; now it was being opened. There it was—at last—the chair he had so often seen in his dreams—that he so dreaded—to which he was now compelled to go. He was being pushed toward that— into that—on—on—through the door which was now open—to receive him—but which was as quickly closed again on all the earthly life he had ever known.

The enormous power of this is not necessarily literary or imaginative; Dreiser, like Poe, had the uncanny quality of being able to tap into our common nightmares. Compulsiveness dominates us here, but we cannot help seeing that Clyde cannot even join himself in these final moments. Like every crucial transition in Clyde's life, this is another mechanical operation of the spirit. The passion of Clyde embraces everything in us that is untouched by the will and the intellect. Dreiser is almost the unique instance in high literature of an author lived by forces he could not understand, forces that strongly did the writing for him.

Willa Cather

(1873–1947)

I T IS BECAUSE Willa Cather was so intensely in love with Ántonia that
the sensitive reader so easily comes to share the passion, but Cather's
art is exquisitely subtle in rendering her love. Shadowed by Henry James,
toward whose social scene she manifested acute ambivalence, Cather can
be said to have moved her master outdoors, onto the western prairie. Pragmatically, that obliged the Virginia-born Cather to be retrospective: she
studies the nostalgias of lost or unfulfillable love, appropriate for her veiled
lesbian stance in early twentieth-century America.

Jim Burden, Cather's surrogate, is obsessed with Virgil's *Aeneid*, and
My Ántonia is a profoundly Virgilian novel. Cather's genius, like Virgil's,
centers upon regret, upon honorable because hopeless erotic defeats.

Cather's aesthetic Americanizes Walter Pater, rather as Wallace Stevens
does. Stevens preferred Cather to almost all their contemporaries, and their
affinities help explain his judgment. She is the novelist of a retrospective
glory of the beauty of loss, even as Stevens is its poet. The Connecticut of
Wallace Stevens necessarily is remote from the Nebraska of Willa Cather,
but both are in the Evening Land aspect of America. East or West, we
represent Europe's last stand. Cather brings the fading culture of Europe
to the prairie as a counterpoise to Henry James's passionate American pil-
grims, who search in European society for those values of moral choice
and aesthetic sensibility that Europe no longer possesses, or holds on to
only in decline.

Geniuses of nostalgia are rare: the only great critic who worked in that
mode was William Hazlitt, the English High Romantic friend of John
Keats. Walter Pater provided Willa Cather with materials for her mastery of
regret, but the evasive Pater would not commit himself to anything. Willa
Cather, searching for antique values, was able to incarnate them beautifully
in her lost ladies.

Willa Cather was one of the major American novelists of the first half of the
twentieth century, fully the peer of Theodore Dreiser, Ernest Hemingway,

and F. Scott Fitzgerald. Only William Faulkner, among her direct contemporaries, has an eminence beyond Cather's. Her genius, for me, emerges most clearly in two lyrical short novels, *My Ántonia* (1918) and *A Lost Lady* (1923). Since what I quest for is insight into the perpetual freshness of these two beautiful narratives, I engage directly with Cather's literary origins and her swerve into her own originality.

Alexander's Bridge (1912), her first novel, is a remarkably successful work, and it appeared when she was thirty-eight, a late start. Cather had published a volume of poetry in 1903 and a book of stories in 1905, but she found herself in the novel. Aside from *My Ántonia* and *A Lost Lady*, her principal fictions are *O Pioneers!* (1913), *One of Ours* (1922), *The Professor's House* (1925), and *Death Comes for the Archbishop* (1927).

In 1916, after a long relationship, Cather lost her first love, Isabelle McClung, to the Jewish violinist Jan Hambourg. This loss is the undersong of *My Ántonia* and still reverberates in *My Lost Lady*. Faithful to Romantic tradition, Cather's imagination transformed experiential loss into aesthetic gain. Unfortunately, her human bitterness manifested itself in a curious assimilation of her resentments of male aggressivity and of Jewishness, as though they were a single entity. *The Professor's House* is gratuitously marred by this mythic blending, and her later essay on the story writer Sarah Orne Jewett expresses her disdain for "Jewish critics." Lionel Trilling delivered a temperate response:

> Miss Cather's later books are pervaded by the air of a broadening ancient wisdom, but if we examine her mystical concern with pots and pans, it does not seem much more than an oblique defense of gentility.

A lament for pots and pans would be well enough in Edward Lear or Lewis Carroll, but not in American fiction of the earlier twentieth century. A Virgilian dirge for a universal erotic bereavement, artfully handled, would be splendid anywhere, and is Cather's lasting glory in *My Ántonia* and *A Lost Lady*.

I have loved *My Ántonia* since I was fifteen, which means that, like the narrator, Jim Burden, I have been in love with Ántonia Shimerda for a lifetime. That seems to me Cather's richest gift; here is Jim Burden's memory of what Walter Pater would have called the "privileged moment" of Jim's falling in love with Ántonia, when they are both children:

We sat down and made a nest in the long red grass. Yulka curled up like a baby rabbit and played with a grasshopper. Ántonia pointed up to the sky and questioned me with her glance. I gave her the word, but she was not satisfied and pointed to my eyes. I told her, and she repeated the word, making it sound like "ice." She pointed up to the sky, then to my eyes, then back to the sky, with movements so quick and impulsive that she distracted me, and I had no idea what she wanted. She got up on her knees and wrung her hands. She pointed to her own eyes and shook her head, then to mine and to the sky, nodding violently.

"Oh," I exclaimed, "blue; blue sky."

She clapped her hands and murmured, "Blue sky, blue eyes," as if it amused her. While we snuggled down there out of the wind, she learned a score of words. She was quick, and very eager. We were so deep in the grass that we could see nothing but the blue sky over us and the gold tree in front of us. It was wonderfully pleasant. After Ántonia had said the new words over and over, she wanted to give me a little chased silver ring she wore on her middle finger. When she coaxed and insisted, I repulsed her quite sternly. I didn't want her ring, and I felt there was something reckless and extravagant about her wishing to give it away to a boy she had never seen before. No wonder Krajiek got the better of these people, if this was how they behaved.

The passage is not sentimental, but myth or magic. Jim's recalcitrance is ambiguous, because as Cather's surrogate, his "repulse" of Ántonia stands for the eternal sorrow of the loss of Isabelle McClung's love. But Jim's only apparent rejection of Ántonia's love is not what will hold on in the reader's memory. "She was quick, and very eager": the sexual promise, never to be fulfilled, will never leave the narrator. Blue sky, gold tree, silver ring: these are the emblems that will haunt Jim, that justify his name of "Burden." Cather wanted to find a woman precursor in Jewett, but she remained always the heir of two great aesthetes, Walter Pater and Henry James.

Like Pater and James, Cather is erotically evasive in her art, homoeroticism in their eros being limited by societal taboos. All three were skilled at intimating their authentic desires, yet Cather seems to me the most original in her intimations, as in Jim's celebrated dream of Ántonia's friend Lena Lingard:

> One dream I dreamed a great many times, and it was always the
> same. I was in a harvest-field full of shocks, and I was lying against
> one of them. Lena Lingard came across the stubble barefoot, in a
> short skirt, with a curved reaping-hook in her hand, and she was
> flushed like the dawn, with a kind of luminous rosiness all about
> her. She sat down beside me, turned to me with a soft sigh and
> said, "Now they are all gone, and I can kiss you as much as I like."

The erotic intensity of this remains undiminished, in force and sugges-
tiveness. Lena becomes the harvest girl of Keats's magnificent ode "To
Autumn," where the stubble-fields testify to a sexual repletion and fulfillment. That curved reaping-hook in the hand of the rosy, short-skirted Lena
testifies to her prowess as a harvester, indeed as a phallic woman. And yet
Jim's dream does not find in Lena a figure of menace, a Belle Dame sans
Merci. Rather she offers completion to female and male alike, as Keats
yields to Cather's mode of lesbian receptivity.

The reader learns to see *My Ántonia* as an antiphony of two goddesses,
Ántonia as Proserpina/Persephone, and Lena as Venus. It hardly matters
that Jim Burden/Willa Cather remains ambiguously unresolved. You can,
if you wish, regard *My Ántonia* as the most persuasive of lesbian novels in
English. To me, that somewhat undervalues the book. Cather, for all her
resentments, had the advanced aesthetic vision of her mentors Walter Pater
and Henry James. The sexual nostalgia of *My Ántonia* touches the universal: whatever one's sexual orientation, one meets one's own nostalgias for a
lost eros in the book. Wallace Stevens, a great student of those nostalgias,
rather startled me by asserting, the one time I met him, that Cather was
the best we had. The judgment was generous but not extravagant.

A Lost Lady is as central to that nostalgia as *My Ántonia*, but something
in me could not clarify my confusions about Cather's most exquisite book
until I first discussed it, decades ago, with the late poet John Hollander. He
caught the sense in which it parallels Eliot's *The Waste Land*, as another
fragment shored against the author's ruin. Though *A Lost Lady* takes us
back to the American 1880s, it is another vision of 1922, when the world
had broken apart. A cultural continuity ends in *A Lost Lady*, where the
nostalgia becomes as cultural as it is erotic.

Niel Herbert, the narrator of *A Lost Lady*, is another surrogate for the
lesbian Cather, but Cather's art has augmented, and Niel coheres as Jim
Burden could not. This protagonist is a Flaubertian young aesthete, but he

is also sturdy enough to be older brother to Hemingway's surrogate, Nick Adams, and to Nick Carraway of Scott Fitzgerald's *The Great Gatsby*. I would cite Pater again as the authentic mentor of Niel Herbert's sensibility, for it is Pater who hovers in Niel Herbert's luminous epiphany of his "lost lady," Mrs. Forrester:

> Her eyes, when they laughed for a moment into one's own, seemed to provide a wild delight that he had not found in life. "I know where it is," they seemed to say, "I could show you!" He would like to call up the shade of the young Mrs. Forrester, as the witch of Endor called up Samuel's, and challenge it, demand the secret of that ardour; ask her whether she had really found some ever-blooming, ever-burning, ever-piercing joy, or whether it was all fine play-acting. Probably she had found no more than another; but she had always the power of suggesting things much lovelier than herself, as the perfume of a single flower may call up the whole sweetness of spring.

If this is illusion, nevertheless we want to dwell in it. There is a particular genius in literature that evokes lost happiness, not so much the happiness we never found anyway, but the illusion of happiness that we saw once (we think), even if only by glimpses. To suggest things much lovelier than herself is a rare gift in a handful of young women, whom one remembers among the pitifully few enlargements of life. Experience darkens Mrs. Forrester throughout *A Lost Lady*, but never to the point of obscuring her. *A Lost Lady* is a permanent book because it holds together, in a coherent vision, the icon of Mrs. Forrester as an image of the love and beauty that may haunt us in the hour of our deaths.

Robert Frost
(1874–1963)

Frost—at his frequent best—rivals Wallace Stevens as the great American poet of this century. He does not much resemble Stevens, ultimately for reasons that have little to do with the "essential gaudiness" of much early Stevens, or even with the austere clairvoyance of the later Stevens, poet of "The Auroras of Autumn" and "The Rock." Both of those aspects of Stevens rise from a powerful, barely repressed influence-relationship to Whitman, a poet who scarcely affected Frost. Indeed, Frost's uniqueness among modern American poets of real eminence partly stems from his independence of Whitman. Eliot, Stevens, Pound, Hart Crane, W. C. Williams, Roethke—all have complex links to Whitman, covert in Eliot and in Stevens. Frost (in this like Whitman himself) is the son of Emerson, of the harsher Emerson that we begin only now to recover. Any deep reader of Frost understands why the poet of "Two Tramps in Mud Time" and "Directive" seriously judged Emerson's "Uriel" to be "the greatest Western poem yet." "Uriel's voice of cherub scorn," once referred to by Frost as "Emersonian scorn," is the essential mode of irony favored throughout Frost's poetry.

"Uriel" is Emerson's own irreverent allegory of the controversy set off by his "Divinity School Address." There are certainly passages in the poem that seem to have been written by Frost and not by Emerson:

> The young deities discussed
> Laws of form, and metre just,
> Orb, quintessence, and sunbeams,
> What subsisteth, and what seems.
> One, with low tones that decide,
> And doubt and reverend use defied,
> With a look that solved the sphere,
> And stirred the devils everywhere,
> Gave his sentiment divine
> Against the being of a line.

"Line in nature is not found;
Unit and universe are round;
In vain produced, all rays return;
Evil will bless, and ice will burn."

At the center of this is Emerson's law of Compensation: "Nothing is got for nothing," as Emerson phrased it later, in the remorseless essay "Power," in his *The Conduct of Life*. The darker Emersonian essays— "Experience," "Power," "Circles," "Fate," "Illusions"—read like manifestos for Frost's poetry. Richard Poirier demonstrated this in some detail, and I follow him here in emphasizing how pervasive and crucial the affinity between Emerson and Freud tends to be. If there is a particular motto that states the dialectic of Frost's best poems, then it is to be found in a formulation of Emerson's "Self-Reliance."

Life only avails, not the having lived. Power ceases in the instant of repose; it resides in the moment of transition from a past to a new state, in the shooting of the gulf, in the darting to an aim.

One thinks of the extraordinary early poem "The Wood-Pile" (1914), where the poet, "out walking in the frozen swamp one gray day," comes upon "a cord of maple, cut and split / and piled" and then abandoned:

I thought that only
Someone who lived in turning to fresh tasks
Could so forget his handiwork on which
He spent himself, the labor of his ax,
And leave it there far from a useful fireplace
To warm the frozen swamp as best it could
With the slow smokeless burning of decay.

That "slow smokeless burning" is the metaphor for Emerson's "instant of repose," where power ceases. Frost's restless turnings are his most Emersonian moments, American and agonistic. His Job, in A *Masque of Reason*, puzzling over God's Reason, deliberately relates Jehovah's dialectic to that of Emerson's "Uriel":

Yet I suppose what seems to us confusion
Is not confusion, but the form of forms,

The serpent's tail stuck down the serpent's throat,
Which is the symbol of eternity
And also of the way all things come round,
Or of how rays return upon themselves,
To quote the greatest Western poem yet.
Though I hold rays deteriorate to nothing:
First white, then red, then ultrared, then out.

Job's last two lines here mark Frost's characteristic swerve away from Emerson, except that Emerson is the most difficult of fathers to evade, having been always so subtly evasive himself. Frost's authentic nihilism is considerable, but is surpassed by "Fate" in *The Conduct of Life*, and by a grand more-than-Frostian late entry in Emerson's journals, set down in the autumn of 1866, when the sage felt burned to the socket by the intensities he had experienced during the Civil War:

There may be two or three or four steps, according to the genius of each, but for every seeing soul there are two absorbing facts, *I and the Abyss*.

Frost's religion, as a poet, was the American religion that Emerson founded. A latecomer exegete of that religion, I once offered its credo as "Everything that can be broken should be broken," a Gnostic motto that eminently suits Frost's poetry, where God, whether in *A Masque of Reason*, *A Masque of Mercy*, or "Once by the Pacific," is clearly animated neither by reason nor mercy but only by the blind necessities of being the Demiurge:

It looked as if a night of dark intent
Was coming, and not only a night, an age.
Someone had better be prepared for rage.
There would be more than ocean-water broken
Before God's last *Put out the Light* was spoken.

A God who echoes Othello at his most murderous is himself also crazed by jealousy. Frost's celebrated negativity is a secularized negative theology, almost wholly derived from Emerson, insofar as it was not purely temperamental. Slyly aware of it, Frost used it as the occasion for lovely jokes, as in the marvelous "Two Tramps in Mud Time":

The water for which we may have to look
In summertime with a witching wand,
In every wheelrut's now a brook,
In every print of a hoof a pond.
Be glad of water, but don't forget
The lurking frost in the earth beneath
That will steal forth after the sun is set
And show on the water its crystal teeth.

"Two Tramps in Mud Time" hymns the Emersonian negativity of refusing to identify yourself with any work, in order instead to achieve the Gnostic identity of the knower with what is known, when the sparks of the
Alien God or true Workman stream through you. A shrewd Gnostic, Frost
refuses to lament confusion, though he also will not follow Whitman in
celebrating it. In Emerson's "Uriel," confusion precedes the dimming of
that Miltonic archangel of the sun, who withers from a sad self-knowledge.
Uriel-Emerson (for which read Frost) is himself not responsible for engendering the confusion, which results from the failure of nerve suffered by
the heavenly powers when they hear Uriel proclaim that "'all rays return;
Evil will bless, and ice will burn'":

As Uriel spoke with piercing eye,
A shudder ran around the sky;
The stern old war-gods shook their heads,
The seraphs frowned from myrtle-beds;
Seemed to the holy festival
The rash word boded ill to all;
The balance-beam of Fate was bent;
The bounds of good and ill were rent;
Strong Hades could not keep his own,
But all slid to confusion.

"Confusion" is a mixing or pouring together of entities that would be
better off if kept apart. Frost's "form of forms," or confusion which is not
confusion, identified by him with the Emersonian rays returning upon
themselves, is a kind of libation poured out to the Alien God, as in the
trope that concludes his great poem "Directive":

Here are your waters and your watering place.
Drink and be whole again beyond confusion.

"Directive" is Frost's poem of poems or form of forms, a meditation
whose rays perpetually return upon themselves. "All things come round,"
even our mental confusion as we blunder morally, since the Demiurge is
nothing but a moral blunderer. Frost shares the fine Emersonian wildness
or freedom, the savage strength of the essay "Power" that suggests a way of
being whole beyond Fate, of arriving at an end to circlings, at a resolution
to all the Emersonian turnings that see unity, and yet behold divisions:
"The world is mathematical, and has no casualty, in all its vast and flowing
curve." "Directive" appears to be the poem in which Frost measures the lot,
and forgives himself the lot, and perhaps even casts out remorse. In some
sense, it was the poem he always wrote and rewrote, in a revisionary process
present already in *A Boy's Will* (1913) but not fully worked out until *Steeple
Bush* (1947), where "Directive" was published, when Frost was seventy-
three. "The Demiurge's Laugh" in *A Boy's Will* features a mocking demonic
derision at the self-realization that "what I hunted was no true god."

North of Boston (1914) has its most memorable poem in the famous
"After Apple-Picking," a gracious hymn to the necessity of yielding up the
quest, of clambering down from one's "long two-pointed [ladder] sticking
through a tree / Toward heaven still." Frost's subtlest of perspectivizings is
the true center of the poem:

I cannot rub the strangeness from my sight
I got from looking through a pane of glass
I skimmed this morning from the drinking trough
And held against the world of hoary grass.
It melted, and I let it fall and break.

The sheet of ice is a lens upon irreality, but so are Frost's own eyes, or
anyone's, in his cosmos. This supposed nature poet represents his harsh
landscapes as a full version of the Gnostic *kenoma*, the cosmological emptiness into which we have been thrown by the mocking Demiurge. This is the
world of *Mountain Interval* (1916), where "the broken moon" is preferred
to the dimmed sun, where the ovenbird sings of "that other fall we name
the fall," and where the birches:

> shed crystal shells
> Shattering and avalanching on the snow-crust—
> Such heaps of broken glass to sweep away
> You'd think the inner dome of heaven had fallen.

Mountain Interval abounds in images of the shattering of human ties, and of humans, as in the horrifying "Out, Out—." But it would be redundant to conduct an overview of all Frost's volumes in pursuit of an experiential darkness that never is dispelled. A measurer of stone walls, as Frost names himself in the remarkable "A Star in a Stoneboat," is never going to be surprised that life is a sensible emptiness. The demiurgic pattern of "Design," with its "assorted characters of death and blight," is the rule in Frost. There are a few exceptions, but they give Frost parodies, rather than poems.

Frost wrote the concluding and conclusive Emersonian irony for all his work in the allegorical "A Cabin in the Clearing," the set piece of *In the Clearing* (1962), published for his eighty-eighth birthday, less than a year before his death. Mist and Smoke, guardian wraiths and counterparts, eavesdrop on the unrest of a human couple, murmuring in their sleep. These guardians haunt us because we are their kindred spirits, for we do not know where we are, since who we are "is too much to believe." We are "too sudden to be credible," and so the accurate image for us is "an inner haze," full kindred to mist and smoke. For all the genial tone, the spirit of "A Cabin in the Clearing" is negative even for Frost. His final letter, dictated just before his death, states an unanswerable question as though it were not a question: "How can we be just in a world that needs mercy and merciful in a world that needs justice." The Demiurge's laugh lurks behind the sentence, though Frost was then in no frame of spirit to indulge a demiurgic imagination.

"Directive," an extraordinary poem, is so rich that readers rarely agree as to its meanings. It has a close relation to two ancestor poems, Wordsworth's tale of Margaret in "The Ruined Cottage," which became Book I of *The Excursion*, and Emerson's genially ironic "Uriel," sparked by the controversy excited by his address to the Harvard Divinity School.

To Wordsworth Frost owes "A broken drinking goblet like the Grail." From "The Ruined Cottage":

> When I stooped to drink
> A spider's web hung to the water's edge,
> And on the wet and slimy foot-stone lay
> The useless fragment of a wooden bowl.
> It moved my very heart.

In Wordsworth's poem, Margaret, pathetic victim of her own hope rather than her despair, benignly gave the water of life to all who passed. She is dead, and the bowl with which she served them has dwindled to a useless fragment. Frost, addressing his directives to himself and to his right readers (as opposed to the "wrong ones" he mentions below), offers only an ambiguous hope to either:

> I have kept hidden in the instep arch
> Of an old cedar at the waterside
> A broken drinking goblet like the Grail
> Under a spell so the wrong ones can't find it,
> So can't get saved, as Saint Mark says they mustn't.
> (I stole the goblet from the children's playhouse.)
> Here are your waters and your watering place.
> Drink and be whole again beyond confusion.

The text from Mark that the poem refers to (4:11–12) is the weirdest in that uncanniest of gospels:

> And he said unto them, Unto you it is given to know the mystery of the kingdom of God: but unto them that are without, all these things are done in parables:
> That seeing they may see, and not perceive; and hearing they may hear, and not understand; lest at any time they should be converted, and their sins should be forgiven them.

In Mark, only the demons know the divinity of Jesus: he himself is uncertain, and his blockhead disciples are puzzled. The author of Mark is a true precursor of the poet who writes "Directive." To understand Mark or Frost, you have to be daemonic. Robert Frost is what the Bible names a watcher: of places, persons, things, and one's solitary inward self. He does not share Whitman's eros, however intransitive.

I am more an Emersonian than a Frostian, and that renders the question relevant to me as I embark upon my own reading of "Directive":

> Back out of all this now too much for us,
> Back in a time made simple by the loss
> Of detail, burned, dissolved, and broken off
> Like graveyard marble sculpture in the weather,
> There is a house that is no more a house
> Upon a farm that is no more a farm
> And in a town that is no more a town.

This monosyllabic backward march is carefully weighed out. The initial line is all monosyllables, the second also except for "simple," an effect repeated in lines 5, 6 (except for "upon"), and 7. This helps produce a kind of parataxis, a biblical style much favored by Walt Whitman, though the Frostian turn is very different.

I am an experiential and personalizing literary critic, which certainly rouses up enmity, but I go on believing that poems matter only if we matter. All criticism of a man's self, said my hero Samuel Johnson, is really oblique praise; it is to show how much he can spare. Frost in "Directive" criticizes himself and his elite readers but only to show how much he and they can spare.

The poem's journey back in time reminds me in my old age of the hazard in memorial simplification: detail is lost. I like to think that such loss is drowsy, but Frost shocks me awake by the hurt "burned, dissolved, and broken off / Like graveyard marble sculpture." After that, house, farm, and town are weathered off into nothingness.

Whether Frost is describing or inventing a home he and Elinor had to abandon is uncertain, but to the poem that scarcely matters. Again, tone is central:

> The road there, if you'll let a guide direct you
> Who only has at heart your getting lost,
> May seem as if it should have been a quarry—
> Great monolithic knees the former town
> Long since gave up pretense of keeping covered.
> And there's a story in a book about it:
> Besides the wear of iron wagon wheels

The ledges show lines ruled southeast-northwest,
The chisel work of an enormous Glacier
That braced his feet against the Arctic Pole.
You must not mind a certain coolness from him
Still said to haunt this side of Panther Mountain.
Nor need you mind the serial ordeal
Of being watched from forty cellar holes
As if by eye pairs out of forty firkins.
As for the woods' excitement over you
That sends light rustle rushes to their leaves,
Charge that to upstart inexperience.
Where were they all not twenty years ago?
They think too much of having shaded out
A few old pecker-fretted apple trees.

Defeat is the burden, but the voice directing us possesses authority. What we hear is a spirit "too lofty and original to rage," to quote a later section of the poem. The prouder word here is "original," since the proof of experiential triumph is the poem itself, permanent survivor beyond house, farm, town, "all this now too much for us." Frost is saturnine in contrasting "Directive" to the "cheering song" he will not write:

Make yourself up a cheering song of how
Someone's road home from work this once was,
Who may be just ahead of you on foot
Or creaking with a buggy load of grain.
The height of the adventure is the height
Of country where two village cultures faded
Into each other. Both of them are lost.
And if you're lost enough to find yourself
By now, pull in your ladder road behind you
And put a sign up CLOSED to all but me.
Then make yourself at home. The only field
Now left's no bigger than a harness gall.

That is the most severe humor in all of Frost, so bitter that it becomes something else, comprehending self-mockery, scorn of sociological jargon of "village cultures faded," and the wonderful cartoon perspective of "pull

in your ladder road behind you." There is a particularly self-directed cruelty in the reduction of the only remaining field cleared by Frost to a sore
inflicted on a workhorse by its harness.

A finer tone enters with the next movement:

> First there's the children's house of make-believe,
> Some shattered dishes underneath a pine,
> The playthings in the playhouse of the children.
> Weep for what little things could make them glad.
> Then for the house that is no more a house,
> But only a belilaced cellar hole,
> Now slowly closing like a dent in dough.
> This was no playhouse but a house in earnest.

That last line confirms the reader's apprehension that the "children"
were Elinor and Robert Frost, playing house in earnest. There is an almost
unique poignance, for Frost, in "Weep for what little things could make
them glad," countered by the grim brilliance of "slowly closing like a dent
in dough."

Tone rises past the earlier irony of "the height of the adventure" to the
intensity of an American Sublime:

> Your destination and your destiny's
> A brook that was the water of the house,
> Cold as a spring as yet so near its source,
> Too lofty and original to rage.
> (We know the valley streams that when aroused
> Will leave their tatters hung on barb and thorn.)

That brook of the blessing is a constant image in Frost, though never
before so urgent as it is now. We are then led on to the grandest of his
conclusions:

> I have kept hidden in the instep arch
> Of an old cedar at the waterside
> A broken drinking goblet like the Grail
> Under a spell so the wrong ones can't find it,
> So can't get saved, as Saint Mark says they mustn't.

(I stole the goblet from the children's playhouse.)
Here are your waters and your watering place.
Drink and be whole again beyond confusion.

Emerson and Frost, both learned classicists, knew that a root meaning of "confusion" was to pour out a libation to the gods. Frost was a profoundly pagan poet, and "Directive" invites its elite readers to a communion with fatal Ananke, the god of contingencies and overdeterminations. This is a cold and clean communion, promising only a Lucretian clarity, a difficult acceptance of the way things are.

Wallace Stevens

(1879–1955)

POETS INFLUENCE US because we fall in love with their poems. All love unfortunately changes, if indeed it does not end, and since nothing is got for nothing, we also get hurt when we abandon, or are abandoned by, poems. Criticism is as much a series of metaphors for the acts of loving what we have read as for the acts of reading themselves. Walter Pater liked to use the word "appreciations" for his critical essays, and I present this particular series of metaphors as an appreciation of Wallace Stevens. Precisely, I mean to appreciate his success in writing the poems of our climate more definitively than any American since Whitman and Dickinson. What justifies an estimate that sets him higher than Frost, Pound, Eliot, and Williams? If he is, as so many readers now believe, a great poet, at least the equal of such contemporaries as Hardy, Yeats, Rilke, and Valéry, what are the qualities that make for greatness in him? How and why does he move us, enlighten us, enlarge our existences, and help us to live our lives?

Though the admirers of Stevens are a mighty band these days, they have not convinced all skeptics or detractors. We have had some difficulty in exporting him to the British, who with a few noble exceptions continue to regard him as a rather luxurious and Frenchified exquisite, a kind of upper-middle-class mock-Platonist who represents at best an American Aestheticism, replete with tropical fruits and aroma-laden invitations to the voyage. Their Stevens is the celebrator of Florida and of pre-Castro Havana, a vulgarian-in-spite-of-himself. Some American apostles of the Pound-Eliot-Williams-Olson axis are holdouts also; thus we find Hugh Kenner's complaint in *The Pound Era* that all Stevens comes to is the ultimate realization of the poetics of Edward Lear. We can find also, apart from different adherents of the Gorgeous Nonsense school, those critics who complain that Stevens increasingly became desiccated and mock-philosophical; here one can remember Randall Jarrell's crack about the later Stevens resembling "G. E. Moore at the spinet." Finally, sometimes we can hear the complaint of those who insist they are weary of poems about poetry, and so are rendered weariest by the recorder of "Notes toward a Supreme Fiction. "Probably new fault-findings, more soundly based upon Stevens's actual limitations, will arrive as the decades pass. Someone will rise to ask the hard question: How many qualifications can you get into a single poem and still have a poem? Do we not get more than enough of these interjections that Stevens himself describes as "a few words, an and yet, and yet, and yet—"?

But an appreciation does not address itself to answering negative critics, or to proposing fresh negations. The reader who loves Stevens learns a passion for Yes, and learns also that such a passion, like the imagination, needs to be indulged. "It must give pleasure," Stevens says, following a supreme tradition, and his poems do give pleasure. This pleasure, though naturalistic, essentially helps to satisfy the never-satisfied mind, and to the pursuit of the meaning of that satisfaction I now turn. Courageously waving before me the gaudy banners of the Affective Fallacy, I ask myself what it is that reading Stevens does for me, and what is it that I then attempt to do for other readers of Stevens? Is it an effectual though reduced Romantic Humanism that is rekindled for us? Is it a last splendid if willfully grotesque triumph of the American Sublime? Is it, O glorious if this be so, an achieved survival of the Genteel Tradition, another final hedge against the barbarians who are, as we all know, not only within the gates but also indistinguishable, alas, except upon certain moonlit nights, from our very selves? Is the prudential Seer of Hartford only the most eloquent elaborater of our way of life, the Grand Defender of our sanctified evasions, our privileged status as the secular clergy of a society we cannot serve, let alone save? Have we committed the further and grievous sin of making a Stevens in our own image, a poet of professors as Auden and Eliot and Arnold used to be? Having employed Stevens as a weapon in the mimic wars of criticism against the anti-Romantic legions of the Eliotics and Arnoldians, are we now confronted by his poems as so many statues in the formal parks of our university culture? Are his poems still Spirit to us, or are they only what Emerson, most prudential of New England seers, shrewdly called Commodity? Have we made him too into Literature? Do we need now to defend him against ourselves?

Several critics have regarded Stevens as essentially a comic poet. I think this characterization is not adequate to even his more sardonic aspect, but at least it reminds us of how humorous he could be. One of my favorite poems in *Harmonium*, which I rarely persuade anyone else to like, is called "Two Figures in Dense Violet Light." I take it as being a superbly American

kind of defeated eroticism, the complaint of a would-be lover who is ruefully content to be discontent, because he rather doubts that high romance
can be domesticated anyway in a world still so ruggedly New. One might
think of this poem's speaker as being a decadent Huckleberry Finn dressed
up to play the part of Romeo:

> I had as lief be embraced by the porter at the hotel
> As to get no more from the moonlight
> Than your moist hand.
>
> Be the voice of night and Florida in my ear.
> Use dusky words and dusky images.
> Darken your speech.
>
> Speak, even, as if I did not hear you speaking,
> But spoke for you perfectly in my thoughts,
> Conceiving words,
>
> As the night conceives the sea-sounds in silence,
> And out of their droning sibilants makes
> A serenade.
>
> Say, puerile, that the buzzards crouch on the ridge-pole
> And sleep with one eye watching the stars fall
> Below Key West.
>
> Say that the palms are clear in a total blue,
> Are clear and are obscure; that it is night;
> That the moon shines.

Though more than usually mocking and self-mocking, this is surely
another of Stevens's hymns to the Interior Paramour, another invocation
of his Muse, his version of Whitman's Fancy. But Whitman's Fancy, though
she rarely emanated very far out from him, did have a touch or two of an
exterior existence. Stevens's Paramour, poor girl, is the most firmly Interior being in Romantic tradition. Compared to her, the epipsyches of Nerval, Poe, Shelley, and the young Yeats are buxom, open-air, Renoir-like
ladies. Stevens knows this, and the violet light of his poem is so dense

that the two figures might as well be one. "What a love affair!" we cannot help exclaiming, as the Grand Solipsist murmurs to his Paramour: "Speak, even, as if I did not hear you speaking, / But spoke for you perfectly in my thoughts." This is a delicious Dialogue of One, all right, and we find its true father in some of Emerson's slyly bland observations on the Self-Reliance of Spheral Man. Recalling one Boscovich, an Italian Newtonian who had formulated a more-than-usually crazy version of the molecular theory of matter, Emerson mused: "Was it Boscovich who found that our bodies never come in contact? Well, souls never touch their objects. An innavigable sea washes with silent waves between us and the things we aim at and converse with."

In Stevens, this "innavigable sea" is called "the dumbfoundering abyss / Between us and the object," and no poet has been more honestly ruthless about the actual dualism of our everyday perceptions and imperceptions. Except for a peculiar roster of fabulistic caricatures, there aren't any *people* in Stevens's poems, and this exclusion is comprehensive enough to include Stevens himself as whole man or as person. But the "whole man" or "person" in a poem is generally only another formalizing device or dramatizing convention anyway, a means of self-presentation that Stevens did not care to employ. In the difficult poem "The Creations of Sound," written against Eliot, who appears in it as X, Stevens declares himself as:

> a separate author, a different poet,
> An accretion from ourselves, intelligent
> Beyond intelligence, an artificial man
>
> At a distance, a secondary expositor,
> A being of sound, whom one does not approach
> Through any exaggeration.

For all his antimythological bias, the old Stevens turned to Ulysses, "symbol of the seeker," to present his own final quest for a transcendental self. Unlike the Ulysses of Tennyson, at once somewhat Homeric, Dantesque, Shakespearean, and Miltonic, the Ulysses of Stevens is not seeking to meet anything even partly external to himself. What other Ulysses would start out by saying: "As I know, I am and have / The right to be"? For Stevens, "the right to know / And the right to be are one," but his Ulysses must go on questing because:

Yet always there is another life,
A life beyond this present knowing,
A life lighter than this present splendor,
Brighter, perfected and distant away,
Not to be reached but to be known,
Not an attainment of the will
But something illogically received,
A divination, a letting down
From loftiness, misgivings dazzlingly
Resolved in dazzling discovery.

There is, despite so many of his critics, no doubt concerning the precursor of this ultimate Stevens. For that "something illogically received," we can recall the divinations of the inescapable father of the American Sublime, who uttered the grand formula "All I know is reception; I am and I have: but I do not get, and when I have fancied I had gotten anything, I found I did not." In the same essay, the superb "Experience," Emerson mused: "I am very content with knowing, if only I could know." Both Emerson and Stevens hold hard to what both call "poverty," imaginative need, and they believe that holding hard long enough will compel the self to attain its due sphericity. Between the skeptically transcendental grandfather and the transcendentally skeptical grandson came the heroic father, spheral man himself, unqualified in his divinations, who tells us what we miss in Emerson and Stevens alike, and what we cannot resist in him:

Encompass worlds, but never try to encompass me,
I crowd your sleekest and best by simply looking toward you.

Writing and talk do not prove me,
I carry the plenum of proof and every thing else in my face,
With the hush of my lips I wholly confound the skeptic.

For the absolutely transcendental self, the man-god, we read Whitman only, but I am astonished always how much of it abides in Stevens, despite nearly all his critics, and despite the Idiot Questioner in Stevens himself. His evasive glory is hardly distinguishable from his imperfect solipsism, or from ours. And there I verge upon what I take as the clue to his greatness: in the curiously esoteric but centrally American tradition of Emerson, Whitman,

Thoreau, and Dickinson, Stevens is uniquely the twentieth-century poet of that solitary and inward glory we can none of us share with others. His value is that he describes and even celebrates (occasionally) our selfhood communings as no one else can or does. He knows that "the sublime comes down / To the spirit and space," and though he keeps acknowledging the spirit's emptiness and space's vacancy, he keeps demonstrating a violent abundance of spirit and a florabundance of the consolations of space. He is the poet we always needed, who would speak for the solitude at our center, who would do for us what his own "Large Red Man Reading" did for those ghosts that returned to earth to hear his phrases, "and spoke the feeling for them, which was what they had lacked." Or, to state this function positively, Stevens, more even than Wordsworth, is the essential poet who can recognize:

> There is a human loneliness,
> A part of space and solitude,
> In which knowledge cannot be denied,
> In which nothing of knowledge fails,
> The luminous companion, the hand,
> The fortifying arm, the profound
> Response, the completely answering voice,
> That which is more than anything else
> The right within us and about us,
> Joined, the triumphant vigor, felt,
> The inner direction on which we depend,
> That which keeps us the little that we are,
> The aid of greatness to be and the force.

There is nothing communal here. Stevens celebrates an apprehension that has no social aspect whatsoever and that indeed appears resistant to any psychological reductions we might apply. As no one is going to be tempted to call Stevens a mystical poet, or in any way religious, we rightly *confront* a considerable problem in description whenever Stevens is most himself. His True Subject appears to be his own sense of glory, and his true value for his readers appears to be that he reminds us of our own moments of solipsistic bliss, or at least of our aspirations for such moments.

The Stevens I begin to sketch has little in common with the poet of "decreation" most of his better critics have described for us. There is indeed a Stevens as seen by Hillis Miller, a poet of the almost Paterian flux of *sensations*, of a cyclic near-nihilism returning always upon itself. There is also truly a Stevens as seen by Helen Vendler: Stevens the venerable ironist, apostle of "the total leaflessness." I do not assert that these are merely peripheral aspects of the poet, but they seem to me aspects only, darker saliences that surround the central man, shadows flickering beyond that crucial light cast by the single candle of Stevens's self-joying imagination, his version of "A Quiet Normal Life":

> His place, as he sat and as he thought, was not
> In anything that he constructed, so frail,
> So barely lit, so shadowed over and naught,
>
> As, for example, a world in which, like snow,
> He became an inhabitant, obedient
> To gallant notions on the part of cold.
>
> It was here. This was the setting and the time
> Of year. Here in his house and in his room,
> In his chair, the most tranquil thought grew peaked
>
> And the oldest and the warmest heart was cut
> By gallant notions on the part of night—
> Both late and alone, above the crickets' chords,
>
> Babbling, each one, the uniqueness of its sound.
> There was no fury in transcendent forms.
> But his actual candle blazed with artifice.

Stevens's customary anxiety about transcendent forms is evident, yet it is also evident that his actual candle is precisely a transcendent form. Wordsworth was sanely English in refusing to go too far into his True Subject, which was his own sense of actual sublimity. Emerson, deliberately and wildly American, made possible for all his descendants the outrageous True Subject of the American Sublime. Mocking as always where he is most vulnerable and most involved, here is Stevens's "The American Sublime":

> How does one stand
> To behold the sublime,

To confront the mockers,
The mickey mockers
And plated pairs?

When General Jackson
Posed for his statue
He knew how one feels.
Shall a man go barefoot
Blinking and blank?

But how does one feel?
One grows used to the weather,
The landscape and that;
And the sublime comes down
To the spirit itself,

The spirit and space,
The empty spirit
In vacant space.
What wine does one drink?
What bread does one eat?

Juxtapose this to one of the pure versions of the American Sublime:

> In the highest moments, we are a vision. There is nothing that can
> be called gratitude nor properly joy. The soul is raised over passion.
> It seeth nothing so much as Identity. It is a Perceiving that Truth
> and Right ARE. Hence it becomes a perfect Peace out of the know-
> ing that all things will go well. Vast spaces of nature, the Atlantic
> Ocean, the South Sea; vast intervals of time, years, centuries, are
> annihilated to it; this which I think and feel underlay that former
> state of life and circumstances, as it does underlie my present, and
> will always all circumstance, and what is called life and what is
> called death.

This excerpt from Emerson's 1838 *Journal* was modified into one of the
most famous passages in the essay "Self-Reliance." Nervous as Stevens is
at confronting possible mockers, his American Sublime is no appreciable
distance from Emerson's. One doesn't see Stevens posing for his statue, but

he still admits that the Sublime comes down to what one feels and what one sees, and his emptiness of spirit and vacancy of space were part of the weather, inner and outer, and not permanent metaphysical reductions. That which he was, that only could he see, and he never wearied of affirming his version of Self-Reliance:

> What
> One believes is what matters. Ecstatic identities
> Between one's self and the weather and the things
> Of the weather are the belief in one's element,
> The casual reunions, the long-pondered
> Surrenders, the repeated sayings that
> There is nothing more and that it is enough
> To believe in the weather and in the things and men
> Of the weather and in one's self, as part of that
> And nothing more.

How can a solipsism present itself in the accents of glory, we may be uneasy enough to ask, and again, can a solipsism be a possible humanism? I begin an answer with the dark Wittgensteinian aphorism: what the solipsist *means* is right. For, though solipsism is refutable by its status as tautology, this is what Wittgenstein means when he speaks of a *deep* tautology, which leads to a true realism. Stevens too knows, as Emerson knew, that what he *says* is wrong, but that his meaning is right. The European Sublime had a communal aspect, however solitary its stimulus, but we are of an even more displaced Protestant national sensibility, and, accordingly, we come to reality only through knowing first the scandalous reality of our own selves. Or, as Stevens said:

> The lean cats of the arches of the churches,
> That's the old world. In the new, all men are priests.

Stevens is a priest, not of the invisible but of that visible he labors to make a little hard to see. He serves that visible, not for its own sake but because he wants to make his own sublimity more visible to himself. Endlessly qualifying his sense of his own greatness, he still endlessly returns to rest upon such a sense. Yet he knows that he needs us, his possible readers, to do for him "what he cannot do for himself, that is to say, receive his poetry." As he proudly tells us, he addresses us as an elite, being in this one respect, at least, more honest than a far more esoteric and difficult poet, Whitman. In "The Noble Rider and the Sound of Words," Stevens says:

> all poets address themselves to someone and it is of the essence of that instinct, and it seems to amount to an instinct, that it should be to an elite, not to a drab but to a woman with the hair of pythoness, not to a chamber of commerce but to a gallery of one's own, if there are enough of one's own to fill a gallery. And that elite, if it responds, not out of complaisance, but because the poet has quickened it, because he has educed from it that for which it was searching in itself and in the life around it and which it had not yet quite found, will thereafter do for the poet what he cannot do for himself, that is to say, receive his poetry.

There are two questions to be asked of this passage: What is it in this poet that gives him the instinct to address himself not to a drab but to a woman with the hair of a pythoness, and what is it that we keep searching for in ourselves that Stevens would quicken in us, that he would educe from us? The answer to both questions must be the same answer: a quality that Stevens calls "nobility." As he knew, it is hardly a word that now moves us, and I suspect he chose the word defiantly and therefore wrongly. Stevens says, in the same essay, that "it is one of the peculiarities of the imagination that it is always at the end of an era." Certainly Stevens now seems peculiarly to have been at the end of an era, where he himself could still be visualized as a *noble* rider moving to the sound of words. I myself have come to think that the principal peculiarity of the imagination is that it does not exist, or to state my thought another way, that people talking about the arts do better when they begin to talk as though the imagination did not exist. Let us reduce to the rocky level and say, as Hobbes did, that "decaying sense" most certainly does exist. Stevens had then a decaying sense of nobility, which he called an imagination of nobility. "Noble," in its root, means to be knowing or seeing, and Stevens had therefore a decaying sense of a certain seeing that was also a knowing. I turn again to Stevens's central precursor for the inevitable vision of this nobility in its American variety:

> This insight, which expresses itself by what is called Imagination, is a very high sort of seeing, which does not come by study, but by

the intellect being where and what it sees; by sharing the path or circuit of things through forms, and so making them translucid to others.

"Leave the many and hold the few," Emerson also advises in his late poem "Terminus," thus sanctioning the democratic poet, like Whitman, in the pragmatic address to an actual elite. Stevens needed little sanctioning as to audience, but he was rather anxious about his own constant emphasis upon the self as solitary "scholar," and his recourse was to plead "poverty." He cannot have been unaware that both "scholar" and "poverty" in his rather precise senses were Emersonian usages. A great coverer of traces, Stevens may be judged nevertheless to have turned more to a tradition than to a man. American Romanticism found its last giant in Stevens, who defines the tradition quite as strongly as it informs him. "The prologues are over. . . . It is time to choose," and the Stevens I think we must choose writes the poems not of an empty spirit in vacant space, but of a spirit so full of itself that there is room for nothing else. This description hardly appears to flatter Stevens, yet I render it in his praise. Another of his still-neglected poems, for which my own love is intense, is entitled simply "Poem With Rhythms":

The hand between the candle and the wall
Grows large on the wall.

The mind between this light or that and space,
(This man in a room with an image of the world,
That woman waiting for the man she loves,)
Grows large against space:

There the man sees the image clearly at last.
There the woman receives her lover into her heart
And weeps on his breast, though he never comes.

It must be that the hand
Has a will to grow larger on the wall,
To grow larger and heavier and stronger than
The wall; and that the mind
Turns to its own figurations and declares,

"This image, this love, I compose myself
Of these. In these, I come forth outwardly.
In these, I wear a vital cleanliness,
Not as in air, bright-blue-resembling air,
But as in the powerful mirror of my wish and will."

The principal difference between Stevens and Whitman appears to be that Stevens admits his mind is alone with its own figurations, while Whitman keeps inaccurately but movingly insisting he wants "contact" with other selves. His "contact" is an Emersonian term, and we know, as Whitman's readers, that he actually cannot bear "contact," any more than Emerson, Dickinson, Frost, or Stevens can tolerate it. "Poem With Rhythms," like so much of Stevens, has a hidden origin in Whitman's "The Sleepers," particularly in a great passage apparently describing a woman's disappointment in love:

I am she who adorn'd herself and folded her hair expectantly,
My truant lover has come, and it is dark.

Double yourself and receive me darkness,
Receive me and my lover too, he will not let me go without him.

I roll myself upon you as upon a bed, I resign myself to the dusk.

He whom I call answers me and takes the place of my lover,
He rises with me silently from the bed.

Darkness, you are gentler than my lover, his flesh was sweaty
    and panting,
I feel the hot moisture yet that he left me.

My hands are spread forth, I pass them in all directions.
I would sound up the shadowy shore to which you are journeying.

Be careful, darkness! already, what was it touch'd me?
I thought my lover had gone, else darkness and he are one,
I hear the heart-beat, I follow, I fade away.

This juxtaposition of major Whitman to relatively minor Stevens is not altogether fair, but then I don't think I hurt Stevens by granting that Whitman, upon his heights, is likely to make his descendant seem only a dwarf of disintegration. Whitman-as-Woman invokes the darkness of birth, and blends himself into the mingled Sublimity of death and the Native Strain. Stevens-as-Interior-Paramour invokes only his mind's own figurations, but he sees himself cleansed in the vitalizing mirror of will as he could never hope to see himself in the mere outwardness of air. Whitman oddly but beautifully persuades us of a dramatic poignance that his actual solipsism does not earn, while Stevens rather less beautifully knows only the nondramatic truth of his own fine desperation.

What then is Stevens giving us? What do we celebrate with and in him when he leads us to celebrate? His vigorous affirmation "The Well Dressed Man With a Beard" centers on "a speech / Of the self that must sustain itself on speech." Is eloquence enough? I turn again to the fountain of our will, Emerson, who had the courage to insist that eloquence was enough, because he identified eloquence with "something unlimited and boundless," in the manner of Cicero. Here is Stevens in "Chocorua to Its Neighbors" mounting through eloquence to his individual sense of "something unlimited and boundless," a "something" not beyond our apprehension:

> Last night at the end of night his starry head,
> Like the head of fate, looked out in darkness, part
> Thereof and part desire and part the sense
> Of what men are. The collective being knew
> There were others like him safely under roof:
>
> The captain squalid on his pillow, the great
> Cardinal, saying the prayers of earliest day;
> The stone, the categorical effigy;
> And the mother, the music, the name; the scholar,
> Whose green mind bulges with complicated hues:
>
> True transfigurers fetched out of the human mountain,
> True genii for the diminished, spheres,
> Gigantic embryos of populations,
> Blue friends in shadows, rich conspirators,
> Confiders and comforters and lofty kin.

To say more than human things with human voice,
That cannot be; to say human things with more
Than human voice, that, also, cannot be;
To speak humanly from the height or from the depth
Of human things, that is acutest speech.

A critic who has learned, ruefully, to accept the reductive view that the imagination is only decaying sense, must ask himself: "Why is he so moved by this transfiguration of language into "acutest speech"? He may remember, in this connection, the prose statement by Stevens that moves him most:

Why should a poem not change in sense when there is a fluctuation of the whole of appearance? Or why should it not change when we realize that the indifferent experience of life is the unique experience, the item of ecstasy which we have been isolating and reserving for another time and place, loftier and more secluded?

The doctrinal voice of Walter Pater, another unacknowledged ancestor, is heard in this passage, as perhaps it must be heard in any modern Epicureanism. Stevens, I suggest, is the Lucretius of our modern poetry, and like Lucretius seeks his truth in mere appearances, seeks his spirit in things of the weather. Both poets are beyond illusions, yet both invest their knowing of the way things are with a certain grim ecstasy. But an American Lucretius, coming after the double alienation of European Romanticism and domestic Transcendentalism, will have lost all sense of the communal in his ecstasy. Stevens fulfilled the unique enterprise of a specifically American poetry by exposing the essential solipsism of our Native Strain. No American feels free when he is not alone, and every American's passion for Yes affirms a hidden belief that his soul's substance is no part of the creation. We are mortal gods, the central strain in our poetry keeps saying, and our aboriginal selves are forbidden to find companionship in one another. Our ecstasy comes only from self-recognition, yet cannot be complete if we reduce wholly to "the evilly compounded, vital I . . . made . . . fresh in a world of white." We need "The Poems of Our Climate" because we are, happily, imperfect solipsists, unhappy in a happily imperfect and still-external world—which is to say, we need Stevens:

There would still remain the never-resting mind,
So that one would want to escape, come back

To what had been so long composed.
The imperfect is our paradise.
Note that, in this bitterness, delight,
Since the imperfect is so hot in us,
Lies in flawed words and stubborn sounds.

"Mrs. Alfred Uruguay" is a comic masterpiece, in a mode that Stevens never developed, a quest-romance not so much parodied, as in "The Comedian as the Letter C," as raised to an unparalleled pitch of sardonic irreality. Mrs. Uruguay is no interior paramour; she is the reductionist in Stevens personified, but personified as she might be in James or Wharton. Her name, as Northrop Frye noted, is meant to suggest the city of Montevideo, the mount of vision she is determined to take by a laborious cure of the ground. But though she is sublimely funny as a reductionist, she is also very formidable, for she represents what Stevens now knows to be the most dangerous element in his own poetic mind, the Snow Man tendency that says no to everything in order to get at itself. The reductive fallacy can be defined as the notion that we cannot know what someone or something really is until we know the very worst that someone or something is or can be. Applied to poetry, this is indeed to wipe away moonlight like mud.

Mrs. Uruguay is an apostle of the total leaflessness, except for the idea of her own elegance, which she cannot surrender even to sacred reductiveness. She climbs the mount of vision all dressed in velvet, though in the pure good of theory she would wish to ride naked. The very likable donkey is Sancho Panza to her Don Quixote, as inexorably "she approached the real, upon her mountain, / With lofty darkness," which is her Sublime contribution to the quest. We too wish for a falsifying bell, but that would spoil this anecdote since "her no and no made yes impossible," and any bell on her dark road upward would be a happily falsifying yes.

Yet that is only one half of this mad poem, the other half belonging to the figure of the youth as a virile poet, the ephebe as reborn Apollo who rushes past her down the mountain, remorselessly abandoning "the real" even as she seeks it. She is all ethos, the limitation of Fate; like the horse he rides, he is "all will," the pathos of Power. She presumably seeks the martyrs' bones, relics of those who attained the mount of vision before her. He is the "figure of capable imagination," a noble synecdoche personified, though "no chevalere and poorly dressed," the poverty of costume representing his eros, his need of the imagination he pursues, the idea of the sun upon which he is intent. His vision is expansionist yet capable, and his blindness is itself an enabling act. Stevens, and we ourselves as readers, are moved by the young man, but Stevens and the reader are more in sympathy with the donkey, with the bells and midnight forms, with the moonlight, and with the charm of the reductive dowager's velvet. The rider's "phosphorescent hair" marks him as being in the tradition of the youth with flashing eyes and floating hair that Coleridge fears to become at the close of "Kubla Khan," the youth who like Keats in "The Fall of Hyperion" has been daemonic enough to reenter the earthly paradise. Mrs. Uruguay seeks the real because the mountaintop is indeed outside and above her. The youth scorns the real, and out of those who have died seeking it he creates, in his mind, his own eventual victory: "The ultimate elegance: the imagined land." "Elegance" is a final irony against Mrs. Uruguay, who had identified herself with elegance, presumably in its Paterian or etymological sense of "chosen out" or "selected"; so we can interpret "the ultimate elegance" as a seeking after evidence of election. This lovely poem's ultimate elegance is that both Mrs. Uruguay and the youth are equally outrageous, each just as elected a quester as the other. To pursue the middle path of invention or discovery is to wish for a falsifying bell, but such a statement takes us beyond this poem and into the doctrinal text "Asides on the Oboe," with its curious balance between transcendental expansiveness and what Stevens hoped to distinguish as a separate mode of discovery.

The deliberately offhand title suggests an anxiety in Stevens, because he is starting to make a definitive formulation and he is wary of finalities. But "It is time to choose," and the mythologies being obsolete, Stevens chooses a crucial Nietzschean notion, though he tries to defend himself against Nietzsche by taking his ideas at second hand (through Hans Vaihinger's *The Philosophy of "As If "*) and by assimilating Nietzsche to Whitman's presentation to the self. The philosophers' man alone who still walks in dew is not Zarathustra but the ephebe of "Out of the Cradle Endlessly Rocking," and also the central man and human globe of Emersonian tradition, at once mimetic and expressive ("responsive / As a mirror with a voice") and recalling Emerson's lament in "Experience": "Temperament also enters fully into the system of illusions and shuts us in a prison of glass which we cannot see. There is an optical illusion about every person we meet." Emerson's ambivalence is also Stevens's, but Frank Doggett is probably right in finding a closer parallel in Schopenhauer, who before Nietzsche had demystified the inner self as being a mere fiction: "As soon as we . . . seek for once to know ourselves fully by means of introspective reflection, we are lost in a bottomless void; we find ourselves like the hollow glass globe, from out of which a voice speaks whose cause is not to be found in it."

And yet because belief is final in this known fiction of the self, the Emersonian emblem of transcendence, "the transparence of the place," is possible; and as Emerson had prophesied, such a self must be a poet's, "and in his poems we find peace." Stevens's acute anxiety at his own affirmativeness is rarely more noticeable than in part 2 of the poem, where the glass man is fictively "cold and numbered" yet cries with the vital voice of the dew and puns brilliantly in "Thou art not August unless I make thee so." The possible poet, abstracted from the anteriority of poetic tradition, has an actual erotic effect, but only upon the mind. Yet we live in the mind, as Stevens kept saying, and "Asides on the Oboe" becomes a more elevated and convincing poem when, in its third part, it engages the problem of a world whose erotic intensities have been mutilated by pain and suffering:

> One year, death and war prevented the jasmine scent
> And the jasmine islands were bloody martyrdoms.
> How was it then with the central man? Did we
> Find peace? We found the sum of men. We found,
> If we found the central evil, the central good.
> We buried the fallen without jasmine crowns.
> There was nothing he did not suffer, no; nor we.

The jasmine here is likelier to be Southern American than East Indian; for Stevens it is a residue of the image of Florida, the venereal soil of *Harmonium*. We can read "jasmine islands" as a trope for Stevens's poetry of earth, his celebration of the marriage of flesh and air. As Emerson and Whitman discovered in the American Civil War, there is no central man if there is no peace. With the expansive or Transcendental vision impaired, Stevens substitutes a subtler if more modest discovery:

> It was not as if the jasmine ever returned.
> But we and the diamond globe at last were one.
> We had always been partly one. It was as we came
> To see him, that we were wholly one, as we heard
> Him chanting for those buried in their blood,

In the jasmine haunted forests, that we knew
The glass man, without external reference.

It is worth noting that this is one of Stevens's most American stanzas. Eros is projected, and an identity with the transcendent poetic self is introjected, in a transumptive trope that abolishes all possibility of putting the will into present time. The effect is Whitmanian, as we hear a universal bard chanting for all of us, for who is not one of "those buried in their blood," even while supposedly alive, and everyone is "in the jasmine haunted forests," studying the nostalgias of lost erotic longings. Yet there is a final knowledge here, and it is of the self, "without external reference," which is a muted anticipation of "It Must Give Pleasure," VIII, the climax of "Notes," when the self proclaims its majesty, "I have not but I am and as I am, I am," and then confirms this Hoon-like glory by dismissing "these external regions" as being relevant only to Cinderella-like wish fulfillments.

I conclude by turning to "The Well Dressed Man with a Beard," the only short poem upon which Stevens congratulated himself at the end. Like so much of Stevens, the poem has a hidden origin in Whitman's "The Sleepers," where the poet wanders all night in his vision, "bending with open eyes over the shut eyes of sleepers." Stevens seem to have assimilated, repressively, the opening of "The Sleepers" to the opening of the most poignant of Whitman's poems, "The Wound-Dresser," where the poet has a proleptic vision of himself telling future children how he nursed the wounded in Washington hospitals during the Civil War:

An old man bending I come among new faces,
Years looking backward resuming in answer to children.

The imageries of "The Wound-Dresser" and "The Sleepers" seem to combine in "Extracts from Addresses to the Academy of Fine Ideas," and the passage of the woman waiting for her lover toward the end of part 1 of "The Sleepers" is repressively echoed in Stevens's "Poem with Rhythms," composed just before "The Well Dressed Man with a Beard." What does the title mean? A man with a beard, to an American poet, tends to mean God, Uncle Sam, or the prophetic Walt, or some combination thereof, but of course neither Jehovah nor Whitman can be called well dressed. I suspect that an idealized version of Stevens's own father gets into the mix also, both here and in "The Auroras of Autumn," since the elder Stevens was a man of splendidly affirmative temperament until he was let down by a business associate. The charm of "The Well Dressed Man with a Beard" is that it celebrates "yet one, / One only, one thing" that is not an actual thing but rather affirmative language itself, the eloquence of "a speech / Of the self that must sustain itself on speech." It is "a petty phrase" that sweetens the meadow, honeys the heart, greens the body. Most striking is the culminating object of this celebration:

> The form on the pillow humming while one sleeps,
> The aureole above the humming house . . .

Doggett relates this humming or living self to a passage in Henri Bergson's *Creative Evolution*, which "suggests that the subjective self cannot conceive of a void or absence of self." But the humming, I think, is more Stevens's misprision of Whitman than of Bergson. Two years before, Stevens had written a wild poem, "The Woman That Had More Babies than That," which he felt was not worthy of being in *Parts of a World*. The poem is Stevens's most obsessive variation upon "Out of the Cradle," for the woman is Whitman's fierce old mother crying for her castaways. And these are her castaways, poets like Whitman and Stevens:

> The children are men, old men,
> Who, when they think and speak of the central man,
> Of the humming of the central man, the whole sound
> Of the sea, the central humming of the sea,
> Are old men breathed on by a maternal voice.

So humming while sleeping is one with the central murmuring or humming of the sea in Whitman. This purchases affirmation at a high price, for it was just this Whitmanian identification that Whitman himself transcended in the 1855 "Song of Myself," only to fall back into it in the 1860 *Leaves of Grass*. And it was again this identification that Hoon transcended when he declared, "I was myself the compass of that sea," or that Stevens was moved to declare when he chanted of the woman at Key West that "she sang beyond the genius of the sea." I think this is why Stevens does not end "The Well Dressed Man with a Beard" with the image of the aureole or crown of light above the central, because humming, house of the mind, for that would not suffice. He remembered the poem thirteen years later as "the one / About the mind as never satisfied," as though the poem's true subject inhered in its final line: "It can never be satisfied, the mind, never." It cannot be satisfied with a central humming because it wants to assert its power, its pathos, over the humming of the sea, and no assertion can convince it of a finality in that exercise of its will. Powerful as *Parts of a World* was, Stevens could not be satisfied with it. He went on to "Notes toward a Supreme Fiction," his truly central humming, where a more capable idea of the hero appears as "the major man." This man called forth a subtler music of thought from his maker. Of him, "Notes" says that he is "the object of / The hum of thoughts evaded in the mind," and for him Stevens commanded a stronger muse: "My dame, sing for this person accurate songs."

William Carlos Williams
(1883–1963)

I N HIS CRITICAL biography *William Carlos Williams: A New World Naked*, Paul Mariani wisely asserts the lasting influence of John Keats's poetry upon even the late phases of Williams:

> The voice he was listening to, and the voice that struck paydirt for him, was a matter of a complex crossing with Keats, especially the Keats of the *Hyperion* fragments and the odes. Why this should have been so is difficult to say with any exactness, for Williams himself probably did not understand why. What *he* thought he was "capturing" was the voice of the classics—the stately rhythms and sharp straightforward idiom of the Greeks as he thought they must sound should they be discovered walking the streets of his Paterson. But there was something more, a kinship Williams had felt with Keats for over half a century, the plight of the romantic poet who would have spoken as the gods speak if only he had had the power to render their speech in the accents of his own debased language. *Hyperion* is in part the portrait of the dying of the ephebe into the life of the major poet, and Keats had aborted it at the very moment that his poet was undergoing that transformation.
>
> And so with Williams, opting for the step-down line as his "classic" signature as he surfaced from the realization of his mortality, the new rhythm providing a stately, slow saraband to echo Keats's Miltonic and Dantesque phase with a difference. The crossing with Keats is there too in the nature of Williams's late iconography, in the stasis of his late images, frozen for eternity in the realized artifact, as in Williams's translation from Theocritus's first idyll, with its images limned on a "two-eared bowl / of ivy-wood," a girl and two young men, an ancient fisherman, and a small boy preoccupied with "plaiting a pretty / cage of locust stalks and asphodel." The images of "Asphodel" too belong to the same strain:

sharply realized but without Williams's earlier breathlessness and jagged line cuttings.

Poetic influence, an intensely problematical process, normally brings together a strong poet's earliest and final phases. Williams's true precursor, necessarily composite and in some sense imaginary, was a figure that fused Keats with Walt Whitman. Such a figure has in it the potential for a serious splitting of the poetic ego in its defense against the poetic past. The "negative capability" of Keats sorts oddly with Whitman's rather positive capability for conveying the powerful press of himself. "Memory is a kind / of accomplishment," Williams wrote in "The Descent," a crucial poem in his *The Desert Music* (1954). The descent to dying beckons to a return of the dead precursors in one's own colors, even as Keats and Whitman beckoned Williams to ascend into his own poetry. But the poem "The Descent" Williams shrewdly quarried from Book 2 of his own major long poem *Paterson*, a quarrying that suggests his pride in his own continuities.

Those continuities are massive throughout Williams's best work, which can be cataloged (against the numerous Williams idolators) as a limited yet still remarkably diverse canon: *Paterson* (Book I), *Kora in Hell*, *Spring and All*, "The Widow's Lament in Springtime," "To Waken an Old Lady," "The Trees," "The Yachts," "A Coronal," "These," "The Poor," "A Marriage Ritual," "Raleigh Was Right," "Burning the Christmas Greens," "A Unison," and the grand return of Keats-as-Williams in "Asphodel, That Greeny Flower." Many critics would select more, much more, but I am of the school of Wallace Stevens, rather than of Williams, and the Williams I honor is the author of about a dozen shorter poems, and four remarkable long poems and prose or verse sequences. If you believe—as I do—that Williams is not of the eminence of Stevens and Robert Frost, of Hart Crane and even of T. S. Eliot, then what is the irreducible achievement that survives even an extreme skepticism as to Williams's poetic greatness?

Of the volumes that collect Williams, I return most often to *Imaginations*, edited by Webster Schott (1970), which gathers together four weird American originals—*Kora in Hell*, *Spring and All*, *The Great American Novel*, *The Descent of Winter*—as well as some miscellaneous prose. *Kora in Hell* was subtitled *Improvisations* by Williams, who had a particular fondness for it. He analogized its astonishing "Prologue" to *On the Sublime* by the pseudo-Longinus, a comparison not so far-fetched as he himself asserted it to be. Essentially it, and all of *Kora*, is a collection of what

Emerson (following Plutarch and Cudworth) called "lustres" (Ezra Pound's *lustra*), aphoristic impressions drawn either from others or from the self. Its center is in Williams's characteristic polemic against Pound and Eliot, with an ironizing boost from Stevens:

> E. P. is the best enemy United States verse has. He is interested, passionately interested—even if he doesn't know what he is talking about. But of course he does know what he is talking about. He does not, however, know everything, not by more than half. The accordances of which Americans have the parts and the colors but not the completions before them pass beyond the attempts of his thought. It is a middle-aging blight of the imagination.
>
> I praise those who have the wit and courage, and the conventionality, to go direct toward their vision of perfection in an objective world where the signposts are clearly marked, viz., to London. But confine them in hell for their paretic assumption that there is no alternative but their own groove.
>
> Dear fat Stevens, thawing out so beautifully at forty! I was one day irately damning those who run to London when Stevens caught me up with his mild: "But where in the world will you have them run to?"

The shrewd link to *On the Sublime* is that Williams (admirably and accurately) shares the conviction of Longinus that the Sublime or strong poetry either is agonistic or it is nothing. Williams too seeks to persuade the reader to forsake easier pleasures (Eliot and Pound) for more difficult pleasures (*Kora in Hell*). And his quest is frankly Emersonian, an overt instance of American cultural nationalism. Unfortunately, *Kora*'s considerable verve and vivacity are shadowed by the immense power of James Joyce's *Ulysses*, still incomplete then, but appearing in magazine installments even as Williams wrote and read. Williams's use of mythology is essentially Joyce's, and to fight Joyce on any ground, let alone his prepared killing field, was beyond Williams's talents:

> Giants in the dirt. The gods, the Greek gods, smothered in filth and ignorance. The race is scattered over the world. Where is its home? Find it if you've the genius. Here Hebe with a sick jaw and a cruel husband,—her mother left no place for a brain to grow. Herakles

rowing boats on Berry's Creek! Zeus is a country doctor without a taste for coin jingling. Supper is of a bastard nectar on rare nights for they will come—the rare nights! The ground lifts and out sally the heroes of Sophokles, of Æschylus. They go seeping down into our hearts, they rain upon us and in the bog they sink again down through the white roots, down—to a saloon back of the rail-road switch where they have that girl, you know, the one that should have been Venus by the lust that's in her. They've got her down there among the railroad men. A crusade couldn't rescue her. Up to jail—or call it down to Limbo—the Chief of Police our Pluto. It's all of the gods, there's nothing else worth writing of. They are the same men they always were—but fallen. Do they dance now, they that danced beside Helicon? They dance much as they did then, only, few have an eye for it, through the dirt and fumes.

The question becomes: Who shall describe the dance of the gods as it is danced now in America? The answer is: Dr. Williams, who brings American babies into the world and who sees exquisitely what we cannot see without him, which is how differently the gods come to dance here in America:

This is a slight stiff dance to a waking baby whose arms have been lying curled back above his head upon the pillow, making a flower—the eyes closed. Dead to the world! Waking is a little hand brushing away dreams. Eyes open. Here's a new world.

This dance figures again in the concluding improvisation of *Kora in Hell*, as an American seasonal rhythm akin to the natural year of Stevens's "Credences of Summer" and Emerson's "Experience":

Seeing the leaves dropping from the high and low branches the thought rises: this day of all others is the one chosen, all other days fall away from it on either side and only itself remains in perfect fullness. It is its own summer, of its leaves as they scrape on the smooth ground it must build its perfection. The gross summer of the year is only a halting counterpart of those fiery days of secret triumph which in reality themselves paint the year as if upon a parchment, giving each season a mockery of the warmth or frozenness which is within ourselves. The true seasons blossom

or wilt not in fixed order but so that many of them may pass in a
few weeks or hours whereas sometimes a whole life passes and the
season remains of a piece from one end to the other.

The world is largest in the American summer, for Williams and Stevens, even as it was for their forefather, Emerson. *Spring and All* celebrates not this world but the more difficult American skepticism of a hard spring, imperishably rendered in its magnificent opening lyric, "By the road to the contagious hospital," with its harsh splendor of inception, at once of vegetation, infants, and of Whitmanian or American poems:

Lifeless in appearance, sluggish
dazed spring approaches—

They enter the new world naked,
cold, uncertain of all
save that they enter. All about them
the cold, familiar wind—

Now the grass, tomorrow
the stiff curl of wildcarrot leaf

One by one objects are defined—
It quickens: clarity, outline of leaf

But now the stark dignity of
entrance—Still, the profound change
has come upon them: rooted, they
grip down and begin to awaken

The ancient fiction of the leaves, a continuous tradition from Homer and Virgil, through Dante and on to Spenser and Milton, Shelley and Whitman, receives one culmination in Stevens, and a very different apotheosis here in Williams. In the prose of *Spring and All*, Williams protests too emphatically that "THE WORLD IS NEW," a protest that has been taken too much at its own self-mystifying evaluation by the most distinguished of the deconstructive critics of Williams, J. Hillis Miller and the late Joseph Riddel. But when the best poems in *Spring and All* unfold themselves, the reader can be persuaded that Williams has invented freshly the accurate metaphors for our American sense of imaginative belatedness: "There is / an approach with difficulty from / the dead—," and "The rose is obsolete / but each petal ends in / an edge." Except for "By the road to the contagious hospital," the best poems in *Spring and All* are the justly famous ones: "The pure products of America / go crazy—," and "so much depends / upon / a red wheel / barrow."

More problematical are *The Great American Novel* and *The Descent of Winter*, pugnacious assaults upon Williams's own formal limits, yet assaults masked as ironies directed against the literary conventionalities of others. I prefer *The Descent of Winter*, where the authentic anxiety of belatedness, the only legitimate point of origin for any American literature, is expressed in relation to that most impossible of all influences, Shakespeare:

> By writing he escaped from the world into the natural world of his mind. The unemployable world of his fine head was unnaturally useless in the gross exterior of his day—or any day. By writing he made this active. He melted himself into that grossness, and colored it with his powers. The proof that he was right and they passing, being that he continues always and naturally while their artificiality destroyed them. A man unable to employ himself in his world.
>
> Therefore his seriousness and his accuracies, because it was not his play but the drama of his life. It is his anonymity that is baffling to nitwits and so they want to find an involved explanation—to defeat the plainness of the evidence.
>
> When he speaks of fools he is one; when of kings he is one, doubly so in misfortune.
>
> He is a woman, a pimp, a prince Hal—
>
> Such a man is a prime borrower and standardizer—No inventor. He lives because he sinks back, does not go forward, sinks back into the mass—
>
> He is Hamlet plainer than a theory—and in everything.
>
> You can't buy a life again after it's gone, that's the way I mean.
>
> He drinks awful bad and he beat me up every single month while I was carrying this baby, pretty nearly every week.

As an overview of Shakespeare, this is unquestionably the weakest commentary available since Tolstoy; but as a representation of Williams's dilemmas, it has a curious force, including the weird parody of Heming-way's agonistic stance in the last sentence I have just quoted. Despite his army of hyperbolic exegetes, Williams's nakedness in relation to the literary past is not so much that of "a new world naked" as it is that of a no longer so very new world awkwardly wrapped round by too many fine rags.

The best lyrics and Book I of *Paterson* are of a higher order, though they also betray darker anxieties of influence than even Williams's defiances dared to confront. They display also another kind of agon, the anxiety as to contemporary rivals, not so much Pound and Eliot as Wallace Stevens and Hart Crane, heirs to Keats and to Whitman, even as Williams was. No two readers are likely to agree upon just which shorter poems by Williams are his strongest, but the one that impresses and moves me most is "A Unison," where the title seems to comprehend most of the dictionary meanings of "unison": an identity of pitch in music; the same words spoken simulta-neously by two or more speakers; musical parts combined in octaves; a concord, agreement, harmony. Thomas R. Whitaker, one of Williams's best and most sympathetic critics but no idolator, gives the best introduction to "A Unison":

> It is like an improvisation from *Kora in Hell*—but one with the quiet maturity of vision and movement that some three decades have brought. . . . As the implicit analogies and contrasts accumulate, we discover (long before the speaker tells us) that we are attending a "unison and a dance." This "death's festival"—*memento mori* and celebration of the *"Undying"*—evades neither the mystery of transience nor that of organic continuance, though neither can be "parsed" by the analytical mind. . . . In this composed testament of acceptance, Williams's saxifrage ("through metaphor to reconcile / the people and the stones") quietly does its work. . . . Not since Wordsworth has this natural piety been rendered so freshly and poignantly.

I would not wish to quarrel with Whitaker's judgment, yet there is very little Wordsworth and (inevitably) much Whitman and considerable Keats in "A Unison." Indeed, the poem opens with what must be called an echo from Whitman, in what I assume was a controlled allusion:

The grass is very green, my friend,
And tousled, like the head of—
your grandson, yes?

We hear one of the uncanniest passages in Whitman, from "Song of Myself" 6:

This grass is very dark to be from the white heads of old mothers,
Darker than the colorless beards of old men,
Dark to come from under the faint red roofs of mouths.

Whitman's great fantasia answers a child's question: *"What is the grass?"* As an Epicurean materialist, Whitman believed that the *what* was unknowable, but his remarkable troping on the grass takes a grand turn after his Homeric line: "And now it seems to me the beautiful uncut hair of graves." Williams simply borrows the trope, and even his "very green" merely follows Whitman's hint that a "very green" becomes a "very dark" color, in the shadow of mortality. "A Unison" insists upon:

—what cannot be escaped: the
mountain riding the afternoon as
it does, the grass matted green,
green underfoot and the air—
rotten wood. *Hear! Hear them!*
the Undying. The hill slopes away,
then rises in the middleground,
you remember, with a grove of gnarled
maples centering the bare pasture,
sacred, surely—for what reason?

Williams does not know whether he can or cannot say the reason, but the allusion is to Keats's characteristic, Saturnian shrine in "Hyperion." For Williams it is "a shrine cinctured there by / the trees," the girdling effect suggested by the natural sculpture of Keats's shrine. Where Keats as the quester in "The Fall of Hyperion" pledges "all the mortals of the world, / And all the dead whose names are in our lips," and where Whitman insists, "The smallest sprout shows there is really no death," Williams neither salutes the living and the dead nor folds the two into a single figuration. Rather, he *hears* and urges us to *"Hear the unison of their voices. . . ."* How are we to interpret such an imaginative gesture? Are we hearing more, or enough more, than the unison of the voices of John Keats and Walt Whitman? Devoted Williamsites doubtless would reject the question, but it always retains its force, nevertheless. It is not less true of *The Waste Land* than it is of Williams. Eliot revises Whitman's "When Lilacs Last in the Dooryard Bloom'd" by fusing it with Tennyson (among others, but prime among those others). Image of voice or the trope of poetic identity then becomes a central problem.

Whitman once contrasted himself to Keats by rejecting "negative capability" and insisting instead that the great poet gave us the "powerful press of himself." Admirable as *Paterson* is (particularly its first book), does even it resolve the antithesis in Williams between his "objectivism" or negative capability and his own agonistic, powerful press of himself? Mariani ends his vast, idealizing biography by asserting that Williams established "an American poetic based on a new measure and a primary regard for the living, protean shape of the language as it was actually used." Hillis Miller, even more generously, tells us that Williams gave us a concept of poetry transcending both Homer and Wordsworth, both Aristotle and Coleridge:

> The word is given reality by the fact it names, but the independence of the fact from the word frees the word to be a fact in its own right and at the same time "dynamizes" it with meaning. The word can then carry the facts named in a new form into the realm of imagination.

Mariani and Miller are quite sober compared to more apocalyptic Williamsites. Not even Whitman gave us "a new measure," and not Shakespeare himself freed a single word "to be a fact in its own right." William Carlos Williams was, at his best, a strong American poet, far better than his hordes of imitators. Like Ezra Pound's, Williams's remains a fairly problematical achievement in the traditions of American poetry. Some generations hence, it will become clear whether his critics have canonized him permanently or subverted him by taking him too much at his own intentions. For now he abides, a live influence, and perhaps with even more fame to come.

Marianne Moore
(1887–1972)

For Plato the only reality that mattered is exemplified best for us in the principles of mathematics. The aim of our lives should be to draw ourselves away as much as possible from the unsubstantial, fluctuating facts of the world about us and establish some communion with the objects which are apprehended by thought and not sense. This was the source of Plato's asceticism. To the extent that Miss Moore finds only allusion tolerable she shares that asceticism. While she shares it she does so only as it may be necessary for her to do so in order to establish a particular reality or, better, a reality of her own particulars.

—WALLACE STEVENS

ALLUSION WAS Marianne Moore's method, a method that was herself. One of the most American of all poets, she was fecund in her progeny—Elizabeth Bishop, May Swenson, and Richard Wilbur being the most gifted among them. Her own American precursors were not Emily Dickinson and Walt Whitman—still our two greatest poets—but the much slighter Stephen Crane, who is echoed in her earliest poems, and in an oblique way Edgar Poe, whom she parodied. I suspect that her nearest poetic father, in English, was Thomas Hardy, who seems to have taught her lessons in the mastery of incongruity and whose secularized version of biblical irony is not far from her own. If we compare her with her major poetic contemporaries—Frost, Stevens, Eliot, Pound, Williams, Aiken, Ransom, Cummings, H. D., Hart Crane—she is clearly the most original American poet of her era, though not quite of the eminence of Frost, Stevens, Crane. A curious kind of devotional poet, with some authentic affinities to George Herbert, she reminds us implicitly but constantly that any distinction between sacred and secular poetry is only a shibboleth of cultural politics. Some day she will remind us also of what current cultural politics obscure: that any distinction between poetry written by women or poetry by men is a mere polemic, unless it follows upon an initial distinction between good and bad poetry. Moore, like Bishop and Swenson, is an extraordinary poet-as-poet. The issue of how gender enters into her vision should arise only after the aesthetic achievement is judged as such.

Moore, as all her readers know, to their lasting delight, is the visionary of natural creatures: the jerboa, frigate pelican, buffalo, monkeys, fish, snakes, mongooses, the octopus (actually a trope for a mountain), snail, peacock, whale, pangolin, wood-weasel, elephants, racehorses, chameleon, jellyfish, arctic ox (or goat), giraffe, blue bug (another trope, this time for a pony), all of La Fontaine's bestiary, not to mention sea and land unicorns, basilisks, and all the weird fabulous roster that perhaps only Borges also, among crucial modern writers, celebrates so consistently. There is something of Blake and of the Christopher Smart of "Jubilate Agno" in Moore, though the affinity does not result from influence but rather is the consequence of election. Moore's famous eye, like that of Bishop after her, is not so much a visual gift as it is visionary, for the beasts in her poems are charged with a spiritual intensity that doubtless they possess, but which I myself cannot see without the aid of Blake, Smart, and Moore.

I remember always in reading Moore again that her favorite poem was the Book of Job. Just as I cannot read Ecclesiastes without thinking of Dr. Johnson, I cannot read certain passages in Job without recalling Marianne Moore:

> But ask now the beasts, and they shall teach thee; and the fowls
>   of the air, and they shall tell thee:
> Or speak to the earth, and it shall teach thee: and the fishes
>   of the sea shall declare unto thee.
> Who knoweth not in all these that the hand of the Lord hath
>   wrought this?
> In whose hand is the soul of every living thing.

This, from chapter 12, is the prelude to the great chant of Yahweh, the Voice out of the whirlwind that sounds forth in the frightening magnificence of chapters 38 through 41, where the grand procession of beasts comprehends lions, ravens, wild goats, the wild ass, the unicorn, peacocks, the ostrich, the sublime battle-horse who "saith among the trumpets, Ha, ha," the hawk, the eagle, and at last behemoth and leviathan. Gorgeously celebrating his own creation, Yahweh through the poet of Job engendered another strong poet in Marianne Moore. Of the Book of Job, she remarked that its agony was veracious and its fidelity of a force "that contrives glory for ashes."

"Glory for ashes" might be called Moore's ethical motto, the basis for the drive of her poetic will toward a reality of her own particulars. Her poetry, as befitted the translator of La Fontaine and the heir of George Herbert, would be in some danger of dwindling into moral essays, an impossible form for our time, were it not for her wild allusiveness, her zest for quotations, and her essentially anarchic stance, the American and Emersonian insistence upon seeing everything in her own way, with "conscientious inconsistency." When her wildness or freedom subsided, she produced an occasional poetic disaster like the patriotic war poems "In Distrust of Merits" and "'Keeping Their World Large.'" But her greatest poems are at just the opposite edge of consciousness: "A Grave," "Novices," "Marriage," "An Octopus," "He 'Digesteth Harde Yron,'" "Elephants," the deceptively light "Tom Fool at Jamaica."

Those seven poems by themselves have an idiosyncratic splendor that restores my faith, as a critic, in what the language of the poets truly is: diction, or choice of words, playing endlessly upon the dialectic of denotation and connotation. The play of diction, or the poet's will over language, is itself constituted by the endless interchanges of denotation and connotation.

> Marriage, through which thought does not penetrate, appeared to Miss Moore a legitimate object for art, an art that would not halt from using thought about it, however, as it might want to. Against marriage, "this institution, perhaps one should say enterprise"—Miss Moore launched her thought not to have it appear arsenaled as in a textbook on psychology, but to stay among apples and giraffes in a poem.
>
> —WILLIAM CARLOS WILLIAMS

If I had to cite a single poem by Moore as representing all of her powers working together, it would be "Marriage" (1923), superficially an outrageous collage but profoundly a poignant comic critique of every society's most sacred and tragic institution. As several critics have ventured, this is Moore's *The Waste Land*, a mosaic of fragments from Francis Bacon, the *Scientific American*, Baxter's *The Saint's Everlasting Rest*, Hazlitt on Burke, William Godwin, Trollope, *The Tempest*, a book on *The Syrian*

Christ, the Bible, Ezra Pound, and even Daniel Webster (from an inscrip-
tion on a statue!), and twenty sources more. Yet it is a poem, and perhaps
is more ruggedly unified than any other poem of such ambition by Moore.

The poet's own headnote to "Marriage" could not be more diffident:
"Statements that took my fancy which I tried to arrange plausibly." The
arrangement is more than plausible; it is quite persuasive, though it begins
with a parody of the societal *apologia* for marriage:

> This institution,
> perhaps one should say enterprise
> out of respect for which
> one says one need not change one's mind
> about a thing one has believed in,
> requiring public promises
> of one's intention
> to fulfil a private obligation.

No one, I believe, could interpret that opening stance with any exacti-
tude. The substitution of "enterprise" for "institution" qualifies the wryness
of "public promises / of one's intention / to fulfil a private obligation," but
adds a note both of commerce and of the human virtue of taking an ini-
tiative. Who could have anticipated that the next movement of the poem
would be this?

> I wonder what Adam and Eve
> think of it by this time,
> this fire-gilt steel
> alive with goldenness;
> how bright it shows—
> "of circular traditions and impostures,
> committing many spoils,"
> requiring all one's criminal ingenuity
> to avoid!

Like nearly every other quotation in this poem, the two lines from Sir
Francis Bacon gain nothing for Moore's own text by being restored to their
own context. Steel burned by fire does not exactly brighten into a golden
bough, so the "gilt" is there partly as anticipation of "criminal ingenuity."

Yet "gilt" is in cognitive sequence with "goldenness" and "bright," even if we rightly expect to behold blackened steel. All who have known marriage (as Moore declined to do) will register an unhappy shudder at the force the Baconian phrases take on when Moore appropriates them. Traditions as treasons become circular, and together with impostures can be read here either as performing many despoilments or as investing many gains of previous despoilments. Either way, it might seem as though an ingenuity avoiding this equivocal enterprise could only be taken as criminal by some dogmatist, whether societal or theological.

The poem proceeds to dismiss psychology, since to explain everything is to explain nothing, and then meditates upon the beauty, talents, and contrariness of Eve, a meditation that suddenly achieves Paterian intensity:

> Below the incandescent stars
> below the incandescent fruit,
> the strange experience of beauty;
> its existence is too much;
> it tears one to pieces
> and each fresh wave of consciousness
> is poison.

The detachment of Moore as watcher is not totally lost but seems (by design) never fully recovered again in the poem. A woman's fine bitterness against the West's endless assault upon Eve is felt in Moore's description of the universal mother as "the central flaw" in the experiment of Eden, itself "an interesting impossibility" ecstatically described by Richard Baxter as "the choicest piece of my life." If Baxter's ecstasy (though not his eloquence) is qualified shrewdly by Moore's contextualizations, Eden is nowhere near so scaled down by her as is Adam, whose male pomp is altogether undermined. He is pretty well identified with Satan, and like Satan is "alive with words, / vibrating like a cymbal / touched before it has been struck."

Moore's genius at her method allows her the joy of exemplifying her borrowings even as she employs them in a corrective polemic against male slanderings of women:

> "Treading chasms
> on the uncertain footing of a spear,"
> forgetting that there is in woman

a quality of mind
which as an instinctive manifestation
is unsafe,
he goes on speaking
in a formal customary strain.

In the first quotation, Hazlitt is praising his precursor Edmund Burke for a paradoxically certain footing: for power, energy, truth set forth in the Sublime style. Burke is a chasm-treader, sure-footed as he edges near the abyss. But men less given to truth than Burke have very uncertain footing indeed, whether they forget or remember their characteristic brutalities in regard to a woman's "quality of mind." The poem's "he" therefore goes on speaking of marriage in Richard Baxter's ecstatic terms, as though marriage itself somehow could become "the saints' everlasting rest." Fatuously joyous, the male is ready to suffer the most exquisite passage in the poem, and perhaps in all of Moore:

Plagued by the nightingale
in the new leaves,
with its silence—
not its silence but its silences,
he says of it:
"It clothes me with a shirt of fire."
"He dares not clap his hands
to make it go on
lest it should fly off;
if he does nothing, it will sleep;
if he cries out, it will not understand."
Unnerved by the nightingale
and dazzled by the apple,
impelled by "the illusion of a fire
effectual to extinguish fire,"
compared with which
the shining of the earth
is but deformity—a fire
"as high as deep
as bright as broad

as long as life itself,"
he stumbles over marriage,
"a very trivial object indeed"
to have destroyed the attitude
in which he stood—.

I hardly know of a more unnerving representation of the male fear and
distrust of the female, uncannily combined with the male quandary of
being obsessed with, fascinated by, not only the female but the enterprise
of marriage as well. Moore imperishably catches the masterpiece of male
emotive ambivalence toward the female, which is the male identification
of woman and the taboo. Here the nightingale, perhaps by way of Keats's
erotic allusions, becomes an emblem of the female, while the male speaker,
ravished by the silences of the emblem, becomes Hercules suicidally aflame
with the shirt of Nessus. The poor male, "unnerved by the nightingale /
and dazzled by the apple," stumbles over the enterprise that is Adam's
experiment, marriage:

its fiddlehead ferns,
lotus flowers, opuntias, white dromedaries,
its hippopotamus—
nose and mouth combined
in one magnificent hopper—
its snake and the potent apple.

We again receive what might be called Moore's Paradox: marriage, considered from either the male or female perspective, is a dreadful disaster,
but as a poetic trope gorgeously shines forth its barbaric splendors. The
male, quoting Trollope's *Barchester Towers*, returns us to the image of
Hercules and commends marriage "as a fine art, as an experiment, / a duty
or as merely recreation." I myself will never get out of my memory Moore's
subsequent deadpan definition of marriage as "the fight to be affectionate."
With a fine impartiality, the poet has a vision of the agonists in this eternal
dispute:

The blue panther with black eyes,
the basalt panther with blue eyes,

entirely graceful—
one must give them the path—.

But this mutual splendor abates quickly, and a rancorous humor emerges:

He says, "What monarch would not blush
to have a wife
with hair like a shaving brush?"
The fact of woman
is "not the sound of the flute
but very poison."
She says, "Men are monopolists
of 'stars, garters, buttons
and other shining baubles'—
unfit to be the guardians
of another person's happiness."
He says, "These mummies
must be handled carefully—
'the crumbs from a lion's meal,
a couple of shins and the bit of an ear';
turn to the letter M
and you will find
that 'a wife is a coffin.'"

This marvelous exchange of diatribes is weirdly stitched together from outrageously heterogeneous "sources," ranging from a parody of *The Rape of the Lock* (in which Moore herself took a hand) to a women's college president's denunciation of the male love of awards and medals on to a surprising misappropriation of a great moment in the prophet Amos, which is then juxtaposed to a brutal remark of Ezra Pound's. Amos associates the lion with Yahweh:

The lion hath roared, who will not fear? the Lord GOD hath spoken, who can but prophesy?
    Thus saith the LORD; As the shepherd taketh out of the mouth of the lion two legs, or a piece of an ear; so shall the children of Israel be taken out that dwell in Samaria in the corner of a bed, and in Damascus in a couch.

Moore slyly revises the roaring prophet, making the lion every male, and the children of Israel every woman. Pound's dictum that "a wife is a coffin" is presumably placed under the letter *M* for "male," and sorts well with Moore's unfair but strong revision of Amos, since the revision suggests that a wife is a corpse. In order to show that her revisionary zeal is savagely if suavely directed against both sexes (or rather their common frailties), Moore proceeds to dissect the narcissism of men and women alike, until she concludes with the most ironic of her visions in the poem:

> "I am such a cow,
> if I had a sorrow
> I should feel it a long time;
> I am not one of those
> who have a great sorrow
> in the morning
> and a great joy at noon";

> which says: "I have encountered it
> among those unpretentious
> protégés of wisdom,
> where seeming to parade
> as the debater and the Roman,
> the statesmanship
> of an archaic Daniel Webster
> persists to their simplicity of temper
> as the essence of the matter:

> 'Liberty and union
> now and forever';

> the Book on the writing-table;
> the hand in the breast-pocket."

Webster, hardly unpretentious, and wise only in his political cunning, is indeed the message inscribed upon his statue: "Liberty and union / now and forever." As a judgment upon marriage, it would be a hilarious irony, if we did not wince so much under Moore's not wholly benign tutelage. That "Book on the writing table," presumably the Bible, is precisely like

Webster's hand in the breast pocket, an equivocal emblem, in this context, of the societal benediction upon marriage. Moore's own *Waste Land*, "Marriage," may outlast Eliot's poem as a permanent vision of the West in its long, ironic decline.

T. S. Eliot

(1888–1965)

E LIOT HAS BEEN lacquered over by hagiographical exegesis, by the proponents of the myth of the Great Western Butterslide, as my late friend and former mentor Northrop Frye memorably termed it. For acolytes like Allen Tate and Cleanth Brooks, Helen Gardner and even Frank Kermode, a much more considerable figure, Eliot was the prophet who proclaimed the onetime existence of a great blob of classical and Christian butter that started to melt in the later seventeenth century, slid down Enlightenment and Romantic slopes, and at last superbly congealed in *The Waste Land*.

As a young scholar-critic in the period 1957–77, I was a Romantic Revivalist, furiously battling to restore many great writers to the canon: Spenser, Milton, Blake, Shelley, Browning, Tennyson, Emerson, Whitman, Thomas Carlyle, Ruskin, Pater, Wilde, Swinburne, Lawrence, Stevens, Hart Crane, and others. Many if not most of these had been exiled by Eliot and his churchwardens. When I was a child, my ear had been ravished by Eliot's poetry, but his criticism—literary and cultural—dismayed me. In my old age I have calmed down: my warfare is accomplished, my grudge ebbing with the ocean of life. The prose Eliot still displeases me; I have just read through three enormous volumes of his letters and my ancient fury almost revives. His scorn for Emerson is so ill-informed that some personal bias has to be noted in it.

With some poets, Shelley and Whitman particularly, sorrows of family romance activate Eliot's defensiveness. Shakespeare, everyone's resource, had a mixed effect upon Eliot: he preferred—he said—*Coriolanus* to *Hamlet*, a weirdness unworthy of refutation, and he echoed Shakespeare both overtly and involuntarily, a general phenomenon. At his best, early and late, Eliot's incantatory style achieves a difficult rightness that only Hart Crane could transume, to very different purposes. Allen Tate, whose poems blended Eliot and Tate's close friend Crane, told me at one of our several uneasy meetings that "Hart's problem was the impossible project of extending Walt Whitman's stance in Eliotic cadences." I recall murmuring that the result was not problematic but triumphant, as Eliot may have concluded when Crane published "The Tunnel," the descent into Avernus in *The Bridge*.

Dickinson and Whitman, of all Americans, most engaged death and dying as adventures in consciousness. Eliot joins this engagement from the early "Death of Saint Narcissus" onward and achieves final splendor in "The Dry Salvages" of *Four Quartets*, where the dark wisdom of Whitman and Mark Twain, enhanced by Hart Crane, merges with Indic traditions, of which the creator of *The Waste Land* was an erudite scholar.

Eliot, with deep knowledge of the original, was immersed in the *Bhagavad Gita*, as Emerson and Thoreau were. Whitman was not (if we are to believe him), though Thoreau and Emerson wondered otherwise. I am haunted by the shade of the great Gershom Scholem, who urged me to associate Walt with Kabbalah, of which the poet had no knowledge. Capacious Whitman intuitively contains traditions he never overtly studied.

The seer of "Passage to India" connected his daemon or real Me to the cosmos. Illuminated from the start, he did not need to quest for release. Emersonian idealism was rejected by Whitman in favor of Lucretian materialism, itself not compatible with Indian speculations. And yet Walt, unlike a consistent Epicurean, sings loss in and to the self. Without having read the *Gita*, Whitman discovered its discipline in himself. The activity of mourning in his elegies moves away from dark inertia to enlightened renunciation of any fruit of sorrow except the poem itself. Immortality departs from literal survival to being joined together with the memory of other selves, with the hope of being included in their memories.

The *Gita* is a severe poem, once compared to Dante by Eliot. Possessing no Sanskrit, I rely most on the spirited version by Barbara Stoler Miller (1986). Certainly it seems far more Eliotic than Whitmanian, since "Song of Myself" and the "Calamus" poems move toward merging Walt and the cosmos by and through sexual exuberance. And yet Eliot discerned that Whitman more profoundly quested for the tally, an image of voice conferred only by a daemonic surrender to a larger sense of death, whose outlet song emerges from the mockingbird in "Out of the Cradle Endlessly Rocking" and the hermit thrush in "When Lilacs Last in the Dooryard Bloom'd." *The Waste Land* owes its hermit thrush to Whitman, as Eliot was slow to acknowledge, for the good reason that its debts are so great as to jeopardize the originality of the Eliotic masterwork. Walt is the daemon of *The Waste Land*, the corpse planted in its forsaken garden.

Eliot's elegiac tonalities are his peculiar strength and account for much of the beauty of his cadences. His long palaver as to his supposed precursors embraced Dante, Baudelaire, Jules Laforgue, Tristan Corbière, Pound, various metaphysicals and Jacobeans, anyone but Shelley, Tennyson, and Whitman, the actual forerunners. Daemonic possession by the poetic voices of Shelley, Whitman, and Tennyson was an endless danger for Eliot, early and late. Vulnerable to the poetics of loss, he recognized masters of regret in Whitman and in Tennyson. "My heart is a handful of dust" is Tennyson's trope in *Maud*, and the corpse planted last year in the garden was buried first in Walt Whitman's "This Compost."

Eliot's Arthur Henry Hallam, a young critic dead at twenty-one whom Tennyson loved, was Jean Verdenal: his version of Whitman's Winter Comrade of the "Calamus" poems, another "awful daring of a moment's surrender, / Which an age of prudence can never retract." That frankly dubious observation makes sense to me only in that Tennyson, Whitman, and Eliot all had androgynous imaginations. The greatest instance of that fecund faculty is William Shakespeare. Tiresias, the Oedipal seer who suffered sexual experience both as woman and as man, is appropriate as a figure for poets and poetry in Tennyson and in Eliot.

Eugene O'Neill

(1888–1953)

IT IS AN INEVITABLE oddity that the principal American dramatist to date should have no American precursors. Eugene O'Neill's art as a playwright owes most to Strindberg's, and something crucial, though rather less, to Ibsen's. Intellectually, O'Neill's ancestry also has little to do with American tradition, with Emerson or William James or any other of our cultural speculators. Schopenhauer, Nietzsche, and Freud formed O'Neill's sense of what little was possible for any of us. Even where American literary tradition was strongest, in the novel and poetry, it did not much affect O'Neill. His novelists were Zola and Conrad; his poets were Dante Gabriel Rossetti and Swinburne. Overwhelmingly an Irish American, with his Jansenist Catholicism transformed into anger at God, he had little active interest in the greatest American writer, Whitman, though his spiritual darkness has a curious, antithetical relation to Whitman's overt analysis of our national character.

Yet O'Neill, despite his many limitations, is the most American of our handful of dramatists who matter most: Williams, Miller, Wilder, Albee, Kushner, perhaps Mamet and Shepard. A national quality that is literary, yet has no clear relation to our domestic literary traditions, is nearly always present in O'Neill's strongest works. We can recognize Hawthorne in Henry James, and Whitman (however repressed) in T. S. Eliot, while the relation of Hemingway and Faulkner to Mark Twain is just as evident as their debt to Conrad. Besides the question of his genre (since there was no vital American drama before O'Neill), there would seem to be some hidden factor that governed O'Neill's ambiguous relation to our literary past. It was certainly not the lack of critical discernment on O'Neill's part. His admiration for Hart Crane's poetry, at its most difficult, was solely responsible for the publication of Crane's first volume, *White Buildings*, for which O'Neill initially offered to write the introduction, withdrawing in favor of Allen Tate when the impossibility of his writing a critical essay on Crane's complexities became clear to O'Neill. But to have recognized Hart Crane's genius, so early and so helpfully, testifies to O'Neill's profound insights into the American literary imagination at its strongest.

The dramatist whose masterpieces are *The Iceman Cometh* and *Long Day's Journey into Night*, and, in a class just short of those, *A Moon for the Misbegotten* and *A Touch of the Poet*, is not exactly to be regarded as a celebrator of the possibilities of American life. The central strain in our literature remains Emersonian, from Whitman to our contemporaries like Saul Bellow and John Ashbery. Even the tradition that reacted against Emerson—from Poe, Hawthorne, and Melville through Gnostics of the abyss like Nathanael West and Thomas Pynchon—remains always alert to transcendental and extraordinary American possibilities. The late Robert Penn Warren must be the most overtly anti-Emersonian partisan in our history, yet even Warren sought an American Sublime in his poetry. O'Neill would appear to be the most non-Emersonian author of any eminence in our literature. Irish American through and through, with a heroic resentment of the New England Yankee tradition, O'Neill from the start seemed to know that his spiritual quest was to undermine Emerson's American religion of self-reliance.

O'Neill's own Irish Jansenism is curiously akin to the New England Puritanism he opposed, but that only increased the rancor of his powerful polemic in *Desire Under the Elms, Mourning Becomes Electra*, and *More Stately Mansions*. The Will to Live is set against New England Puritanism in what O'Neill himself once called "the battle of moral forces in the New England scene" to which he said he felt closest as an artist. But since this is Schopenhauer's rapacious Will to Live, and not Bernard Shaw's genial revision of that Will into the Life Force of a benign Creative Evolution, O'Neill is in the terrible position of opposing one death drive with another. Only the inescapable Strindberg comes to mind as a visionary quite as negative as O'Neill, so that *The Iceman Cometh* might as well have been called *The Dance of Death*, and *Long Day's Journey into Night* could be retitled *The Ghost Sonata*. O'Neill's most powerful self-representations—as Edmund in *Long Day's Journey* and Larry Slade in *Iceman*—are astonishingly negative identifications, particularly in an American context.

Edmund and Slade do not long for death in the mode of Whitman and his descendants—Wallace Stevens, T. S. Eliot, Hart Crane, and Theodore Roethke—all of whom tend to incorporate the image of a desired death into the great, triple trope of night, the mother, and the sea. Edmund Tyrone and Larry Slade long to die because life without transcendence is impossible, and yet transcendence is totally unavailable. O'Neill's true polemic against his country and its spiritual tradition is not, as he insisted, that "its main idea is that everlasting game of trying to possess your own soul by the possession of something outside it." Though uttered in 1946, in remarks before the first performance of *The Iceman Cometh*, such a reflection is banal and represents a weak misreading of *The Iceman Cometh*. The play's true argument is that your own soul cannot be possessed, whether by possessing something or someone outside it, or by joining yourself to a transcendental possibility, to whatever version of an Emersonian Oversoul that you might prefer. The United States, in O'Neill's dark view, was uniquely the country that had refused to learn the truths of the spirit, which are that good and the means of good, love and the means of love, are irreconcilable. Such a formulation is Shelleyan and reminds one of O'Neill's High Romantic inheritance, which reached him through pre-Raphaelite poetry and literary speculation. O'Neill seems a strange instance of the Aestheticism of Rossetti and Pater, but his metaphysical nihilism, desperate faith in art, and phantasmagoric naturalism stem directly from them. When Jamie Tyrone quotes from Rossetti's "Willowwood" sonnets, he gives the epigraph not only to *Long Day's Journey* but to all of O'Neill: "Look into my face. My name is Might-Have-Been; / I am also called No More, Too Late, Farewell." In O'Neill's deepest polemic, the lines are quoted by, and for, all Americans of imagination whatsoever.

By common consent, *Long Day's Journey into Night* is Eugene O'Neill's masterpiece. Since O'Neill, rather than Williams or Miller, Wilder or Albee, is recognized as our leading dramatist, *Long Day's Journey* must be the best play in our more than two centuries as a nation. One rereads it therefore with awe and a certain apprehension, but with considerable puzzlement also. Strong work it certainly is, and twice I have been moved by watching it well directed and well performed. Yet how can this be the best stage play that an exuberantly dramatic people has produced? Is it equal to the best of our imaginative literature? Can we read it in the company of *The Scarlet Letter* and *Moby-Dick*, *The Adventures of Huckleberry Finn* and *The Portrait of a Lady*, *As I Lay Dying* and *Gravity's Rainbow*? Does it have the aesthetic distinction of our greatest poets, of Whitman, Dickinson, Frost, Stevens, Eliot, Hart Crane, Elizabeth Bishop, and John Ashbery? Can it stand intellectually with the crucial essays of Emerson and of William James?

These questions, alas, are self-answering. O'Neill's limitations are obvious and need not be surveyed intensively. Perhaps no major dramatist has ever been so lacking in rhetorical exuberance, in what Yeats once praised Blake for having: "beautiful, laughing speech." O'Neill's convictions were deeply held but were in no way remarkable, except for their incessant sullenness. It is embarrassing when O'Neill's exegetes attempt to expound his ideas, whether about his country, his own work, or the human condition. When one of them speaks of "two kinds of nonverbal, tangential poetry in *Long Day's Journey into Night*" as the characters' longing "for a mystical union of sorts," and the influence of the setting, I am compelled to reflect that insofar as O'Neill's art is nonverbal it must also be nonexistent.

My reflection, however, is inaccurate, and O'Neill's dramatic art is considerable, though it does make us revise our notions of just how strictly literary an art drama necessarily has to be. Sophocles, Shakespeare, and Molière are masters alike of language and of a mimetic force that works through gestures that supplement language, but O'Neill is mastered by language and relies instead upon a drive-toward-staging that he appears to have learned from Strindberg. Consider the close of *Long Day's Journey*. How much of the power comes from what Tyrone and Mary say, and how much from the extraordinarily effective stage directions?

Critics have remarked on how fine it is that the three alcoholic Tyrone males slowly lower their drinks to the table, forgetting them, as the morphine-laden wife and mother begins to speak. One can go further; her banal if moving address to herself, and Tyrone's petulant outbursts, are considerably less eloquent than the stage directions. I had not remembered anything that was spoken, returning to the text after a decade, but I had held on to that grim family tableau of the three Tyrones slowly lowering their glasses. Again, I had remembered nothing actually said between Edmund and his mother at the end of Act I, but the gestures and glances between them always abide with me, and Mary's reactions when she is left alone compel in me the Nietzschean realization that the truly memorable is always associated with what is most painful.

That grim ballet of looks between mother and son, followed by the terrible, compulsive drumming of her long fingers, has a lyric force that only the verse quotations from Baudelaire, Swinburne, and others in O'Neill's text are able to match. Certainly a singular dramatic genius is always at work in O'Neill's stage directions and can be felt also, most fortunately, in the repressed intensities of inarticulateness in all of the Tyrones.

It seems to me a marvel that this can suffice, and in itself probably it could not. But there is also O'Neill's greatest gift, more strongly present in *Long Day's Journey* than it is even in *The Iceman Cometh*. Lionel Trilling, subtly and less equivocally than it seemed, once famously praised Theodore Dreiser for his mixed but imposing representation of "reality in America" in his best novels, *Sister Carrie* and *An American Tragedy*. One cannot deny the power of the mimetic art of *Long Day's Journey into Night*. No dramatist to this day, among us, has matched O'Neill in depicting the nightmare realities that can afflict American family life, indeed family life in the twentieth-century Western world. And yet that is the authentic subject of our dramatists who matter most after O'Neill: Williams, Miller, Albee, with the genial Thornton Wilder as the grand exception. It is a terrifying distinction that O'Neill earns, and more decisively in *Long Day's Journey into Night* than anywhere else. He is the elegist of the Freudian "family romance," of the domestic tragedy of which we all die daily, a little bit at a time. The helplessness of family love to sustain, let alone heal, the wounds of marriage, of parenthood, and of sonship have never been so remorselessly and so pathetically portrayed, and with a force of gesture too painful ever to be forgotten by any of us.

Like its great precursor play, Strindberg's *The Dance of Death*, O'Neill's *The Iceman Cometh* must be one of the most remorseless of what purport to be tragic dramas since the Greeks and the Jacobeans. Whatever tragedy meant to the incredibly harsh Strindberg, to O'Neill it had to possess a "transfiguring nobility," presumably that of the artist like O'Neill himself in his relation to his time and his country, of which he observed that "we are tragedy, the most appalling yet written or unwritten." O'Neill's strength was never conceptual, and so we are not likely to render his stances into a single coherent view of tragedy.

Whitman could say that "these States are themselves the greatest poem," and we know what he meant, but I do not know how to read O'Neill's "we are tragedy." When I suffer through *The New York Times* every morning, am I reading tragedy? Does *The Iceman Cometh* manifest a "transfiguring nobility"? How could it? Are Larry Slade in *Iceman* or Edmund Tyrone in *Long Day's Journey into Night*, both clearly O'Neill's surrogates, either of them tragic in relation to his time and country? Or to ask all this in a single question: Are the crippling sorrows of what Freud called "family romances" tragic or are they not primarily instances of strong pathos, reductive processes that cannot, by definition, manifest an authentic "transfiguring nobility"?

I think that we need to ignore O'Neill on tragedy if we are to learn to watch and read *The Iceman Cometh* for the dramatic values it certainly possesses. Its principal limitation, I suspect, stems from its tendentious assumption that "we are tragedy," that "these States" have become the "most appalling" of tragedies. Had O'Neill survived into the Age of Reagan, and observed the phalanxes of yuppies on the march, doubtless he would have been even more appalled. And what would he have made of Silicon Valley's corporate campuses? But societies are not dramas, and O'Neill was not Jeremiah the prophet. His strength was neither in stance nor style but in the dramatic representation of illusions and despairs, in the persuasive imitation of human personality, particularly in its self-destructive weaknesses.

Critics have rightly emphasized how important O'Neill's lapsed Irish Catholicism was to him and to his plays. But "importance" is a perplexing notion in this context. Certainly the absence of the Roman Catholic faith is the given condition of *The Iceman Cometh*. Yet we would do O'Neill's play wrong if we retitled it *Waiting for the Iceman* and tried to assimilate it to the Gnostic cosmos of Samuel Beckett, just as we would destroy *Long Day's Journey into Night* if we retitled it *Endgame in New London*. All that O'Neill and Beckett have in common is Schopenhauer, with whom they share a Gnostic sense that our world is a great emptiness, the *kenoma*, as the Gnostics of the second century of the common era called it. But Beckett's post-Protestant cosmos could not be redeemed by the descent of the alien god. O'Neill's post-Catholic world longs for the suffering Christ and is angry at him for not returning. Such a longing is by no means in itself dramatic, unlike Beckett's ironically emptied-out cosmos.

A comparison of O'Neill to Beckett is hardly fair, since Beckett is infinitely the better artist, subtler mind, and finer stylist. Beckett writes apocalyptic farce, or tragicomedy raised to its greatest eminence. O'Neill doggedly tells his one story and one story only, and his story turns out to be himself. *The Iceman Cometh*, being O'Neill at his most characteristic, raises the vexed question of whether and just how dramatic value can survive a paucity of eloquence, too much commonplace religiosity, and a thorough lack of understanding of the perverse complexities of human nature. Plainly *Iceman* does survive, and so does *Long Day's Journey*. They stage remarkably, and hold me in the audience, though they give neither aesthetic pleasure nor spiritually memorable pain when I reread them in the study.

For sheer bad writing, O'Neill's only rival among significant American authors is Theodore Dreiser, whose *Sister Carrie* and *An American Tragedy* demonstrate a similar ability to evade the consequences of rhetorical failure. Dreiser has some dramatic effectiveness, but his peculiar strength appears to be mythic. O'Neill, unquestionably a dramatist of genius, fails also on the mythic level; his anger against God, or the absence of God, remains petulant and personal, and his attempt to universalize that anger by turning it against his country's failure to achieve spiritual reality is simply misguided. No country, by definition, achieves anything spiritual anyway. We live and die, in the spirit, in solitude, and the true strength of *Iceman* is its intense dramatic exemplification of that somber reality.

Whether the confessional impulse in O'Neill's later plays ensued from Catholic *praxis* is beyond my surmise, though John Henry Raleigh and other critics have urged this view. I suspect that here too the influence of the non-Catholic Strindberg was decisive. A harsh expressionism dominates *Iceman* and *Long Day's Journey*, where the terrible confessions are not made to priestly surrogates but to fellow sinners, and with no hopes of absolution. Confession becomes another station on the way to death, whether by suicide, or by alcohol, or by other modes of slow decay.

Iceman's strength is in three of its figures, Hickman (Hickey), Slade, and Parritt, of whom only Slade is due to survive, though in a minimal sense. Hickey, who preaches nihilism, is a desperate self-deceiver and so a deceiver of others, in his self-appointed role as evangelist of the abyss. Slade, evasive and solipsistic, works his way to a more authentic nihilism than Hickey's. Poor Parritt, young and self-haunted, cannot achieve the sense of nothingness that would save him from Puritanical self-condemnation.

Life, in *Iceman*, is what it is in Schopenhauer: illusion. Hickey, once a great sustainer of illusions, arrives in the company of "the Iceman of Death," hardly the "sane and sacred death" of Whitman, but insane and impious death, our death. One feels the refracted influence of Ibsen in Hickey's twisted de-idealizings, but Hickey is an Ibsen protagonist in the last ditch. He does not destroy others in his quest to destroy illusions, but only himself. His judgments of Harry Hope's patrons are intended not to liberate them but to teach his old friends to accept and live with failure. Yet Hickey, though pragmatically wrong, means only to have done good.

In an understanding strangely akin to Wordsworth's in the sublime *Tale of Margaret; or The Ruined Cottage*, Hickey sees that we are destroyed by vain hope more inexorably than by the anguish of total despair. And that is where I would locate the authentic mode of tragedy in *Iceman*. It is Hickey's tragedy, rather than Slade's (O'Neill's), because Hickey is slain between right and right, as in the Hegelian theory of tragedy. To deprive the derelicts of hope is right, and to sustain them in their illusory "pipe dreams" is right also.

Caught between right and right, Hickey passes into phantasmagoria, and in that compulsive condition he makes the ghastly confession that he murdered his unhappy, dreadfully saintly wife. His motive, he asserts perversely, was love, but here too he is caught between antitheses, and we are not able to interpret with certainty whether he was more moved by love or hatred:

> HICKEY: (*Simply*) So I killed her. (*There is a moment of dead silence. Even the detectives are caught in it and stand motionless.*)
> PARRITT: (*Suddenly gives up and relaxes limply in his chair—in a low voice in which there is a strange exhausted relief.*) I may as well confess, Larry. There's no use lying any more. You know, anyway. I didn't give a damn about the money. It was because I hated her.
> HICKEY: (*Obliviously*) And then I saw I'd always known that was the only possible way to give her peace and free her from the misery of loving me. I saw it meant peace for me, too, knowing she was at peace. I felt as though a ton of guilt was lifted off my mind. I remember I stood by the bed and suddenly I had to laugh. I couldn't help it, and I knew Evelyn would forgive me. I remember I heard myself speaking to her, as if it was something I'd always wanted to say: "Well, you know what you can do with your pipe dream now, you damned bitch!" (*He stops with a horrified start, as if shocked out of a nightmare, as if he couldn't believe he heard what he had just said. He stammers*) No! I never—!
> PARRITT: (*To* LARRY *sneeringly*) Yes, that's it! Her and the damned old Movement pipe dream! Eh, Larry?
> HICKEY: (*Bursts into frantic denial*) No! That's a lie! I never said—! Good God, I couldn't have said that! If I did, I'd gone insane! Why, I loved Evelyn better than anything in life! (*He appeals brokenly to the crowd*) Boys, you're all my old pals! You've known old Hickey

for years! You know I'd never—(*His eyes fix on* HOPE) You've known me longer than anyone, Harry. You know I must have been insane, don't you, Governor?

Rather than a demystifier, whether of self or others, Hickey is revealed as a tragic enigma who cannot sell himself a coherent account of the horror he has accomplished. Did he slay Evelyn because of a hope, hers or his—or because of a mutual despair? He does not know, nor does O'Neill, nor do we. Nor does anyone know why Parritt betrayed his mother, the anarchist activist, and her comrades and his. Slade condemns Parritt to a suicide's death, but without persuading us that he has uncovered the motive for so hideous a betrayal. Caught in a moral dialectic of guilt and suffering, Parritt appears to be entirely a figure of pathos, without the weird idealism that makes Hickey an interesting instance of High Romantic tragedy.

Parritt at least provokes analysis; the drama's failure is Larry Slade, much against O'Neill's palpable intentions, which were to move his surrogate from contemplation to action. Slade ought to end poised on the threshold of a religious meditation on the vanity of life in a world from which God is absent. But his final speech, expressing a reaction to Parritt's suicide, is the weakest in the play:

> LARRY: (*In a whisper of horrified pity*) Poor devil! (*A long-forgotten faith returns to him for a moment and he mumbles*) God rest his soul in peace. (*He opens his eyes—with a bitter self-derision*) Ah, the damned pity—the wrong kind, as Hickey said! Be God, there's no hope! I'll never be a success in the grandstand—or anywhere else! Life is too much for me! I'll be a weak fool looking with pity at the two sides of everything till the day I die! (*With an intense bitter sincerity*) May that day come soon! (*He pauses startledly, surprised at himself—then with a sardonic grin*) Be God, I'm the only real convert to death Hickey made here. From the bottom of my coward's heart I mean that now!

The momentary return of Catholicism is at variance with the despair of the death drive here, and Slade does not understand that he has not been converted to any sense of death, at all. His only strength would be in emulating Hickey's tragic awareness between right and right, but of course without following Hickey into violence: "I'll be a weak fool looking with pity at the two sides of everything till the day I die!" That vision of the two sides, with compassion, is the only hope worthy of the dignity of any kind of tragic conception. O'Neill ended by exemplifying Yeats's great apothegm: he could embody the truth, but he could not know it.

Katherine Anne Porter
(1890–1980)

BY THE TIME she was fifty, Katherine Anne Porter had written and published nearly all the fiction for which she would be remembered. Her single novel, *Ship of Fools* (1962), seemed to me an interesting failure when I first read it, many years ago, and I now find it very difficult to read through for a second time. Its critical defenders have been numerous and distinguished, including Robert Penn Warren (certainly Porter's best critic), yet it is one of those books that calls out for defense. Perhaps its author waited too long to compose *Ship of Fools*, or perhaps her genius was so admirably suited to the short novel and the short story that it was condemned to languish at greater length. What seems clear is that Porter's lasting achievement is not in *Ship of Fools* but in "Flowering Judas," "He," "Old Mortality," "Noon Wine," "Pale Horse, Pale Rider," "The Grave," and many of their companions. She is a supreme lyricist among story writers, molding her tales with the care and delicacy that Willa Cather (whom she greatly admired) gave to such novels as *My Ántonia* and *The Lost Lady*. Like Cather, she found her truest precursor in Henry James, though her formative work seems to me rather more indebted to Joyce's *Dubliners*. But, again like Cather, her sensibility is very different from that of her male precursors, and her art, original and vital, swerves away into a rhetorical stance and moral vision peculiarly her own.

I confess to loving "Flowering Judas" most among her works, though I recognize that the aesthetic achievement of "Old Mortality," "Noon Wine," and the stories grouped as "The Old Order" is a larger one. Still, "Flowering Judas" established Porter and rhetorically set a standard even she never surpassed. Its two most famous passages retain their aura:

> A brown, shock-haired youth came and stood in her patio one night and sang like a lost soul for two hours, but Laura could think of nothing to do about it. The moonlight spread a wash of gauzy silver over the clear spaces of the garden, and the shadows were cobalt

blue. The scarlet blossoms of the Judas tree were dull purple, and the names of the colors repeated themselves automatically in her mind, while she watched not the boy, but his shadow, fallen like a dark garment across the fountain rim, trailing in the water. . . .

. . . No, said Laura, not unless you take my hand, no; and she clung first to the stair rail, and then to the topmost branch of the Judas tree that bent down slowly and set her upon the earth, and then to the rocky ledge of a cliff, and then to the jagged wave of a sea that was not water but a desert of crumbling stone. Where are you taking me, she asked in wonder but without fear. To death, and it is a long way off, and we must hurry, said Eugenio. No, said Laura, not unless you take my hand. Then eat these flowers, poor prisoner, said Eugenio in a voice of pity, take and eat: and from the Judas tree he stripped the warm bleeding flowers, and held them to her lips. She saw that his hand was fleshless, a cluster of small white petrified branches, and his eye sockets were without light, but she ate the flowers greedily for they satisfied both hunger and thirst. Murderer! said Eugenio, and Cannibal! This is my body and my blood. Laura cried No! and at the sound of her own voice, she awoke trembling, and was afraid to sleep again.

The allusiveness of these passages has been analyzed as being in the mode of T. S. Eliot; indeed the allusions generally are taken to involve Eliot's "Gerontion," where "Christ the tiger" came: "In depraved May, dogwood and chestnut, flowering judas, / To be eaten, to be divided, to be drunk / Among whispers." But Porter's story, intensely erotic, is neither a *Waste Land* allegory nor a study of Christian nostalgia. Its beautiful, sleepwalking Laura is neither a betrayer nor a failed believer, but an aesthete, a storyteller poised upon the threshold of crossing over into her own art. Porter alternately dated "Flowering Judas" in December 1929 or January 1930. She was not much aware of Freud, then or later, but he seemed to be aware of her, so to speak, in his extraordinary essay of 1914 on narcissism, which can be read, in some places, as a portrait of Porter's Laura, the beautiful enigma of "Flowering Judas":

There arises in the woman a certain self-sufficiency (especially when there is a ripening into beauty) which compensates her for the social restrictions upon her object-choice. Strictly speaking, such women love only themselves with an intensity comparable to that of the man's love for them. Nor does their need lie in the direction of loving, but of being loved; and that man finds favour with them who fulfills this condition. The importance of this type of woman for the erotic life of mankind must be recognized as very great.

Freud goes on to observe that "one person's narcissism has a great attraction for those others who have renounced part of their own narcissism." Laura's curious coolness, which charms us into a sense of her inaccessibility, is the product not of her disillusion with either the Revolution or the Church but of her childlike narcissism. Much of the lyrical strength of "Flowering Judas" comes from its superb contrast between the gray-eyed, grave Laura, who walks as beautifully as a dancer, and her obscene serenader, the professional revolutionist Braggioni, with his tawny yellow cat's eyes, his snarling voice, his gross intensity. Yet Braggioni is accurate when he tells Laura: "We are more alike than you realize in some things." Narcissist and self-loving leader of men share in a pragmatic cruelty, and in a vanity that negates the reality of all others:

> No matter what this stranger says to her, nor what her message to him, the very cells of her flesh reject knowledge and kinship in one monotonous word. No. No. No. She draws her strength from this one holy talismanic word which does not suffer her to be led into evil. Denying everything, she may walk anywhere in safety, she looks at everything without amazement.

It is Porter's art to place Laura beyond judgment. The dream-vision that ends the story is hardly a representation of a dream, since it is anything but a wish fulfillment. It is the narcissist's ultimate reverie, an image of the Judas tree representing not betrayal so much as a revelation that the flowering Judas is oneself, one's perfect self-sufficiency. Laura, in the supposed dream or visionary projection, rightly transposes her status to that of Eugenio, the "poor prisoner," and greedily eats the Judas flowers "for they satisfied both hunger and thirst," as they must, being emblems of narcissistic self-passion, of the ego established by the self's investment in itself. When Eugenio cries out: "This is my body and my blood," he is mistaken, and we ought to give credence rather to Laura's outcry of "No!," which wakens her from her dream. It is again the same "one holy talismanic word which does not suffer her to be led into evil," the narcissist's rejection of any love-object except herself. It is Laura's body and Laura's blood that she never ceases to absorb, and it does satisfy her hunger and her thirst.

Porter is a superb instance of what Frank O'Connor called *The Lonely Voice*, his title for his book on the short story, where he begins by rejecting the traditional term for the genre:

> All I can say from reading Turgenev, Chekhov, Katherine Anne Porter, and others is that the very term "short story" is a misnomer. A great story is not necessarily short at all, and the conception of the short story as a miniature art is inherently false. Basically, the difference between the short story and the novel is not one of length. It is a difference between pure and applied storytelling, and in case someone has still failed to get the point, I am not trying to decry applied storytelling. Pure storytelling is more artistic, that is all, and in storytelling I am not sure how much art is preferable to nature.

Porter too was not sure, and she deserves Robert Penn Warren's praise that hers "is a poetry that shows a deep attachment to the world's body." I add only that it shows also a deeper attachment to her own body, but I insist that is all to the good. Narcissism has gotten an absurdly bad name, but Freud certainly would snort at that, and so should we. A beautiful lyricist and a beautiful woman necessarily celebrate their own beauty, and Porter surpassingly was both. Even her stories' titles haunt me, just as photographs depicting her hold on in the memory. Warren rather surprisingly compares her to Faulkner, whose magnificence, unlike hers, generally does not come in particular phrases. I would prefer to compare her to Hart Crane, her difficult friend and impossible guest in Mexico, yet her truest contemporary, in the sense of a profound affinity in art. Porter's ambivalent account of Crane is at once a story by Porter and a visionary lyric of Hart Crane's:

> It was then that he broke into the monotonous obsessed dull obscenity which was the only language he knew after reaching a certain point of drunkenness, but this time he cursed things and elements as well as human beings. His voice at these times . . .

stunned the ears and shocked the nerves and caused the heart to contract. In this voice and with words so foul there is no question of repeating them, he cursed separately and by name the moon, and its light the heliotrope, the heaven-tree, the sweet-by-night, the star jessamine, and their perfumes. He cursed the air we breathed together, the pool of water with its two small ducks huddled at the edge, and the vines on the wall and house. But those were not the things he hated. He did not even hate us, for we were nothing to him. He hated and feared himself.

This is a great poet rushing toward self-destruction, his wounded narcissism converted into aggressivity against the self, which in turn fuels the death drive, beyond the pleasure principle. Implicit in Porter's memory of Crane is the trauma of betrayed affinity, as one great lyrical artist watches another take, not her downward path to wisdom, but the way down and out to death by water. Porter, a survivor, makes the paragraph into a frighteningly effective elegy for Crane, for that supreme lyricist whose gift has become a curse, to himself and to others. Like Crane, Porter concentrated her gift, and her stories match his lyrics in their economy and in their sublime eloquence. Unlike him, she took care to survive, and perhaps we should praise her Laura, in "Flowering Judas," for the wisdom to survive, rather than condemn her for not offering herself up to be devoured by a violent though beautiful reality.

Zora Neale Hurston

(1891–1960)

M OSES: MAN OF THE MOUNTAIN is an impressive book in its mode
and ambitions, but a mixed achievement, unable to resolve problems
of diction and of rhetorical stance. Essentially, Hurston is the author of one
superb and moving novel, *Their Eyes Were Watching God*, unique not in its
kind but in its isolated excellence among other stories of the kind.

The wistful opening of *Their Eyes Were Watching God* pragmatically
affirms greater repression in women as opposed to men, by which I mean
"repression" only in Freud's sense: unconscious yet purposeful forgetting:

> Now, women forget all those things they don't want to remember,
> and remember everything they don't want to forget. The dream is
> the truth. Then they act and do things accordingly.

Hurston's Janie is now necessarily a paradigm for women, of whatever
race, heroically attempting to assert their own individuality in contexts
that continue to resent and fear any consciousness that is not male. In a
larger perspective, should the contexts modify, the representation of Janie
will take its significant place in a long tradition of such representations in
English and American fiction. This tradition extends from Samuel Richardson to Doris Lessing and other contemporaries, but only rarely has been
able to visualize authentically strong women who begin with all the depri-
vations that circumstance assigns to Janie. It is a crucial aspect of Hurston's
subtle sense of limits that the largest limitation is that imposed upon Janie
by her grandmother, who loves her best, yet fears for her the most.

As a former slave, the grandmother, Nanny, is haunted by the compensatory dream of making first her daughter, and then her granddaughter,
something other than "the mule of the world," customary fate of the black
woman. The dream is both powerful enough and sufficiently unitary to
have driven Janie's mother away, and to condemn Janie herself to a double disaster of marriages, before the tragic happiness of her third match

completes as much of her story as Hurston desires to give us. As readers, we carry away with us what Janie never quite loses, the vivid pathos of her grandmother's superb and desperate displacement of hope:

> "And, Janie, maybe it wasn't much, but Ah done de best Ah kin by you. Ah raked and scraped and bought dis lil piece uh land so you wouldn't have to stay in de white folks' yard and tuck yo' head befo' other chillun at school. Dat was all right when you was little. But when you got big enough to understand things, Ah wanted you to look upon yo'self. Ah don't want yo' feathers always crumpled by folks throwin' up things in yo' face. And Ah can't die easy thinkin' maybe de menfolks white or black is makin' a spit cup outa you: Have some sympathy fuh me. Put me down easy, Janie, Ah'm a cracked plate."

Hurston's rhetorical strength, even in *Their Eyes Were Watching God*, is frequently too overt, and threatens an excess, when contrasted with the painful simplicity of her narrative line and the reductive tendency at work in all her characters except for Janie and Nanny. Yet the excess works, partly because Hurston is so considerable and knowing a mythologist. Hovering in *Their Eyes Were Watching God* is the Mosaic myth of deliverance, the pattern of revolution and exodus that Hurston reimagines as her prime trope of power:

> But there are other concepts of Moses abroad in the world. Asia and all the Near East are sown with legends of this character. They are so numerous and so varied that some students have come to doubt if the Moses of the Christian concept is real. Then Africa has her mouth on Moses. All across the continent there are the legends of the greatness of Moses, but not because of his beard nor because he brought the laws down from Sinai. No, he is revered because he had the power to go up the mountain and to bring them down. Many men could climb mountains. Anyone could bring down laws that had been handed to them. But who can talk with God face to face? Who has the power to command God to go to a peak of a mountain and there demand of Him laws with which to govern a nation? What other man has ever commanded the wind and the

hail? The light and darkness? That calls for power, and that is what Africa sees in Moses to worship. For he is worshipped as a god.

Power in Hurston is always *potentia*, the demand for life, for more life. Despite the differences in temperament, Hurston has affinities both with Dreiser and with Lawrence, heroic vitalists. Her art, like theirs, exalts an exuberance that is beauty, a difficult beauty because it participates in reality-testing. What is strongest in Janie is a persistence akin to Dreiser's Carrie and Lawrence's Ursula and Gudrun, a drive to survive in one's own fashion. Nietzsche's vitalistic injunction, that we must try to live as though it were morning, is the implicit basis of Hurston's true religion, which in its American formulation (Thoreau's) reminds us that only that day dawns to which we are alive. Something of Lawrence's incessant sense of the sun is paralleled by Hurston's trope of the solar trajectory, in a cosmos where "They sat on the boarding house porch and saw the sun plunge into the same crack in the earth from which the night emerged" and where "Every morning the world flung itself over and exposed the town to the sun."

Janie's perpetual sense of the possibilities of another day propels her from Nanny's vision of safety first to the catastrophe of Joe Starks and then to the love of Tea Cake, her true husband. But to live in a way that starts with the sun is to become pragmatically doom-eager, since mere life is deprecated in contrast to the possibility of glory, of life more abundant, rather than Nanny's dream of a refuge from exploitation. Hurston's most effective irony is that Janie's drive toward her own erotic potential should transcend her grandmother's categories, since the marriage with Tea Cake is also Janie's pragmatic liberation from bondage toward men. When he tells her, in all truth, that she has the keys to the kingdom, he frees her from living in her grandmother's way.

A more pungent irony drove Hurston to end Janie's idyll with Tea Cake's illness and the ferocity of his subsequent madness. The impulse of her own vitalism compels Janie to kill him in self-defense, thus ending necessarily life and love in the name of the possibility of more life again. The novel's conclusion is at once an elegy and a vision of achieved peace, an intense realization that indeed we are all asleep in the outer life:

The day of the gun, and the bloody body, and the courthouse came and commenced to sing a sobbing sigh out of every corner in the room; out of each and every chair and thing. Commenced to sing, commenced to sob and sigh, singing and sobbing. Then Tea Cake came prancing around her where she was and the song of the sigh flew out of the window and lit in the top of the pine trees. Tea Cake, with the sun for a shawl. Of course he wasn't dead. He could never be dead until she herself had finished feeling and thinking. The kiss of his memory made pictures of love and light against the wall. Here was peace. She pulled in her horizon like a great fish-net. Pulled it from around the waist of the world and draped it over her shoulder. So much of life in its meshes! She called in her soul to come and see.

Hurston herself was refreshingly free of all the ideologies that currently obscure the reception of her best book. Her sense of power has nothing in common with politics of any persuasion, with contemporary modes of feminism, or even with those questers who search for a black aesthetic. As a vitalist, she was of the line of the Wife of Bath and Sir John Falstaff and Mynheer Peeperkorn. Like them, she was outrageous, heroically larger than life, witty in herself and the cause of wit in others. She belongs now to literary legend, which is as it should be. Her famous remark in response to Carl Van Vechten's photographs is truly the epigraph to her life and work: "I love myself when I am laughing. And then again when I am looking mean and impressive." Walt Whitman would have delighted in that as in her assertion: "When I set my hat at a certain angle and saunter down Seventh Avenue . . . the cosmic Zora emerges. . . . How can any deny themselves the pleasure of my company? It's beyond me." With Whitman, Hurston herself is now an image of American literary vitality, and a part also of the American mythology of exodus, of the power to choose the party of Eros, of more life.

F. Scott Fitzgerald
(1896–1940)

IT IS DIFFICULT to imagine John Keats writing the fictions of Joseph Conrad, since there is nothing in common between the Great Odes and "The Secret Sharer" or "Heart of Darkness." But such an imagining is not useless, since in some sense that was Scott Fitzgerald's accomplishment. *The Great Gatsby* does combine the lyrical sensibility of Keats and the fictive mode of Conrad, and makes of so odd a blending a uniquely American story, certainly a candidate for *the* American story of its time (1925). *Gatsby* has more in common with T. S. Eliot's "The Hollow Men," also published in 1925, than it does with such contemporary novels as the *Arrowsmith* of Sinclair Lewis or the *Manhattan Transfer* of John Dos Passos. Eliot's admiration for *The Great Gatsby* is understandable; the book, like the visionary lyric of Hart Crane, struggles against Eliot's conclusions while being compelled to appropriate Eliot's language and procedures. Fitzgerald, the American Keats, and Crane, even more the American Shelley, both sought to affirm a High Romanticism in the accents of a belated countertradition. The Keatsian belief in the holiness of the heart's affections is central to Fitzgerald, and *Tender Is the Night* owes more than its title to the naturalistic humanism of the Great Odes.

Fitzgerald's canonical status is founded more upon *Gatsby* and his best short stories, such as "Babylon Revisited," than it is upon the seriously flawed *Tender Is the Night*, let alone upon the unfinished *The Last Tycoon*. Oddly praised as "the best Hollywood novel" despite its manifest inferiority to Nathanael West's *The Day of the Locust*, *The Last Tycoon* is more an embryo than it is a torso. Edmund Wilson's affectionate overestimation of this fragment has been influential but will fade away each time the book is actually read. *Tender Is the Night* demonstrates that Fitzgerald, unlike Conrad and Lawrence, cannot sustain too long a narrative. The book, though coming relatively late in his career, is Fitzgerald's *Endymion*, while *Gatsby* is, as it were, his "Fall of Hyperion." Keats desired to write epic but was more attuned to romance and to lyric. Fitzgerald desired to write novels on the scale of Thackeray and of Conrad, but his genius was more fitted to *Gatsby* as his mode of romance and to "Babylon Revisited" as his version of the ode or of the reflective lyric.

The aesthetic of Scott Fitzgerald is quite specifically a personal revision of Keats's hope for Negative Capability, which Fitzgerald called "a romantic readiness" and attributed to his Gatsby. It is certainly part of the achievement of Fitzgerald's best novel that its hero possesses an authentic aesthetic dignity. By an effective troping of form, Fitzgerald made this a book in which nothing is aesthetically wasted, even as the narrative shows us everyone being humanly wasted. Edith Wharton rather nastily praised Fitzgerald for having created the "perfect Jew" in the gambler Meyer Wolfsheim. Had she peered closer, she might have seen the irony of her patrician prejudice reversed in the ancient Jewish wisdom that even Wolfsheim is made to express:

> "Let us learn to show our friendship for a man when he is alive and not after he is dead," he suggested. "After that, my own rule is to let everything alone."

Whether Nick Carraway is capable of apprehending this as wisdom is disputable but Fitzgerald evidently could, since Wolfsheim is not wholly devoid of the dignity of grief. Lionel Trilling commended *The Great Gatsby* for retaining its freshness. After eighty years, it has more than retained its moral balance and affective rightness. Those qualities seem augmented through the perspective of lapsed time. What has been augmented also is the Eliotic phantasmagoria of the *Waste Land* imagery that is so effectively vivid throughout Fitzgerald's vision. Carraway begins by speaking of "what preyed on Gatsby, what foul dust floated in the wake of his dreams." These are also "the spasms of bleak dust," above which you perceive the blue and gigantic eyes of Doctor T. J. Eckleburg, which brood on over the dumping ground of the gray land. "My heart is a handful of dust," the monologist of Tennyson's *Maud* had proclaimed in a great phrase stolen by Eliot for his *Waste Land*. Fitzgerald's dust is closer to Tennyson's heart than to Eliot's fear:

> to where Myrtle Wilson, her life violently extinguished, knelt in the road and mingled her thick dark blood with the dust.
> Michaelis and this man reached her first, but when they had torn

open her shirtwaist, still damp with perspiration, they saw that her left breast was swinging loose like a flap, and there was no need to listen for the heart beneath.

Fitzgerald's violence has that curious suddenness we associate with the same narrative quality in E. M. Forster. Something repressed in the phantasmagoria of the ordinary returns, all too often, reminding us that Fitzgerald shares also in Conrad's sense of reality and its treacheries, particularly as developed in *Nostromo*, a novel that we know Fitzgerald rightly admired. *Heart of Darkness*, which Fitzgerald also admired, is linked to "The Hollow Men" by that poem's epigraph, and many critics have seen Carraway as Fitzgerald's version of Marlow, somewhat sentimentalized but still an authentic secret sharer in Gatsby's fate. Like the Eliot of "The Hollow Men," Fitzgerald found in Conrad a seer of the contemporary abyss of

Shape without form, shade without color,
Paralysed force, gesture without motion;

or, in the language of *Heart of Darkness*: "A vision of grayness without form."

Writing to his daughter about the "Ode on a Grecian Urn," Fitzgerald extravagantly observed "For awhile after you quit Keats all other poetry seems to be only whistling or humming." Fitzgerald's deepest affinity to Keats is in the basic stance of his work, at once rhetorical, psychological, and even cosmological. In both Keats and Fitzgerald, the perpetual encounter is between the mortal poet or man-of-imagination (Gatsby, Diver) and an immortal or perpetually youthful goddess-woman. Fitzgerald's women— Daisy, Nicole, Rosemary—are not so much American dreams as they are Keatsian Lamias or perpetually virgin moon-maidens. "Virginity renews itself like the moon" is a Keatsian apothegm of Yeats's and the quester in Fitzgerald would have concurred. The murdered Gatsby is truly Daisy's victim; rather more grimly, Diver is emptied out by his relationship with Nicole, and to some degree by his repetition of that pattern with Rosemary.

This has been read as misogyny in Fitzgerald but, as in Keats, it tends largely to be the reverse. Confronting his immortal women, the Keatsian quester seeks what at last Keats himself obtains from the harshly reluctant Muse, Moneta, in "The Fall of Hyperion": recognition that he is *the* poet in and for his own time. "I sure should see / Other men here; but

I am here alone." Fitzgerald was greatly ambitious, but his audacity did not extend quite that far. Yet his surrogates—Gatsby and Diver—are no more deceived than Keats's poets are deceived. Daisy, Nicole, and Rosemary do not matter as personalities, not to us as readers and not much more to Gatsby or Diver. Gatsby, the more sublime quester, is allowed his famous touch of genius when he dismisses Daisy's love for her husband, the brutal Tom Buchanan: "In any case, it was just personal." Diver, less magnificently, also knows better, but is just as doom-eager as Gatsby. The inadequacies of the actual women do not matter, because the drive is not for satisfaction or for happiness. It is Freud's uncanny death drive, which replaces the drive for self-preservation and exists in a dialectical balance with the libido. Gatsby somehow chooses to die in his own fashion, while Diver chooses the death-in-life of erotic and professional defeat.

Tender Is the Night survives the weakness of its characterizations and the clumsiness of its narrative structure precisely because of Diver's own fated sense that there are no accidents. His character is his fate, and his relationship with Nicole is not so much a failed counter-transference as it is another pathetic version of the sublime Romantic vision of sexual entropy set forth overtly in Blake's "The Mental Traveller" and implicitly in James's *The Sacred Fount*: "And she grows young as he grows old." For the Blakean "young" we can substitute "whole," yet for the "old" we cannot quite substitute "weak" but something closer to Fitzgerald's "interior laughter," the quality in Diver that drives him down and out until he ends up practicing medicine in progressively smaller towns in the Finger Lakes section in western New York State. The pathos of that dying fall is anything but Keatsian and may have been Fitzgerald's trope for his own self-destructiveness.

A curious self-appropriation, or perhaps indeliberate self-repetition, links the close of *Tender Is the Night* to the close of "Babylon Revisited," which seems to me Fitzgerald's most impressive single short story. On the day before he leaves the Riviera for America, after his rejection by Nicole, Diver spends all his time with his children: "He was not young any more with a lot of nice thoughts and dreams to have about himself, so he wanted to remember them well." The penultimate sentence of "Babylon Revisited" is "He wasn't young anymore, with a lot of nice thoughts and dreams to have about himself."

Whichever came first, the repetition is central to Fitzgerald. "Nice thoughts and dreams" are the essence, and Fitzgerald's regressive vision, like Gatsby's and Diver's and Charlie Wales's, is a Keatsian and Stevensian study of the nostalgias. Keats, staring at the face of the unveiled Moneta, prophesies the Stevens of "The Auroras of Autumn," with his unabashed, Freudian celebration of the imago: "The mother's face, the purpose of the poem, fills the room." Charlie Wales, in "Babylon Revisited," longing for his daughter, remembers his dead wife as any man remembers his mother: "He was absolutely sure Helen wouldn't have wanted him to be so alone." As the last sentence of what may be Fitzgerald's most memorable story, it reverberates with a peculiar plangency in American Romantic tradition.

William Faulkner

(1897–1962)

B Y COMMON AGREEMENT, William Faulkner is the canonical Ameri-can writer of prose fiction since the death of Henry James. No one else among Faulkner's contemporaries or in later generations achieved compa-rable eminence. He shared nothing with Henry James except a relation-ship to Hawthorne, who, with Melville, Twain, and Eliot, is a vital part of Faulkner's American literary heritage. Honoré de Balzac, Sir Walter Scott, Shakespeare, the King James Bible, James Joyce, and Joseph Conrad are crucial influences on Faulkner as well, but what matters most is Faulkner's own daemonic originality. Nothing in him is other than idiosyncratic, yet what I care most for are *As I Lay Dying* (1930) and *Light in August* (1932), astonishing inventions without precedents. Between the two books came a revised *Sanctuary* (1931), composed, according to Faulkner, "in order to make money," though to me it seems a permanent work, one I prefer to *The Sound and the Fury* (1929) and to *Absalom, Absalom!* (1936), grand yet over-schematized narratives.

This in no way suggests limitations, beyond my own as a reader. I know *The Sound and the Fury* almost by heart and sometimes find the stylistic traces of James Joyce distracting, but in the orchestral sonorities of *Absa-lom, Absalom!*, Thomas Sutpen's saga, I hear only Faulkner's voice at its richest, in the most comprehensive and ambitious of all his superb prose romances. Sometimes I think that I am so overwhelmed by *Absalom, Absa-lom!* that I cannot take it all in, despite a score or so of readings throughout its panoramas.

The crucial personages I find most memorable in Faulkner are Darl Bun-dren of *As I Lay Dying* and Lena Grove of *Light in August*. Doubtless it reveals an oddity in me that I add to this list the murderous gangster Pop-eye of *Sanctuary*. They certainly are a trio: the visionary Darl; the Keatsian harvest girl Lena, who will be light in August when her baby is born; the impotent Popeye, infamous for violating Temple Drake with a corncob.

Emerson, Hawthorne, Whitman, Dickinson, Melville, Henry James, Stevens, Frost, and Hart Crane start with a recognition of the god or daemon within themselves and compose through moving outward. On the other side, Twain, Eliot, and Faulkner begin in the outside world and only gradually encounter inside themselves an affirmation of their outward vision. Twain is found by his daemon only through his Mississippi writings, which give him the new name "Mark Twain." Eliot, resisting his daemon, constructs an antithetical self of critic-philosopher-theologian, but the poetry breaks through nevertheless, High Romantic and daemonic from the start. Faulkner, more than Twain or Eliot, nurtures a new self when he moves from his early, quite bad poetry to prose fiction. The territory all of them light out for is ultimately themselves.

There had been a sense of otherness in Faulkner's verse, a blend of Swinburne and Eliot, but the desire to be different was diffuse and halting. In the early novel (his third) alternately titled *Sartoris* and *Flags in the Dust*, he began to be found by his own daemon.

That daemon belonged to family tradition and particularly to the singular Old Colonel, William Clark Falkner, great-grandfather of the novelist. Colonel Falkner (1825–89) was almost a parody of the Southern myth: plantation slaveowner, gallant soldier, aggressive lawyer, political opponent of Reconstruction, popular novelist (*The White Rose of Memphis*), and duelist; he was eventually shot to death in the streets by a business associate. In the Civil War, as a Cavalier sporting a knightly black plume, he led the Magnolia Rifles to victory at Manassas, winning the admiration of General J. E. Johnston and of J. E. B. Stuart. The sublimely absurd litany (all factual) goes on: he was a blockade runner and a railroad pioneer, both of which brought him wealth.

The child William Faulkner (who added a *u* to the family name) grew up hearing stories exalting the Old Colonel, an impressive model for personal emulation and a superb stimulus for heroic fiction like *Flags in the Dust* and *The Unvanquished*, in which he becomes Colonel John Sartoris.

The pride, love, and horror of familial connections became Faulkner's decisive tropes for fiction and life alike. This is the burden of his initial breakthroughs into canonical achievement, *The Sound and the Fury* and *As I Lay Dying*. I recall amiable disagreements with Malcolm Cowley and rather sharp ones with Cleanth Brooks when I argued, in some essays and introductions during the mid-1980s, that in Faulkner the ambivalent sufferings and dooms of familial love far outweighed the joy and solace. The common reader of the Compson and Bundren sagas will decide for herself.

Like Balzac and Dickens, Faulkner peopled his own cosmos. All three need to be absorbed as seers of *The Human Comedy* but also as tacticians of individual dooms. More than with Hawthorne and Henry James, we do Faulkner violence when we isolate a single narrative and weigh it by itself. Dead before he was sixty-five, Faulkner left his region, his nation, and the world a wealth of story, character, heightened language, and a visionary stance to rival his greatest American precursors: Hawthorne, Melville, and Twain.

The finest opening section of any twentieth-century American novel belongs to William Faulkner's masterpiece, *As I Lay Dying* (1930). The book consists of fifty-nine interior monologues, forty-three of them spoken by members of the Bundren family, a proud clan of poor whites, who struggle heroically through flood and fire to carry the coffin containing the corpse of their mother, Addie, back to the graveyard in Jefferson, Mississippi, where she wished to be buried next to her father. Nineteen of the sections, including the first, are spoken by the remarkable Darl Bundren, a visionary who finally crosses the border into madness. We hear Darl speaking the novel's opening, as he follows his enemy brother, Jewel, up to the house where Addie is dying:

> Jewel and I come up from the field, following the path in single file. Although I am fifteen feet ahead of him, anyone watching us from the cottonhouse can see Jewel's frayed and broken straw hat a full head above my own.

As Darl and Jewel mount the path, Darl hears the saw of his carpenter brother, Cash, who is making the coffin for their mother, and we listen to Darl's dispassionate observation:

> A good carpenter. Addie Bundren could not want a better one, a better box to lie in. It will give her confidence and comfort.

Unloved by Addie, the dissociated Darl insists he has no mother, and his extraordinary consciousness reflects his conviction. Stark, simple, dignified, suggestive—the opening of *As I Lay Dying* intimates the superb originality of Faulkner's most surprising novel. Faulkner's principal rivals have nothing comparable; F. Scott Fitzgerald's *The Great Gatsby* begins with Nick Carraway's father telling him: "Just remember that all the people in this world haven't had the advantages that you've had," which is a healthy admonition not to criticize others, but a long way from the Faulknerian sublimity. Hemingway's *The Sun Also Rises* begins with the ironical observation that "Robert Cohn was once middleweight boxing champion of Princeton." Again, Faulkner is rather beyond that. The only possible rival for an opening in Faulkner's class seems to me the start of Cormac McCarthy's astonishing *Blood Meridian* (1985), where the narrator introduces us to the Kid, the tragic protagonist who will finally be destroyed by the uncanny and Iago-like Judge Holden:

> See the child. He is pale and thin, he wears a thin and ragged linen shirt. He stokes the scullery fire. Outside lie dark turned fields with rags of snow and darker woods beyond that harbor yet a few last wolves. His folk are known for hewers of wood and drawers of water but in truth his father has been a schoolmaster. He lies in drink, he quotes from poets whose names are now lost. The boy crouches by the fire and watches him.

The accents of Herman Melville and of Faulkner fuse in this great prose. I return us to *As I Lay Dying*. A deliberate tour de force, the book refers in its title to Addie Bundren, who dies soon after it begins, but Faulkner quoted from memory the bitter speech of the ghost of Agamemnon to Odysseus (*Odyssey*, Book XI, "The Descent to the Dead"):

> As I lay dying the woman with the dog's eyes would not close my eyes for me as I descended into Hades.

Murdered by his wife and her lover, Agamemnon, and his fate, have little to do with Faulkner's novel. Faulkner wanted the phrase, rather than its context, and took it, though he may also have wished to suggest that the lack of love between Addie Bundren and her son Darl has elements in it akin to the Clytemnestra relationship with Orestes and Electra. Clytemnestra is "the woman with the dog's eyes" who sends Agamemnon open-eyed into Hades, and Addie is, if anything, more unpleasant than Clytemnestra.

Though Faulkner does not number the sections or fifty-nine interior monologues that make up his book, I suggest that the reader do so in her paperback copy of *As I Lay Dying*, for convenience of cross-reference (the best edition is the current Vintage reprint, which has the Library of America corrected text). Addie speaks only one section, the fortieth, but it is more than sufficient to alienate every reader:

> I could just remember how my father used to say that the reason for living was to get ready to stay dead a long time. And when I would have to look at them day after day, each with his and her secret and selfish thought, and blood strange to each other blood and strange to mine, and think that this seemed to be the only way I could get ready to stay dead, I would hate my father for having ever planted me. I would look forward to the times when they faulted, so I could whip them. When the switch fell I could feel it upon my flesh; when it welted and ridged it was my blood that ran, and I would think with each blow of the switch: Now you are aware of me! Now I am something in your secret and selfish life, who have marked your blood with my own for ever and ever.

One sees why this sadistically disturbed woman wishes to be buried next to her father. Addie, dead, is even more of a curse than when alive, as we are told the grotesque, heroic, sometimes hilarious, always outrageous saga of how her five children and husband go through flood and fire to carry her corpse back to her desired resting place. Faulkner's *As I Lay Dying* is tragic farce, yet it has enormous aesthetic dignity and is a sustained nightmare of what Freud grimly called "family romances." Some pious critics have tried to interpret *As I Lay Dying* as an affirmation of Christian family values, but the reader will be baffled by such a judgment. As elsewhere in Faulkner's great decade as a novelist (1929–39), the novelist's vision founds itself upon a horror of families and of community, and offers the one value of stoic endurance, which does not suffice to save the gifted Darl Bundren from the madhouse.

So ironical are the tonalities of Faulkner's interior monologues, partic-ularly of Darl's nineteen soliloquies, that the reader may feel at first that Faulkner does too little to guide our responses. There is no genre we can turn to in aiding our understanding of this epic narrative of Mississippi poor whites fulfilling the dying request of their quite dreadful mother. Family honor is almost the only principle holding the Bundrens together, since the father, Anse, is in his own way as destructive as Addie. Anse is given three monologues—numbers 9, 26, 28 (if you have numbered them)—and they establish him as wily, shiftless, a trickster and manipulator, as selfish as his wife, Addie, was.

Dewey Dell, the one Bundren daughter, has her own dignity but cannot find strength to mourn her mother's death, because as an unmarried, pregnant, poor white young woman, she is compelled to seek vainly for a secret abortion. The child Vardaman simply denies Addie's death; he bores holes in her coffin so that she can breathe, and finally identifies her with a large fish he caught as she lay dying: "My mother is a fish." Faulkner centers the novel on the consciousness of Darl Bundren and on the heroic actions of the other sons, Cash the carpenter and Jewel the horseman (Addie's natural son through an adulterous relationship with the Reverend Mr. Whitfield).

Jewel is fierce, fearless, and capable of expressing himself only through intense action. His one monologue (number 4), in protest against Cash's coffin-making, concludes with a possessing vision of guarding his dying mother against the family and all the world:

> It would not be happening with every bastard in the county coming in to stare at her because if there is a God what the hell is He for. It would just be me and her on a high hill and me rolling the rocks down the hill at their faces, picking them up and throwing them down the hill faces and teeth and all by God until she was quiet.

Jewel and Darl hate one another with mutual passion, and there is a dark, implicitly incestuous hostility between Darl and Dewey Dell. Cash, who is on warm terms with all his siblings, is simple, direct, and heroically enduring, and like Jewel a man of unreflective, physical courage. But Darl is the heart, and the greatness, of *As I Lay Dying*, and clearly Faulkner's surrogate narrator.

Darl ends in what looks like what we call schizophrenia, but his uncanniness and visionary power cannot be reduced to madness. All of his nineteen interior monologues are remarkable, as here in the conclusion to number 17:

> . . . And since sleep is is-not and rain and wind are *was*, it is not. Yet the wagon *is*, because when the wagon is *was*, Addie Bundren

will not be. And Jewel *is*, so Addie Bundren must be. And then I
must be, or I could not empty myself for sleep in a strange room.
And so if I am not emptied yet, I am *is*.

How often have I lain beneath rain on a strange roof, thinking
of home.

Doubting his own identity, Darl has a Shakespearean awareness of nothingness, which is a version of Faulkner's own nihilism (again, in his great
phase, 1929–39) and of Faulkner's wartime experience, of training for the
British Royal Air Force but never taking off in a plane. Darl too has been
away at World War I, but it has left little mark upon his consciousness.
Hating the terrible wagon odyssey of bringing Addie's corpse back to its
birthplace, Darl nearly sabotages the effort with a barn-burning, but this
only inspires Jewel to fresh heroics.

Darl is a *knower*, as Faulkner continuously emphasizes. He knows that
his sister is pregnant, that Jewel is not Anse's son, that his mother is in
no true sense *his* mother, and that the human predicament is a kind of
aboriginal disaster. And he knows that even the landscape is an emptiness,
a falling-away from a prior reality, as here in section number 34:

> Above the ceaseless surface they stand—trees, cane, vines—root-
> less, severed from the earth, spectral above a scene of immense
> yet circumscribed desolation filled with the voice of the waste and
> mournful water.

An intuitive poet and metaphysician, Darl is dangerously close to a verge
over which he must fall. His psychic wounds are the legacy in him of Addie's
coldness and Anse's selfishness; he is fated for alienation. No escape is possible for Darl; his only sexual desires are for his own sister, and his family
is his doom.

In Darl's final monologue (number 57), he is so dissociated from himself
that all his perceptions, uncannier than ever, observe him in the third person. Two guards escort him to the state asylum on the train, and we hear
his voice at its most shattering:

> One of them sat beside him, the other sat on the seat facing him,
> riding backward. One of them had to ride backward because the
> state's money has a face to each backside and a backside to each

face, and they are riding on the state's money which is incest. A nickel has a woman on one side and a buffalo on the other; two faces and no back.

Darl, split in half, holds conversations with himself, yet remains a seer: "the state's money which is incest." The passage is haunted by Iago's Rabelaisian jest of heterosexual love being a beast with two backs, yet there is a deeper Shakespeareanism in seeing the state's money as being incest; *Measure for Measure* is close by.

The reader must find *As I Lay Dying* difficult: it *is* difficult, yet legitimately so. Faulkner, who acutely felt the need to be his own father, infuriates some feminists by his obsessive, implicit identification of death and female sexuality. Darl's sanity dies with his mother, but in some sense his derangement makes explicit what is muted in his siblings. Nature, in *As I Lay Dying*, is itself a wound. André Gide oddly observed that Faulkner's characters lacked souls; what Gide meant to say is that the Bundrens, like the Compsons in *The Sound and the Fury*, had no hope, could not believe that their doom would ever lift. God will not make any covenant with the Bundrens or the Compsons, perhaps because they come out of an abyss and must go into it again. That may be why Dewey Dell cries out so desperately that she believes in God. *As I Lay Dying* portrays the human condition as being catastrophic, with the nuclear family the most terrible of the catastrophes.

Except for *As I Lay Dying*, I take *Light in August* to be Faulkner's finest aesthetic achievement. It tends to defeat criticism, perhaps because the false touchstone of "unity" is applied to it. The sagas of Joe Christmas, Hightower, and Lena are separate stories, and the links between them are minor. But narrative power sustains all three recitals, and each is aided by juxtaposition with the others. The existence of Joe Christmas is a continuous nightmare, while Hightower dwells in an unreal dream, and Lena moves on like the natural process she both exemplifies and enhances. Faulkner gives Lena the opening and closing visions, framing the violence, hatred, self-destructive drive of the rest of the novel. Faulkner's esteem for her is palpable and clearly redeems much of the misogyny that feminists assert to be his stance.

So intricate is the plot of *Light in August* that I find it helpful to note its more labyrinthine and sinuously elaborate aspects. As Lena travels to Jefferson, she sees a burning house in the middle distance. Only later will we learn that this is Joanna Burden's house, torched by Joe Christmas, who has murdered her.

Byron Bunch, who falls in love with Lena at first glance, is Hightower's friend. The two represent polarities of being, though both are humane and decent persons. Byron lives in reality, Hightower in a Tennysonian dream of the past and all its illusions. Civil War legends of his grandfather—a daring raid or an ignoble immolation by shotgun while chicken-stealing—mingle with bizarre memories of his wife's infidelity and his subsequent expulsion by his parish congregation. These also are gilded by dream-distancing. It is not until Hightower delivers Lena's baby that he encounters reality. This leads to his culminating attempt to save Joe Christmas from a lynch mob of the Ku Klux Klan, akin to Byron Bunch's beating by Lucas Burch, Lena's perpetually illusive despoiler.

Light in August is the book of Joe Christmas, a man neither black nor white, decent nor evil, who is doomed by his region, upbringing, and election as a born, total victim. His symbolic relation to Jesus Christ has nothing to do with redemption or divinity but only with the exemplary status of Jesus as infinite sufferer.

Faulkner's sympathy with Joe Christmas is not shared by the reader, because the novelist renders the outcast in terms that are antipathetic: Christmas is murderous, vicious to all women as such, and loathes his own sexual desires while abominating theirs. He *is* the death drive beyond the pleasure principle and contaminates Joanna Burden with what becomes her own northern Puritan version of the same destructive malady.

Is he a tragic protagonist? Not in the Shakespearean sense: he is a more complex cartoon than Popeye but a caricature nevertheless. For tragic, almost Shakespearean figures in Faulkner, you turn to Darl Bundren and Quentin Compson, who possess consciousness, while Thomas Sutpen seems to me precariously balanced between Marlovian caricature and Shakespearean inwardness.

And yet there seems no end to Joe Christmas; like Darl Bundren, he intimates no limits. Faulkner has managed to catch in Joe something permanently American, not just southern. Not knowing yet fearing personal "blackness," Christmas in one sense is the American everyman, wondering just who or what he or she is or madly fearing madness, murderous impulses, suicide, lovelessness, or the curse of sundered parentage. I never will understand Cleanth Brooks on Faulkner. Somehow that archetypal southern critic thought Faulkner exalted both supposed community values and family cohesiveness. *Light in August* acutely shows the malign influence of both Mississippi social mores and family romance.

And yet the novel is Faulkner's richest in the novelty of its tonalities and human stances. Balancing Christmas and the increasingly deranged Joanna, and the dubious grouping of Lucas Burch, McEachern, and Doc Hines, are the book's extremes: the Nazi stormtrooper-in-advance, Percy Grimm, who murders and mutilates Joe Christmas; the benignly deluded Hightower; Byron Bunch; and, above all, there is Lena Grove, the unfallen Eve of an otherwise desolated world.

Indeed *Light in August* is the book of Joe Christmas; and yet whenever I recall it, I think first of Lena. Her relevance to the book has been questioned but not by any deep reader of Faulkner. Her serene presence contributes to what can be termed Faulkner's "ecstasy of the ordinary," curious moments that are secular epiphanies.

Like his ancestor Melville in *Moby-Dick* and his disciple Cormac McCarthy in *Blood Meridian*, Faulkner alternates violent action with a quietism akin to that which calms Melville's "tornadoed Atlantic of my being." There are in Faulkner uncanny moments of listening, as if his narrative art sought a still center, where racial and personal violence, and the agonies of copulation and dying, could never intrude.

Vladimir Nabokov

(1899–1977)

NABOKOV WAS GIVEN to lamenting that his American English could never match the richness of his native Russian style, a lament that seems an irony when the reader confronts the baroquely rich textures of his story "The Vane Sisters." Our narrator, himself French in origin, instructs in French literature at a New England women's college. Nabokovian through and through, this nameless narrator is a finicky aesthete, a harmless version of Oscar Wilde's Dorian Gray. The Vane sisters are Cynthia and Sybil, whose name and suicide are borrowed from Dorian Gray's victimized girlfriend, though both young women are more Henry Jamesian than Wildean, since they are evanescent and indirect personalities. The nameless French professor was the teacher of Sybil, and the estranged close friend of Cynthia, but the lover of neither.

The narrator begins with a chance hearing of Cynthia's death by heart attack. He is taking his usual Sunday afternoon stroll and stops "to watch a family of brilliant icicles drip-dropping from the eaves of a frame house." A long paragraph is devoted to these icicles, and later he observes: "The lean ghost, the elongated umbra cast by a parking meter upon some damp snow, had a strange ruddy tinge." At the story's end, he wakes from a vague dream of Cynthia, but cannot unravel it:

> I could isolate, consciously, little. Everything seemed blurred, yellow-clouded, yielding nothing tangible. Her inept acrostics, maudlin evasions, theopathies—every recollection formed ripples of mysterious meaning. Everything seemed yellowly blurred, illusive, lost.

The self-parody of Nabokov's own style here testifies that Sybil's acrostics are not as inept as Cynthia's. Work out the acrostic formed by the initial letters of this passage and you get *Icicles by Cynthia, meter from me, Sybil.* Our narrator is haunted then by both women, but why? Probably because the Vane sisters glided ghostlike through their existence anyway; death seems hardly to alter them. But why the French professor as the object of these charmingly mischievous shades? It is possible that the narrator, being a Nabokovian self-parody, is being punished for Nabokov's own aestheticism and skepticism. Unlike Maupassant's "The Horla," which represents a gathering madness, "The Vane Sisters" is an authentic though highly original ghost story

Sybil Vane, the day after taking a midyear examination in French literature, given by the narrator, kills herself in reaction to being abandoned by her married lover. We get to know the older sister, Cynthia, rather better, after Sybil's death. Cynthia is a painter and a spiritualist, and has evolved a "theory of intervenient auras." These auras of the deceased intervene benignly in the lives of their survivors. After the narrator's skepticism alienates Cynthia—she accurately also calls him a prig and a snob—he breaks with her and forgets her until he is told of her death. Discreetly, she haunts him, until the climactic dream he cannot decipher, and the final acrostic, which we can.

Nabokov's story, though brief, is replete with literary allusions—to Emerson's "transparent eyeball" (from his *Nature*) and Coleridge's person from Porlock (who supposedly interrupted the composition of "Kubla Khan"). There are also vivid manifestations of Oscar Wilde and of Tolstoy at a séance, and an extraordinary general atmosphere of literary preciosity. What makes "The Vane Sisters" magical is that the reader's own skepticism is overcome by the curious charm of these amiable women whose existences, and after-auras, alike are so tenuous. The reader is separated by Nabokov from the narrator's priggishness, but not necessarily from his skepticism. Pragmatically, though, skepticism makes little difference here; these ghosts are persuasive precisely because they are so uninsistent upon persuasion. One doesn't think of the author of *Pale Fire* and *Lolita* as a Chekhovian writer. Nabokov adored Nikolai Gogol, whose spirit was fiercer (and more lunatic) than Chekhov's. But Cynthia and Sybil Vane would be at home in Chekhov; like so many of his women they represent the pathos of the unlived life. Nabokov, not much interested in pathos, prefers them as whimsical ghosts.

Hart Crane
(1899–1932)

CRANE COMPOSED "Repose of Rivers" in 1926 before leaving for the Isle of Pines in the Caribbean to continue work on *The Bridge*. He was able to place the poem in *White Buildings*, where its excellence vies with "Possessions" and the "Voyages" sequence.

The incarnation of the poetical character crucial to the Romantic Sublime takes place in the scene of instruction in "Repose of Rivers." Crane chooses *Moby-Dick* and "Song of Myself" as his poem's allusive starting points because he stands upon the threshold of his *annus mirabilis* and wishes his strongest American precursors to aid his own quest. Sexual orientation and poetic maturation are allied here: Whitman's love of comrades and the Ishmael-Queequeg "marriage" are part of the forerunners' role.

Once I ventured the interpretation that Crane's "How much I would have bartered!" in "Repose of Rivers" intimated an exchange of "nature for poetry," but that was simplistic. Who is to define "nature"? King Lear's "nature" is antithetical to Edmund the Bastard's, and Allen Tate's and Yvor Winters's conviction that their friend Crane's sexual orientation was unnatural is now of little interest. Crane was scarcely happy in his homoeroticism but would have been unhappier still as a lover of women. He had been a battleground upon which his selfish and stupid parents pursued their narcissistic motives, thus rending his psyche: his mother, highly neurotic and immature, whose beauty faded quickly, and his business magnate father couldn't get along almost from the start, and they sought to alienate each other from their child. So intense was his daemonic genius that he survived to become a great poet, but his self-destructiveness became the cost of that confirmation.

Crane is fiercely subtle, even for him, in blending his voice with that of the river:

> The willows carried a slow sound,
> A sarabande the wind mowed on the mead.

I could never remember
That seething, steady leveling of the marshes
Till age had brought me to the sea.

In chapter 58 of *Moby-Dick*, the right-whales feed on brit:

As morning mowers, who side by side slowly and seethingly advance their scythes through the long wet grass of marshy meads; even so these monsters swam, making a strange, grassy, cutting sound . . .

A sarabande is a slow, stately Spanish dance of past centuries. The poem being visionary and scarcely natural, phantasmagoria is everywhere: rivers that speak, winds that dance, mammoth turtles slow in cruel coition and destroyed by the sun's heat. Crane's likely source was "The Encantadas" in Melville's *Piazza Tales*, but there is a clear parallel in D. H. Lawrence's tortoise poems in *Birds, Beasts, and Flowers*.

In the following stanza, "flags, weeds" suggests Whitman in "Song of Myself," as does the poet's incestuous entry into the mothering waters. Whitman merges with the mother in the hermit thrush's song of death in the "Lilacs" elegy:

Flags, weeds. And remembrance of steep alcoves
Where cypresses shared the noon's
Tyranny; they drew me into hades almost.
And mammoth turtles climbing sulphur dreams
Yielded, while sun-silt rippled them
Asunder . . .

How much I would have bartered! the black gorge
And all the singular nestings in the hills
Where beavers learn stitch and tooth.
The pond I entered once and quickly fled—
I remember now its singing willow rim.

The cypress traditionally represents erotic suffering, while the willow is the emblem of mourning and also the signature of Orpheus. Crane employs the "alcoves"/"almost" pararhyme to intensify the hazard of heterosexual incest: "the pond I entered once and quickly fled." Anyone who has watched the violent courtship of beavers will appreciate "stitch and tooth."

The slow sound of the willows swells into the pond's singing willow rim and preludes the poem's superb resolution:

> And finally, in that memory all things nurse;
> After the city that I finally passed
> With scalding unguents spread and smoking darts
> The monsoon cut across the delta
> At gulf gates . . . There, beyond the dykes
>
> I heard wind flaking sapphire, like this summer,
> And willows could not hold more steady sound.

The city is at once Hart Crane's New York and the Mississippi's New Orleans, as it will be in the extraordinary close of "The River" in *The Bridge*. The stinging rancidity of the homoerotic "scalding unguents spread and smoking darts" is poetically offset by the Shelleyan and Orphic close of the last two lines.

The flaking of the sapphire sky is at once an Orphic breaking and a Shelleyan showering of the azure of vision. As Langdon Hammer noted, this is apocalyptic, another falling away of nature. "Repose of Rivers" shares the stance of Blake and of Shelley and is worthy of them.

Crane wrote this superb tribute to Herman Melville in October 1925 and printed it in *White Buildings*, where it is placed just before the six "Voyages." Melville's "tomb" is the ocean and *Moby-Dick* but also the primal abyss below the waves.

> Often beneath the wave, wide from this ledge
> The dice of drowned men's bones he saw bequeath
> An embassy. Their numbers as he watched,
> Beat on the dusty shore and were obscured.
>
> And wrecks passed without sound of bells,
> The calyx of death's bounty giving back
> A scattered chapter, livid hieroglyph,
> The portent wound in corridors of shells.

Then in the circuit calm of one vast coil,
Its lashings charmed and malice reconciled,
Frosted eyes there were that lifted altars;
And silent answers crept across the stars.

Compass, quadrant and sextant contrive
No farther tides . . . High in the azure steeps
Monody shall not wake the mariner.
This fabulous shadow only the sea keeps.

Several of my departed friends, lovers alike of Melville and of Crane, requested that this poem be read at their final services. It is a last word for Melville, Hart Crane, and all readers who share their tragic vision of materialism in matters pertaining to death.

Crane's control is a miracle of firmness and restraint in this very formal lyric. Like Hamlet, Melville is death's ambassador to us. The "numbers" refer to the dice into which the sea has rendered the bodies of the drowned men but also to Crane's metric. "Calyx" is at once a vortex of a sinking ship, like Ahab's *Pequod*, and also a cornucopia. The Greek word "calyx," which refers to a flower's outer whorl, also meant a chalice or drinking vessel. John Irwin, the great authority on the image of hieroglyphics in the American Renaissance, reminds us that tattooed Queequeg is himself a hieroglyphic, but so are Ahab and his entire book. The White Whale and livid Ahab become the largest of daemonic hieroglyphics.

With the "coil" and "lashings," we are still in the world of *Moby-Dick*, where both refer to the mode of Ahab's death. The "frosted eyes" are those of the floating Ishmael gazing up at the constellation Ara (the altar), while the silent answers are from the constellations Cetus (the whale) and Argo Navis (the boat *Argo*).

In a dramatic moment in *Moby-Dick*, Ahab destroys his quadrant, a navigational device, while later in the novel the *Pequod*'s compass suffers reversal. Crane, in a letter to Harriet Monroe, remarked that instruments like the compass, quadrant, and sextant have extended concepts of space in the imagination so that now metaphorically they have expanded the boundaries of both the seen and unseen.

The poet's monody will not wake Melville the mariner, since neither the author of *Moby-Dick* nor of *The Bridge* believes in resurrection. What remains is a fabulous shadow both of Ahab and his crew and of Hart Crane himself, another drowned man whom only the sea keeps.

Crane's "Voyages II" is the equivalent in the twentieth century of Coleridge's "Kubla Khan" in the nineteenth: an absolute cognitive music caught in a single lyric with immense reverberation. I memorized both poems long ago, before I comprehended either, and only now is my appreciation flowering into full clarity.

Sea change, a great Shakespearean trope, haunts both *The Waste Land* and "Voyages." Crane, in his love for Emil Opffer, the Danish merchant mariner with whom he had a short but passionate relationship, suffers sa ea change even as the poet overhears his own poem and tallies his losses. Ecstatic celebration of mutual passion ebbs with an ebb of the ocean of life. Following in the wake of Shelley, Crane also discovers that love and the means of love are irreconcilable.

Shelley's *Alastor, or The Spirit of Solitude*, composed in 1815 when he was twenty-three, is a young poet's remorseless quest to unite with a dream woman. Narcissistic and solipsistic, he is haunted by his daemon, a nemesis who is an avenging spirit. Voyaging in a little shallop down the shores of Asia Minor, the poet wastes away into death. Crane takes from *Alastor* a unity of "sleep, death, desire" and the poet's voyage, which becomes the slow, rocking movement of the boat carrying the lovers through "adagios of islands." "Voyages I," composed earlier, introduces the menace of its final line: "the bottom of the sea is cruel." Until then it weaves together the children playing upon the shore from Wordsworth's "Immortality" ode and Whitman's fantasia of the twenty-nine bathers from "Song of Myself," with Crane in the role of the female twenty-ninth bather. In "Voyages II," we inhabit a different world, Hart Crane's heterocosm. Though it is a realm of total sexual fulfillment, the daemonic sense of loss floods the poem, foretelling total surrender to death.

Crane loads every rift with ore (the agonistic advice of Keats to Shelley in a letter that suggests Shelley's poetry is being composed too profusely and hastily) and achieves a rhetorical richness that rivals Coleridge, Shelley, Keats, and Tennyson. The poem's surge of erotic ecstasy is carried by a rhapsodic intensity beyond anything created earlier by the American Orphic poet, whose muse is not so much Emil Opffer as it is Crane's own daemon, potential divinity but also the guilt of the slayers of Dionysus.

"Voyages II" returns us to Melville's tomb, at once the ocean and the language of *Moby-Dick*:

—And yet this great wink of eternity,
Of rimless floods, unfettered leewardings,
Samite sheeted and processioned where
Her undinal vast belly moonward bends,
Laughing the wrapt inflections of our love;

Take this Sea, whose diapason knells
On scrolls of silver snowy sentences,
The sceptered terror of whose sessions rends
As her demeanors motion well or ill,
All but the pieties of lovers' hands.

And onward, as bells off San Salvador
Salute the crocus lustres of the stars,
In these poinsettia meadows of her tides,—
Adagios of islands, O my Prodigal,
Complete the dark confessions her veins spell.

Mark how her turning shoulders wind the hours,
And hasten while her penniless rich palms
Pass superscription of bent foam and wave,—
Hasten, while they are true,—sleep, death, desire,
Close round one instant in one floating flower.

Bind us in time, O Seasons clear, and awe.
O minstrel galleons of Carib fire,
Bequeath us to no earthly shore until
Is answered in the vortex of our grave
The seal's wide spindrift gaze toward paradise.

In "The Spirit-Spout" chapter of *Moby-Dick*, "all the waves rolled by like scrolls of silver; and, by their soft, suffusing seethings, made what seemed a silvery silence." The mark of Melville is strong throughout: *Moby-Dick* is the American epic "of rimless floods, unfettered leewardings."

The Tennysonian "samite sheeted and processioned," with its silken aura of the Lady of the Lake, clashes with the "undinal vast belly" of the sea bending moonward, seeking a lover who might give her a soul. Punning on "wrapped" and "rapt," Crane implicitly begins the sea's negative judgment of the lovers, whose inflected tonalities of passion are mocked.

Nevertheless, Crane remains bold: "Take this Sea." Its rush of sound "knells" on scrolls that are sentences of death, delivered by an authority whose supposed benignity instead "rends" in sessions of "sceptered terror" the bodies of the lovers yet cannot end the pieties of their joined hands.

After the knelling come the "bells," which perhaps came about from a story Emil Opffer told Crane about the lost city of Port Royal, Jamaica, which was sucked into the sea following a great earthquake in 1692. Crane was excited at the legend which claimed that standing on the shore one still could hear sunken church bells ringing, tolling with the tide—a story Crane assimilated with the legend of lost Atlantis. That he refers to San Salvador instead of Jamaica is another of Crane's brilliant transpositions, as legend also had it that Columbus first set foot in the New World on the coast of San Salvador.

Two stanzas into this lyric of implication, I stand back to ask: What has Crane subtly left out? This is not the mothering sea of Walt Whitman but the estranging element in Herman Melville.

In Hart Crane's gnosis—as in Melville's—the sea is part of the broken world, the universe of death. "Voyages II," in its desire to celebrate (though unable to prolong) Crane's authentic love, has to exercise the poet's power of mind over the universe of death. Can it? Is it so exercised? The sea's demeanors capriciously can motion well or ill, but I dissent from John Irwin, Crane's best critic, when he speaks of the sea's sympathy for the lovers. Like its lover the moon, the sea is time and destroys love and lovers.

Against time and the sea, Crane sets one of his best-known tropes: "adagios of islands." At once the reference is to the slow, rocking motion of a small boat as it winds through islets, the sexual exchange between the lovers, and also an assertion against the rapid pace that will end them.

The sea becomes a clock, compelling haste. Yet it is sleep, death, desire, and not the sea, that will fail and become false. A closing prayer asks for the lovers to be covenanted "in time" yet only to be reprieved long enough to achieve both clarity and awe, in Emily Dickinson's sense of her love for Judge Otis Lord.

The *Pequod's* fate is invoked again in "the vortex," the conceptual image of whirlpool that will end Crane and his lover in the yearning glance of *Moby-Dick's* young seals seeking their lost mothers, a paradise unknown.

But why the Melvillean "spindrift" for spray? The lovers, like the bereft seals, will receive an answer but only one indistinctly seen through spray.

The harmonies of "Voyages II" are deliberately at odds with its implicit sense of destruction. Yet Crane's rhetorical art achieves an apotheosis that even he could not often match.

Readers are so accustomed to seeing "To Brooklyn Bridge" as a proem, or opening dedication to *The Bridge,* that it can be initially startling to realize how differently it works in the compositional sequence. It was written in January 1927, just after "The Tunnel" and directly before "The Harbor Dawn." A daemonic Hand of Fire traces a path from the quester "searching, thumbing the midnight on the piers" through the dawn and on to night again, "under thy shadow by the piers," and then on to another dawn awakening, with Crane in his room overlooking Brooklyn Bridge. More inwardly, the movement is an ascent from Hades through "prayer of pariah, and the lover's cry," on to the waking dream of union with an unknown woman.

However contextualized, "To Brooklyn Bridge" is one of Crane's aesthetically perfect lyrics, standing with "Voyages II," "Repose of Rivers," and "The Broken Tower." Its eleven quatrains echo Blake yet are more in the mode of the Spanish mystical poet John of the Cross, whom Crane had not read:

> O harp and altar, of the fury fused,
> (How could mere toil align thy choiring strings!)
> Terrific threshold of the prophet's pledge,
> Prayer of pariah, and the lover's cry,—

> Again the traffic lights that skim thy swift
> Unfractioned idiom, immaculate sigh of stars,
> Beading thy path—condense eternity:
> And we have seen night lifted in thine arms.

> Under thy shadow by the piers I waited;
> Only in darkness is thy shadow clear.
> The City's fiery parcels all undone,
> Already snow submerges an iron year . . .

O Sleepless as the river under thee,
Vaulting the sea, the prairies' dreaming sod,
Unto us lowliest sometime sweep, descend
And of the curveship lend a myth to God.

It is astonishing how Crane, addressing his bridge, invokes the diction and drive of a Catholic baroque mystic to adumbrate a vision of his personal transcendentalism, with its superb apotheosis of the American Sublime. I recite these three final stanzas to myself several times a day, because they capture so well the theurgy of Gnostic traditions: Hermetic, neo-Platonic, Kabbalistic.

Crane relies on his own "Atlantis" for the trope of Brooklyn Bridge as an Aeolian harp and as giving birth upon its altar to a God unknown. The evocation of Michelangelo's *Pietà*, where the Virgin Mary holds her cruci-fied son upon her lap with one of her hands beneath his armpit, as if she could raise him, is a poetic absolute in "and we have seen night lifted in thine arms." Audaciously, that transmembers Brooklyn Bridge into God's bride, lending thus of its curveship "a myth to God," who badly needs one.

The dark night of the soul of Saint John of the Cross, where the poet seeks God as his beloved, in the mode of the Song of Songs, has a fit com-panion in Crane's vigil under the shadow of the bridge. Master of trope, Crane surpasses himself in "the City's fiery parcels all undone." Envision, as he does, the towers of Manhattan ablaze with light, as though you'd unpacked gifts and the wrappings unfolded into points of flame. "An iron year" of suffering vanishes into the snow, and Crane utters the prayer of the pariah he was to become for many in 1929 through 1932.

The poet who had prophesied "new thresholds, new anatomies" and who had sought to memorialize the lover's cry renders instead the cry of the human lowliest, hoping only for the accolade of anonymity.

Like "the chartered Thames" of Blake's "London," the bay waters shed by the seagull are "chained," while the bridge, like Blake's sunflower, counts the steps of the sun. Keats is subtly invoked through his faith in the unspent motion of power-in-reserve.

Crane, when asked to select his best lyric, once chose "To Brooklyn Bridge" and "Voyages II" and "VI." This judgment was similar to his sense that *The Bridges'* "The Dance" was as good as he could do. Beyond his darkening consciousness, he could not have anticipated what must be his greatest poem, "The Broken Tower," written in Mexico from December

1931 to January 1932, before he plunged to his death-by-water on April 27, 1932, just thirty-two years and nine months old.

In *Voyager* (1969), his distinguished biographical study of Crane, John Unterecker quotes Lesley Simpson, a friend of the poet during his tumultuous year in Mexico:

> I was with Hart Crane in Taxco, Mexico, the morning of January 27, this year, when he first conceived the idea of "The Broken Tower." The night before, being troubled with insomnia, he had risen before daybreak and walked down to the village square. . . . Hart met the old Indian bell-ringer who was on his way down to the church. He and Hart were old friends, and he brought Hart up into the tower with him to help ring the bells. As Hart was swinging the clapper of the great bell, half drunk with its mighty music, the swift tropical dawn broke over the mountains. The sublimity of the scene and the thunder of the bells woke in Hart one of those gusts of joy of which only he was capable. He came striding up the hill afterwards in a sort of frenzy, refused his breakfast, and paced up and down the porch impatiently waiting for me to finish my coffee. Then he seized my arm and bore me off to the plaza, where we sat in the shadow of the church, Hart the while pouring out a magnificent cascade of words. It was . . . an experience I shall never forget.

Simpson recently had heard Crane, in a resonant voice, chant aloud the entire *Bridge*. There are, alas, no recordings of Crane's performances: they would enhance our ability to master his difficulties. Though "The Broken Tower" fuses so many echoes and allusions into its swift, unfractioned idiom, its elegy for the poetic self achieves memorable clarity.

As he ceaselessly revised, Crane changed the manuscript version from "Those stark / Black shadows in the tower" to "shadows in the tower" in his opening stanzas:

> The bell-rope that gathers God at dawn
> Dispatches me as though I dropped down the knell
> Of a spent day—to wander the cathedral lawn
> From pit to crucifix, feet chill on steps from hell.

Have you not heard, have you not seen that corps
Of shadows in the tower, whose shoulders sway
Antiphonal carillons launched before
The stars are caught and hived in the sun's ray?

The image of a broken tower begins in English with Chaucer's "The Knight's Tale," where Saturn as the God of Time proclaims his sway:

Min is the ruine of the highe halles,
The falling of the towers and of the walles.

Spenser directly anticipates Crane in Book I, Canto II, of *The Faerie Queene*:

The old Ruines of a broken tower . . .

Milton's "Il Penseroso" created the Hermetic image of "some high lonely tower" of meditation, which influenced Shelley's "Prince Athanase":

His soul had wedded Wisdom, and her dower
Is love and justice, clothed in which he sate
Apart from men, as in a lonely tower.

Yeats, haunted by Shelley's image, employs it frequently, including in his book of the daemon, *Per Amica Silentia Lunae*: "the ringers in the tower have appointed for the hymen of the soul a passing bell."

Crane's sacred book was *Moby-Dick*, and he read widely elsewhere in Melville. *The Piazza Tales*, now most esteemed for "Benito Cereno" and "Bartleby, the Scrivener," also contains "The Encantadas," which influences both "Repose of Rivers" and "O Carib Isle!", while "The Bell-Tower" affects "The Broken Tower." Melville's allegory examines the fate of Bannadonna; the visionary architect is destroyed by his mechanical sexton slave Talus, who rings the titanic bell of a three-hundred-foot tower: "So the bell was too heavy for the tower. So the bell's main weakness was where man's blood had flawed it."

One of the fragments shored against Eliot's ruins as he concludes *The Waste Land* are the words from the French poet Gérard de Nerval's poem "El Desdichado," "la tour abolie," while earlier the poem gives us its own ruined towers:

And upside down in air were towers
Tolling reminiscent bells, that kept the hours
And voices singing out of empty cisterns and exhausted wells.

Though in anguish and suicidal despair, Crane keeps to his lifelong program of so transuming his wealth of forerunners as to make them seem belated and himself their ever-early if sacrificial displacement:

The bells, I say, the bells break down their tower;
And swing I know not where. Their tongues engrave
Membrane through marrow, my long-scattered score
Of broken intervals . . . And I, their sexton slave!

Oval encyclicals in canyons heaping
The impasse high with choir. Banked voices slain!
Pagodas, campaniles with reveilles outleaping—
O terraced echoes prostrate on the plain! . . .

After the supreme eloquence of his poetic gift breaking down his whole sense of being, unable to sustain his own daemonic inspiration, Crane relegates *Moby-Dick* and *The Waste Land* to "heaping / The impasse high with choir," recalling Captain Ahab saying of the White Whale: "he heaps me."

Crane then surpasses himself:

And so it was I entered the broken world
To trace the visionary company of love, its voice
An instant in the wind (I know not whither hurled)
But not for long to hold each desperate choice.

My word I poured. But was it cognate, scored
Of that tribunal monarch of the air
Whose thigh embronzes earth, strikes crystal Word
In wounds pledged once to hope,—cleft to despair?

More than a half century ago, I published a book on Romantic poetry called (after Crane) *The Visionary Company*. Many years later, I read Walter Pater's unfinished novel *Gaston de Latour* and tracked Crane's presence before me in chapter 1:

Seen from the incense-laden sanctuary, where the bishop was assuming one by one the pontifical ornaments, La Beauce, like a many-coloured carpet spread under the great dome, with the white double house-front quivering afar through the heat, though it looked as if you might touch with the hand its distant spaces, was for a moment the unreal thing. Gaston alone, with all his mystic preoccupations, by the privilege of youth, seemed to belong to both, and link the visionary company about him to the external scene.

Crane's poignant longing to be "healed, original now, and pure," quoted in the verses below, is consonant with Pater's scene. "My word I poured," but Apollyon, Revelation's blending of Satan and Apollo, scores with a hand of fire all of Crane's poetry, with its record of rage and partial appetite.

In loving desperation, Crane turns to his first and only woman, the sleeping Peggy Baird Cowley:

The steep encroachments of my blood left me
No answer (could blood hold such a lofty tower
As flings the question true?)—or is it she
Whose sweet mortality stirs latent power?—

And through whose pulse I hear, counting the strokes
My veins recall and add, revived and sure
The angelus of wars my chest evokes:
What I hold healed, original now, and pure . . .

The open question "is it she?" was soon answered negatively, but the brief relationship nevertheless is tenderly conveyed. The two final stanzas achieve Crane's last sublimity:

And builds, within, a tower that is not stone
(Not stone can jacket heaven)—but slip
Of pebbles,—visible wings of silence sown
In azure circles, widening as they dip

The matrix of the heart, lift down the eye
That shrines the quiet lake and swells a tower . . .

The commodious, tall decorum of that sky
Unseals her earth, and lifts love in its shower.

"Slip / Of pebbles" transmembers the slip of finely ground clay employed in pottery-making into the mingling of female and male sexual fluids, reminding us of the red clay of Adam's creation. A tribute to the close of Wallace Stevens's "Sunday Morning" can be heard in the "extended wings" that cunningly "dip / The matrix of the heart."

For his final image, Crane turned to Dante, *Paradiso*, Canto 14:

Qual si lamenta perché qui si moia
per viver colà sù, non vide quive
lo refrigerio de l'etterna ploia.

Whoever laments that here we must die in order to live up above
    does not see that the refreshment of the eternal shower is here.

Perhaps the spiritual force of Dante was too strong for Crane to subsume, yet he is yearning rather than asserting. His dying music was worthy of the greatness of his daemonic gift.

Ernest Hemingway
(1899–1961)

HEMINGWAY FREELY PROCLAIMED his relationship to *Huckleberry Finn*, and there is some basis for the assertion, except that there is little in common between the rhetorical stances of Twain and Hemingway. Kipling's *Kim*, in style and mode, is far closer to *Huckleberry Finn* than anything Hemingway wrote. The true accent of Hemingway's admirable style is to be found in an even greater and more surprising precursor:

> This grass is very dark to be from the white heads of old mothers,
> Darker than the colorless beards of old men,
> Dark to come from under the faint red roofs of mouths.

Or again:

> I clutch the rails of the fence, my gore drips, thinn'd with the
>   ooze of my skin,
> I fall on the weeds and stones,
> The riders spur their unwilling horses, haul close,
> Taunt my dizzy ears and beat me violently over the head with
>   whip-stocks.
>
> Agonies are one of my changes of garments,
> I do not ask the wounded person how he feels, I myself become
>   the wounded person,
> My hurts turn livid upon me as I lean on a cane and observe.

Hemingway is scarcely unique in not acknowledging the paternity of Walt Whitman; T. S. Eliot and Wallace Stevens are far closer to Whitman than William Carlos Williams and Hart Crane were, but literary influence is a paradoxical and antithetical process, about which we continue to know all too little. The profound affinities between Hemingway, Eliot, and Stevens are not accidental, but are family resemblances due to the repressed but crucial relation each had to Whitman's work. Hemingway characteristically boasted (in a letter to Sara Murphy, February 27, 1936) that he had knocked Stevens down quite handily: ". . . for statistics sake Mr. Stevens is 6 feet 2 weighs 522 lbs. and . . . when he hits the ground it is highly spectaculous." Since this match between the two writers took place in Key West on February 19, 1936, I am moved, as a loyal Stevensian, for statistics' sake to point out that the victorious Hemingway was born in 1899, and the defeated Stevens in 1879, so that the novelist was then going on thirty-seven, and the poet verging on fifty-seven. The two men doubtless despised one another, but in the letter celebrating his victory Hemingway calls Stevens "a damned fine poet" and Stevens always affirmed that Hemingway was essentially a poet, a judgment concurred in by Robert Penn Warren when he wrote that Hemingway "is essentially a lyric rather than a dramatic writer." Warren compared Hemingway to Wordsworth, which is feasible, but the resemblance to Whitman is far closer. Wordsworth would not have written, "I am the man, I suffer'd, I was there," but Hemingway almost persuades us he would have achieved that line had not Whitman set it down first.

It is now many years since Hemingway's suicide, and some aspects of his permanent canonical status seem beyond doubt. Only a handful of modern American novels seem certain to endure: *A Lost Lady, The Sun Also Rises, The Great Gatsby, Miss Lonelyhearts, Call It Sleep, The Crying of Lot 49, Mason & Dixon, American Pastoral, Sabbath's Theater, Blood Meridian,* and at least several by Faulkner, including *As I Lay Dying, Sanctuary, Light in August, The Sound and the Fury, Absalom, Absalom!* Two dozen stories by Hemingway could be added to the group, indeed perhaps all of *The First Forty-Nine Stories.* Faulkner is an eminence apart, but critics agree that Hemingway and Fitzgerald are his nearest rivals, largely on the strength of their shorter fiction. What seems unique is that Hemingway is the only American writer of prose fiction in this century who, as a stylist, rivals the principal poets: Stevens, Eliot, Frost, Hart Crane, aspects of Pound, W. C. Williams, Robert Penn Warren, and Elizabeth Bishop. This is hardly to say that Hemingway, at his best, fails at narrative or the representation of character. Rather, his peculiar excellence is closer to Whitman than to Twain, closer to Stevens than to Faulkner, and even closer to Eliot than to Fitzgerald, who was his friend and rival. He is an elegiac poet who mourns the self, who celebrates the self (rather less effectively), and who suffers divisions in the self. In the broadest tradition of American litera- ture, he stems ultimately from the Emersonian reliance on the god within, which is the line of Whitman, Thoreau, and Dickinson. He arrives late and dark in this tradition, and is one of its negative theologians, as it were, but as in Stevens the negations, the cancelings, are never final. Even the most ferocious of his stories, say "God Rest You Merry, Gentlemen" or "A Natural History of the Dead," can be said to celebrate what we might call the Real Absence. Doc Fischer, in "God Rest You Merry, Gentlemen," is a precursor of Nathanael West's Shrike in *Miss Lonelyhearts*, and his savage, implicit religiosity prophesies not only Shrike's Satanic stance but the entire demonic world of Pynchon's explicitly paranoid or Luddite visions. Perhaps there was a nostalgia for a Catholic order always abiding in Hemingway's consciousness, but the cosmos of his fiction, early and late, is American Gnostic, as it was in Melville, who first developed so strongly the negative side of the Emersonian religion of self-reliance.

Hemingway notoriously and splendidly was given to overtly agonistic images whenever he described his relationship to canonical writers, includ- ing Melville, a habit of description in which he has been followed by his true ephebe, Norman Mailer. In a grand letter (September 6–7, 1949) to his publisher Charles Scribner, he charmingly confessed, "Am a man with- out any ambition, except to be champion of the world, I wouldn't fight Dr. Tolstoi in a 20 round bout because I know he would knock my ears off." This modesty passed quickly, to be followed by, "If I can live to 60 I can beat him. (MAYBE)." Since the rest of the letter counts Turgenev, Maupassant, Henry James, even Cervantes, as well as Melville and Dostoevsky among the defeated, we can join Hemingway, himself, in admiring his extraordi- nary self-confidence. How justified was it, in terms of his ambitions?

It could be argued persuasively that Hemingway is the best short story writer in the English language from Joyce's *Dubliners* until the present. The aesthetic dignity of the short story need not be questioned, and yet we seem to ask more of a canonical writer. Hemingway wrote *The Sun Also Rises* and not *Ulysses*, which is only to say that his true genius was for very short stories, and hardly at all for extended narrative. Had he been primar- ily a poet, his lyrical gifts would have sufficed: we do not hold it against Yeats that his poems, not his plays, are his principal glory. Alas, neither Turgenev nor Henry James, neither Melville nor Mark Twain, provides true agonists for Hemingway. Instead, Maupassant is the apter rival. Of

Hemingway's intensity of style in the briefer compass, there is no question, but even *The Sun Also Rises* reads now as a series of epiphanies, of brilliant and memorable vignettes.

Much that has been harshly criticized in Hemingway, particularly in *For Whom the Bell Tolls*, results from his difficulty in adjusting his gifts to the demands of the novel. Robert Penn Warren suggested that Hemingway is successful when his "system of ironies and understatements is coherent." When incoherent, then, Hemingway's rhetoric fails as persuasion, which is to say, we read *To Have and Have Not* or *For Whom the Bell Tolls* and we are all too aware that the system of tropes is primarily what we are offered. Warren believes this not to be true of *A Farewell to Arms*, yet even the celebrated close of the novel seems now a worn understatement:

> But after I had got them out and shut the door and turned off the light it wasn't any good. It was like saying good-by to a statue. After a while I went out and left the hospital and walked back to the hotel in the rain.

Contrast this to the close of "Old Man at the Bridge," a story only two and a half pages long:

> There was nothing to do about him. It was Easter Sunday and the Fascists were advancing toward the Ebro. It was a gray overcast day with a low ceiling so their planes were not up. That and the fact that cats know how to look after themselves was all the good luck that old man would ever have.

The understatement continues to persuade here because the stoicism remains coherent and is admirably fitted by the rhetoric. A very short story concludes itself by permanently troping the mood of a particular moment in history. Vignette is Hemingway's natural mode, or call it hard-edged vignette: a literary sketch that somehow seems to be the beginning or end of something longer, yet truly is complete in itself. Hemingway's style encloses what ought to be unenclosed, so that the genre remains subtle yet trades its charm for punch. But a novel of 340 pages (*A Farewell to Arms*) which I have just finished reading again (after many years away from it) cannot sustain itself upon the rhetoric of vignette. After many understatements, too many, the reader begins to believe that he is reading a Hemingway imitator, like the accomplished John O'Hara, rather than the master himself. Hemingway's notorious fault is the monotony of repetition, which becomes a dulling litany in a somewhat less accomplished imitator like Nelson Algren, and sometimes seems self-parody when we must confront it in Hemingway.

Nothing is got for nothing, and a great style generates defenses in us, particularly when it sets the style of an age, as the Byronic Hemingway did. As with Byron, the color and variety of the artist's life become something of a veil between the work and our aesthetic apprehension of it. Hemingway's career included four marriages (and three divorces); service as an ambulance driver for the Italians in World War I (with an honorable wound); activity as a war correspondent in the Greek-Turkish War (1922), the Spanish Civil War (1937–39), the Chinese-Japanese War (1941), and the War against Hitler in Europe (1944–45). Add big-game hunting and fishing, safaris, expatriation in France and Cuba, bullfighting, the Nobel Prize, and ultimate suicide in Idaho, and you have an absurdly implausible life, apparently lived in imitation of Hemingway's own fiction. The final effect of the work and the life together is not less than mythological, as it was with Byron and with Whitman and with Oscar Wilde. Hemingway now is myth, and so is permanent as an image of American heroism, or perhaps more ruefully the American illusion of heroism. The best of Hemingway's work, the stories and *The Sun Also Rises*, are also a permanent part of the American mythology. Faulkner, Stevens, Frost, perhaps Eliot, and Hart Crane were stronger writers than Hemingway, but he alone in this American century has achieved the enduring status of myth.

Hemingway's best short stories surpass even *The Sun Also Rises*. Wallace Stevens, the strongest of modern American poets, once termed Hemingway "the most significant of living poets, so far as the subject of extraordinary reality is concerned." By "poet" here, Stevens meant the remarkable stylist of Hemingway's short stories, and by "extraordinary reality" he meant a poetic realm in which "consciousness takes the place of imagination." This high praise is merited by Hemingway's permanent achievements in the short story, some fifteen or so masterpieces, easy to parody (frequently by Hemingway himself) but impossible to forget.

Frank O'Connor, who disliked Hemingway as intensely as he liked Chekhov, remarks in *The Lonely Voice* that Hemingway's stories "illustrate a

technique in search of a subject" and therefore become "a minor art." Let
us see. Read the famous sketch called "Hills Like White Elephants," five
pages that are almost all dialogue, between a young woman and her lover,
while they wait for a train at a station in a provincial Spanish town. They
are continuing a disagreement as to the abortion he wishes her to undergo
when they reach Madrid. The story catches the moment of her defeat, and
very likely of the death of their relationship. And that is all. The dialogue
makes clear that the woman is vital and decent, while the man is a sensible
emptiness, selfish and unloving. The reader is wholly with her when she
responds to his "I'd do anything for you" with "Would you please please
please please please please please stop talking." Seven *pleases* are a lot,
but as repetition they are precise and persuasive in "Hills Like White Elephants." The story is beautifully prefigured in that simile of a title. Long
and white, the hills across the valley of the Ebro "look like white elephants"
to the woman, not to the man. White elephants, proverbial Siamese royal
gifts to courtiers who would be ruined by the expense of their upkeep,
become a larger metaphor for unwanted babies, and even more for erotic
relationships too spiritually costly when a man is inadequate.

Hemingway's personal mystique—his bravura poses as warrior, big-
game hunter, bullfighter, and boxer—is as irrelevant to "Hills Like White
Elephants" as its male protagonist's insistence that "You know I love you."
More relevant is the remark of Hemingway's surrogate Nick Adams, in
"The End of Something," when he terminates a relationship: "It isn't fun
any more." I don't know many women readers who like that sentence, but
it hardly is an *apologia*, only a very young man's self-indictment.

The Hemingway story that wounds me most is another five-pager, "God
Rest You Merry, Gentlemen," which is almost entirely dialogue, after its
opening paragraphs, including an outrageous initial sentence:

> In those days the distances were all very different, the dirt blew off
> the hills that now have been cut down, and Kansas City was very
> like Constantinople.

You can parody that by saying: "In those days Bridgeport, Connecticut, was very like Haifa." Still, we are in Kansas City on Christmas Day,
and listening to the conversation between two physicians: the incompetent
Doctor Wilcox, who relies upon a limp, leather, indexed volume, *The Young
Doctor's Friend and Guide*, and the mordant Doc Fischer, who begins by

quoting his coreligionist Shylock: "What news along the Rialto?" The news is very bad, as we learn soon enough: a boy of about sixteen, obsessed with purity, had come into the hospital to ask for castration. Turned away, he had mutilated himself with a razor and will probably die from loss of blood.

The interest of the story centers in Doc Fischer's lucid nihilism, prophetic of Nathanael West's Shrike in *Miss Lonelyhearts*:

> "Ride you, Doctor, on the day, the very anniversary, of our Savior's birth?"
>
> "*Our* Savior? Ain't you a Jew?" Doctor Wilcox said.
>
> "So I am. So I am. It always is slipping my mind. I've never given it its proper importance. So good of you to remind me. *Your* Savior. That's right. *Your* Savior, undoubtedly *your* Savior—and the ride for Palm Sunday."

"You, Wilcox, are the donkey upon whom I ride into Jerusalem" is the implication of that last phrase. Rancid and brilliant, Doc Fischer has peeked, as he says, into hell. His Shylockian intensity is a Hemingwayesque tribute to Shakespeare, described by Colonel Cantwell (Hemingway's surrogate) in *Across the River and into the Trees* as "the winner and still the undisputed champion." When he is most ambitious in his stories, Hemingway is most Shakespearean, as in the famous, quasi-autobiographical "The Snows of Kilimanjaro," its author's favorite. Of the story's protagonist, the failed writer Harry, Hemingway observes: "He had loved too much, demanded too much, and he wore it all out." That would be a superb critical remark to make about King Lear, Hemingway's most admired character in all of Shakespeare. More than anywhere else, Hemingway attempts and achieves tragedy in the relatively brief compass of "The Snows of Kilimanjaro."

The meditation of a dying man rather than the description of an action, this baroque story is Hemingway's most intense self-chastisement, and I think that Chekhov himself, much given to that mode, would have been impressed by it. One doesn't think of Hemingway as a visionary writer, but "The Snows of Kilimanjaro" begins with an epigraph telling us that the snow-covered western summit of the mountain is called the House of God, and close to it is the carcass, dried and frozen, of a leopard. There is no explanation as to what a leopard could have been seeking nearly twenty thousand feet above sea level.

Very little is gained by saying that the leopard is a symbol of the dying Harry. Originally, in ancient Greek, a *simbolon* was a token for identification that could be compared to a counterpart. Commonly, we use *symbol* more loosely, as something that stands for something else, whether by association or resemblance. If you identify the corpse of the leopard with Harry's lost but still-residual ambition or aesthetic idealism as a writer, then you plunge Hemingway's story into bathos and grotesquerie. Hemingway himself did that in *The Old Man and the Sea*, but not in the masterful "The Snows of Kilimanjaro."

Harry is dying, slowly, of gangrene in an African hunting camp, surrounded by vultures and hyenas, palpably unpleasant presences that need not be interpreted as symbolic. Neither need the leopard be so interpreted. Like Harry, it is out of place, but the writer's vision of Kilimanjaro does seem another of Hemingway's nostalgic visions of a lost spirituality, qualified as always by a keen sense of nothingness, a Shakespearean nihilism. It seems useful to regard the uncanny presence of the dead leopard as a strong irony, a forerunner of Harry's vain quest to recover his identity as a writer at Kilimanjaro, rather than, say, at Paris, Madrid, Key West, or Havana. The irony is at Hemingway's own expense, insofar as Harry prophesies the Hemingway who, nineteen days short of his sixty-second birthday, turned a double-barreled shotgun on himself in the mountains of Idaho. Yet the story is not primarily ironical and need not be read as a personal prophecy. Harry is a failed Hemingway; Hemingway, by being able to compose "The Snows of Kilimanjaro," is precisely not a failure, at least as a writer.

The best moment in the story is hallucinatory and comes just before the end. It is Harry's dying vision, though the reader cannot know that, until Harry's wife, Helen, realizes she can no longer hear him breathing. As he died, Harry dreamed that the rescue plane had come for him, but could carry only one passenger. On the visionary flight, Harry is taken up to see the square top of Kilimanjaro: "great, high, and unbelievably white in the sun." This apparent image of transcendence is the most illusive moment in the story; it represents death, and not the House of God. A dying man's phantasmagoria is not to be regarded as triumphal, when the entire story conveys Harry's conviction that he has wasted his gifts as a writer.

Yet Hemingway may have remembered King Lear's dying fantasy, in which the old, mad king is persuaded that his beloved daughter Cordelia breathes again, despite her murder. If you love too much, and demand too much, then you, like Lear and Harry (and, at last, Hemingway), will wear it all out. Fantasy, for Harry, takes the place of art.

Hemingway was so wonderful and unexpected a story writer that I choose to end my account of him here with one of his unknown masterpieces, the splendidly ironic "A Sea Change," which prefigures his posthumously published novel *The Garden of Eden*, with its portrayal of ambiguous sexualities. In "A Sea Change" we are in a Parisian bar, where an archetypal Hemingwayesque couple are engaged in a crisp dialogue on infidelity. It takes the reader only a few exchanges to realize that the "sea change" of the title does not refer to the woman, who is determined to begin (or continue) a lesbian relationship, yet wishes also to return to the man. It is the man who is suffering a sea change, presumably into the writer who will compose the rich and strange *The Garden of Eden*.

"I'm a different man," he twice announces to the uncomprehending bartender, after the woman has left. Looking into the mirror, he *sees* the difference, but what he sees we are not told. Though he remarks to the bartender that "vice is a very strange thing," it cannot be a consciousness of "vice" that has made him a different man. Rather, it is his imaginative yielding to the woman's persuasive defense that has altered him forever. "We're made up of all sorts of things. You've known that. You've used it well enough," she has said to him, and he tacitly acknowledges some crucial element in the sexuality they have shared. He suffers now a sea change, but nothing of him fades in this moment of only apparent loss. Almost too deft for irony, "A Sea Change" is a subtle self-recognition, an erotic autobiography remarkable for its indirection and its nuanced self-acceptance. Only the finest American master of the short story could have placed so much in so slight a sketch.

Nathanael West

(1903–1940)

NATHANAEL WEST, who died in an automobile accident in 1940 at the age of thirty-seven, wrote one remorseless masterpiece, *Miss Lonelyhearts* (1933). Despite some astonishing sequences, *The Day of the Locust* (1939) is an overpraised work, a waste of West's genius. Of the two lesser fictions, *The Dream Life of Balso Snell* (1931) is squalid and dreadful, with occasional passages of a rancid power, while *A Cool Million* (1934), though an outrageous parody of American picaresque, is a permanent work of American satire and seems to me underpraised. To call West uneven is therefore a litotes; he is a wild medley of magnificent writing and inadequate writing, except in *Miss Lonelyhearts*, which excels *The Sun Also Rises*, *The Great Gatsby*, and even *Sanctuary* as the perfected instance of a negative vision in modern American fiction. The greatest Faulkner, of *The Sound and the Fury*, *As I Lay Dying*, *Absalom, Absalom!*, and *Light in August*, is the only American writer of prose fiction in the twentieth century who can be said to have surpassed *Miss Lonelyhearts*. West's spirit lives again in *The Crying of Lot 49* and some sequences in *Gravity's Rainbow*, but the negative sublimity of *Miss Lonelyhearts* proves to be beyond Pynchon's reach, or perhaps his ambition.

West, born Nathan Weinstein, is a significant episode in the long and tormented history of Jewish Gnosticism. The late Gershom Scholem's superb essay "Redemption Through Sin," in his *The Messianic Idea in Judaism*, is the best commentary I know upon *Miss Lonelyhearts*. I once attempted to convey this to Scholem, who shrugged West off, quite properly from Scholem's viewpoint, when I remarked to him that West was manifestly a Jewish anti-Semite, and admitted that there were no allusions to Jewish esotericism or Kabbalah in his works. Nevertheless, for the stance of literary criticism, Jewish Gnosticism, as defined by Scholem, is the most illuminating context in which to study West's novels. It is a melancholy paradox that West, who did not wish to be Jewish in any way at all, remains the most indisputably Jewish writer yet to appear in America, a judgment at once aesthetic and moral. Nothing by Bellow, Malamud, Mailer, or Ozick can compare to *Miss Lonelyhearts* as an achievement. Philip Roth's *Sabbath's Theater* may stand with any American novel. But West's Jewish heir, if he has one, may be Joshua Cohen, whose *Book of Numbers* can be regarded as another powerful instance of Jewish Gnosis, free of West's hatred of his own Jewishness.

Stanley Edgar Hyman, in his pamphlet on West (1962), concluded that "his strength lay in his vulgarity and bad taste, his pessimism, his nastiness." Hyman remains West's most useful critic, but I would amend this by observing that these qualities in West's writing emanate from a negative theology, spiritually authentic, and given aesthetic dignity by the force of West's eloquent negations. West, like his grandest creation, Shrike, is a rhetorician of the abyss, in the tradition of Sabbatian nihilism that Scholem has expounded so masterfully. One thinks of ideas such as "the violation of the Torah has become its fulfillment, just as a grain of wheat must rot in the earth" or such as Jacob Frank's: "We are all now under the obligation to enter the abyss." The messianic intensity of the Sabbatians and Frankists results in a desperately hysterical and savage tonality which prophesies West's authentically religious book, *Miss Lonelyhearts*, a work profoundly Jewish but only in its negations, particularly the negation of the normative Judaic assumption of total sense in everything, life and text alike. *Miss Lonelyhearts* takes place in the world of Freud, where the fundamental assumption is that everything already has happened, and that nothing can be made new because total sense has been achieved but then repressed or negated. Negatively Jewish, the book is also negatively American. Miss Lonelyhearts is a failed Walt Whitman (hence the naming of the cripple as Peter Doyle, Whitman's pathetic friend) and a fallen American Adam to Shrike's very American Satan. Despite the opinions of later critics, I continue to find Hyman's argument persuasive and agree with him that the book's psychosexuality is marked by a repressed homosexual relation between Shrike and Miss Lonelyhearts. Hyman's Freudian observation that all the suffering in the book is essentially female seems valid, reminding us that Freud's "feminine masochism" is mostly encountered among men, according to Freud himself. Shrike, the butcherbird impaling his victim, Miss Lonelyhearts, upon the thorns of Christ, is himself as much an instance of "feminine masochism" as his victim. If Miss Lonelyhearts is close to pathological frenzy, Shrike is also consumed by religious hysteria, by a terrible nostalgia for God.

The book's bitter stylistic negation results in a spectacular verbal economy, in which literally every sentence is made to count, in more than one sense of "count." Freud's "negation" involves a cognitive return of the repressed, here through West's self-projection as Shrike, spit out but not disavowed. The same Freudian process depends upon an affective continuance of repression, here by West's self-introjection as Miss Lonelyhearts, at once West's inability to believe and his disavowed failure to love. Poor Miss Lonelyhearts, who receives no other name throughout the book, has been destroyed by Shrike's power of Satanic rhetoric before the book even opens. But then Shrike has destroyed himself first, for no one could withstand the sustained horror of Shrike's impaling rhetoric, which truly can be called West's horror:

> "I am a great saint," Shrike cried, "I can walk on my own water. Haven't you ever heard of Shrike's Passion in the Luncheonette, or the Agony in the Soda Fountain? Then I compared the wounds in Christ's body to the mouths of a miraculous purse in which we deposit the small change of our sins. It is indeed an excellent conceit. But now let us consider the holes in our own bodies and into what these congenital wounds open. Under the skin of man is a wondrous jungle where veins like lush tropical growths hang along overripe organs and weed-like entrails writhe in squirming tangles of red and yellow. In this jungle, flitting from rock-gray lungs to golden intestines, from liver to lights and back to liver again, lives a bird called the soul. The Catholic hunts this bird with bread and wine, the Hebrew with a golden ruler, the Protestant on leaden feet with leaden words, the Buddhist with gestures, the Negro with blood. I spit on them all. Phooh! And I call upon you to spit. Phooh! Do you stuff birds? No, my dears, taxidermy is not religion. No! A thousand times no. Better, I say unto you, better a live bird in the jungle of the body than two stuffed birds on the library table."

I have always associated this great passage with what is central to West: the messianic longing for redemption, through sin if necessary. West's humor is almost always apocalyptic, in a mode quite original with him, though so influential since his death that we have difficulty seeing how strong the originality was. Originality, even in comic writing, becomes a difficulty. How are we to read the most outrageous of the letters sent to

Miss Lonelyhearts, the one written by the sixteen-year-old girl without a nose?

> *I sit and look at myself all day and cry. I have a big hole in the middle of my face that scares people even myself so I cant blame the boys for not wanting to take me out. My mother loves me, but she crys terrible when she looks at me.*
>
> *What did I do to deserve such a terrible bad fate? Even if I did do some bad things I didnt do any before I was a year old and I was born this way. I asked Papa and he says he doesnt know, but that maybe I did something in the other world before I was born or that maybe I was being punished for his sins. I dont believe that because he is a very nice man. Ought I commit suicide?*
>
> *Sincerely yours,*
> *Desperate*

Defensive laughter is a complex reaction to grotesque suffering. In his 1928 essay on humor, Freud concluded that the above-the-I, the superego, speaks kindly words of comfort to the intimidated ego, and this speaking is humor, which Freud calls "the triumph of narcissism, the ego's victorious assertion of its own invulnerability." Clearly, Freud's "humor" does not include the Westian mode. Reading Desperate's "What did I do to deserve such a terrible bad fate?", our ego knows that it is defeated all the time, or at least is vulnerable to undeserved horror. West's humor has *no* liberating element whatsoever, but is the humor of a vertigo ill-balanced on the edge of what ancient Gnosticism called the *kenoma*, the cosmological emptiness.

Shrike, West's superb Satanic tempter, achieves his apotheosis at the novel's midpoint, the eighth of its fifteen tableaux, accurately titled "Miss Lonelyhearts in the Dismal Swamp." As Miss Lonelyhearts, sick with despair, lies in bed, the drunken Shrike bursts in, shouting his greatest rhetorical set piece, certainly the finest tirade in modern American fiction. Cataloging the methods that Miss Lonelyhearts might employ to escape out of the Dismal Swamp, Shrike begins with a grand parody of the later D. H. Lawrence, in which the vitalism of *The Plumed Serpent* and *The Man Who Died* is carried into a gorgeous absurdity, a heavy sexuality that masks Shrike's Satanic fears of impotence:

"You are fed up with the city and its teeming millions. The ways and means of men, as getting and lending and spending, you lay waste your inner world, are too much with you. The bus takes too long, while the subway is always crowded. So what do you do? So you buy a farm and walk behind your horse's moist behind, no collar or tie, plowing your broad swift acres. As you turn up the rich black soil, the wind carries the smell of pine and dung across the fields and the rhythm of an old, old work enters your soul. To this rhythm, you sow and weep and chivy your kine, not kin or kind, between the pregnant rows of corn and taters. Your step becomes the heavy sexual step of a dance-drunk Indian and you tread the seed down into the female earth. You plant, not dragon's teeth, but beans and greens."

Confronting only silence, Shrike proceeds to parody the Melville of *Typee* and *Omoo*, and also Somerset Maugham's version of Gauguin in *The Moon and Sixpence*:

"You live in a thatch hut with the daughter of a king, a slim young maiden in whose eyes is an ancient wisdom. Her breasts are golden speckled pears, her belly a melon, and her odor is like nothing so much as a jungle fern. In the evening, on the blue lagoon, under the silvery moon, to your love you croon in the soft sylabelew and vocabelew of her langorour tongorour. Your body is golden brown like hers, and tourists have need of the indignant finger of the missionary to point you out. They envy you your breech clout and carefree laugh and little brown bride and fingers instead of forks. But you don't return their envy, and when a beautiful society girl comes to your hut in the night, seeking to learn the secret of your happiness, you send her back to her yacht that hangs on the horizon like a nervous racehorse. And so you dream away the days, fishing, hunting, dancing, swimming, kissing, and picking flowers to twine in your hair."

As Shrike says, this is a played-out mode, but his savage gusto in rendering it betrays his hatred of the religion of art, of the vision that sought a salvation in imaginative literature. What Shrike goes on to chant is an even more effective parody of the literary stances West rejected. Though Shrike calls it "Hedonism," the curious amalgam here of Hemingway and Ronald Firbank, with touches of Fitzgerald and the earlier Aldous Huxley, might better be named an aesthetic stoicism:

> "You dedicate your life to the pursuit of pleasure. No overindulgence, mind you, but knowing that your body is a pleasure machine, you treat it carefully in order to get the most out of it. Golf as well as booze, Philadelphia Jack O'Brien and his chestweights as well as Spanish dancers. Nor do you neglect the pleasures of the mind. You fornicate under pictures by Matisse and Picasso, you drink from Renaissance glassware, and often you spend an evening beside the fireplace with Proust and an apple. Alas, after much good fun, the day comes when you realize that soon you must die. You keep a stiff upper lip and decide to give a last party. You invite all your old mistresses, trainers, artists and boon companions. The guests are dressed in black, the waiters are coons, the table is a coffin carved for you by Eric Gill. You serve caviar and blackberries and licorice candy and coffee without cream. After the dancing girls have finished, you get to your feet and call for silence in order to explain your philosophy of life. 'Life,' you say, 'is a club where they won't stand for squawks, where they deal you only one hand and you must sit in. So even if the cards are cold and marked by the hand of fate, play up, play up like a gentleman and a sport. Get tanked, grab what's on the buffet, use the girls upstairs, but remember, when you throw box cars, take the curtain like a dead game sport, don't squawk.'"

Even this is only preparatory to Shrike's bitterest phase in his tirade, an extraordinary send-up of High Aestheticism proper, of Pater, George Moore, Wilde, and the earlier W. B. Yeats:

> "Art! Be an artist or a writer. When you are cold, warm yourself before the flaming tints of Titian, when you are hungry, nourish yourself with great spiritual foods by listening to the noble periods of Bach, the harmonies of Brahms and the thunder of Beethoven. Do you think there is anything in the fact that their names all begin with a B? But don't take a chance, smoke a 3 B pipe, and remember these immortal lines: *When to the suddenness of mel-*

ody the echo parting falls the failing day. What a rhythm! Tell
them to keep their society whores and pressed duck with oranges.
For you *l'art vivant,* the living art, as you call it. Tell them that you
know that your shoes are broken and that there are pimples on
your face, yes, and that you have buck teeth and a club foot, but
that you don't care, for to-morrow they are playing Beethoven's
last quartets in Carnegie Hall and at home you have Shakespeare's
plays in one volume."

That last sentence, truly and deliciously Satanic, is one of West's greatest triumphs, but he surpasses it in the ultimate Shrikean rhapsody, after
Shrike's candid avowal: "God alone is our escape." With marvelous appro-
priateness, West makes this at once the ultimate Miss Lonelyhearts letter
and also Shrike's most Satanic self-identification in the form of a letter to
Christ dictated for Miss Lonelyhearts by Shrike, who speaks absolutely for
both of them:

> *Dear Miss Lonelyhearts of Miss Lonelyhearts—*
> *I am twenty-six years old and in the newspaper game. Life for*
> *me is a desert empty of comfort. I cannot find pleasure in food,*
> *drink, or women—nor do the arts give me joy any longer. The*
> *Leopard of Discontent walks the streets of my city; the Lion of*
> *Discouragement crouches outside the walls of my citadel. All*
> *is desolation and a vexation of spirit. I feel like hell. How can I*
> *believe, how can I have faith in this day and age? Is it true that*
> *the greatest scientists believe again in you?*
> *I read your column and like it very much. There you once wrote:*
> *"When the salt has lost its savour, who shall savour it again?" Is*
> *the answer: "None but the Saviour?"*
> *Thanking you very much for a quick reply, I remain yours truly,*
> *A Regular Subscriber*

"I feel like hell," the Miltonic "Myself am Hell," is Shrike's credo, and
West's.

What is the relation of Shrike to West's rejected Jewishness? The question may seem illegitimate to many admirers of West, but it acquires considerable force in the context of the novel's sophisticated yet unhistorical

Gnosticism. The way of nihilism means, according to Scholem, "to free oneself of all laws, conventions, and religions, to adopt every conceivable attitude and to reject it, and to follow one's leader step for step into the abyss." Scholem is paraphrasing the daemonic Jacob Frank, an eighteenth-century Jewish Shrike who brought the Sabbatian messianic movement to its final degradation. Frank would have recognized something of his own negations and nihilistic fervor in the closing passages that form a pattern in West's four novels:

> His body screamed and shouted as it marched and uncoiled; then, with one heaving shout of triumph, it fell back quiet.
> The army that a moment before had been thundering in his body retreated slowly—victorious, relieved.
> (*The Dream Life of Balso Snell*)

> While they were struggling, Betty came in through the street door. She called to them to stop and started up the stairs. The cripple saw her cutting off his escape and tried to get rid of the package. He pulled his hand out. The gun inside the package exploded and Miss Lonelyhearts fell, dragging the cripple with him. They both rolled part of the way down the stairs.
> (*Miss Lonelyhearts*)

> "Alas, Lemuel Pitkin himself did not have this chance, but instead was dismantled by the enemy. His teeth were pulled out. His eye was gouged from his head. His thumb was removed. His scalp was torn away. His leg was cut off. And, finally, he was shot through the heart.
> "But he did not live or die in vain. Through his martyrdom the National Revolutionary Party triumphed, and by that triumph this country was delivered from sophistication, Marxism and International Capitalism. Through the National Revolution its people were purged of alien diseases and America became again American."
> "Hail the martyrdom in the Bijou Theater!" roar Shagpoke's youthful hearers when he is finished.
> "Hail, Lemuel Pitkin!"
> "All hail, the American Boy!"
> (*A Cool Million*)

He was carried through the exit to the back street and lifted into a police car. The siren began to scream and at first he thought he was making the noise himself. He felt his lips with his hands. They were clamped tight. He knew then it was the siren. For some reason this made him laugh and he began to imitate the siren as loud as he could.

(*The Day of the Locust*)

All four passages mutilate the human image, the image of God that normative Jewish tradition associates with our origins. "Our forefathers were always talking, only what good did it do them and what did they accomplish? But we are under the burden of silence," Jacob Frank said. What Frank's and West's forefathers always talked about was the ultimate forefather, Adam, who would have enjoyed the era of the Messiah, had he not sinned. West retains of tradition only the emptiness of the fallen image, the scattered spark of creation. The screaming and falling body, torn apart and maddened into a siren-like laughter, belongs at once to the American Surrealist poet, Balso Snell; to the American Horst Wessel, poor Lemuel Pitkin; to Miss Lonelyhearts, the Whitmanian American Christ; and to Tod Hackett, painter of the American apocalypse. All are nihilistic versions of the mutilated image of God, or of what the Jewish Gnostic visionary Nathan of Gaza called the "thought-less" or nihilizing light.

West was a prophet of American violence, which he saw as augmenting progressively throughout our history. His satirical genius, for all its authentic and desperate range, has been defeated by American reality. Shagpoke Whipple, the Calvin Coolidge–like ex-President who becomes the American Hitler in *A Cool Million*, talks in terms that West intended as extravagant, but that now can be read all but daily in our media. Here is Shagpoke at his best, urging us to hear what the dead Lemuel Pitkin has to tell us:

"Of what is it that he speaks? Of the right of every American boy to go into the world and there receive fair play and a chance to make his fortune by industry and probity without being laughed at or conspired against by sophisticated aliens."

And here are some lines from a speech given by President Trump on October 18, 2018:

But the choice could not be more clear. Democrats produce mobs. Republicans produce jobs. It's true. It's true. By the way, this is the most beautiful sky. Well, it's big sky. I guess there's a reason for everything, right? No, it's just—I got out and I'm looking—I've been here many times—but I got out and I'm looking—I say, that really is big sky. That's beautiful. It's not only big, it's really beautiful sky. Someday one of you will explain exactly why, but that is a beautiful, beautiful, big sky. But Nancy Pelosi, crying Chuck Schumer, and the radical Democrats, they want to raise your taxes, they want to impose socialism on our incredible nation, make it Venezuela, because that's what's going to happen.

Reality may have triumphed over poor West, but only because he, doubtless as a ghost, inspired or wrote these presidential remarks. Perhaps West's ghost now writes not only Shagpokian speeches, but the very text of reality in our America.

Eudora Welty

(1909–2001)

EUDORA WELTY divides her remarkable brief autobiography, *One Writer's Beginnings*, into three parts: "Listening," "Learning to See," "Finding a Voice." Gentle yet admonitory, these titles instruct us in how to read her stories and novels, a reading that necessarily involves further growth in our sense of inwardness. Certain of her stories never cease their process of journeying deep into interior regions we generally reserve only for personal and experiential memories. Doubtless they differ from reader to reader; for me they include "A Still Moment" and "The Burning."

Mark Twain has had so varied a progeny among American writers that we hardly feel surprise when we reflect that Welty and Hemingway both emerge from *Huckleberry Finn*. All that Welty and Hemingway share as storytellers is Twain's example. Their obsessive American concern is Huck's: the freedom of a solitary joy, intimately allied to a superstitious fear of solitude. Welty's people, like Hemingway's, and like the self-representations of our major poets—Whitman, Dickinson, Stevens, Frost, Eliot, Hart Crane, R. P. Warren, Roethke, Elizabeth Bishop, Ashbery, Merrill, and Ammons—all secretly believe themselves to be no part of the creation and all feel free only when they are quite alone.

In *One Writer's Beginnings*, Welty comments upon "A Still Moment":

> "A Still Moment"—another early story—was a fantasy, in which the separate interior visions guiding three highly individual and widely differing men marvelously meet and converge upon the same single exterior object. All my characters were actual persons who had lived at the same time, who would have been strangers to one another, but whose lives had actually taken them at some point to the same neighborhood. The scene was in the Mississippi wilderness in the historic year 1811—"*anno mirabilis*," the year the stars fell on Alabama and lemmings, or squirrels perhaps, rushed straight down the continent and plunged into the Gulf of Mexico,

and an earthquake made the Mississippi River run backwards and New Madrid, Missouri, tumbled in and disappeared. My real characters were Lorenzo Dow the New England evangelist, Murrell the outlaw bandit and murderer on the Natchez Trace, and Audubon the painter; and the exterior object on which they all at the same moment set their eyes is a small heron, feeding.

Welty's choices—Lorenzo Dow, James Murrell, Audubon—are all obsessed solitaries. Dow, the circuit rider, presumably ought to be the least solipsistic of the three, yet his fierce cry as he rides on at top speed—"I must have souls! And souls I must have!"—is evidence of an emptiness that never can be filled:

> It was the hour of sunset. All the souls that he had saved and all those he had not took dusky shapes in the mist that hung between the high banks, and seemed by their great number and density to block his way, and showed no signs of melting or changing back into mist, so that he feared his passage was to be difficult forever. The poor souls that were not saved were darker and more pitiful than those that were, and still there was not any of the radiance he would have hoped to see in such a congregation.

As Dow himself observes, his eyes are in a "failing proportion to my loving heart always," which makes us doubt his heart. He loves his wife, Peggy, effortlessly since she is in Massachusetts and he is galloping along on the Old Natchez Trace. Indeed, their love can be altogether effortless, consisting as it does of a marriage proposal, accepted as his first words to her, a few hours of union, and his rapid departure south for evangelical purposes, pursued by her first letter declaring that she, like her husband, fears only death, but never mere separation.

This remarkable hunter of souls, intrepid at evading rapacious Indians or Irish Catholics, can be regarded as a sublime lunatic, or merely as a pure product of America:

> Soon night would descend, and a camp-meeting ground ahead would fill with its sinners like the sky with its stars. How he hungered for them! He looked in prescience with a longing of love over the throng that waited while the flames of the torches threw

change, change, change over their faces. How could he bring them enough, if it were not divine love and sufficient warning of all that could threaten them? He rode on faster. He was a filler of appointments, and he filled more and more, until his journeys up and down creation were nothing but a shuttle, driving back and forth upon the rich expanse of his vision. He was homeless by his own choice, he must be everywhere at some time, and somewhere soon. There hastening in the wilderness on his flying horse he gave the night's torch-lit crowd a premature benediction, he could not wait. He spread his arms out, one at a time for safety, and he wished, when they would all be gathered in by his tin horn blasts and the inspired words would go out over their heads, to brood above the entire and passionate life of the wide world, to become its rightful part.

He peered ahead. "Inhabitants of Time! The wilderness is your souls on earth!" he shouted ahead into the treetops. "Look about you, if you would view the conditions of your spirit, put here by the good Lord to show you and afright you. These wild places and these trails of awesome loneliness lie nowhere, nowhere, but in your heart."

Dow is his own congregation, and his heart indeed contains the wild places and awesomely lonesome trails through which he endlessly rushes. His antithesis is provided by the murderous James Murrell, who suddenly rides at Dow's side, without bothering to look at him. If Dow is a mad angel, Murrell is a scarcely sane devil, talking to slow the evangelist down, without realizing that the sublimely crazy Lorenzo listens only to the voice of God:

Murrell riding along with his victim-to-be, Murrell riding, was Murrell talking. He told away at his long tales, with always a distance and a long length of time flowing through them, and all centered about a silent man. In each the silent man would have done a piece of evil, a robbery or a murder, in a place of long ago, and it was all made for the revelation in the end that the silent man was Murrell himself, and the long story had happened yesterday, and the place *here*—the Natchez Trace. It would only take one dawning look for the victim to see that all of this was another story and he himself had listened his way into it, and that he too was about to recede in time (to where the dread was forgotten) for some listener and to live for a listener in the long ago. Destroy the present!—that must have been the first thing that was whispered in Murrell's heart—the living moment and the man that lives in it must die before you can go on. It was his habit to bring the journey—which might even take days—to a close with a kind of ceremony. Turning his face at last into the face of the victim, for he had never seen him before now, he would tower up with the sudden height of a man no longer the tale teller but the speechless protagonist, silent at last, one degree nearer the hero. Then he would murder the man.

Since Murrell is capable of observing nothing whatsoever, he does not know what the reader knows, which is that Lorenzo is not a potential victim for this self-dramatizing Satanist. Whatever the confrontation between angel and devil might have brought (and one's surmise is that Murrell might not have survived), the crucial moment is disturbed by the arrival of a third, the even weirder Audubon:

Audubon said nothing because he had gone without speaking a word for days. He did not regard his thoughts for the birds and animals as susceptible, in their first change, to words. His long playing on the flute was not in its origin a talking to himself. Rather than speak to order or describe, he would always draw a deer with a stroke across it to communicate his need of venison to an Indian. He had only found words when he discovered that there is much otherwise lost that can be noted down each item in its own day, and he wrote often now in a journal, not wanting anything to be lost the way it had been, all the past, and he would write about a day, "Only sorry that the Sun Sets."

These three extraordinarily diverse obsessives share a still moment, in which "a solitary snowy heron flew down not far away and began to feed beside the marsh water." To Lorenzo, the heron's epiphany is God's love become visible. To Murrell, it is "only whiteness ensconced in darkness," a prophecy of the slave, brigand, and outcast rebellion he hopes to lead in the Natchez country. To Audubon it is precisely what it is, a white heron he must slay if he is to be able to paint, a model that must die in order to become a model. Welty gives us no preference among these three:

What each of them had wanted was simply *all*. To save all souls, to destroy all men, to see and record all life that filled this world—all, all—but now a single frail yearning seemed to go out of the three of them for a moment and to stretch toward this one snowy, shy bird in the marshes. It was as if three whirlwinds had drawn together at some center, to find there feeding in peace a snowy heron. Its own slow spiral of flight could take it away in its own time, but for a little it held them still, it laid quiet over them, and they stood for a moment unburdened. . . .

To quest for *all* is to know anything but peace, and "a still moment" is only shared by these three questers in a phantasmagoria. When the moment ends with Audubon's killing of the bird, only Lorenzo's horrified reaction is of deep import or interest. Murrell is content to lie back in ambush and await travelers more innocent, who will suit his Satanic destiny as Lorenzo and Audubon could not. Audubon is also content to go on, to fulfill his vast design. But Lorenzo's epiphany has turned into a negative moment and though he will go on to gather in the multitudes, he has been darkened:

> In the woods that echoed yet in his ears, Lorenzo riding slowly looked back. The hair rose on his head and his hands began to shake with cold, and suddenly it seemed to him that God Himself, just now, thought of the Idea of Separateness. For surely He had never thought of it before, when the little white heron was flying down to feed. He could understand God's giving Separateness first and then giving Love to follow and heal in its wonder; but God had reversed this, and given Love first and then Separateness, as though it did not matter to Him which came first. Perhaps it was that God never counted the moments of Time; Lorenzo did that, among his tasks of love. Time did not occur to God. Therefore— did He even know of it? How to explain Time and Separateness back to God, Who had never thought of them, Who could let the whole world come to grief in a scattering moment?

This is a meditation on the verge of heresy, presumably Gnostic, rather than on the border of unbelief. Robert Penn Warren, in a classical early essay on "Love and Separateness in Eudora Welty" (1944), reads the dialectic of Love and Separateness here as the perhaps Blakean contraries of

Innocence and Experience. On this reading, Welty is an ironist of limits and of contamination, for whom knowledge destroys love, almost as though love could survive only upon enchanted ground. That may underestimate both Lorenzo and Welty. Pragmatically, Lorenzo has been unchanged by the still moment of love and its shattering into separateness; indeed he is as unchanged as Murrell or Audubon. But only Lorenzo remains haunted by a vision, by a particular beauty greater than he can account for, and yet never can deny. He will change someday, though Welty does not pursue that change.

The truth of Welty's fictive cosmos, for all her preternatural gentleness, is that love always does come first, and always does yield to an irreparable separateness. Like her true mentor, Twain, she triumphs in comedy because her deepest awareness is of a nihilistic "unground" beyond consciousness or metaphysics, and comedy is the only graceful defense against that cosmological emptiness. Unlike Faulkner and Flannery O'Connor, she is, by design, a genial writer, but the design is a subtler version of Twain's more urgent desperation. "A Still Moment," despite its implications, remains a fantasy of the continuities of quest. Rather than discuss one of her many masterpieces of humorous storytelling, I choose instead "The Burning," which flamboyantly displays her gift for a certain grim sublimity, and which represents her upon her heights, as a stylist and narrator who can rival Hemingway in representing the discontinuities of war and disaster.

"The Burning" belongs to the dark genre of Southern Gothic, akin to Faulkner's "A Rose for Emily" and O'Connor's "A Good Man Is Hard to Find." Welty, as historical a storyteller as Robert Penn Warren, imagines an incident from Sherman's destructive march through Georgia. The imagining is almost irrealistic in its complexity of tone and indirect representation, so that "The Burning" is perhaps the most formidable of all Welty's stories, with the kind of rhetorical and allusive difficulties we expect to encounter more frequently in modern poetry than in modern short stories. Writing on form in D. H. Lawrence's stories, Welty remarked on "the unmitigated shapelessness of Lawrence's narrative" and sharply noted that his characters would only appear deranged if they began to speak on the streets as they do in the stories:

> For the truth seems to be that Lawrence's characters don't really
> speak their words—not conversationally, not to one another; they

are not speaking on the street, but are playing like fountains or
radiating like the moon or storming like the sea, or their silence is
the silence of wicked rocks. It is borne home to us that Lawrence
is writing of our human relationships on earth in terms of eternity,
and these terms set Lawrence's form. The author himself appears
in authorship in places like the moon, and sometimes smites us
while we stand there under him.

The characters of Welty's "The Burning" fit her description of Lawrence's men and women; their silence too is the silence of wicked rocks.
Essentially they are only three: two mad sisters, Miss Theo and Miss Myra,
and their slave, called Florabel in the story's first published version (*Harp-
er's Bazaar*, March 1951). The two demented high born ladies are very
different; Miss Theo is deep-voiced and domineering, Miss Myra gentler
and dependent. But little of the story is seen through their eyes or refracted
through either's consciousness. Florabel, an immensely passive being, sees
and reacts, in a mode not summarized until nearly the end of the story, in
its first printed form:

> Florabel, with no last name, was a slave. By the time of that
> moment on the hill, her kind had been slaves in a dozen countries
> and that of their origin for thousands of years. She let everything
> be itself according to its nature—the animate, the inanimate, the
> symbol. She did not move to alter any of it, not unless she was told
> to and shown how. And so she saw what happened, the creation
> and the destruction. She waited on either one and served it, not
> expecting anything of it but what she got; only sooner or later she
> would seek protection somewhere. Herself was an unknown, like
> a queen, somebody she had heard called, even cried for. As a slave
> she was earth's most detached visitor. The world had not touched
> her—only possessed and hurt her, like a man; taken away from
> her, like a man; turned another way from her and left her, like a
> man. Her vision was clear. She saw what was there and had not
> sought it, did not seek it yet. (It was *her* eyes that were in the back
> of her head, her vision that met itself coming the long way back,
> unimpeded, like the light of stars.) The command to loot was one
> more fading memory. Many commands had been given her, some
> even held over from before she was born; delayed and miscarried

and interrupted, they could yet be fulfilled, though it was safer for one once a slave to hear things a second time, a third, fourth, hundredth, thousandth, if they were to be carried out to the letter. In that noon quiet after conflict there might have been only the two triumphant, the mirror which was a symbol in the world and Florabel who was standing there; it was the rest that had died of it.

The mirror, "a symbol in the world," is in this first version of "The Burning" a synecdoche for the fragmented vision of both mad sisters and their slave. In rewriting the story, Welty uses the mirror more subtly. Delilah (as Florabel is now named) sees Sherman's soldiers and their apocalyptic white horse directly as they enter the house, and she runs to tell Miss Theo and Miss Myra. They deign to look up and observe the intruders in the mirror over the fireplace. Throughout the rest of the catastrophic narrative, the sisters behold everything that transpires as though in a mirror. Clearly they have spent their lives estranging reality as though looking in a mirror, and they move to their self-destruction as though they saw themselves only as images. The violence that prepares for the burning is thus rendered as phantasmagoria:

> The sisters showed no surprise to see soldiers and Negroes alike (old Ophelia in the way, talking, talking) strike into and out of the doors of the house, the front now the same as the back, to carry off beds, tables, candlesticks, washstands, cedar buckets, china pitchers, with their backs bent double; or the horses ready to go; or the food of the kitchen bolted down—and so much of it thrown away, this must be a second dinner; or the unsilenceable dogs, the old pack mixed with the strangers and fighting with all their hearts over bones. The last skinny sacks were thrown on the wagons—the last flour, the last scraping and clearing from Ophelia's shelves, even her pepper-grinder. The silver Delilah could count was counted on strange blankets and then, knocking against the teapot, rolled together, tied up like a bag of bones. A drummer boy with his drum around his neck caught both Miss Theo's peacocks, Marco and Polo, and wrung their necks in the yard. Nobody could look at those bird-corpses; nobody did.

The strangling of the peacocks is a presage of the weirdest sequence in "The Burning," in which Miss Theo and Miss Myra hang themselves from a tree, with Delilah assisting as ordered. It is only when the sisters are dead that we begin to understand that "The Burning" is more Delilah's story than it ever could have been theirs. A baby, Phinny, who had been allowed to perish in the fire (Welty does not allow us to know why), turns out to have been begotten by Miss Theo's and Miss Myra's brother Benton upon Delilah:

> The mirror's cloudy bottom sent up minnows of light to the brim where now a face pure as a water-lily shadow was floating. Almost too small and deep down to see, they were quivering, leaping to life, fighting, aping old things Delilah had seen done in this world already, sometimes what men had done to Miss Theo and Miss Myra and the peacocks and to slaves, and sometimes what a slave had done and what anybody now could do to anybody. Under the flicker of the sun's licks, then under its whole blow and blare, like an unheard scream, like an act of mercy gone, as the wall-less light and July blaze struck through from the opened sky, the mirror felled her flat.
>
> She put her arms over her head and waited, for they would all be coming again, gathering under her and above her, bees saddled like horses out of the air, butterflies harnessed to one another, bats with masks on, birds together, all with their weapons bared. She listened for the blows, and dreaded that whole army of wings—of flies, birds, serpents, their glowing enemy faces and bright kings' dresses, that banner of colors forked out, all this world that was flying, striking, stricken, falling, gilded or blackened, mortally splitting and falling apart, proud turbans unwinding, turning like the spotted dying leaves of fall, spiraling down to bottomless ash; she dreaded the fury of all the butterflies and dragonflies in the world riding, blades unconcealed and at point—descending, and rising again from the waters below, down under, one whale made of his own grave, opening his mouth to swallow Jonah one more time.
>
> Jonah!—a homely face to her, that could still look back from the red lane he'd gone down, even if it was too late to speak. He was her Jonah, her Phinny, her black monkey; she worshiped him still, though it was long ago he was taken from her the first time.

Delilah, hysterical with fear, shock, and anguish, has fallen into the mirror world of the mad sisters, her self-slain mistresses. She is restored to some sense of reality by her search for Phinny's bones. Carrying them, and what she can save of the sisters' finery, she marches on to what is presented ambiguously either as her own freedom or her death, or perhaps both together:

> Following the smell of horses and fire, to men, she kept in the wheel tracks till they broke down at the river. In the shade underneath the burned and fallen bridge she sat on a stump and chewed for a while, without dreams, the comb of a dirtdauber. Then once more kneeling, she took a drink from the Big Black, and pulled the shoes off her feet and waded in.
>
> Submerged to the waist, to the breast, stretching her throat like a sunflower stalk above the river's opaque skin, she kept on, her treasure stacked on the roof of her head, hands laced upon it. She had forgotten how or when she knew, and she did not know what day this was, but she knew—it would not rain, the river would not rise, until Saturday.

This extraordinary prose rises to an American sublime that is neither grotesque nor ironic. Welty, in her *On Short Stories*, asked the question: "Where does beauty come from, in the short story?" and answered only that beauty was a result:

> It *comes*. We are lucky when beauty comes, for often we try and it should come, it could, we think, but then when the virtues of our story are counted, beauty is standing behind the door.

I do not propose to count the virtues of "The Burning," or even of "A Still Moment." Both narratives are as thoroughly written through, fully composed, as the best poems of Wallace Stevens or of Hart Crane, or the strongest of Hemingway's stories, or Faulkner's *As I Lay Dying*. American writing in the twentieth century touches the sublime mode only in scattered instances, and always by reaching the frontier where the phantasmagoric, and the realism of violence, are separated only by ghostlier demarcations, keener sounds. Welty's high distinction is that in her the demarcations are as ghostly, the sounds as keen, as they are in her greatest narrative contemporaries, Faulkner and Hemingway.

Elizabeth Bishop

(1911–1979)

T HE PRINCIPAL POETS of Elizabeth Bishop's generation included
Roethke, Lowell, Berryman, Jarrell, and, in a different mode, Olson.
Whether any of these articulated an individual rhetorical stance with a skill
as sure as hers may be questioned. Her way of writing was closer to that of
Stevens and Marianne Moore, in the generation just beyond, than to any of
her exact contemporaries. Despite the differences in scale, her best poems
rival the Stevens of the shorter works, rather than the perhaps stronger
Stevens of the sequences.

Bishop stands then securely in a tradition of American poetry that began
with Emerson, Jones Very, and Dickinson, and culminated in aspects of
Frost as well as of Stevens and Moore. This tradition is marked by firm
rhetorical control, overt moral authority, and sometimes a fairly strict economy of means. The closing lines in *Geography III* epitomize the tradition's
self-recognition:

> He and the bird know everything is answered,
> all taken care of,
> no need to ask again.
> —Yesterday brought to today so lightly!
> (A yesterday I find almost impossible to lift.)

These poignant lines have more overt pathos than the poet ever allowed
herself elsewhere. But there is a paradox always in the contrast between a
poetry of deep subjectivity, like Wordsworth's or Stevens's or Bishop's, and
a confessional poetry, like Coleridge's or that of Bishop's principal contemporaries. When I read, say, "The Poems of Our Climate," by Stevens, or
"The End of March," by Bishop, I encounter eventually the overwhelming
self-revelation of a profoundly subjective consciousness. When I read, say,
"Skunk Hour" by Lowell or one of Berryman's sonnets, I confront finally
an opacity, for that is all the confessional mode can yield. It is the strength

of Bishop's tradition that its clarity is more than a surface phenomenon. Such strength is cognitive, even analytical, and surpasses philosophy and psychoanalysis in its power to expose human truth.

There are grander poems by Bishop than the relatively early "The Unbeliever," but I center upon it here because I love it best of all her poems. It does not compare in scope and power to "The Monument," "Roosters," "The Fish," "The Bight," "At the Fishhouses," "Brazil, January 1, 1502," "First Death in Nova Scotia," or the extraordinary late triad of "Crusoe in England," "The Moose," and "The End of March." Those ten poems have an authority and a possible wisdom that transcend "The Unbeliever." But I walk around, certain days, chanting "The Unbeliever" to myself, it being one of those rare poems you never evade again, once you know it (and it knows you). Its five stanzas essentially are variations upon its epigraph, from Bunyan: "He sleeps on the top of a mast." Bunyan's trope concerns the condition of unbelief; Bishop's does not. Think of the personae of Bishop's poem as exemplifying three rhetorical stances, and so as being three kinds of poet, or even three poets: cloud, gull, unbeliever. The cloud is Wordsworth or Stevens. The gull is Shelley or Hart Crane. The unbeliever is Dickinson or Bishop. None of them has the advantage; the spangled sea wants to destroy them all. The cloud, powerful in introspection, regards not the sea but his own subjectivity. The gull, more visionary still, beholds neither sea nor air but his own aspiration. The unbeliever observes nothing, but the sea is truly observed in his dream:

> which was, "I must not fall.
> The spangled sea below wants me to fall.
> It is hard as diamonds; it wants to destroy us all."

I think that is the reality of Bishop's famous eye. Like Dickinson's, its truest precursor, it confronts the truth, which is that what is most worth seeing is impossible to see, at least with open eyes. A poetry informed by that mode of observation will station itself at the edge where what is most worth saying is all but impossible to say. I will conclude here by contrasting Bishop's wonderful trope of the lion, in "The End of March," to Stevens's incessant use of the same figure. In Stevens, the lion tends to represent poetry as a destructive force, as the imposition of the poet's will-to-power over reality. This image culminates in "An Ordinary Evening in New Haven":

> Say of each lion of the spirit
>
> It is a cat of a sleek transparency
> That shines with a nocturnal shine alone.
> The great cat must stand potent in the sun.

Against that destructive night in which all cats are black, even the transparent ones, Stevens sets himself as a possible lion, potent in the light of the idea-of-ideas. Here, I take it, is Bishop's affectionate riposte:

> They could have been teasing the lion sun,
> except that now he was behind them
> —a sun who'd walked the beach the last low tide,
> making those big, majestic paw-prints,
> who perhaps had batted a kite out of the sky to play with.

A somewhat Stevensian lion sun, clearly, but with something better to do than standing potent in itself. The path away from poetry as a destructive force can only be through play, the play of trope. Within her tradition so securely, Bishop profoundly plays at trope. Dickinson, Moore, and Bishop resemble Emerson, Frost, and Stevens, in that tradition, with a difference due not to mere nature or mere ideology but to superb art.

Tennessee Williams

(1911–1983)

IT IS A SAD and inexplicable truth that the United States, a dramatic nation, continues to have so limited a literary achievement in drama. American literature, from Emerson to the present moment, is a distinguished tradition. The poetry of Whitman, Dickinson, Frost, Stevens, Eliot, W. C. Williams, Hart Crane, R. P. Warren, and Elizabeth Bishop down through the generation of my own contemporaries—John Ashbery, James Merrill, A. R. Ammons, and others—has an unquestionable eminence, and takes a vital place in Western literature. Prose fiction from Hawthorne and Melville on through Mark Twain and Henry James to Cather and Dreiser, Faulkner, Hemingway, Fitzgerald, Nathanael West, and Pynchon has almost a parallel importance. The line of essayists and critics from Emerson and Thoreau to Kenneth Burke and beyond constitutes another crucial strand of our national letters. But where is the American drama in comparison to all this, and in relation to the long cavalcade of Western drama from Aeschylus to Beckett?

The American theater, by the common estimate of its most eminent critics, touches an initial strength with Eugene O'Neill, and then proceeds to the more varied excellences of Thornton Wilder, Tennessee Williams, Arthur Miller, Edward Albee, Sam Shepard, and Tony Kushner. That sequence is clearly problematical and becomes even more worrisome when we move from playwrights to plays. Which are our dramatic works that matter most? *Long Day's Journey into Night*, certainly; perhaps *The Iceman Cometh*; evidently *A Streetcar Named Desire* and *Death of a Salesman*; perhaps again *The Skin of Our Teeth* and *The Zoo Story*—it is not God's plenty. And I will venture the speculation that our drama palpably is not yet literary enough. By this I do not just mean that O'Neill writes very badly, or Miller very baldly; they do, but so did Dreiser, and *Sister Carrie* and *An American Tragedy* prevail nevertheless. Nor do I wish to be an American Matthew Arnold (whom I loathe above all other critics) and proclaim that our dramatists simply have not known enough. They know more than enough, and that is part of the trouble.

Literary tradition, as I have come to understand it, masks the agon between past and present as a benign relationship, whether personal or societal. The actual transferences between the force of the literary past and the potential of writing in the present tend to be darker, even if they do not always or altogether follow the defensive patterns of what Sigmund Freud called "family romances." Whether or not an ambivalence, however repressed, toward the past's force is felt by the new writer and is manifested in his work seems to depend entirely upon the ambition and power of the oncoming artist. If he aspires after strength, and can attain it, then he must struggle with both a positive and a negative transference, false connections because necessarily imagined ones, between a composite precursor and himself. His principal resource in that agon will be his own native gift for interpretation, or as I am inclined to call it, strong misreading. Revising his precursor, he will create himself, make himself into a kind of changeling, and so he will become, in an illusory but highly pragmatic way, his own father.

The most literary of our major dramatists, and clearly I mean "literary" in a precisely descriptive sense, neither pejorative nor eulogistic, was Tennessee Williams. Wilder, with his intimate connections to *Finnegans Wake* and Gertrude Stein, might seem to dispute this placement, and Wilder was certainly more literate than Williams. But Wilder had a benign relation to his crucial precursor, Joyce, and did not aspire after a destructive strength. Williams did, and suffered the fate he prophesied and desired; the strength destroyed his later work, and his later life, and thus joined itself to the American tradition of self-destructive genius. Williams truly had one precursor only: Hart Crane, the greatest of our lyrical poets, after Whitman and Dickinson, and the most self-destructive figure in our national literature, surpassing all others in this, as in so many regards.

Williams asserted he had other precursors also: D. H. Lawrence, and Chekhov in drama. These were outward influences and benefited Williams well enough, but they were essentially formal, and so not the personal and societal family romance of authentic poetic influence. Hart Crane made Williams into more of a dramatic lyricist, though writing in prose, than the lyrical dramatist that Williams is supposed to have been. Though this influence—perhaps more nearly an identification—helped form *The Glass*

Menagerie and (less overtly) *A Streetcar Named Desire*, and in a lesser mode *Summer and Smoke* and *Suddenly Last Summer*, it also led to such disasters of misplaced lyricism as the dreadful *Camino Real* and the dreary *The Night of the Iguana*. (*Cat on a Hot Tin Roof*, one of Williams's best plays, does not seem to me to show any influence of Crane.) Williams's long aesthetic decline covered thirty years, from 1953 to 1983, and reflected the sorrows of a seer who, by his early forties, had outlived his own vision. Hart Crane, self-slain at thirty-two, had set for Williams a High Romantic paradigm that helped cause Williams, his heart as dry as summer dust, to burn to the socket.

It is difficult to argue for the aesthetic achievement of Tennessee Williams's long, final phase as a dramatist. Rereading persuades me that his major plays remain *The Glass Menagerie*, *A Streetcar Named Desire*, *Suddenly Last Summer*, and the somewhat undervalued *Summer and Smoke*. *Cat on a Hot Tin Roof* was a popular and critical success, onstage and as a film. I have just reread it in the definitive Library of America edition, which prints both versions of Act III, the original, which Williams greatly preferred, and the Broadway revision, made to accommodate the director Elia Kazan. Here is the ambiguous original conclusion, followed by the revision:

> MARGARET: And so tonight we're going to make the lie true, and when that's done, I'll bring the liquor back here and we'll get drunk together, here, tonight, in this place that death has come into . . . —What do you say?
> BRICK: I don't say anything. I guess there's nothing to say.
> MARGARET: Oh, you weak people, you weak, beautiful people!— who give up.—What you want is someone to—(*She turns out the rose-silk lamp.*)—take hold of you.—Gently, gently, with love! And—
> (*The curtain begins to fall slowly.*)
> I do love you, Brick, I do!
> BRICK: (*smiling with charming sadness*): Wouldn't it be funny if that was true?
>
> MARGARET: And you lost your driver's license! I'd phone ahead and have you stopped on the highway before you got halfway to Ruby Lightfoot's gin mill. I told a lie to Big Daddy, but we can make that lie come true. And then I'll bring you liquor, and we'll

get drunk together, here, tonight, in this place that death has come into! What do you say? What do you say, baby?

BRICK: (*X to L side bed*)

I admire you, Maggie.

(*Brick sits on edge of bed. He looks up at the overhead light, then at Margaret. She reaches for the light, turns it out; then she kneels quickly beside Brick at foot of bed.*)

MARGARET: Oh, you weak, beautiful people who give up with such grace. What you need is someone to take hold of you—gently, with love, and hand your life back to you, like something gold you let go of—and I can! I'm determined to do it—and nothing's more determined than a cat on a tin roof—is there? Is there, baby?

(*She touches his cheek, gently.*)

As Williams noted, his Maggie augments in charm between the two versions; his Brick modulates subtly, and is a touch more receptive to her. Shakespeare demonstrates how difficult it is to resist vitality in a stage role by creating Sir John Falstaff with a vivacity and wit that carries all before him. There is nothing Shakespearean about Williams: he sketches archetypes, caricatures, grotesques, and cannot represent inwardness. And yet, with all his limitations, he writes well, unlike Eugene O'Neill, who is leaden, and Arthur Miller, who is drab. Thornton Wilder, Edward Albee, and Tony Kushner also have their eloquences, but Williams remains the most articulate and adequate of American dramatists up to this moment.

Yet his inability to dramatize inwardness is a considerable limitation. What is Brick's spiritual malady? His homoeroticism is palpably less a burden than is his homophobia: he will not accept Big Daddy's earlier bisexuality, any more than he could yield to love for Skipper (or to Maggie). Brick's narcissism is central to the play, but even more crucial would be his nihilism, if only Williams could tell us something about it. As a Hamlet, Brick does not work at all; he hasn't enough mind to express what most deeply torments him, and I fear that Williams shares this lack. What deprives *Cat on a Hot Tin Roof* of any authentic aesthetic eminence is its obscurantism, which may be indeliberate, unlike Joseph Conrad's in *Heart of Darkness*. It is as though both Williams and Brick were saying: "The horror! The horror!" without ever quite knowing what they were trying to talk about.

The ultimately benign and loving Big Daddy and the adoring Big Mama are *not* the cause of Brick's despair. Were it not for his nihilistic malaise, it seems likely that Brick eventually would turn into his dying father and would become pragmatically bisexual or pansexual. Brick's attachment to Maggie is ambivalent, but so was his affection for Skipper. As a pure narcissist, Brick is autoerotic, in the manner of Walt Whitman.

The play's epigraph, from Dylan Thomas's "Do not go gentle into that good night," is a gesture of tribute to Big Daddy, who, with Maggie the Cat, saves the play. Brick, without them, would freeze the audience, particularly now, when homosexuality is no longer an issue for an audience not dominated by Fundamentalists, Trump Republicans, and assorted other mossbacks. Read side by side with the wistful *Summer and Smoke*, *Cat on a Hot Tin Roof* seems more a film script than an achieved drama.

In Hart Crane's last great Pindaric ode, "The Broken Tower," the poet cries aloud, in a lament that is also a high celebration, the destruction of his battered self by his overwhelming creative gift:

> The bells, I say, the bells break down their tower;
> And swing I know not where. Their tongues engrave
> Membrane through marrow, my long-scattered score
> Of broken intervals . . . And I, their sexton slave!

This Shelleyan and Whitmanian catastrophe creation, or death by inspiration, was cited once by Williams as an omen of Crane's self-immolation. "By the bells breaking down their tower," in Williams's interpretation, Crane meant "the romantic and lyric intensity of his vocation." Gilbert Debusscher has traced the intensity of Crane's effect upon Williams's Romantic and lyric vocation, with particular reference to Tom Wingfield's emergent vocation in *The Glass Menagerie*. More than seventy years after its first publication, the play provides an absorbing yet partly disappointing experience of rereading.

A professed "memory play," *The Glass Menagerie* seems to derive its continued if wavering force from its partly repressed representation of the quasi-incestuous and doomed love between Tom Wingfield and his crippled, "exquisitely fragile," ultimately schizophrenic sister Laura. Incest, subtly termed the most poetical of circumstances by Shelley, is the dynamic of the erotic drive throughout Williams's more vital writings. Powerfully displaced, it is the secret dynamic of what is surely Williams's masterwork, *A Streetcar Named Desire*.

The Glass Menagerie scarcely bothers at such a displacement, and the transparency of the incest motif is at once the play's lyrical strength and, alas, its dramatic weakness. Consider the moment when Williams chooses to end the play, which times Tom's closing speech with Laura's gesture of blowing out the candles:

> TOM: I didn't go to the moon, I went much further—for time is the longest distance between two places. Not long after that I was fired for writing a poem on the lid of a shoebox. I left St. Louis. I descended the steps of this fire escape for a last time and followed, from then on, in my father's footsteps, attempting to find in motion what was lost in space. I traveled around a great deal. The cities swept about me like dead leaves, leaves that were brightly colored but torn away from the branches. I would have stopped, but I was pursued by something. It always came upon me unawares, taking me altogether by surprise. Perhaps it was a familiar bit of music. Perhaps it was only a piece of transparent glass. Perhaps I am walking along a street at night, in some strange city, before I have found companions. I pass the lighted window of a shop where perfume is sold. The window is filled with pieces of colored glass, tiny transparent bottles in delicate colors, like bits of a shattered rainbow. Then all at once my sister touches my shoulder. I turn around and look into her eyes. Oh, Laura, Laura, I tried to leave you behind me, but I am more faithful than I intended to be! I reach for a cigarette, I cross the street, I run into the movies or a bar, I buy a drink, I speak to the nearest stranger—anything that can blow your candles out!
>
> (*Laura bends over the candles.*)
>
> For nowadays the world is lit by lightning! Blow out your candles, Laura—and so goodbye. . . .
>
> (*She blows the candles out.*)

The many parallels between the lives and careers of Williams and Crane stand behind this poignant passage, though it is fascinating that the actual allusions and echoes here are to Shelley's poetry, but then Shelley increasingly appears to be Crane's heroic archetype, and one remembers Robert Lowell's poem where Crane speaks and identifies himself as the Shelley of his age. The cities of aesthetic exile sweep about Wingfield/Williams like the dead, brightly colored leaves of the "Ode to the West Wind," dead leaves that are at once the words of the poet and lost human souls, like the beloved sister Laura.

What pursues Tom is what pursues the Shelleyan Poet of *Alastor*, an avenging daemon or shadow of rejected, sisterly eros that manifests itself in a further Shelleyan metaphor, the shattered, colored transparencies of Shelley's dome of many-colored glass in *Adonais*, the sublime, lyrical elegy for Keats. That dome, Shelley says, is a similitude for life, and its many colors stain the white radiance of Eternity until death tramples the dome into fragments. Williams beautifully revises Shelley's magnificent trope. For Williams, life itself, through memory as its agent, shatters itself and scatters the colored transparencies of the rainbow, which ought to be, but is not, a covenant of hope.

As lyrical prose, this closing speech has its glory, but whether the dramatic effect is legitimate seems questionable. The key sentence, dramatically, is: "Oh, Laura, Laura, I tried to leave you behind me, but I am more faithful than I intended to be!" In his descriptive list of the characters, Williams says of his surrogate, Wingfield: "His nature is not remorseless, but to escape from a trap he has to act without pity." What would pity have been? And in what sense is Wingfield more faithful, after all, than he attempted to be?

Williams chooses to end the play as though its dramatic center had been Laura, but every reader and every playgoer knows that every dramatic element in the play emanates out from the mother, Amanda. Dream and its repressions, guilt and desire, have remarkably little to do with the representation of Amanda in the play and everything to do with her children. The split between dramatist and lyricist in Williams is manifested in the play as a generative divide. Williams's true subject, like Crane's, is the absolute identity between his artistic vocation and his homosexuality. What is lacking in *The Glass Menagerie* is that Williams could not have said of Amanda, what, Flaubert-like, he did say of the heroine of *Streetcar*: "I am Blanche DuBois." There, and there only, Williams could fuse Chekhov and Hart Crane into one.

The epigraph to *A Streetcar Named Desire* is a quatrain from Hart Crane's "The Broken Tower," the poet's elegy for his gift, his vocation, his life, and so Crane's precise equivalent of Shelley's *Triumph of Life*, Keats's "Fall of

Hyperion," and Whitman's "When Lilacs Last in the Dooryard Bloom'd."
Tennessee Williams, in his long thirty years of decline after composing
A Streetcar Named Desire, had no highly designed, powerfully executed
elegy for his own poetic self. Unlike Crane, his American Romantic precursor and aesthetic paradigm, Williams had to live out the slow degradation
of the waning of his potential, and so endured the triumph of life over his
imagination.

Streetcar sustains a first rereading, after thirty years away from it, more
strongly than I had expected. It is, inevitably, more remarkable on the stage
than in the study, but the fusion of Williams's lyrical and dramatic talents in
it has prevailed over time, at least so far. The play's flaws, in performance,
ensue from its implicit tendency to sensationalize its characters, Blanche
DuBois in particular. Directors and actresses have made such sensational-
izing altogether explicit, with the sad result prophesied by Kenneth Tynan.
The playgoer forgets that Blanche's only strengths are "nostalgia and hope,"
that she is "the desperate exceptional woman," and that her fall is a parable,
rather than an isolated squalor:

> When, finally, she is removed to the mental home, we should feel
> that a part of civilization is going with her. Where ancient drama
> teaches us to reach nobility by contemplation of what is noble,
> modern American drama conjures us to contemplate what might
> have been noble, but is now humiliated, ignoble in the sight of all
> but the compassionate.

Tynan, though accurate enough, still might have modified the image of
Blanche taking a part of civilization away with her into madness. Though
Blanche yearns for the values of the aesthetic, she scarcely embodies them,
being in this failure a masochistic self-parody on the part of Williams himself. His *Memoirs* portray Williams incessantly in the role of Blanche,
studying the nostalgias, and inching along the wavering line between hope
and paranoia. Williams, rather than Blanche, sustains Tynan's analysis
of the lost nobility, now humiliated, that American drama conjures us to
contemplate.

The fall of Blanche is a parable, not of American civilization's lost nobility, but of the failure of the American literary imagination to rise above its
recent myths of recurrent defeat. Emerson admonished us, his descendants,

to go beyond the Great Defeat of the Crucifixion and to demand Victory instead, a victory of the senses as well as of the soul. Walt Whitman, taking up Emerson's challenge directly, set the heroic pattern so desperately emulated by Hart Crane, and which is then repeated in a coarser tone in Williams's life and work.

It must seem curious, at first, to regard Blanche DuBois as a failed Whitmanian, but essentially that is her aesthetic identity. Confronted by the revelation of her young husband's preference for an older man over herself, Blanche falls downwards and outwards into nymphomania, phantasmagoric hopes, pseudo-imaginative collages of memory and desire. Her Orphic, psychic rending by the amiably brutal Stanley Kowalski, a rough but effective version of D. H. Lawrence's vitalistic vision of male force, is pathetic rather than tragic, not because Stanley necessarily is mindless, but because she unnecessarily has made herself mindless, by failing the pragmatic test of experience.

Williams's most effective blend of lyrical vision and dramatic irony in the play comes in the agony of Blanche's cry against Stanley to Stella, his wife and her sister:

> He acts like an animal, has an animal's habits! Eats like one, moves like one, talks like one! There's even something—subhuman—something not quite to the stage of humanity yet! Yes, something—ape-like about him, like one of those pictures I've seen in—anthropological studies! Thousands and thousands of years have passed him right by, and there he is—Stanley Kowalski—survivor of the stone age! Bearing the raw meat home from the kill in the jungle! And you—*you* here—*waiting* for him! Maybe he'll strike you or maybe grunt and kiss you! That is, if kisses have been discovered yet! Night falls and the other apes gather! There in the front of the cave, all grunting like him, and swilling and gnawing and hulking! His poker night!—you call it—this party of apes! Somebody growls—some creature snatches at something—the fight is on! *God!* Maybe we are a long way from being made in God's image, but Stella—my sister—there has been *some* progress since then! Such things as art—as poetry and music—such kinds of new light have come into the world since then! In some kinds of people some tenderer feelings have had some little beginning! That we have got to make *grow*! And *cling* to, and hold as our flag!

In this dark march toward whatever it is we're approaching. . . .
Don't—don't hang back with the brutes!

The lyricism here takes its strength from the ambivalence of what at once attracts and dismays both Blanche and Williams. Dramatic irony, terrible in its antithetical pathos, results here from Blanche's involuntary self-condemnation, since she herself has hung back with the brutes while merely blinking at the new light of the aesthetic. Stanley, being what he is, is clearly less to blame than Blanche, who was capable of more but failed in will.

Williams in his *Memoirs*, haunted as always by Hart Crane, refers to his precursor as "a tremendous and yet fragile artist," and then associates both himself and Blanche with the fate of Crane, a suicide by drowning in the Caribbean:

> I am as much of an hysteric as . . . Blanche; a codicil to my will pro-
> vides for the disposition of my body in this way. "Sewn up in a clean
> white sack and dropped over board, twelve hours north of Havana,
> so that my bones may rest not too far from those of Hart Crane . . ."

At the conclusion of *Memoirs*, Williams again associated Crane with both his own vocation and his own limitations, following Crane even in an identification with the young Rimbaud:

> A poet such as the young Rimbaud is the only writer of whom
> I can think, at this moment, who could escape from words into
> the sensations of being, through his youth, turbulent with revolu-
> tion, permitted articulation by nights of absinthe. And of course
> there is Hart Crane. Both of these poets touched fire that burned
> them alive. And perhaps it is only through self-immolation of such
> a nature that we living beings can offer to you the entire truth of
> ourselves within the reasonable boundaries of a book.

It is the limitation of *Memoirs*, and in some sense even of *A Streetcar Named Desire*, that we cannot accept either Williams or poor Blanche as a Rimbaud or a Hart Crane. Blanche cannot be said to have touched fire that burned her alive. Yet Williams earns the relevance of the play's great epigraph to Blanche's terrible fate:

And so it was I entered the broken world
To trace the visionary company of love, its voice
An instant in the wind (I know not whither hurled)
But not for long to hold each desperate choice.

Ralph Ellison

(1913–1994)

IT SEEMS REASONABLE to judge that the greatest aesthetic achievement by African Americans is the work of the major masters of jazz:
Louis Armstrong, Charlie Parker, Bud Powell, and others. But then jazz
is the only indigenous American art. African American writers, despite
critical confusions among some of their politicized academic cheerleaders,
were in no position to found an original literary art. *Invisible Man* (1952)
by Ralph Ellison remains much the strongest novel by an American black,
and its palpable (and, by Ellison, acknowledged) debts are to Melville,
Mark Twain, Faulkner, Dostoevsky, and to the poetic language of T. S.
Eliot. Toni Morrison, though she passionately argues otherwise, is also
a child of Faulkner, as well as of Virginia Woolf. Ellison was a writer of
immense and mordant sensibility, and his pride at having composed *Invisible Man* was the largest single factor in his refusal to publish a second
novel during his lifetime. I urge the reader toward *Invisible Man* and not
to *Juneteenth*, edited from Ellison's manuscripts. I do not believe he would
have sanctioned its publication: more than once, he had asked me if any
American novelist, except for Henry James, had really composed a second
masterwork.

Presumably he was thinking of Melville, Twain, Hemingway, Fitzgerald—among others—and I would have been tactless to suggest candidates,
and so did not. Yet he was well aware of Faulkner, who in his grand early
phase had created *The Sound and the Fury, As I Lay Dying, Light in
August,* and *Absalom, Absalom!* Faulkner, a southern white, faced many
cultural pressures, but nothing like those that bothered Ellison in the last
quarter century of his life. Feminist critics, Marxists, and African American
nationalists complained of Ellison's insistence at setting art above ideology.
Refusing polemic, the novelist partly withdrew into his massive dignity.
There are essays galore (he commented upon some of them, to me, with
ironical dismissal) that chide Ellison, and his narrator-protagonist, Invisible Man, for not embracing the true "political" faith. Though Ellison, as

the reader will see for herself, ends with an ambiguity tinged with hope, the typical condemnation is that Invisible Man will never come up from underground, because he lacks the black mother, black Muse, or Marxist wiliness that could propel him back to society. Ellison wrote his own novel, and we do best to learn how to read it, and why. Another age will come, with other cultural politics, while *Invisible Man* will retain the American, and universal, imaginative vitality with which Ralph Waldo Ellison endowed it.

At *Invisible Man's* conclusion, the narrator again invokes Louis Armstrong, who throughout has been his chosen precursor, indeed his spiritual guide, Virgil to his Dante:

> And there's still a conflict within me: With Louis Armstrong one half of me says, "Open the window and let the foul air out," while the other says, "It was good, green corn before the harvest."

In the prologue, Invisible Man listens to Armstrong playing and singing "What Did I Do to Be So Black and Blue," and reflects: "Perhaps I like Louis Armstrong because he's made poetry of being invisible." Ellison, a deep student of Armstrong's work, understood that jazz changed from a music of the folk to a high art of innovation because of Armstrong. In some sense, Ellison transformed Charles Chesnutt and Richard Wright rather as Armstrong transcended his precursors in jazz, a movement from folklore to High Modernism.

Invisible Man is a historical novel, because most of it takes place in the 1920s and 1930s, when the United States was hardly less racist a society than it had been in the 1870s and 1880s. Though we need not congratulate ourselves that much of what goes on in Ellison's novel could not happen now (it can and does), public attitudes have altered (to some degree), and the law at least is different. The book's Brotherhood (the Communist Party) scarcely exists, and the remarkable Ras the Exhorter has been replaced by the more mundane Reverend Al Sharpton. The even more remarkable Rinehart, reverend and drug-runner, has a host of contemporary equivalents, but here nature falls short of Ellison's art, and the exuberant Rinehart remains larger than life.

Invisible Man, Melvillean-Faulknerian like *Miss Lonelyhearts, The Crying of Lot 49*, and *Blood Meridian*, shares the negative sublimity of these novels, and shares also in their greatness. Kenneth Burke, most admirable of twentieth-century American critics, several times in conversation urged me to meditate upon Ellison as the American master of the novel of education, the genre of the German bildungsroman, of Thomas Mann's *The Magic Mountain* and Goethe's *Wilhelm Meister.* Mann's novel is a lovingly ironic parody of the genre but Ellison's seems to me a daemonic or tragic parody. His Invisible Man in some respects is closer to Dostoevsky's Underground Man than to a developmental hero of the Goethean-Mannian sort.

Ellison himself cited Malraux, T. S. Eliot, Hemingway, Faulkner, and Dostoevsky as his literary "ancestors." Interestingly, he excluded *Moby-Dick*, which lends *Invisible Man* its crucial Jonah component. I suspect that Melville, like Faulkner, was a touch too close, while Dostoevsky was safely distant, in place and in time. The hero of Dostoevsky's *Notes from Underground* suffers humiliations and narrates his subsequent rejection of the world, withdrawing to a hovel. This symbolic withdrawal is to some extent a rejection of Western values and ideas, though the Underground Man is well aware that European rationalism has an inescapable position in his own consciousness. But he rebels against it, profoundly believing that it violates his integrity. Ellison's Invisible Man is considerably more gifted than Dostoevsky's angry protagonist, and as an African American he has a more complex predicament. Dostoevsky wanted to reject Europe; Ellison passionately refuses to give up on America, though his Invisible Man will not accept it upon its hypocritical terms.

Moby-Dick is haunted by the Book of Jonah, and so is *Invisible Man.* I don't know whether Melville knew that the Book of Jonah is read aloud to the congregation on the Jewish Day of Atonement, but Ellison certainly did. The Book of Jonah is not apocalyptic but survivalist; Jonah, the evasive prophet, is resurrected from the belly of the whale, after he has repented fleeing from Yahweh out of pique. Humor clearly dominates the Hebrew text, since Jonah's vexation against Yahweh is that the prophecy proved successful and the people of Nineveh turned away from evil, thus averting the city's destruction.

The Invisible Man, like Jonah, is always in repression, to which Freud assigned the metaphor of fleeing. False fathers—Bledsoe, Lucius Brockway, Jack of the Brotherhood—continually betray him, even as Jonah feels betrayed by God the Father, who declined to obliterate Nineveh. Chased by whites into a manhole, Invisible Man becomes Jonah in the whale's belly, thus beginning his underground existence, from which (as I read it) he is about to emerge as the novel concludes. The book's prologue, with its lyrical power, sweeps the reader downwards to a Dantesque vision, as Invisible Man, listening to Armstrong play and sing "What Did I Do to Be So Black and Blue," descends the levels of an African-American Inferno. In his phantasmagoria, he hears a preacher who takes as his text the "Blackness of Blackness," which touches its nadir in the Jonah-motif of the whale's belly: "... *It'll put you, glory, glory, Oh my Lawd, in the* WHALE'S BELLY."

Covertly, Ellison alludes to Father Mapple's great sermon on Jonah in *Moby-Dick*, where each of us is adjured to be "only a patriot to Heaven." And yet Ellison enforces the African American difference. Blackness puts you in the whale's belly, and blackness alone is insufficient to resurrect you (though nothing American society offers is going to resurrect you either). Self-reliance (even if you are named for Emerson) will not send you out of the whale's belly, and yet it can change the nature of your sojourn. *Invisible Man* is as intricate and rich in texture as *Moby-Dick* and *As I Lay Dying*, and the reader is best advised to take the book slowly and steadily, reading aloud to herself (and others) whenever the prose is richest. The rewards are immense. This is a novel that transcends politics and ideology, while never for a moment evading the Invisible Man's obligation to prophesy the destruction of the new Nineveh, the United States of America, unless it turns, now, away from the hatefulness of the final consequences of African American slavery.

Since his symbolic function is so dominant, the reader may slight the Invisible Man's personality and character, which would be a loss. Ellison, perhaps with an eye upon James Joyce's *Ulysses*, magnificently fuses naturalism and symbolism in his novel, rather as Faulkner (also influenced by Joyce) did in *As I Lay Dying*. Though necessarily nameless, Invisible Man's personality renders any name redundant. We hear his voice incessantly: ironic, eloquent, jazz-influenced, sometimes furious with outrage, yet always open to a vision that others yet might match his own humane sensibility. Perhaps he is the black Ulysses, on the implicit model of Joyce's Poldy, who abhors all violence and hatred. Far more of an outsider even than Poldy, the Invisible Man, to survive, answers violence with violence and hatred with fierce irony. A surrogate for Ellison, the Invisible Man takes as his cultural aesthetic jazz. Ellison, with profound insight into jazz, defined it as a perpetual contest, a "cutting" in which each innovator transcends his forerunners while ironically incorporating them. That is the secret of the Invisible Man's language and is the basis of the continuous stylistic splendor of Ellison's novel. Its narrative techniques and evolving styles have set a standard for what should be called novelistic jazz that no one else has been able to attain.

The fusion of a jazz aesthetic with an essentially Faulknerian style made *Invisible Man* a book that remains unique, though Toni Morrison has come closest to Ellison's synthesis. There is a subtle polyphony that goes on throughout *Invisible Man*: the narrative line is clear, but something else frequently plays against it, as in the great epiphany of Rinehart—holy man, pimp, drug racketeer—who appears in a cardinal's robe in front of his congregation, under the gold rubric LET THERE BE LIGHT! Backing away from Rinehart's apotheosis, the Invisible Man, who has weathered nearly anything you can imagine, is shocked into the realization that Rinehart and truth are one:

> It was too much for me. I removed my glasses and tucked the white hat carefully beneath my arm and walked away. Can it be, I thought, can it actually be? And I knew that it was. I had heard of it before but I'd never come close. Still, could he be all of them: Rine the runner and Rine the gambler and Rine the briber and Rine the lover and Rinehart the Reverend? Could he himself be both rind and heart? What is real anyway? But how could I doubt it? He was a broad man, a man of parts who got around. Rinehart the rounder. It was true as I was true. His world was possibility and he knew it. He was years ahead of me and I was a fool. I must have been crazy and blind. The world in which we lived was without boundaries. A vast seething, hot world of fluidity, and Rine the rascal was at home. Perhaps *only* Rine the rascal was at home in it. It was unbelievable, but perhaps only the unbelievable could be believed. Perhaps the truth was always a lie.

This is a paradigm for Ellison's achievement of an intricate verbal jazz. Playing just off the beat are the variations on a refrain, "Could he himself be both rind and heart?" and "Rinehart the rounder" and "Rine the rascal," triumphantly repeated. Ras the Exhorter, vividly and sympathetically portrayed by Ellison, is not a temptation for the Invisible Man, but the metamorphic Rinehart heartbreakingly (and hilariously) is. Though Ellison's picaresque hero finally identifies Rinehart's freedom with chaos rather than imagination, again we may trust the tale and not the teller. Ras the Destroyer is a figure of sinister pathos, but still we are moved because, in the background, we can hear the jazz of Ras the Exhorter. What do we hear in Rinehart's great music?

It would be difficult to disengage Rinehart from the contexts in which jazz originated. One might go further and mention Rinehart's literary comrades: Villon, Marlowe, Rimbaud—major poets who were cutthroats, thieves, spies, runners. The Invisible Man accepts Rinehart as context, but not as forerunner. There he chooses Louis Armstrong, who broke through context. Ellison, not quite willing to assert as much for himself, famously ends the novel by implicating the reader in the imagination of invisibility: "Who knows but that, on the lower frequencies, I speak for you?"

Robert Hayden

(1913–1980)

I MET ROBERT HAYDEN only once, when sometime in the early 1970s I
lectured at Ann Arbor and had the privilege of a personal conversation
with him for rather more than an hour or so. We talked about the Bahá'í
gardens in Haifa, which I had visited in the later 1950s, and also about the
poetry of W. B. Yeats, on which I had recently published a long book, and
of Hart Crane, who still seems to me an unexamined presence in several
of Hayden's strongest poems.

Like Jay Wright, Hayden is a major modern American poet, as well as
forming a quartet, together with Ralph Ellison, Toni Morrison, and Jay
Wright, one that seems to me the crown of African American literary
achievement up to this moment. Hayden is a permanent poet, canonical in
a sense that current politicism continues to deride. Cultural fashions fade
away, and literary survival always depends upon three criteria: aesthetic
splendor, cognitive power, and wisdom. A time will come when much current rant and cant will dwindle into period pieces, at best. Hayden, a maker
and not an image of political correctness, will be read long after louder
voices have vanished into the void.

Hayden was at his best in poetic sequences, though some of his lyrical
poems are as rewarding. Like Yeats and Hart Crane (and the young Jay
Wright of *The Homecoming Singer*), at his most memorable, Hayden is
an incantatory poet. His characteristic rhetorical movement is invocation,
rather as Yeats invokes his Tower or Hart Crane, Brooklyn Bridge. Most of
Hayden's critics regard him as invoking black history, but they oversimplify
the basis for his rhetorical art. You can be a very bad poet no matter how
incessantly you call upon the West African past, or the horrific sadism
of the English, Spanish, and Portuguese slave traders and owners of the
Americas. Hayden matters because he is an authentic poet, one of the best
of his generation (which included Elizabeth Bishop, Theodore Roethke,
May Swenson, and the still-overesteemed Robert Lowell). He told me,
with a reticence worthy of his best poems, that he was fascinated by the

impacted quality of Hart Crane's rhetoric, and in some respects he resembles Crane more than he does Yeats, whom his teacher W. H. Auden had commended to him as a model.

Like Crane, who hymned an Unknown God, Hayden was a religious poet, but of the highly eclectic Bahá'í persuasion, a heresy from Iranian Islam. Inwardness and aesthetic elitism mark Hayden's highest achievements, as they do the Pindaricism of Jay Wright, for whom Hayden's freedom from spuriously black ideological "criticism" provided a beacon. Hayden's poetic integrity, like Jay Wright's, was absolute, and invariably courageous, in the mode of Ralph Ellison, who insisted that the American and European literary traditions were as much his possession as was the example of Richard Wright.

All this is merely preamble to a rather rapid survey of a few of Hayden's superb sequences, of which "Middle Passage" is the most famous. Both Hart Crane and T. S. Eliot are drawn upon and evaded in section III in particular, where an Eliotic allusion, in *The Waste Land*, to Shakespeare's *The Tempest*, fuses with the high rhetoric of Crane's Columbus approaching the New World in the "Ave Maria" canto of *The Bridge*:

> Shuttles in the rocking loom of history,
> the dark ships move, the dark ships move,
> their bright ironical names
> like jests of kindness on a murderer's mouth;
> plough through thrashing glister toward
> fata morgana's lucent melting shore,
> weave toward New World littorals that are
> mirage and myth and actual shore.
>
> Voyage through death,
> voyage whose chartings are unlove.
>
> A charnel stench, effluvium of living death
> spreads outward from the hold,
> where the living and the dead, the horribly dying,
> lie interlocked, lie foul with blood and excrement.
> *Deep in the festering hold thy father lies,*
> *the corpse of mercy rots with him,*
> *rats eat love's rotten gelid eyes.*

The dispassionate tonalities of this extraordinary passage stem from Hayden's poetic reticence, his characteristic rhetoric of litotes or understatement, in a reaction-formation against Crane's ecstatic hyperboles and Eliot's hyperbolic ironies. For Crane, Columbus is a mystical (if cruel) disciple of the prophet Isaiah, while Eliot's Tiresias is death-in-life desperately waiting for the grace of Anglican conversion. Hayden, a black Bahá'í, longs for a more universal salvation. His Cinquez, hero of the *Amistad* Mutiny, is the emblem of all those, of whatever origin, who sought the Blessing that America ought to constitute, however far from that ideal it continues to fall:

> Voyage through death
> to life upon these shores.

"Runagate Runagate" is not as intricate and fully written as "Middle Passage," but it too dares and sustains a high rhetoric:

> Tell me, Ezekiel, oh tell me do you see
> mailed Jehovah coming to deliver me?

My late friend, the great poet-novelist Robert Penn Warren, fiercely hated John Brown, upon whom he had written his first book. One day, at lunch with Warren, I commended John Brown as a prophet, though violent in the extreme, yet in the best of causes. Warren, too urbane to argue, presented me at the next week's lunch with a copy of his *John Brown: The Making of a Martyr*. Loving and honoring Warren's memory, I still follow Emerson and Thoreau and vote for Hayden's sequence "John Brown," which honestly admits the prophet's responsibility for "Bleeding Kansas":

> Doing The Lord's work with saber
> sharpened on the grindstone
> of The Word:
> Bleeding Kansas:
>
> the cries of my people the cries
> of their oppressors harrowed
> hacked—poison meat for Satan's maw.
>
> I slew no man but blessed
> the Chosen, who in the name
> of justice killed at my command.

Bleeding Kansas:

a son martyred
there: I am tested I am trued
made worthy of my servitude.

Oh the crimes of this guilty
guilty land:

let Kansas bleed.

Of John Brown, Hayden says simply: "he died / for us." Few American poets have understood so well their hopelessly paradoxical country. Hayden, in the concluding stanza of his "American Journal," joins Walt Whitman in apprehending what may be beyond comprehension:

confess i am curiously drawn unmentionable to
the americans doubt i could exist among them for
long however psychic demands far too severe
much violence much that repels i am attracted
none the less their variousness their ingenuity
their elan vital and that some thing essence
quiddity i cannot penetrate or name

Carson McCullers

(1917–1967)

"I BECOME THE characters I write about and I bless the Latin poet Terence who said 'Nothing human is alien to me.'" That was the aesthetic credo of Carson McCullers and was her program for a limited yet astonishingly intense art of fiction. Rereading her after nearly twenty years away from her novels and stories, I discover that time has enhanced *The Heart Is a Lonely Hunter* and *The Ballad of the Sad Café*, and perhaps rendered less problematic *Reflections in a Golden Eye*. What time cannot do is alter the burden for critics that McCullers represents. Her fiction, like her person, risked that perpetual crisis of Eros of which D. H. Lawrence was the poet and Freud the theoretician. Call it the tendency to make false connections, as set forth by Freud with mordant accuracy in the second paragraph of his crucial paper of 1912, "The Dynamics of the Transference":

> Let us bear clearly in mind that every human being has acquired, by the combined operation of inherent disposition and of external influences in childhood, a special individuality in the exercise of his capacity to love—that is, in the conditions which he sets up for loving, in the impulses he gratifies by it, and in the aims he sets out to achieve in it. This forms a *cliché* or stereotype in him, so to speak (or even several), which perpetually repeats and reproduces itself as life goes on, in so far as external circumstances and the nature of the accessible love-objects permit, and is indeed itself to some extent modifiable by later impressions. Now our experience has shown that of these feelings which determine the capacity to love only a part has undergone full psychical development; this part is directed towards reality, and can be made use of by the conscious personality, of which it forms part. The other part of these libidinal impulses has been held up in development, withheld from the conscious personality and from reality, and may either expend itself only in phantasy, or may remain completely buried in

the unconscious so that the conscious personality is unaware of its existence. Expectant libidinal impulses will inevitably be roused, in anyone whose need for love is not being satisfactorily gratified in reality, by each new person coming upon the scene, and it is more than probable that both parts of the libido, the conscious and the unconscious, will participate in this attitude.

All of McCullers's characters share a particular quirk in the exercise of their capacity to love—they exist, and eventually expire, by falling in love with a hopeless hope. Their authentic literary ancestor is Wordsworth's poignant Margaret, in *The Ruined Cottage*, and like his Margaret they are destroyed, not by despair, but by the extravagance of erotic hope. It is no accident that McCullers's first and best book should bear, as title, her most impressive, indeed unforgettable metaphor: *The Heart Is a Lonely Hunter*.

McCullers's few ventures into literary criticism, whether of Gogol, Faulkner, or herself, were not very illuminating, except in their obsession with loneliness. Her notes on writing, "The Flowering Dream," record her violent, physical response to reading Anne Frank's diary, which caused a rash to break out on her hands and feet. The fear of insulation clearly was the enabling power of McCullers's imagination. When she cited Faulkner and Eugene O'Neill as her major influences, she surprisingly added the Flaubert of *Madame Bovary*, where we might have expected the Lawrence of *The Rainbow* and "The Prussian Officer." But it was Emma's *situation* rather than Flaubert's stance or style that engrossed her.

Mick Kelly, McCullers's surrogate in *The Heart Is a Lonely Hunter*, remains her absolute achievement at representing a personality, presumably a vision of her own personality at the age of twelve. Vivid as the other lonely hunters are—the deaf mute John Singer; Biff Brannon, the café proprietor; Jake Blount, alcoholic revolutionary; Dr. Benedict Mady Copeland, black liberal and reformer—the book still lives in the tormented intensity of Mick Kelly, who knows early to be "grieved to think how power and will / In opposition rule our mortal day, / And why God made irreconcilable / Good and the means of Good." That is the dark wisdom of Shelley in *The Triumph of Life*, but it is also a wisdom realized perfectly and independently by Mick Kelly, who rightly fears the triumph of life over her own integrity, her own hope, her own sense of potential for achievement or for love. The Shelleyan passage becomes pure McCullers if we transpose it to "And why God made irreconcilable / Love and the means of Love."

The Heart Is a Lonely Hunter would not maintain its force if its only final vision were to be the triumph of life, in Shelley's ironic sense. McCullers gives us a tough-grained last sense of Mick Kelly, bereaved, thrown back into an absolute loneliness, but ongoing nevertheless:

> But now no music was in her mind. That was a funny thing. It was like she was shut out from the inside room. Sometimes a quick little tune would come and go—but she never went into the inside room with music like she used to do. It was like she was too tense. Or maybe because it was like the store took all her energy and time. Woolworth's wasn't the same as school. When she used to come home from school she felt good and was ready to start working on the music. But now she was always tired. At home she just ate supper and slept and then ate breakfast and went off to the store again. A song she had started in her private notebook two months before was still not finished. And she wanted to stay in the inside room but she didn't know how. It was like the inside room was locked somewhere away from her. A very hard thing to understand.
>
> Mick pushed her broken front tooth with her thumb. But she did have Mister Singer's radio. All the installments hadn't been paid and she took on the responsibility. It was good to have something that had belonged to him. And maybe one of these days she might be able to set aside a little for a second-hand piano. Say two bucks a week. And she wouldn't let anybody touch this private piano but her—only she might teach George little pieces. She would keep it in the back room and play on it every night. And all day Sunday. But then suppose some week she couldn't make a payment. So then would they come to take it away like the little red bicycle? And suppose like she wouldn't let them. Suppose she hid the piano under the house. Or else she would meet them at the front door. And fight. She would knock down both the two men so they would have shiners and broke noses and would be passed out on the hall floor.
>
> Mick frowned and rubbed her fist hard across her forehead. That was the way things were. It was like she was mad all the time. Not how a kid gets mad quick so that soon it is all over—but in another way. Only there was nothing to be mad at. Unless the store. But the store hadn't asked her to take the job. So there was nothing to be mad at. It was like she was cheated. Only nobody had cheated

her. So there was nobody to take it out on. However, just the same she had that feeling. Cheated.

But maybe it would be true about the piano and turn out O.K. Maybe she would get a chance soon. Else what the hell good had it all been—the way she felt about music and the plans she had made in the inside room? It had to be some good if anything made sense. And it was too and it was too and it was too and it was too. It was some good.

All right!

O.K.!

Some good.

One can call this "Portrait of the Artist as a Young Girl" and see Mick as a visionary of "the way things were." She has the strength of McCullers's endings that are not wholly negations:

Biff wet his handkerchief beneath the water tap and patted his drawn, tense face. Somehow he remembered that the awning had not yet been raised. As he went to the door his walk gained steadiness. And when at last he was inside again he composed himself. (*The Heart Is a Lonely Hunter*)

Even in death the body of the soldier still had the look of warm, animal comfort. His grave face was unchanged, and his sun-browned hands lay palm upwards on the carpet as though in sleep. (*Reflections in a Golden Eye*)

The most remarkable of these conclusions is the vignette called "The Twelve Mortal Men" that serves as epilogue or coda to *The Ballad of the Sad Café*:

The Forks Falls highway is three miles from the town, and it is here the chain gang has been working. The road is of macadam, and the county decided to patch up the rough places and widen it at a certain dangerous place. The gang is made up of twelve men, all wearing black and white striped prison suits, and chained at the ankles. There is a guard, with a gun, his eyes drawn to red slits by the glare. The gang works all the day long, arriving huddled in the prison cart soon after daybreak, and being driven off again in the gray August twilight. All day there is the sound of the picks striking into the clay earth, hard sunlight, the smell of sweat. And every day there is music. One dark voice will start a phrase, halfsung, and like a question. And after a moment another voice will join in, soon the whole gang will be singing. The voices are dark in the golden glare, the music intricately blended, both somber and joyful. The music will swell until at last it seems that the sound does not come from the twelve men on the gang, but from the earth itself, or the wide sky. It is music that causes the heart to broaden and the listener to grow cold with ecstasy and fright. Then slowly the music will sink down until at last there remains one lonely voice, then a great hoarse breath, the sun, the sound of the picks in the silence.

And what kind of gang is this that can make such music? Just twelve mortal men, seven of them black and five of them white boys from this county. Just twelve mortal men who are together.

The rhetorical stance or tone of this is wholly McCullers's and is rather difficult to characterize. In context, its reverberation is extraordinary, working as it does against our incapacity to judge or even comprehend the grotesque tragedy of the doomed love between Miss Amelia Evans and Cousin Lymon, with its consequence in the curious flowering and subsequent demise of the sad café. We, as readers, also would rather love than be loved, a preference that, in the aesthetic register, becomes the defense of reading more intensely lest we ourselves be read, whether by ourselves or by others. The emotion released by the juxtaposition between the music and its origin in the chain gang is precisely akin to the affect arising from McCullers's vision of the tragic dignity of the death of love arising so incongruously from the story of Miss Amelia, Cousin Lymon, and the hideous Marvin Macy.

James Baldwin

(1924–1987)

W HATEVER THE ULTIMATE canonical judgment upon James Baldwin's fiction may prove to be, his nonfictional work has permanent status in American literature. Baldwin is a considerable moral essayist, comparable to George Orwell as a prose Protestant in stance. The evangelical heritage never abandoned the author of *Go Tell It on the Mountain*, and Baldwin, like so many American essayists since Emerson, possesses the fervor of a preacher. Unlike Emerson, Baldwin lacks the luxury of detachment, since he speaks, not for a displaced Yankee majority, but for a sexual minority within a racial minority, indeed for an aesthetic minority among black homosexuals.

Ultimately, Baldwin's dilemma as a writer compelled to address social torments and injustices is that he was a minority of one, a solitary voice breaking forth against himself (and all others) from within himself. Like Carlyle (and a single aspect of the perspectivizing Nietzsche), Baldwin is of the authentic lineage of Jeremiah, most inward of prophets. What Baldwin opposes is what might be called, in Jeremiah's language, the injustice of outwardness, which means that Baldwin's stance is always protest, even in the rather unlikely event that his country turned from selfishness and cruelty to justice and compassion in confronting its underclass of the exploited poor, whether blacks, Hispanics, or others cast out by the Reagan Revolution.

It seems accurate to observe that we remember Jeremiah, unlike Amos or Micah, for his individuation of his own suffering, rather than for his social vision, such as it was. Baldwin might have preferred to have been an Amos or a Micah, forerunners of Isaiah, rather than a Jeremiah, but like Jeremiah he is vivid as a rhetorician of his own psychic anguish and perplexities, and most memorable as a visionary of a certain involuntary isolation, an election that requires a dreadful cost of confirmation. As Baldwin puts it, the price of the ticket is to accept the real reasons for the human journey:

The price the white American paid for his ticket was to become white—: and, in the main, nothing more than that, or, as he was to insist, nothing less. This incredibly limited not to say dimwitted ambition has choked many a human being to death here: and this, I contend, is because the white American has never accepted the real reasons for his journey. I know very well that my ancestors had no desire to come to this place: but neither did the ancestors of the people who became white and who require of my captivity a song. They require of me a song less to celebrate my captivity than to justify their own.

The biblical text that Baldwin alludes to here, Psalm 137, does begin with the song of the exiles from Zion ("and they that wasted us required of us mirth") but ends with a ferocious prophecy against the wasters, ourselves. No writer—black or white—warns us so urgently of "the fire next time" as Baldwin and Jeremiah do, but I hear always in both prophets the terrible pathos of origins:

Then the word of the Lord came unto me, saying,
     Before I formed thee in the belly I knew thee; and before thou camest forth out of the womb I sanctified thee, and I ordained thee a prophet unto the nations.
     Then said I, Ah, Lord God! behold, I cannot speak: for I am a child.

We: my family, the living and the dead, and the children coming along behind us. This was a complex matter, for I was not living with my family in Harlem, after all, but "down-town," in the "white world," in alien and mainly hostile territory. On the other hand, for me, then, Harlem was almost as alien and in a yet more intimidating way and risked being equally hostile, although for very different reasons. This truth cost me something in guilt and confusion, but it was the truth. It had something to do with my being the son of an evangelist and having been a child evangelist, but this is not all there was to it—that is, guilt is not all there was to it.
     The fact that this particular child had been born when and where he was born had dictated certain expectations. The child does not really know what these expectations are—does not know

how real they are—until he begins to fail, challenge, or defeat them. When it was clear, for example, that the pulpit, where I had made so promising a beginning, would not be my career, it was hoped that I would go on to college. This was never a very realistic hope and—perhaps because I knew this—I don't seem to have felt very strongly about it. In any case, this hope was dashed by the death of my father.

Once I had left the pulpit, I had abandoned or betrayed my role in the community—indeed, my departure from the pulpit and my leaving home were almost simultaneous. (I had abandoned the ministry in order not to betray myself by betraying the ministry.)

Reluctant prophets are in the position of Jonah; they provide texts for the Day of Atonement. Baldwin was forever at work reexamining everything, doing his first works over; as he says: "Sing or shout or testify or keep it to yourself: but *know whence you came.*" We came crying hither because we came to this great stage of fools, but Baldwin, like Jeremiah and unlike Shakespeare, demands a theology of origins. He finds it in self-hatred, which he rightly insists is universal, though he seems to reject or just not be interested in the Freudian account of our moral masochism, our need for punishment. The evangelical sense of conscious sin remains strong in Baldwin. Yet, as a moral essayist, he is post-Christian and persuades us that his prophetic stance is not so much religious as aesthetic. A kind of aesthetic of the moral life governs his vision, even in the turbulence of *The Fire Next Time* and *No Name in the Street.*

The center of Baldwin's prophecy can be located in one long, powerful paragraph of *The Fire Next Time*:

"The white man's Heaven," sings a Black Muslim minister, "is the black man's Hell." One may object—possibly—that this puts the matter somewhat too simply, but the song is true, and it has been true for as long as white men have ruled the world. The Africans put it another way: When the white man came to Africa, the white man had the Bible and the African had the land, but now it is the white man who is being, reluctantly and bloodily, separated from the land, and the African who is still attempting to digest or to vomit up the Bible. The struggle, therefore, that now begins in the world is extremely complex, involving the historical role of Christianity in the realm of power—that is, politics—and in the realm of morals. In the realm of power, Christianity has operated with an unmitigated arrogance and cruelty—necessarily, since a religion ordinarily imposes on those who have discovered the true faith, the spiritual duty of liberating the infidels. This particular true faith, moreover, is more deeply concerned about the soul than it is about the body, to which fact the flesh (and the corpses) of countless infidels bears witness. It goes without saying, then, that whoever questions the authority of the true faith also contests the right of the nations that hold this faith to rule over him—contests, in short, their title to his land. The spreading of the Gospel, regardless of the motives or the integrity or the heroism of some of the missionaries, was an absolutely indispensable justification for the planting of the flag. Priests and nuns and schoolteachers helped to protect and sanctify the power that was so ruthlessly being used by people who were indeed seeking a city, but not one in the heavens, and one to be made, very definitely, by captive hands. The Christian church itself—again, as distinguished from some of its ministers—sanctified and rejoiced in the conquests of the flag, and encouraged, if it did not formulate, the belief that conquest, with the resulting relative well-being of the Western populations, was proof of the favor of God. God had come a long way from the desert—but then so had Allah, though in a very different direction. God, going north, and rising on the wings of power, had become white, and Allah, out of power, and on the dark side of Heaven, had become—for all practical purposes, anyway—black. Thus, in the realm of morals the role of Christianity has been, at best, ambivalent. Even leaving out of account the remarkable arrogance that assumed that the ways and morals of others were inferior to those of Christians, and that they therefore had every right, and could use any means, to change them, the collision between cultures—and the schizophrenia in the mind of Christendom—had rendered the domain of morals as chartless as the sea once was, and as treacherous as the sea still is. It is not too much to say that whoever wishes to become a truly moral human being (and let us not ask whether or not this is possible; I think we must *believe* that it is possible) must first divorce himself from all the prohibitions, crimes, and hypocrisies of the Christian church. If the concept of God has any validity or any use, it can only be to make us larger, freer, and more loving. If God cannot do this, then it is time we got rid of Him.

This superb instance of Baldwin's stance and style as a moral essayist depends for its rhetorical power upon a judicious blend of excess and restraint. Its crucial sentence achieves prophetic authority:

> It is not too much to say that whoever wishes to become a truly moral human being (and let us not ask whether or not this is possible; I think we must *believe* that it is possible) must first divorce himself from all the prohibitions, crimes, and hypocrisies of the Christian church.

The parenthesis, nobly skeptical, is the trope of a master rhetorician, and placing "believe" in italics nicely puts into question the problematics of faith. "Divorce," denounced by St. Paul as having been introduced because of our hardness of hearts, acquires the antithetical aura of the Church itself, while Christian prohibitions are assimilated (rather wickedly) to Christian crimes and hypocrisies. This is, rhetorically considered, good, unclean fun, but the burden is savage, and steeped in moral high seriousness. The strength of *The Fire Next Time* comes to rest in its final paragraph, with the interplay between two italicized rhetorical questions, an interplay kindled when *"then"* is added to the second question:

> When I was very young, and was dealing with my buddies in those wine- and urine-stained hallways, something in me wondered, *What will happen to all that beauty?* For black people, though I am aware that some of us, black and white, do not know it yet, are very beautiful. And when I sat at Elijah's table and watched the baby, the women, and the men, and we talked about God's— or Allah's—vengeance, I wondered, when that vengeance was achieved, *What will happen to all that beauty then?* I could also see that the intransigence and ignorance of the white world might make that vengeance inevitable—a vengeance that does not really depend on, and cannot really be executed by, any person or organization, and that cannot be prevented by any police force or army: historical vengeance, a cosmic vengeance, based on the law that

we recognize when we say, "Whatever goes up must come down." And here we are, at the center of the arc, trapped in the gaudiest, most valuable, and most improbable water wheel the world has ever seen. Everything now, we must assume, is in our hands; we have no right to assume otherwise. If we—and now I mean the relatively conscious whites and the relatively conscious blacks, who must, like lovers, insist on, or create, the consciousness of the others—do not falter in our duty now, we may be able, handful that we are, to end the racial nightmare, and achieve our country, and change the history of the world. If we do not now dare everything, the fulfillment of that prophecy, recreated from the Bible in song by a slave, is upon us: "God gave Noah the rainbow sign, No more water, the fire next time!"

The shrewd rhetorical movement here is from the waterwheel to the ambivalent divine promise of no second flood, the promise of covenant with its dialectical countersong of the conflagration ensuing from our violation of covenant. That vision of impending fire re-illuminates the poignant question: "*What will happen to all that beauty then?*" All that beauty that is in jeopardy transcends even the beauty of black people, and extends to everything human, and to bird, beast, and flower.

No Name in the Street takes its fierce title from Job 18:16–19, where it is spoken to Job by Bildad the Shuhite, concerning the fate of the wicked:

> His roots shall be dried up beneath, and above shall his branch
> be cut off.
> His remembrance shall perish from the earth, and he shall have
> no name in the street.
> He shall be driven from light into darkness, and chased out of the
> world.
> He shall neither have son nor nephew among his people, nor any
> remaining in his dwellings.
> They that come after him shall be astonished at his day, as they
> that went before were affrighted.

I have to admit, having just read (and reread) my way through the 690 pages of *The Price of the Ticket*, that frequently I am tempted to reply to Baldwin with Job's response to Bildad:

> How long will ye vex my soul, and break me in pieces with
> words?
> These ten times have ye reproached me: ye are not ashamed
> that ye make yourselves strange to me. And be it indeed that
> I have erred, mine error remaineth with myself.
> If indeed ye will magnify yourselves against me, and plead
> against me my reproach.

Baldwin's rhetorical authority as prophet would be seriously impaired if he were merely a Job's comforter, Bildad rather than Jeremiah. *No Name in the Street* cunningly evades the risk that Baldwin will magnify himself against the reader, partly by the book's adroitness at stationing the author himself in the vulnerable contexts of his own existence, both in New York and in Paris. By not allowing himself (or his readers) to forget how perpetually a black homosexual aesthete and moralist, writer and preacher, must fight for his life, Baldwin earns the pathos of the prophetic predicament.

The discomfort of having lost bearings is itself a prophetic trope, and comes to its fruition in the book's searing final paragraph:

> To be an Afro-American, or an American black, is to be in the situation, intolerably exaggerated, of all those who have ever found themselves part of a civilization which they could in no wise honorably defend—which they were compelled, indeed, endlessly to attack and condemn—and who yet spoke out of the most passionate love, hoping to make the kingdom new, to make it honorable and worthy of life. Whoever is part of whatever civilization helplessly loves some aspects of it, and some of the people in it. A person does not lightly elect to oppose his society. One would much rather be at home among one's compatriots than be mocked and detested by them. And there is a level on which the mockery of the people, even their hatred, is moving because it is so blind: it is terrible to watch people cling to their captivity and insist on their own destruction. I think black people have always felt this about America, and Americans, and have always seen, spinning above the thoughtless American head, the shape of the wrath to come.

Not to be at home among one's compatriots is to avoid the catastrophe of being at ease in the new Zion that is America. A reader, however moved by Baldwin's rhetorical authority, can be disturbed here by the implication that all blacks are prophets, at least in our society. Would to God indeed that all the Lord's people were prophets, but they are not, and cannot be.

The final utterance in *The Price of the Ticket* seems to me Baldwin's most poignant ever:

> Freaks are called freaks and are treated as they are treated—in the main, abominably—because they are human beings who cause to echo, deep within us, our most profound terrors and desires.
>
> Most of us, however, do not appear to be freaks—though we are rarely what we appear to be. We are, for the most part, visibly male or female, our social roles defined by our sexual equipment.
>
> But we are all androgynous, not only because we are all born of a woman impregnated by the seed of a man but because each of us, helplessly and forever, contains the other—male in female, female in male, white in black and black in white. We are a part of each other. Many of my countrymen appear to find this fact exceedingly inconvenient and even unfair, and so, very often, do I. But none of us can do anything about it.

Baldwin is most prophetic, and most persuasive, when his voice is as subdued as it is here. What gives the rhetorical effect of self-subdual is the precise use of plural pronouns throughout. Moving from his own predicament to the universal, the prophet achieves an effect directly counter to Jeremiah's pervasive trope of individualizing the prophetic alternative. The ultimate tribute that Baldwin has earned is his authentic share in Jeremiah's most terrible utterance:

> O Lord, thou has deceived me, and I was deceived: thou art stronger than I, and hast prevailed: I am in derision daily, every one mocketh me.
>
> For since I spake, I cried out, I cried violence and spoil; because the word of the Lord was made a reproach unto me, and a derision, daily.
>
> Then I said, I will not make mention of him, nor speak any more

in his name. But his word was in mine heart as a burning fire shut up in my bones, and I was weary with forbearing, and I could not stay.

Flannery O'Connor
(1925–1964)

D. H. LAWRENCE, a superb writer of short stories, gave the reader a permanent wisdom in one brief remark: "Trust the tale, not the teller." That seems to me an essential principle in reading the stories of Flannery O'Connor, who may have been the most original tale-teller among Americans since Hemingway. Her sensibility was an extraordinary blend of Southern Gothic and severe Roman Catholicism. So fierce a moralist is O'Connor that readers need to be wary of her tendentiousness: she has too palpable a design upon us, to shock us by violence into a need for traditional faith. As teller, O'Connor was very shrewd, yet I think her best tales are far shrewder and enforce no moral except an awakened moral imagination.

O'Connor's South is wildly Protestant, not the Protestantism of Europe, but of the indigenous American Religion, whether it calls itself Baptist, Pentecostal, or whatever. The prophets of that religion—"snake-handlers, Free Thinking Christians, Independent Prophets, the swindlers, the mad, and sometimes the genuinely inspired"—O'Connor named as "natural Catholics." Except for this handful of "natural Catholics," the people who throng O'Connor's marvelous stories are the damned, a category in which Flannery O'Connor cheerfully included most of her readers. I think that the best way to read her stories is to begin by acknowledging that one is among her damned, and then go on from there to enjoy her grotesque and unforgettable art of telling.

"A Good Man Is Hard to Find" remains a splendid introduction to O'Connor. A grandmother, her son and daughter-in-law and their three children, are on a car journey when they encounter an escaped convict, the Misfit, and his two subordinate killers. Upon seeing the Misfit, the grandmother foolishly declares his identity, thus dooming herself and all her family. The old lady pleads with the Misfit while her family is taken away to be shot, but O'Connor gives us one of her masterpieces in this natural theologian of a killer. Jesus, the Misfit declares, "thrown everything off balance" by raising the dead, in a cosmos where there is "No pleasure but meanness." Dizzy and hallucinating, the terrified grandmother touches the Misfit while murmuring: "Why you're one of my babies. You're one of my own children!" He recoils, shoots her three times in the chest, and pronounces her epitaph: "She would of been a good woman if it had been somebody there to shoot her every minute of her life."

The tale and the teller came together here, since the Misfit clearly speaks for something fierce and funny in O'Connor herself. O'Connor gives us a hypocritical and banal old lady, and a killer who is, in O'Connor's view, an instrument of Catholic grace. This is meant to be and certainly *is* outrageous because, being damned, *we* are outraged by it. We would be good, O'Connor thinks, if someone were there to shoot us every minute of our lives.

Why do we not resent O'Connor's palpable designs upon us? Her comic genius is certainly part of the answer; someone who can entertain us so profoundly can damn us pretty much as she pleases. In her "Good Country People," we meet the unfortunate Joy Hopewell, who possesses both a PhD in philosophy and a wooden leg, and the fancy first name Hulga, which she has given herself. A brash young Bible salesman, with the improbably phallic name of Manley Pointer, divests Hulga of her wooden leg in a haystack and then runs off with it. Hulga accurately knows herself as of the damned (is she not a philosopher?) and we can draw what moral we will from her cruelly hilarious fate. Shall we say of her: "She would of been a good woman if it had been somebody there to seduce her and run off with her wooden leg every minute of her life?"

O'Connor would have disdained my skepticism, and I am aware that my parody is defensive. But her early stories, though lively, are not her greatest. That comes in such later work as "A View of the Woods" and "Parker's Back," and in her second novel, *The Violent Bear It Away.* "A View of the Woods" is a sublimely ugly tale, featuring the seventy-nine-year-old Mr. Fortune and his nine-year-old granddaughter, Mary Fortune Pitts. Both are dreadful: selfish, stubborn, mean, sullen monuments of pride. At the story's end, a nasty fight between the two closes with the grandfather killing the little girl, having throttled her and smashed her head upon a rock. In his excitement and exhaustion, Mr. Fortune has a final "view of the woods" during a fatal heart attack. This is all grimly impressive, but how should we interpret it?

O'Connor remarked that Mary Fortune Pitts was saved and Mr. Fortune damned, but she could not explain why, since they are equally abominable persons, and the death struggle might have gone either way. It is splendid that O'Connor was so outrageous, because our skepticism outraged her, and inspired her art. And yet her obsessive spirituality and absolute moral judgments cannot just sustain themselves at the reader's expense. But when I think that, I suddenly recall how close her literary tastes were to my own: she preferred Faulkner's *As I Lay Dying* and Nathanael West's *Miss Lonelyhearts* to all other works of modern American fiction, and so do I. Reading Flannery O'Connor's stories and *The Violent Bear It Away*, I am exhilarated to the brink of fear, as I am by Faulkner and West in their grandest works, and by Cormac McCarthy's *Blood Meridian*, which surely O'Connor would have admired had she survived to read it.

The Violent Bear It Away, a professedly Roman Catholic prose romance, begins with the death of an eighty-four-year-old Southern American Protestant, self-called prophet, and professional moonshiner, as set forth in this splendidly comprehensive sentence:

> Francis Marion Tarwater's uncle had been dead for only half a day when the boy got too drunk to finish digging his grave and a Negro named Buford Munson, who had come to get a jug filled, had to finish it and drag the body from the breakfast table where it was still sitting and bury it in a decent and Christian way, with the sign of its Saviour at the head of the grave and enough dirt on top to keep the dogs from digging it up.

Flannery O'Connor's masterwork ends with the fourteen-year-old Tarwater marching toward the city of destruction, where his own career as prophet is to be suffered:

> Intermittently the boy's jagged shadow slanted across the road ahead of him as if it cleared a rough path toward his goal. His singed eyes, black in their deep sockets, seemed already to envision the fate that awaited him but he moved steadily on, his face set toward the dark city, where the children of God lay sleeping.

In Flannery O'Connor's fierce vision, the children of God, all of us, always are asleep in the outward life. Young Tarwater, clearly O'Connor's surrogate, is in clinical terms a borderline schizophrenic, subject to auditory hallucinations in which he hears the advice of an imaginary friend who is overtly the Christian Devil. But clinical terms are utterly alien to O'Connor, who accepts only theological namings and unnamings. This is necessarily a spiritual strength in O'Connor, yet it can be an aesthetic distraction also, since *The Violent Bear It Away* is a fiction of preternatural power, and not a religious tract. Rayber, the antagonist of both prophets, old and young Tarwater, is an aesthetic disaster, whose defects in representation alone keep the book from making a strong third with Faulkner's *As I Lay Dying* and Nathanael West's *Miss Lonelyhearts*. O'Connor despises Rayber and cannot bother to make him even minimally persuasive. We wince at his unlikely verbal mixture of popular sociology and confused psychology, as even Sally Fitzgerald, O'Connor's partisan, is compelled to admit:

> Her weaknesses—a lack of perfect familiarity with the terminology of the secular sociologists, psychologists, and rationalists she often casts as adversary figures, and an evident weighting of the scales against them all—are present in the character of Rayber (who combines all three categories).

One hardly believes that a perfect familiarity with the writings, say, of David Riesman, Erik Erikson, and Karl Popper would have enabled O'Connor to make poor Rayber a more plausible caricature of what she despised. We remember *The Violent Bear It Away* for its two prophets, and particularly young Tarwater, who might be called a Gnostic version of Huckleberry Finn. What makes us free is the Gnosis, according to the most ancient of heresies. O'Connor, who insisted upon her Catholic orthodoxy, necessarily believed that what makes us free is baptism in Christ, and for her the title of her novel was its most important aspect, since the words are spoken by Jesus himself:

> But what went ye out for to see? A prophet? yea, I say unto you, and more than a prophet.
> For this is *he*, of whom it is written, Behold, I send my messenger before thy face, which shall prepare thy way before thee.
> Verily I say unto you, Among them that are born of women there

> hath not risen a greater than John the Baptist: notwithstanding
> he that is least in the kingdom of heaven is greater than he.
> And from the days of John the Baptist until now the kingdom of
> heaven suffereth violence, and the violent take it by force.

I have quoted the King James Version of Matthew 11:9–12, where "and the violent take it by force" is a touch more revealing than O'Connor's Catholic version, "and the violent bear it away." For O'Connor, we are back in or rather never have left Christ's time of urgency, and her heart is with those like the Tarwaters who know that the kingdom of heaven will suffer them to take it by force:

> The lack of realism would be crucial if this were a realistic novel
> or if the novel demanded the kind of realism you demand. I don't
> believe it does. The old man is very obviously not a Southern Bap-
> tist, but an independent, a prophet in the true sense. The true
> prophet is inspired by the Holy Ghost, not necessarily by the dom-
> inant religion of his region. Further, the traditional Protestant
> bodies of the South are evaporating into secularism and respect-
> ability and are being replaced on the grass roots level by all sorts of
> strange sects that bear not much resemblance to traditional Prot-
> estantism—Jehovah's Witnesses, snake-handlers, Free Thinking
> Christians, Independent Prophets, the swindlers, the mad, and
> sometimes the genuinely inspired. A character has to be true to his
> own nature and I think the old man is that. He was a prophet, not
> a church-member. As a prophet, he has to be a natural Catholic.
> Hawthorne said he didn't write novels, he wrote romances; I am
> one of his descendants.

O'Connor's only disputable remark in this splendid defense of her book is the naming of old Tarwater as "a natural Catholic." Hawthorne's descendant she certainly was, by way of Faulkner, T. S. Eliot, and Nathanael West, but though Hawthorne would have approved her mode, he would have been shocked by her matter. To ignore what is authentically shocking about O'Connor is to misread her weakly. It is not her incessant violence that is troublesome but rather her passionate endorsement of that violence as the only way to startle her secular readers into a spiritual awareness. As a visionary writer, she is determined to take us by force, to bear us away so that we may be open to the possibility of grace.

O'Connor anticipates our wounded outcries of nature against grace, since we understandably prefer a vision that corrects nature without abolishing it. Young Tarwater himself, as finely recalcitrant a youth as Huckleberry Finn, resists not only Rayber but the tuition of old Tarwater. A kind of swamp fox, like the Revolutionary hero for whom he was named, the boy Tarwater waits for his own call, and accepts his own prophetic election only after he has baptized his idiot cousin Bishop by drowning him, and even then only in consequence of having suffered a homosexual rape by the Devil himself. O'Connor's audacity reminds us of the Faulkner of *Sanctuary* and the West of *A Cool Million*. Her theology purports to be Roman Catholicism, but her sensibility is Southern Gothic, Jacobean in the mode of the early T. S. Eliot, and even Gnostic, in the rough manner of Carlyle, a writer she is likely never to have read.

I myself find it a critical puzzle to read her two novels, *Wise Blood* and *The Violent Bear It Away*, and her two books of stories, *A Good Man Is Hard to Find* and *Everything That Rises Must Converge*, and then to turn from her fiction to her occasional prose in *Mystery and Manners*, and her letters in *The Habit of Being*. The essayist and letter-writer denounces Manichaeism, Jansenism, and all other deviations from normative Roman Catholicism, while the storyteller seems a curious blend of the ideologies of Simone Weil reading the New Testament into the *Iliad*'s "poem of force" and of René Girard assuring us that there can be no return of the sacred without violence. Yet the actual O'Connor, in her letters, found Weil "comic and terrible," portraying the perpetual waiter for grace as an "angular intellectual proud woman approaching God inch by inch with ground teeth," and I suspect she would have been as funny about the violent thematicism of Girard.

To find something of a gap between O'Connor as lay theologue and O'Connor as a storyteller verging upon greatness may or may not be accurate but in any case intends to undervalue neither the belief nor the fiction. I suspect though that the fiction's implicit theology is very different from what O'Connor thought it to be, a difference that actually enhances the power of the novels and stories. It is not accidental that *As I Lay Dying* and *Miss Lonelyhearts* were the only works of fiction that O'Connor urged upon Robert Fitzgerald, or that her own prose cadences were haunted always by the earlier rather than the later Eliot. *The Waste Land*, *As I Lay Dying*, and *Miss Lonelyhearts* are not works of the Catholic imagination but rather of that Gnostic pattern Gershom Scholem termed "redemption through sin." *Wise Blood, The Violent Bear It Away*, and stories like "A Good Man Is Hard to Find" and the merciless "Parker's Back" take place in the same cosmos as *The Waste Land, As I Lay Dying*, and *Miss Lonelyhearts*. This world is the American version of the cosmological emptiness that the ancient Gnostics called the *kenoma*, a sphere ruled by a demiurge who has usurped the alien God, and who has exiled God out of history and beyond the reach of our prayers.

In recognizing O'Connor's fictive universe as being essentially Gnostic, I dissent not only from her own repudiation of heresy but from the sensitive reading of Jefferson Humphries, who links O'Connor to Proust in an "aesthetic of violence":

> For O'Connor, man has been his own demiurge, the author of his own fall, the keeper of his own cell. . . .
>
> The chief consequence of this partly willful, partly inherited alienation from the sacred is that the sacred can only intrude upon human perception as a violence, a rending of the fabric of daily life.

On this account, which remains normative, whether Hebraic or Catholic, we are fallen into the *kenoma* through our own culpability. In the Gnostic formulation, creation and fall were one and the same event, and all that can save us is a certain spark within us, a spark that is no part of the creation but rather goes back to the original abyss. The grandeur or sublimity that shines through the ruined creation is a kind of abyss-radiance, whether in Blake or Carlyle or the early Eliot or in such novelistic masters of the grotesque as Faulkner, West, and O'Connor.

O'Connor's final visions are more equivocal than she evidently intended. Here is the conclusion of "Revelation," where Mrs. Turpin sees "a vast horde of souls . . . rumbling toward heaven":

> There were whole companies of white-trash, clean for the first time in their lives, and bands of black niggers in white robes, and battalions of freaks and lunatics shouting and clapping and leaping like frogs. And bringing up the end of the procession was a tribe of people whom she recognized at once as those who, like herself and Claud, had always had a little of everything and the God-given wit to use it right. She leaned forward to observe them closer. They were marching behind the others with great dignity, accountable

as they had always been for good order and common sense and respectable behavior. They alone were on key. Yet she could see by their shocked and altered faces that even their virtues were being burned away. She lowered her hands and gripped the rail of the hog pen, her eyes small but fixed unblinkingly on what lay ahead. In a moment the vision faded but she remained where she was, immobile.

At length she got down and turned off the faucet and made her slow way on the darkening path to the house. In the woods around her the invisible cricket choruses had struck up, but what she heard were the voices of the souls climbing upward into the starry field and shouting hallelujah.

This is meant to burn away false or apparent virtues, and yet consumes not less than everything. In O'Connor's mixed realm, which is neither nature nor grace, southern reality nor private phantasmagoria, all are necessarily damned, not by an aesthetic of violence, but by a Gnostic aesthetic in which there is no knowing unless the knower becomes one with the known. Her Catholic moralism masked from O'Connor something of her own aesthetic of the grotesque. Certainly her essay on "Some Aspects of the Grotesque in Southern Fiction" evades what is central in her own praxis:

Whenever I'm asked why Southern writers particularly have a penchant for writing about freaks, I say it is because we are still able to recognize one. To be able to recognize a freak, you have to have some conception of the whole man, and in the South the general conception of man is still, in the main, theological. That is a large statement, and it is dangerous to make it, for almost anything you say about Southern belief can be denied in the next breath with equal propriety. But approaching the subject from the standpoint of the writer, I think it is safe to say that while the South is hardly Christ-centered, it is most certainly Christ-haunted. The Southerner, who isn't convinced of it, is very much afraid that he may have been formed in the image and likeness of God. Ghosts can be very fierce and instructive. They cast strange shadows, particularly in our literature. In any case, it is when the freak can be sensed as a figure for our essential displacement that he attains some depth in literature.

The freakish displacement here is from "wholeness," which is then described as the state of having been made in the image or likeness of God. But that mode, displacement, is not what is operative in O'Connor's fiction. Her own favorite, among her people, is young Tarwater, who is not a freak, and who is so likeable because he values his own freedom above everything and anyone, even his call as a prophet. We are moved by Tarwater because of his recalcitrance, because he is the Huck Finn of visionaries. But he moves O'Connor, even to identification, because of his inescapable prophetic vocation. It is the interplay between Tarwater fighting to be humanly free, and Tarwater besieged by his great-uncle's training, by the internalized Devil, and most of all by O'Connor's own ferocious religious zeal, that constitutes O'Connor's extraordinary artistry. Her pious admirers to the contrary, O'Connor would have bequeathed us even stronger novels and stories, of the eminence of Faulkner's, if she had been able to restrain her spiritual tendentiousness.

James Merrill

(1926–1995)

IN JAMES MERRILL'S first book, *The Black Swan* (privately printed, 1946), there are intimations of his visionary epic, *The Changing Light at Sandover*, published in its complete form in 1983. Across the thirty-seven intervening years, the voice of the outsetting bard echoes in the extraordinary cadences of the matured seer. Here is the third stanza of "The Broken Bowl" from *The Black Swan*, written by a poet in his teens:

> No lucid, self-containing artifice
>   At last, but fire, ice,
> A world in jeopardy. What lets the bowl
> Nonetheless triumph by inconsequence
> And wrestle harmony from dissonance
> And with the fragments build another, whole,
>   Inside us, which we feel
> Can never break, or grow less bountiful?

Love, not unexpectedly, turns out to be the answer, early and late. Merrill, like Yeats, is both an occultist and an erotic poet, and again like Yeats he is a curious kind of religious poet, "curious" because the religion is a variety of Gnosticism, derived by Yeats from sources as troublesome and inauthentic as Madame Helena Petrovna Blavatsky, and by Merrill from sources just as troublesome and inauthentic, such as Dr. Carl Gustav Jung. I assume that Merrill would have been delighted by Yeats's early defense of Madame Blavatsky: "Of course she gets up spurious miracles, but what *is* a woman of genius to do in the Nineteenth Century?" As a man of genius, rather late on in the twentieth century, Merrill insouciantly also gets up spurious miracles, which he calls *The Book of Ephraim, Mirabell: Books of Number*, and *Scripts for the Pageant*. They *are* miracles of poetic achievement, and if I call them "spurious" I only confess my own bewilderment or startled skepticism at being confronted by a contemporary Dante or Blake who follows Victor Hugo and Yeats by spending thousands of evenings at the Ouija board in touch with alarmingly familiar spirits.

The stanza I quoted above, from "The Broken Bowl," displays already what several critics have noted as a fundamental trope of creation-by-catastrophe in Merrill, the ancient Gnostic and Kabbalistic image of the Breaking of the Vessels. But the image appears with a grand difference in Merrill, if only because he is a poet *for whom there are no catastrophes.*

Like Proust, his truest precursor, Merrill studies the nostalgias, but the study in each is just that: wonder, and not elegy. Grief is not a Merrillean or a Proustian emotion, and neither is guilt. Even Yeats, despite his passionate occultries, could mourn his peers, but Merrill is so wholehearted a preternaturalist that dead friends instantly manifest themselves in the Higher Keys of his Spirit World. What is most original and unnerving in Merrill is his emotional stance or metaphoric affect, which too readily can be mistaken for a psychic remoteness or a stylistic coldness. I note this in some contrition, since I myself was a late convert to Merrill, struck down upon my own road to Damascus by the blinding white light of trope in *Divine Comedies* (1976), after a quarter century of weakly misreading Merrill with a merely technical admiration. *The Book of Ephraim* and its companion poems, such as "Lost in Translation" and "The Will," converted me, and sent me back to read again the major lyrics and meditations I had resisted too stubbornly and for too long a time, very much to my own loss.

The canonical judgment should be ventured that Merrill is one of the three permanent poets of his own American generation, together with John Ashbery and A. R. Ammons. His immediate precursors are Elizabeth Bishop, in the generation just before, and, in a more engendering sense, Wallace Stevens, whose language and vision are prevalent in *The Black Swan* and in *First Poems* (1951), to become more subtly internalized in *The Country of a Thousand Years of Peace* (1959) and afterwards. Though W. H. Auden is invoked throughout Merrill's epic, both as sage and as archetype of the poet, his example and career seem to play the same part in Merrill as in Ashbery. He is a benign presence for both, precisely because he is not the true father, but more like an amiable uncle on the mother's side, as it were. Stevens, the veritable precursor, is a very dangerous poetic father, whether one takes after his formal self, as Merrill does, or comes up out of his repressed Whitmanian depths, which is Ashbery's authentic origin. Wallace Stevens, one of the dandies, an American, is not the same as Stevens the Real Me or Me Myself, Whitmanian celebrant of Night, Death, the Mother, and the Sea. Merrill's Stevens is closer to Alexander Pope than to Whitman, but then Merrill himself is, in some aspects, the reincarnation of Pope. *The Book of Ephraim* is less like Dante than it is like *The Rape of the Lock*, or rather *Ephraim* and its successors have the same relation to the *Commedia* that Pope's exquisite fantasy has to *Paradise Lost*.

Merrill is Popean as an artist, but hardly as a visionary, where the Proustian influence dominates, as early as the poignant poem "For Proust" in *Water Street* (1962). Merrill too is always in search of lost time, a quest that aims "to work / The body's resurrection, sense by sense," according to the "Venice" section of *The Book of Ephraim*. The epigraph to *Ephraim* is that extraordinary tercet in *Paradiso XV* where Dante's ancestor, Cacciaguida, addresses the poet as root to his branch:

> You believe the truth, for the lesser and the great of this life gaze into that mirror in which, before you think, you display your thought.

Whether Dante's vision can be reconciled with Proust's is a considerable difficulty, but it is characteristic of Merrill to make the attempt. That mirror, for Proust and for Merrill, is what Freud called the bodily ego, a precarious "frontier concept" on the edge between mind and body. Introjection, for Merrill, is a defense of identification almost invariably accomplished through the eye, so that sight is for Merrill the sense closest both to thinking and to sexual longing. Such an identification is more American than European, more like Emerson and Whitman than like Dante and Proust. The mirror of the self, in Merrill, is an overdetermining mechanism, just as it is in Freud, despite Merrill's curious debt to Jung's *Answer to Job*. "There are no accidents" is the law of Freud's psychic cosmos, and this law is taught also by Ephraim and his fellow Spirits. We gaze into the mirror and behold the bodily ego, as it were, and so behold our thought before ever we think it:

> One speaks. *How superficial*
> *Appearances are!* Since then, as if a fish
> Had broken the perfect silver of my reflectiveness,
> I have lapses. I suspect
> Looks from behind, where nothing is, cool gazes

Through the blind flaws of my mind. As days,
As decades lengthen, this vision
Spreads and blackens. I do not know whose it is,
But I think it watches for my last silver
To blister, flake, float leaf by life, each milling-
Downward dumb conceit, to a standstill
From which not even you strike any brilliant
Chord in me, and to a faceless will,
Echo of mine, I am amenable.

That is Merrill's "Mirror" ending its monologue in *The Country of a Thousand Years of Peace*, 1959. But, by then, poor Mirror is paranoid, though with the madness of mirrors, not humans. Mirror's breakdown ensues from the betrayal of covenant by the children who, at the start of the monologue, had trusted Mirror to teach them how to live. To have become amenable to a faceless will is surely catastrophe if one has been, before that, the glass in which the children beheld their thought ere cognition began. Yet Mirror, like Merrill, acknowledges no catastrophes.

In *Nights and Days* (1966), there is a celebrated sonnet-sequence, "The Broken Home," which takes as subject the history of marriage and divorce of Merrill's parents. Each of the seven irregular sonnets is the most astonishing at controlling what cannot be controlled, knowing what cannot be known. Led by his Irish setter, "head / Passionately lowered," the child enters his mother's bedroom, where

Blinds beat sun from the bed.
The green-gold room throbbed like a bruise.
Under a sheet, clad in taboos
Lay whom we sought, her hair undone, outspread.

And of a blackness found, if ever now, in old
Engravings where the acid bit.
I must have needed to touch it
Or the whiteness—was she dead?
Her eyes flew open, startled strange and cold.
The dog slumped to the floor. She reached for me. I fled.

Is there trauma here? My question intends only the poem itself as refer-
ent, and not the poem as act of the mind. In Stevens, these are not separa-
ble, but in Merrill I think they are. I do not read hurt or pain *in the poem*,
though it clearly renders what ought to be the trauma of the barely evaded
Oedipal taboo. Contrast Hart Crane's beautifully oblique "Repose of Rivers" where the traumatic pain, *in the poem*, is dominant:

> How much I would have bartered! the black gorge
> And all the singular nestings in the hills
> Where beavers learn stitch and tooth.
> The pond I entered once and quickly fled—
> I remember now its singing willow rim.

Crane's pond is Merrill's shut bedroom, yet Crane's lyric is compounded
of hurt, with its superb images of mammoth turtles mounting one another in
a terrible love-death, and of his own homosexual initiation: "With scalding
unguents spread and smoking darts." Where Crane obliquely renders the
evaded Oedipal trespass with a traumatic affect, Merrill directly presents
it without any intense affect at all. I do not contrast the two poems or poets
in terms of aesthetic achievement; few poets, I believe, can survive a close
comparison with Hart Crane, and Merrill has no poetic affinities to Crane
whatsoever. It is Merrill's strangeness that is my concern. Oedipal catastrophe is for Crane catastrophe; psychic trauma does not become poetic gain.
But for Merrill, trauma and grief do become precisely poetic gains, "Ill-
gotten gains," as he calls them with his customary wit and self-knowledge:

> A sense comes late in life of too much death,
> Of standing wordless, with head bowed beneath
>
> The buffeting of losses which we see
> At once, no matter how reluctantly,
>
> As gains. Gains to the work. Ill-gotten gains . . .
> Under the skull-and-crossbones, rigging strains
>
> Our craft to harbor, and salt lashings plow
> The carved smile of a mermaid on the prow.

Merrill is *not* an elegiac poet, as he keeps making clear, yet nothing about his work is more difficult than its stance. Erotic poetry always has been elegiac, but Merrill is the grand and unnerving exception. In a very sensitive essay upon what he calls "elegiac aspects" of *The Changing Light at Sandover*, Peter Sacks reads the decasyllabics I have quoted above as a "balance of loss and gain," but such a reading reflects the consequences of bringing a profound experience of poetic elegy to the consideration of Merrill's very different mode. At the close of his huge poem, Merrill movingly contrasts his gain to a close friend's loss, as if to admit again that traditional elegiac consolation is not revelant to his occult sublimities:

> . . . our poor friend's
> Somber regard—captive like Gulliver
> Or like the mortal in an elfin court
> Pining for wife and cottage on this shore
> Beyond whose depthless dazzle he can't see.

Some part of Merrill's *otherness*, of his authentic uncanniness as a poet, is more attuned to an elfin court than to a wife and cottage on this shore. What is most original and valuable in Merrill's poetry comes out of this otherness, out of a quality that transcends even a sensibility from the highest Camp, as it were, let alone the witty homosexual onto-theology of the *Sandover* epic. A temperament for which there are no accidents and no catastrophes, a consciousness somehow beyond trauma and beyond mourning, is also astonishingly capable of an erotic wisdom that can balance experiential contraries that cannot be balanced:

> Where I hid my face, your touch, quick, merciful,
> Blindfolded me. A god breathed from my lips.
> If that was illusion, I wanted it to last long;
> To dwell, for its daily pittance, with us there,
> Cleaning and watering, sighing with love or pain.
> I hoped it would climb when it needed to the heights
> Even of degradation, as I for one
> Seemed, those days, to be always climbing
> Into a world of wild
> Flowers, feasting, tears—or was I falling, legs

Buckling, heights, depths,
Into a pool of each night's rain?
But you were everywhere beside me, masked,
As who was not, in laughter, pain, and love.

The heights of degradation presumably are the only possible habitation of that illusion where a god breathes through one's lips. Not even paraphrase, this is the ancient formula of a Gnosticism that forsakes asceticism and chooses instead the upward release of the sparks.

It would comfort *me* to say that the central trope of *The Changing Light at Sandover* is the Ouija board, and that Merrill's spooks, like Yeats's, have come to bring him metaphors for poetry. Unhappily, this is not so. Merrill quests for the truth at the Ouija board and receives a heap of gorgeous nonsense, dreadful science fiction, and a considerable swatch of the best poetry written since the death of Wallace Stevens in 1955. My own experience as a reader is that *The Book of Ephraim* is almost continuously superb and can sustain endless rereadings. But *Mirabell: Books of Number* can numb one, in between bouts of sublimity, while *Scripts for the Pageant* all too frequently compels me to believe I may be an invited guest at a post-Wildean tea party, where I wander lost among the cucumber sandwiches and hashish fudge, plaintively mewing for something closer to my usual unhealthy diet. And yet Milton and Blake also have their expositional excesses, and Merrill never ceases to surprise and even astonish, more even in *Scripts* than in *Mirabell*, more in *Mirabell* than in *Ephraim*. Uncommon readers like Richard Saez and Stephen Yenser evidently do not experience my difficulties, but then, like my own hero, Dr. Samuel Johnson, I seem to age into a common reader, and fretfully I wince at yet another uppercase angelical revelation coming at me, and long instead for more lyric interludes and intercessions by the voice of Merrill himself.

The fullness of time doubtless will settle these matters and reveal whether *Mirabell* and *Scripts* are wholly successful in their own terms, or magnificent and picturesque poetic ruins, where one can wander almost endlessly, beholding giant splendors simply not available anywhere else. That many of these splendors are comic enhances their value, though the comedy is often rather specialized. I do not share the anticipation of Richard Saez that in this "masterpiece of sustained camp . . . the camp element may distract some readers from the seriousness of the work." That seems unlikely in an apocalyptic epic whose true starting point is Hiroshima. Charles Berger suggestively has compared *The Changing Light at Sandover* to *Gravity's Rainbow*. The comparison is just, encompassing as it does the shared thematicism, the equal aesthetic dignity, and the comic apocalypticism of the two works. Though the emergent theology of these two essentially religio-erotic seers is a mutual Gnosticism, Merrill's sexual vision is considerably healthier than Pynchon's sado-anarchism, while Pynchon's Tarot coal-tar Kabbalism impresses me spiritually more than Merrill's Ouijian revelations.

Like Pynchon (and John Ashbery), Merrill remains the poet of our moment, a great artist perfectly consonant with what insist upon seeming perpetually the very last days of humankind. If there is a civilized future, then the poet of "Lost in Translation" and "McKane's Falls" (both in *Divine Comedies*, 1976), of *The Book of Ephraim*, of the canzone "Samos" in *Scripts*, and of "The Ballroom at Sandover," which transcendentally fulfills as well as ends the epic, cannot fail to constitute part of what will be civilized in that future. Though he himself scoffed at what he calls his earlier "word-painting," he is indisputably a verse artist comparable to Milton, Tennyson, and Pope. Surely he will be remembered as the Mozart of American poetry, classical rather than mannerist or baroque, master of the changing light or perfection that consoles, even though, like every true manifestation of the strong light of the canonical, it is also necessarily the perfection that destroys.

A. R. Ammons, John Ashbery, W. S. Merwin
(1926–2001) · (1927–2017) · (1927–2019)

> I mean we have yet no man who has leaned entirely on his character,
> and eaten angels' food; who, trusting to his sentiments, found life made
> of miracles; who, working for universal aims, found himself fed, he knew
> not how; clothed, sheltered, and weaponed, he knew not how, and yet it
> was done by his own hands.
>
> EMERSON, "The Transcendentalist" (1842)

THE PROBLEM of American poetry after Emerson might be defined as "Is it possible to be un-Emersonian, rather than, at best, anti-Emersonian?" Poe is not an Emersonian poet, but then he is also not a good poet. Perhaps only our southern poets, down to James Tate and Robert Penn Warren, could be as un-Emersonian as they were anti-Emersonian; others, like Ammons, are wholly Emersonian. Even in Emerson's own time, irreconcilable poets emerged from his maelstrom: Dickinson, Thoreau, Whitman, James Very, even Frederick GoddardTuckerman, whom Yvor Winters judged to be as firm a reaction against Emerson as Hawthorne and Melville were. American Romanticism is larger than Emersonianism, but in our time it may no longer be possible to distinguish between the two phenomena. The prophet of a national poetic sensibility in America was the Concord rhapsode, who contains in the dialectical mysteries of his doctrines and temperament very nearly everything that has come after.

Let me begin with a representative text by the indubitably representative poet of my generation, the protean Merwin. The poem is the wonderful "The Way to the River" from the volume *The Moving Target*, of 1963. As the poem is about fifty lines, I will summarize rather than quote it entire. Addressed to the poet's wife, the poem is a kind of middle-of-the-journey declaration, a creedal hymn reaffirming a covenant of love and a sense of poetic vocation. Historically (and prophetically) the poem sums up the dilemma of "the Silent Generation" of young Americans, on the eve of the astonishing change (or collapse) of sensibility that was to begin at Berkeley in 1964. Merwin, with his curious proleptic urgency, memorably caught the prelude to that time:

> The way to the river leads past the names of
> Ash the sleeves the wreaths of hinges
> Through the song of the bandage vendor
>
> I lay your name by my voice
> As I go
>
> The way to the river leads past the late
> Doors and the games of the children born looking backwards
> They play that they are broken glass
> The numbers wait in the halls and the clouds
> Call
> From windows
> They play that they are old they are putting the horizon
> Into baskets they are escaping they are
> Hiding
>
> I step over the sleepers the fires the calendars
> My voice turns to you

This is the "poverty" of Emerson and Stevens: imaginative need. Merwin joins a tradition that includes the E. A. Robinson of "The Man Against the Sky," the Frost of "Directive," the Stevens of "The Auroras of Autumn," as he too follows Emerson in building an altar to the Beautiful Necessity:

> To the city of wires I have brought home a handful
> Of water I walk slowly
> In front of me they are building the empty
> Ages I see them reflected not for long
> Be here I am no longer ashamed of time it is too brief its hands
> Have no names
> I have passed it I know
>
> > *Oh Necessity you with the face you with*
> > *All the faces*

This is written on the back of everything

But we
Will read it together

The Merwin of this phase began with the central poem "Lemuel's Blessing," which follows the Christopher Smart of "Jubilate Agno" for its form
but which is also an Emersonian manifesto. Addressing a Spirit ("You that
know the way") Merwin prayed: "Let the memory of tongues not unnerve
me so that I stumble or quake." This hymn to Self-Reliance expanded into
the most ambitious poem of *The Moving Target*, a majestic celebration of
what Emerson called the Newness, "For Now:" "Goodbye what you learned
for me I have to learn anyway / You that forgot your rivers they are gone /
Myself I would not know you." In *The Lice*, his next volume (and his best),
Merwin defined the gods as "what has failed to become of us," a dark post-
script to the Emersonian insistence that the poets are as liberating gods.
The poems of *The Lice* are afflicted by light, as in this wholly characteristic
brief lyric, the poignant "How We Are Spared":

> At midsummer before dawn an orange light returns to
>   the mountains
> Like a great weight and the small birds cry out
> And bear it up

With his largest volume, *The Carrier of Ladders*, Merwin completed his
metamorphosis into an American visionary poet. The book's most astonishing yet most problematic poems are four ode-like "Psalms," subtitled: "Our
Fathers," "The Signals," "The September Vision," and "The Cerements."
No recent American poet, not even the Roethke of *The Far Field* or the
later James Dickey of "The Firebombing," "Slave Quarters," "Falling, " and
The Zodiac, has attempted so exalted a style:

> I am the son of hazard but does my prayer reach you O star of
>   the uncertain
> I am the son of blindness but nothing that we have made
>   watches us
> I am the son of untruth but I have seen the children in Paradise
>   walking in pairs each hand in hand with himself

I am the son of the warder but he was buried with his keys
I am the son of the light but does it call me Samuel or Jonah
I am the son of a wish older than water but I needed till now
I am the son of ghosts clutching the world like roads but tomorrow
   I will go a new way

The form is again that of the "Jubilate Agno," but the most important line in this first "Psalm," and in all of Merwin, is very far from Smart's pious spirit:

I am the son of the future but my own father

As a poet, Merwin hardly approaches that impossible self-begetting; the accent of the Pound-Eliot tradition hovers everywhere in even the most self-consciously bare of these verses. Merwin is more impressive for his terrible need, his lust for discontinuity, than for any actual inventiveness. The poignance of Merwin is the constant attempt at self-reliance, in the conviction that only thus will the poet *see*. Merwin's true precursors are three honorable, civilized representative poets: Longfellow and MacLeish and Wilbur, none of whom attempted to speak a Word that was his own Word only. In another time, Merwin would have gone on with the cultivation of a more continuous idiom, as he did in his early volumes, and as Longfellow did even in the Age of Emerson. The pressures of the quasi-apocalyptic 1960s made of Merwin an American Orphic bard despite the sorrow that his poetic temperament is not at home in suffering the Native Strain. No poet legitimately speaks a Word whose burden is that his generation will be the very last. Merwin's litanies of denudation will read very oddly when a fresh generation proclaims nearly the same dilemma, and then yet another generation trumpets finality.

Merwin's predicament (and I hope I read it fairly, as I am not unsympathetic to his work) is that he has no Transcendental vision, and yet feels impelled to prophesy. What is fascinating is that after these many years, the situation of American poetry is precisely as it was when Emerson wrote his loving but ironic essay on his younger contemporaries and followers, "The Transcendentalist," where they are seen as exposing our poverty but also their own. With that genial desperation (or desperate geniality) that is so endearing (and enraging) a quality in his work, Emerson nevertheless urged his followers out into the wilderness:

But all these of whom I speak are not proficients; they are novices; they only show the road in which man should travel, when the soul has greater health and prowess. Yet let them feel the dignity of their charge, and deserve a larger power. Their heart is the ark in which the fire is concealed which shall burn in a broader and universal flame. Let them obey the Genius then most when his impulse is wildest; then most when he seems to lead to uninhabitable deserts of thought and life; for the path which the hero travels alone is the highway of health and benefit to mankind. What is the privilege and nobility of our nature but its persistency, through its power to attach itself to what is permanent?

Merwin prays to be sustained during his time in the desert, but his poems hardly persuade us that his Genius or Spirit has led him into "uninhabitable deserts of thought and life." Readers distrustful of *The Carrier of Ladders* either emphasize what they feel is a dominance of style over substance or they complain of spiritual pretentiousness. What I find more problematic is something that Emerson foresaw when he said of his Transcendentalist that "he believes in miracle, in the perpetual openness of the human mind to new influx of light and power; he believes in inspiration, and in ecstasy," and yet went on to observe that such a youth was part of an American literature and spiritual history still "in the optative mood." Merwin's optative mood seems only to concern his impersonal identity as poet-prophet; instead of a belief in an influx of light and power, he offers us what we might contrive to know anyway, even if we had not been chilled with him by his artful mutations:

To which I make my way eating the silence of animals
Offering snow to the darkness

Today belongs to few and tomorrow to no one

Emerson's favorite oracular guise was as an Orphic poet. Of the Orphic deities—Eros, Dionysus, and Ananke—Merwin gives us some backward glances at the first, and a constant view of the last, but the Dionysiac has gone out of his poetry. Without the Bacchic turbulence, and haunted by a light that he presents as wholly meaningless, Merwin seems condemned to write a poetry that is as bare of true content as it is so elegantly bare in diction and design. Only the *situation* of the Emersonian Transcendentalist or Orphic Poet survives in Merwin; it is as though for him the native strain were pure strain, to be endured because endurance is value enough, or even because the eloquence of endurance is enough.

Except for their excellence, Ashbery and Ammons have no common qualities. Ashbery has been misunderstood because of his association with the "New York School" of Kenneth Koch, Frank O'Hara, and other comedians of the spirit, but also because of the dissociative phase of his work as represented by much of a peculiar volume, *The Tennis Court Oath*. But the poet of *The Double Dream of Spring* and the prose book *Three Poems* is again the Stevensian meditator of the early *Some Trees*. No other American poet ever labored quite so intensely to exorcise all the demons of discursiveness, and no contemporary American poet is so impressively at one with himself in expounding a discursive wisdom. Like his master, Stevens, Ashbery is essentially a ruminative poet, turning a few subjects over and over, knowing always that what counts is the mythology of self, blotched out beyond unblotching.

Ashbery's various styles have suggested affinities to composer-theorists like Cage and Cowell, to painters of the school of Kline and Pollock, and to an assortment of French bards like Roussel, Reverdy, and even Michaux. But the best of Ashbery, from the early *Some Trees* on through "A Last World" and "The Skaters" to the wonderful culminations of his great book *The Double Dream of Spring* and *Three Poems*, shows a clear descent from the major American tradition that began in Emerson. Even as his poetic father is Stevens, Ashbery's largest ancestor is Whitman, and it is the Whitmanian strain in Stevens that found Ashbery. I would guess that Ashbery, like Stevens, turned to French poetry as a deliberate evasion of continuities, a desperate quest for freedom from the burden of poetic influence. The beautiful group called "French Poems" in *The Double Dream of Spring* were written in French and then translated into English, Ashbery notes, "with the idea of avoiding customary word-patterns and associations." This looks at first like the characteristic quarrel with discursiveness that is endemic in modern verse, but a deeper familiarity with the "French Poems" will evoke powerful associations with Stevens at his most central, the seer of "Credences of Summer":

> And it does seem that all the force of
> The cosmic temperature lives in the form of contacts

That no intervention could resolve,
Even that of a creator returned to the desolate
Scene of this first experiment: this microcosm.
. . . .

and then it's so natural

That we experience almost no feeling
Except a certain lightness which matches
The recent closed ambiance which is, besides,
Full of attentions for us. Thus, lightness and wealth.

But the existence of all these things and especially
The amazing fullness of their number must be
For us a source of unforgettable questions:
Such as: whence does all this come? and again:
Shall I some day be a part of all this fullness?

The poet of these stanzas is necessarily a man who must have absorbed
"Credences of Summer" when he was young, perhaps even as a Harvard
undergraduate. Every strong poet's development is a typology of evasions,
a complex misprision of his precursor. Ashbery's true precursor is the composite father Whitman-Stevens, and the whole body to date of Ashbery's
work manifests nearly every possible revisionary ratio in regard to so formidable an American ancestry. Though the disjunctiveness of so much of
Ashbery suggests his usual critical placement with the boisterousness of
Koch or the random poignances of O'Hara, he seems most himself when
most ruefully and intensely Transcendental, the almost involuntary celebrator "of that *invisible light* which spatters the silence / Of our everyday
festivities." Ashbery is a kind of invalid of American Orphism, perpetually
convalescing from the strenuous worship of that dread Orphic trinity of
draining gods: Eros, Dionysus, Ananke, who preside over the Native Strain
of our poetry.

Ashbery's poetry is haunted by the image of transparence, but this comes
to him, from the start, as "a puzzling light," or carried by beings who are "as
dirty handmaidens / To some transparent witch." Against Transcendental
influx, Ashbery knows the wisdom of what he calls "learning to accept / The
charity of the hard moments as they are doled out," and knows also that
"one can never change the core of things, and light burns you the harder for

it." Burned by a visionary flame beyond accommodation (one can contrast Galway Kinnell's too-easy invocations of such fire), Ashbery gently plays with Orphic influx ("Light bounced off the ends / Of the small gray waves to tell / Them in the observatory / About the great drama that was being won"). Between Emerson and Whitman, the seers of this tradition, and Ashbery, Ammons, and other legatees, there comes the mediating figure of Stevens:

> My house has changed a little in the sun.
> The fragrance of the magnolias comes close,
> False flick, false form, but falseness close to kin.
>
> It must be visible or invisible,
> Invisible or visible or both:
> A seeing and unseeing in the eye.

These are hardly the accents of transport, yet Stevens does stand, precariously, in the renewed light. But even the skepticism is Emerson's own; his greatest single visionary oration is "Experience," a text upon which Dickinson, Stevens, and Ashbery always seem to be writing commentaries:

> Thus inevitably does the universe wear our color, and every object fall successively into the subject itself. The subject exists, the subject enlarges; all things sooner or later fall into place. As I am, so I see; use what language we will, we can never say anything but what we are. . . . And we cannot say too little of our constitutional necessity of seeing things under private aspects, or saturated with our humors. And yet is the God the native of these bleak rocks. . . . We must hold hard to this poverty, however scandalous, and by more vigorous self-recoveries, after the sallies of action, possess our axis more firmly.

The Old Transcendentalism in America, like the New, hardly distinguishes itself from a visionary skepticism, and makes no assertions without compensatory qualifications. Still, we tend to remember Emerson for his transparencies, and not the opaquenesses that more frequently haunted him and his immediate disciples. I suspect that this is because of Emerson's *confidence*, no matter where he places his emphases. When Stevens attains to a rare transparence, he generally *sees* very little more than is customary, but he *feels* a greater peace, and this peace reduces to a confidence in the momentary capability of his own imagination. Transcendentalism, in its American formulation, centers upon Emerson's stance of Self-Reliance, which is primarily a denial of the anxiety of influence. Like Nietzsche, who admired him for it, Emerson refuses to allow us to believe we must be latecomers. In a gnomic quatrain introducing his major essay on Self-Reliance, Emerson manifested a shamanistic intensity still evident in his descendents:

> Cast the bantling on the rocks,
> Suckle him with the she-wolf's teat,
> Wintered with the hawk and fox,
> Power and speed be hands and feet.

This is splendid, but Emerson had no more been such a bantling than any of my contemporaries are, unless one wants the delightful absurdity of seeing Wordsworth or Coleridge as a she-wolf. "Do not seek yourself outside yourself" is yet another motto to "Self-Reliance," and there is one more, from Beaumont and Fletcher, assuring us that the soul of an honest man

> Commands all light, all influence, all fate
> Nothing to him falls early or too late.

These are all wonderful idealisms. Whitman, who had been simmering, read "Self-Reliance" and was brought to the boil of the 1855 "Song of Myself." Ashbery, by temperament and choice, always seems to keep simmering, but whether he took impetus from Whitman, Stevens, or even the French partisans of poetic Newness, he has worked largely and overtly in this Emersonian spirit. Unfortunately, like Merwin and Merwin's precursor, Pound, Ashbery truly absorbed from the Emerson-Whitman tradition the poet's over-idealizing tendency to lie to himself, against his origins and against experience. American poets since Emerson are all antithetical completions of one another, which means mostly that they develop into grotesque truncations of what they might have been. Where British poets swerve away from their spiritual fathers, ours attempt to rescue their supposedly benighted sires. American bards, like Democritus, deny the swerve, so as to save divination, holding on to the Fate that might make them liberating gods. Epicurus affirmed the swerve, ruining divination, and all poetry since is caught between the two. Emerson, though close to

Democritus, wants even divination to be a mode of Self-Reliance. That is, he genuinely shares the Orphic belief that the poet is already divine, and realizes more of this divinity in writing his poems. Lucretian poets like Shelley who find freedom by swerving away from fathers (Wordsworth and Milton, for Shelley) do not believe in divination, and do not worship an Orphic Necessity as the final form of divinity. Orphic poets, particularly American or Emersonian Orphics, worship four gods only: Ananke, Eros, Dionysus, and—most of all surely—themselves. They are therefore peculiarly resistant to the idea of poetic influence, for divination—to them—means primarily an apprehension of their own possible sublimity, the gods they are in process of becoming. The gentle Ashbery, despite all his quite genuine and hard-won wisdom, is as much in this tradition as those spheral men, Emerson, Whitman, Thoreau, and that sublime egoist, Stevens, or the American Wordsworth.

The Double Dream of Spring has a limpidly beautiful poem called "Clouds," which begins

> All this time he had only been waiting,
> Not even thinking, as many had supposed.
> Now sleep wound down to him its promise of dazzling
>   peace
> And he stood up to assume that imagination.
>
> There were others in the forest as close as he
> To caring about the silent outcome, but they had gotten lost
> In the shadows of dreams so that the external look
> Of the nearby world had become confused with the cobwebs
>   inside.

Sleep here has a Whitmanian-Stevensian cast ("The Sleepers," "The Owl in the Sarcophagus") and the gorgeous solipsism so directly celebrated here has its sources in the same ultimately Emersonian tradition. Though "he," the poet or quest-hero, is distinguished from his fellows as not having yielded to such solipsism, the poem ends in a negative apotheosis:

> He shoots forward like a malignant star.
> The edges of the journey are ragged.
> Only the face of night begins to grow distinct
> As the fainter stars call to each other and are lost.

Day re-creates his image like a snapshot:
The family and the guests are there,
The talking over there, only now it will never end.
And so cities are arranged, and oceans traversed,

And farms tilled with especial care.
This year again the corn has grown ripe and tall.
It is a perfect rebuttal of the argument. And Semele
Moves away, puzzled at the brown light above the fields.

The harvest of natural process, too ripe for enigmas, refutes quest, and confirms the natural realism of all solipsists. This poem, urging us away from the Emersonian or Central Self, concludes by yielding to that Self, and to the re-birth of Dionysus, Semele's son. Like his precursor Stevens, Ashbery fears and evades the Native Strain of American Orphism, and again like Stevens he belongs as much to that strain as Hart Crane or John Wheelwright does. In the prose book *Three Poems*, he ruefully accepts his tradition and his inescapable place in it:

> Why, after all, were we not destroyed in the conflagration of the moment our real and imaginary lives coincided, unless it was because we never had a separate existence beyond that of those two static and highly artificial concepts whose fusion was nevertheless the cause of death and destruction not only for ourselves but in the world around us. But perhaps the explanation lies precisely here: what we were witnessing was merely the reverse side of an event of cosmic beatitude for all except us, who were blind to it because it took place inside us. Meanwhile the shape of life has changed definitively for the better for everyone on the outside. They are bathed in the light of this tremendous surprise as in the light of a new sun from which only healing and not corrosive rays emanate; they comment on the miraculous change as people comment on the dazzling beauty of a day in early autumn, forgetting that for the blind man in their midst it is a day like any other, so that its beauty cannot be said to have universal validity but must remain fundamentally in doubt.

The closest (though dialectically opposed) analogue to this passage is the great concluding rhapsody of Emerson's early apocalypse, *Nature*, when the Orphic Poet returns to prophesy:

> As when the summer comes from the south the snow-banks melt and the face of the earth becomes green before it, so shall the advancing spirit create its ornaments along its path, and carry with it the beauty it visits and the song which enchants it; it shall draw beautiful faces, warm hearts, wise discourse, and heroic acts, around its way, until evil is no more seen. The kingdom of man over nature, which cometh not with observation,—a dominion such as now is beyond his dream of God,—he shall enter without more wonder than the blind man feels who is gradually restored to perfect sight.

Ashbery's apocalyptic transformation of the Self, its elevation to the Over-Soul, is manifest to everyone and everything outside the Self, but not to the blind man of the Self. The Emersonian Self will know the metamorphic redemption of others and things only by knowing first its gradual freedom from blindness as to its own glory. Ashbery's forerunners, the makers of "Song of Myself" and "Notes toward a Supreme Fiction," were primary Emersonians, involuntary as Stevens was in this identity. Ashbery is that American anomaly, an antithetical Transcendentalist, bearer of an influx of the Newness that he cannot know himself.

In turning to A. R. Ammons, the wisest and, I prophesy, most enduring poet of his generation, we confront the most direct Emersonian in American poetry since Frost. Here I wish to describe the great achievement of Ammons in the large *Collected Poems 1951–1971* (1972), particularly three long poems: "Essay on Poetics," "Extremes and Moderations," "Hibernaculum," but also two crucial recent lyrics.

The "Essay on Poetics" begins by giving us Ammons's central signature, the process by which he has made a cosmos:

> Take in a lyric information
> totally processed, interpenetrated into
> wholeness where
>
> a bit is a bit, a string a string, a
> cluster a cluster, everything beefing up
> and verging out

for that point in the periphery where
salience bends into curve
and all saliences bend to the same angle of

curve and curve becomes curve, one curve, the whole curve:
that is information actual
at every point

but taking on itself at every point
the emanation of curvature, of meaning, all
the way into the high

recognition of wholeness, that synthesis,
feeling, aroused, controlled, and released . . .

Ammons's "periphery" is at once the "circumference" of Emerson and Dickinson, and also the nerve ending of the quester who goes out upon circumference. Ammons's "salience" is the further projecting or out-leaping from the longest periphery that the seer has attained. That makes Ammons's "salience" his equivalent of the Pound-Williams "image" or the Stevensian "solar single, / Man-sun, man-moon, man-earth, man-ocean." Far back, but indubitably the starting-place, Ammons's "Essay on Poetics" touches Whitman's 1855 "Preface" and Whitman's fecund ground, Emerson's "The Poet," a prose rhapsody mostly of 1842. Ammons expounds a "science" that now seems curious, but Emerson called it "true science." More than Whitman, or even Thoreau or Dickinson or Frost, Ammons is the Poet that Emerson prophesied as necessary for America:

For through that better perception he stands one step nearer to things, and sees the flowing or metamorphosis; perceives that thought is multiform; that within the form of every creature is a force impelling it to ascend into a higher form; and following with his eyes the life, uses the forms which express that life, and so his speech flows with the flowing of nature. All the facts of the animal economy, sex, nutriment, gestation, birth, growth, are symbols of the passage of the world into the soul of man, to suffer there a change and reappear a new and higher fact. He uses forms according to the life, and not according to the form. This is true science. The poet alone knows astronomy, chemistry, vegetation and animation, for he does not stop at these facts, but employs them as signs. He knows why the plain or meadow of space was strown with these flowers we call suns and moons and stars; why the great deep is adorned with animals, with men, and gods; for in every word he speaks he rides on them as the horses of thought.

As in "Tintern Abbey," standing closer to things is to see into their life, to see process and not particulars. But it is not Wordsworthian nor even neo-Platonic to possess a speech that is magic, to speak words that are themselves the metamorphosis. This violent Idealism is Emerson's Transcendental science, a knowing too impatient for the disciplines of mysticism, let alone rational dialectic. To read Emerson's "The Poet" side-by-side with any British Romantic on poetry, except Blake, is to see how peculiar the Emersonian wildness is. Only a step away and Emerson will identify a true poet's words with Necessity, as though nature's absolute confounding of our faculties simultaneously could make us skeptics and scientists affirming an inevitable insight. Emerson, here as so often, seems to break down the humanly needful distinctions between incoherence and coherence, relying upon his tone to persuade us of an intelligibility not wholly present. Ammons, like any strong poet, handles influence by misprision. His Emersonianism is so striking and plausible a twisting askew of that heritage as to raise again the labyrinthine issue of what poetic influence is, and how it works.

To talk about a poem by Ammons in terms of Emerson or Whitman is to invoke what one might term the Human Analogue, as opposed to Coleridge's Organic Analogue. No poem rejoices in its own solitary inscape, any more than we can do so. We have to be talked about in terms of other people, for no more than a poem is, can we be "about" ourselves. To say that a poem is about itself is killing, but to say it is about another poem is to go out into the world where we live. We idealize about ourselves when we isolate ourselves, just as poets deceive themselves by idealizing what they assert to be their poems' true subjects. The actual subjects move toward the anxiety of influence, and now frequently *are* that anxiety. But a deeper apparent digression begins to loom here, even as I attempt to relate the peripheries and saliences of Ammons to the great circumference of his ancestors.

Reductively, the anxiety of influence *is* the fear of death, and a poet's vision of immortality includes seeing himself free of all influence. Perhaps sexual jealousy, a closely related anxiety, also reduces to the fear of death, or of the ultimate tyranny of space and time, since influence-anxiety is related to our horror of space and time as a dungeon, as the danger of domination by the Not-Me. Anxiety of influence is due then partly to fear of the natural body, yet poetry is written by the natural man who is one with the body. Blake insisted that there was also the Real Man—the Imagination. Perhaps there is, but he cannot write poems, at least not yet.

The poem attempts to relieve the poet-as-poet from fears that *there is not enough for him*, whether of space (imaginative) or time (priority). A subject, a mode, a voice: all these lead to the question "What, besides my death, is my own?" Poets of the Pound-Williams school, more than most contemporary poets, scoff at the notion of an anxiety of influence, believing as they think they do that a poem is a machine made out of words. Perhaps, but mostly in the sense that we, alas, appear to be machines made out of words, for poems actually are closer to—as Stevens said—men made up out of words. Men make poems as Dr. Frankenstein made his daemon, and poems too acquire the disorders of the human. The people in poems do not have fathers, but the poems do.

Ammons, like Merwin and Ashbery, was aware of all this, for strong poets become strong by meeting the anxiety of influence, not by evading it. Poets adept at forgetting their ancestry write very forgettable poems. Ammons's "Essay on Poetics" swerves away from Emerson by the exercise of a variety of revisionary ratios, cunningly set against mere repetition:

> the very first actions of contact with an ocean say ocean over and
> over: read a few lines along the periphery of any of the truly
> great and the knowledge delineates an open shore:
>
> what is to be gained from the immortal person except the experience
> of ocean: take any line as skiff, break the breakers, and go out
> into the landless, orientationless, but perfectly contained, try
>
> the suasions, brief dips and rises, and the general circulations,
> the wind, the abundant reductions, stars, and the experience is
> obtained: but rivers, brooks, and trickles have their uses and

special joys and achieve, in their identities, difficult absoluteness
but will you say, what of the content—why they are all made of
  water
but will you, because of the confusion, bring me front center as

a mere mist or vapor . . .

This is the faith of Emersonian Self-Reliance, yet severely mitigated by
the consciousness of latecoming. At the close of the poem, Ammons attains
a majestic bleakness not wholly compatible with this apparent humility:

. . . along the periphery of integrations, then, is an exposure
to demons, thralls, witcheries, the maelstrom black of
possibility, costly, chancy, lethal, open: so I am not so much

arguing with the organic school as shifting true organisms from
the already organized to the bleak periphery of possibility,
an area transcendental only by its bottomless entropy . . .

The later Ammons writes out of a vision "transcendental only by its
bottomless entropy," yet still Emersonian, though this is the later Emerson of *The Conduct of Life*, precursor of Stevens in "The Rock" and Frost
throughout *In The Clearing*. "Extremes and Moderations" is Ammons's
major achievement in the long poem, written in "the flow-breaking four-
liner," starting out in an audacious Transcendentalism and modulating
into the prophetic voice Ammons rarely seeks, yet always attains at the
seeking:

                          . . . O city, I cry at
the gate, the glacier is your
mother, the currents of the deep father you, you sleep

in the ministry of trees, the boulders are your brother sustaining
you: come out, I cry, into the lofty assimilations: women, let
down your hair under the dark leaves of the night grove, enter
the currents with a sage whining, rising into the circular

dance: men, come out and be with the wind, speedy and lean, fall
into the moon-cheered waters, plunge into the ecstasy of rapids:

children, come out and play in the toys of divinity: glass, brick,
stone, curb, rail are freezing you out of your motions, the

uncluttered circulations: I cry that, but perhaps I am too secular
or pagan: everything, they say, is artificial: nature's the
artwork of the Lord: but your work, city is aimed unnaturally
against time: your artifice confronts the Artifice: beyond

the scheduled consummation, nothing's to be recalled: there is
memory enough in the rock, unscriptured history in
the wind, sufficient identity in the curve
of the valley . . .

This is the extreme of which Ammons's earlier and masterly lyric "The
City Limits" was the moderation. By "extremes" Ammons signifies what
Emerson's circle called the Newness, onsets of transcendental influx. "Moderations" are the rescues of these evaded furies that Ammons attempts for
the poetry of life, while carefully distinguishing even the extremes from
mere phantasmagorias:

. . . that there should have been possibilities enough to
include all that has occurred is beyond belief, an extreme the
strictures and disciplines of which prevent loose-flowing
phantasmagoria . . .

Though the poem concludes in a moving ecological outrage, an outrage the poet appears to believe is his theme, its concerns hover where
Ammons's obsessions always congregate, his resistance to his own transcendental experience. This resistance is made, as all constant readers of
Ammons learn, in the name of a precarious naturalism, but the concealed
undercurrent is always the sense of an earlier bafflement of vision, a failure
to have attained a longed-for unity with an Absolute. The later Ammons
rarely makes reference to this spent seership, but the old longing beautifully haunts all of the difficult later radiances. Here is a typical late lyric,
"Day," manifesting again the extraordinary and wholly deceptive ease that
Ammons has won for himself, an ease of mode and not of spirit, which
continues to carry an exemplary burden of torment:

On a cold late
September morning,
wider than sky-wide
discs of lit-shale clouds

skim the hills,
crescents, chords
of sunlight
now and then fracturing

the long peripheries:
the crow flies
silent,
on course but destinationless,

floating:
hurry, hurry,
the running light says,
while anything remains.

The mode goes back through Dickinson to Emerson, and is anything but the Pound-Williams "machine made out of words" that Hugh Kenner describes and praises in his crucially polemical *The Pound Era.* "The long peripheries," for Ammons, are identical with poems, or rather with what he would like his poems to be, outermost perceptions within precise boundaries, or literally "carryings-over" from the eye's tyranny to the relative freedom of a personally achieved idiom. What now distinguishes a lyric like "Day" from the characteristic earlier work in the Ammons canon is the urgency of what another late long poem, "Hibernaculum," calls "a staying change," this seer's response to our current time-of-transition from our recent confusions to whatever is coming upon us: "I think we are here to give back our possessions before / they are taken away." This is the motto preceding an immense intimation of another Newness:

                                        . . . I
accost the emptiness saying let all men turn their
eyes to the emptiness that allows adoration's life:
that is my whole saying, though I have no intention to

stop talking: our immediate staying's the rock but
the staying of the rock's motion: motion, that spirit!
we could veer into, dimpling, the sun or into the cold

orbital lofts, but our motion, our weight, our speed
are organized here like a rock, our spiritual stay:
the blue spruce's become ponderous with snow: brief

melt re-froze and knitted ice to needles and ice
to snow so the ridges eight inches high hold: the
branches move back and forth, stiff wailers:

the cloud-misty moonlight fills small fields, plots,
woodnooks with high light, snow transluminant as
fire . . .

Contrast to this an equally superb Emersonian epiphany:

Last night the moon rose behind four distinct pine-tree tops in
the distant woods and the night at ten was so bright that I walked
abroad. But the sublime light of night is unsatisfying, provoking;
it astonishes but explains not. Its charm floats, dances, disappears,
comes and goes, but palls in five minutes after you have left the
house. Come out of your warm, angular house, resounding with
few voices, into the chill, grand, instantaneous night, with such
a Presence as a full moon in the clouds, and you are struck with
poetic wonder. In the instant you leave far behind all human relations, wife, mother and child, and live only with the savages—
water, air, light, carbon, lime, and granite. . . . I become a moist,
cold element. "Nature grows over me." Frogs pipe; waters far off
tinkle; dry leaves hiss; grass bends and rustles, and I have died
out of the human world and come to feel a strange, cold, aqueous,
terraqueous, aerial, ethereal sympathy and existence. I sow the sun
and moon for seeds.

Emerson and Ammons share a nature that on the level of experience or
confrontation cannot be humanized. Yet they share also a Transcendental
belief that one can come to unity, at least in the pure good of theory. Their
common tone is a curious chill, a tang of other-than-human relationship to

an Oversoul or Overall that is not nature, yet breaks through into nature. Like Emerson, its founder, Ammons is a poet of the American Sublime, and a residue of this primordial strength abides in all of his work.

Edward Albee

(1928–2016)

ANY GROUPING of the strongest American dramas would have to include *The Iceman Cometh* and *Long Day's Journey into Night*, *Death of a Salesman* and *The Skin of Our Teeth*, *A Streetcar Named Desire* and *The Zoo Story*. A play in one scene, *The Zoo Story* remains a marvel of economy. The highest tribute one can make to it is to say that it is worthy of its stage history. I saw it during its first American production, in early 1960, when it shared a double bill, off Broadway, with Beckett's extraordinary *Krapp's Last Tape*. The Gnostic sublimity of Beckett's most powerful stage work (except for *Endgame*) ought to have destroyed any companion of the evening, but Albee's mordant lyrical encounter not only survived but took on an added lustre through the association.

I am not certain that *The Zoo Story* has any peers among the shorter works of O'Neill, Wilder, and Williams. Albee's first play, after more than a quarter-century, remains a shot out of Hell, worthy of such authentic American visions of the abyss as West's *Miss Lonelyhearts* and Pynchon's *The Crying of Lot 49*. Both Peter and Jerry are triumphs of representation; rereading the play is to renew one's surprise as to how vivid they both remain, particularly Peter, so apparently pale and stale compared to the daemonic and indeed psychotic Jerry. Yet Peter retains an intense aesthetic dignity, without which the play could neither be staged—nor read. Essentially Peter represents us, the audience, rather in the way that Horatio represents us. Jerry is a New York City Hamlet—mad in all directions, even when the wind blows from the south, and manifestly he is a kind of Christ also. Peter is therefore Peter the denier as well as Horatio, the institutional rock upon which the church of the commonplace must be built.

The psychosexual relationship between Jerry and Peter necessarily is the center of *The Zoo Story*, since the zoo story is, as Jerry desperately observes, that indeed we all are animals, dying animals, in Yeats's phrase:

> JERRY: Now I'll let you in on what happened at the zoo; but first, I should tell you why I went to the zoo. I went to the zoo to find out

more about the way people exist with animals, and the way animals exist with each other, and with people too. It probably wasn't a fair test, what with everyone separated by bars from everyone else, the animals for the most part from each other, and always the people from the animals. But, if it's a zoo, that's the way it is. (*He pokes* PETER *on the arm*) Move over.

PETER (*Friendly*): I'm sorry, haven't you enough room? (*He shifts a little*)

JERRY (*Smiling slightly*): Well, all the animals are there, and all the people are there, and it's Sunday and all the children are there. (*He pokes* PETER *again*) Move over.

PETER (*Patiently, still friendly*): All right. (*He moves some more, and* JERRY *has all the room he might need*)

JERRY: And it's a hot day, so all the stench is there, too, and all the balloon sellers, and all the ice cream sellers, and all the seals are barking, and all the birds are screaming. (*Pokes* PETER *harder*) Move over!

PETER (*Beginning to be annoyed*): Look here, you have more than enough room! (*But he moves more, and is now fairly cramped at one end of the bench*)

JERRY: And I am there, and it's feeding time at the lions' house, and the lion keeper comes into the lion cage, one of the lion cages, to feed one of the lions. (*Punches* PETER *on the arm, hard*) MOVE OVER!

PETER (*Very annoyed*): I can't move over any more, and stop hitting me. What's the matter with you?

Jerry begins with a cruel parody of Walt Whitman's "Song of Myself," section 32, where the American bard idealizes the supposed difference between animals and ourselves:

> I think I could turn and live with animals, they are so placid and
>   self-contain'd,
> I stand and look at them long and long.
>
> They do not sweat and whine about their condition,
> They do not lie awake in the dark and weep for their sins,
> They do not make me sick discussing their duty to God . . .

The mounting hysteria of Jerry demystifies Whitman, and is answered by a rising terror in Peter. Only the catastrophic impaling of Jerry allows Jerry's zoo story to be finished:

> PETER (*Breaks away, enraged*): It's a matter of genetics, not man-hood, you . . . you monster.
> (*He darts down, picks up the knife and backs off a little; he is breathing heavily*)
> I'll give you one last chance; get out of here and leave me alone!
> (*He holds the knife with a firm arm, but far in front of him, not to attack, but to defend*)
> JERRY (*Sighs heavily*): So be it!
> (*With a rush he charges* PETER *and impales himself on the knife. Tableau: For just a moment, complete silence,* JERRY *impaled on the knife at the end of* PETER'S *still firm arm. Then* PETER *screams, pulls away, leaving the knife in* JERRY. JERRY *is motion-less, on point. Then he, too, screams, and it must be the sound of an infuriated and fatally wounded animal. With the knife in him, he stumbles back to the bench that* PETER *had vacated. He crumbles there, sitting, facing* PETER, *his eyes wide in agony, his mouth open*)
> PETER (*Whispering*): Oh my God, oh my God, oh my God. (*He repeats these words many times, very rapidly*)
> JERRY (JERRY *is dying; but now his expression seems to change. His features relax, and while his voice varies, sometimes wrenched with pain, for the most part he seems removed from his dying. He smiles*): Thank you, Peter. I mean that, now; thank you very much.
> (PETER'S *mouth drops open. He cannot move; he is transfixed*) Oh, Peter, I was so afraid I'd drive you away. (*He laughs as best he can*) You don't know how afraid I was you'd go away and leave me. And now I'll tell you what happened at the zoo. . .

Screaming with the fury of a fatally wounded animal, Jerry begins his final moments, attempting to tell Peter and the audience just what hap-pened at the zoo, yet failing to do so, because he himself does not quite know what happened to him there. Though he speaks the language of annunciation, reversed ("I came unto you and you have comforted me"), his only revelation to Peter, and to us, is that "it's all right, you're an animal. You're an animal, too." The battle for the park bench, a territorial imperative, has exposed to Peter, our Horatio and surrogate, that we are all animals also. Jerry's mission ends with that message, and so he is happy to die. What is superb and dreadful about Albee's great short drama is that its apocalyptic burden is both Freudian and Christian. Through Peter, we are taught again that we are all bisexual, though many if not most of us repress that psychic component. Yet we are taught also that, without the transcendental and extraordinary, we are animals indeed. The zoo story is that, without grace or a selfless love, we impale or are impaled.

The fame of *Who's Afraid of Virginia Woolf?*, primarily because of the popular if flawed Mike Nichols film with Elizabeth Taylor and Richard Burton, tends to obscure its close resemblance to *The Zoo Story*, since again we have a drama of impaling, of love gone rancid because of a metaphysical lack. That is Albee's characteristic and obsessive concern, marked always by its heritage, which is a similar sense of the irreconcilability of love and the means of love that dominates the plays of Tennessee Williams. Unfortunately, *Who's Afraid of Virginia Woolf?* is a kind of blowup of *The Zoo Story* and aesthetically is inferior to it, whether in the study or on the stage. Martha and George paradoxically are a less memorable couple than Jerry and Peter, perhaps because both of them, like Peter, are surrogates for the audience. Neither of them has Jerry's Hamlet-like quality of being ourselves, yet considerably beyond us. Instead, both Martha and George are Horatios, who survive only to endure the endless repetition of drawing their breaths, in this harsh world, in order to go on telling our story.

The undenied power as representation of Albee's *Virginia Woolf* is that it has become as much our contemporary version of middle-class marriage as O'Neill's *Long Day's Journey into Night* has established itself as our modern version of the American family. Yet that raises the issue of social mythology rather than of the mimesis of human reality. Albee, like O'Neill and like his own precursor, Williams, is open to the accusation that he has become more a caricaturist than a dramatist. George and Martha are cartoon figures; they cannot surprise us any more than they can surprise one another. They are shrewd imitations of a conventional foreshortening of reality, psychic and societal, a foreshortening that, alas, many of us live. But they do not compel aspects of reality, that we could not see without them, to appear, and they are incapable of change. In some sense, they cannot even listen to themselves, let alone one another. If you cannot hear yourself speak, then you cannot change by pondering what you yourself have said, which is one of the great implicit Shakespearean lessons. *The Zoo Story* had learned that lesson, but *Who's Afraid of Virginia Woolf?* has forgotten it.

One way of observing Albee's decline in power of representation between *The Zoo Story* and *Virginia Woolf* is to contrast our first and last visions of George and Martha, and then juxtapose that contrast to the shocking difference between our first and last visions of Jerry and Peter, the protagonists of *The Zoo Story*. Jerry ends as a pragmatic suicide, and Peter as an involuntary murderer, or manslaughterer, yet their more profound change is from being total strangers to being something like fatal lovers. But, because they are caricatures, can George and Martha change at all? George talks, ineffectually; Martha brays, ineffectually; that is their initial reality when we come upon them. Martha barely talks, or is silent; George is almost equally monosyllabic when we leave them. A silent or monosyllabic ineffectuality has replaced chattering and braying, both ineffectual. Nothing has happened, because nothing has changed, and so this couple will be rubbed down to rubbish in the end. Is that enough to constitute a dramatic image? Albee, who began, in *The Zoo Story*, with the rhetorical strength and exacerbated vision of a strong dramatist, seems to have slain his own powers of representation almost before he himself can have understood them. *Who's Afraid of Virginia Woolf?*, whatever its impact upon contemporary audiences, clearly is of an age, and hardly for all time.

Ursula K. Le Guin
(1929–2018)

I N THE PARABLE "She Unnames Them," the best contemporary author of literary fantasy sums up the consequences of Eve's unnaming of the animals that Adam had named:

> None were left now to unname, and yet how close I felt to them when I saw one of them swim or fly or trot or crawl across my way or over my skin, or stalk me in the night, or go along beside me for a while in the day. They seemed far closer than when their names had stood between myself and them like a clear barrier: so close that my fear of them and their fear of me became one same fear. And the attraction that many of us felt, the desire to smell one another's scales or skin or feathers or fur, taste one another's blood or flesh, keep one another warm—that attraction was now all one with the fear, and the hunter could not be told from the hunted, nor the eater from the food.

This might serve as a coda for all Ursula Kroeber Le Guin's varied works. She is essentially a mythological fantasist; the true genre for her characteristic tale is romance, and she has a high place in the long American tradition of the romance, a dominant mode among us from Hawthorne down to Pynchon's *The Crying of Lot 49*. Because science fiction is a popular mode, she is named as a science-fiction writer, and a certain defiance in her proudly asserts that the naming is accurate. But no one reading, say, Philip K. Dick, as I have been doing after reading Le Guin's discussion of his work in *The Language of the Night*, is likely to associate the prose achievement of Le Guin with that of her acknowledged precursor. She is a fierce defender of the possibilities for science fiction, to the extent of calling Philip K. Dick "our own homegrown Borges" and even of implying that Dick ought not to be compared to Kafka only because Dick is "not an absurdist" and his work "is not (as Kafka's was) autistic."

After reading Dick, one can only murmur that a literary critic is in slight danger of judging Dick to be "our Borges" or of finding Dick in the cosmos of Kafka, the Dante of our century. But Le Guin as critic, loyal to her colleagues who publish in such periodicals as *Fantastic*, *Galaxy*, *Amazing*, *Orbit*, and the rest, seems to me not the same writer as the visionary of The Earthsea Cycle, *The Left Hand of Darkness*, *The Dispossessed*, and *The Beginning Place*. Better than Tolkien, far better than Doris Lessing, Le Guin is the overwhelming contemporary instance of a superbly imaginative creator and major stylist who chose (or was chosen by) "fantasy and science fiction." At her most remarkable, as in what still seems to me her masterpiece, *The Left Hand of Darkness*, she offers a sexual vision that strangely complements Pynchon's *Gravity's Rainbow* and James Merrill's *The Changing Light at Sandover*. I can think of only one modern fantasy I prefer to *The Left Hand of Darkness*, and that is David Lindsay's *Voyage to Arcturus* (1920), but Lindsay's uncanny nightmare of a book survives its dreadful writing, while Le Guin seems never to have written a wrong or bad sentence. One has only to quote some of her final sentences to know again her absolute rhetorical authority:

> But he had not brought anything. His hands were empty, as they had always been.
> (*The Dispossessed*)

> Gravely she walked beside him up the white streets of Havnor, holding his hand, like a child coming home.
> (*The Tombs of Atuan*)

> There is more than one road to the city.
> (*The Beginning Place*)

> But the boy, Therem's son, said stammering, "Will you tell us how he died?—Will you tell us about the other worlds out among the stars—the other kinds of men, the other lives?"
> (*The Left Hand of Darkness*)

When her precise, dialectical style—always evocative, sometimes sublime in its restrained pathos—is exquisitely fitted to her powers of invention, as in *The Left Hand of Darkness*, Le Guin achieves a kind of sensibility very nearly unique in contemporary fiction. It is the pure storyteller's sensibility that induces in the reader a state of uncertainty, of not knowing what comes next. What Walter Benjamin praised Nikolai in Leskov is exactly relevant to Le Guin:

> Death is the sanction of everything that the storyteller can tell. He has borrowed his authority from death. . . .
>   . . .The first true storyteller is, and will continue to be, the teller of fairy tales. Whenever good counsel was at a premium, the fairy tale had it, and where the need was greatest, its aid was nearest. This need was the need created by the myth. The fairy tale tells us of the earliest arrangements that mankind made to shake off the nightmare which the myth had placed upon its chest.

Elsewhere in his essay on Leskov, Benjamin asserts that "the art of storytelling is reaching its end because the epic side of truth, wisdom, is dying out." One can be skeptical of Benjamin's Marxist judgment that such a waning, if waning it be, is "only a concomitant symptom of the secular productive forces of history." Far more impressively, Benjamin once remarked of Kafka's stories that in them "narrative art regains the significance it had in the mouth of Scheherazade: to postpone the future." Le Guin's narrative art, though so frequently set in the future, not only borrows its authority from death but also works to postpone the future, works to protect us against myth and its nightmares.

I am aware that this is hardly consonant with the accounts of her narrative purposes that Le Guin gives in the essays of *The Language of the Night*. But Lawrence's adage is perfectly applicable to Le Guin: trust the tale, not the teller. Her true credo is spoken by one of her uncanniest creations, Faxe the Weaver, master of the Foretelling, to conclude the beautiful chapter "The Domestication of Hunch" in *The Left Hand of Darkness*:

> "The unknown," said Faxe's soft voice in the forest, "the unforetold, the unproven, that is what life is based on. Ignorance is the ground of thought. Unproof is the ground of action. If it were proven that there is no God there would be no religion. No Handdara, no Yomesh, no hearthgods, nothing. But also if it were proven that

there is a God, there would be no religion. . . . Tell me, Genry, what is known? What is sure, predictable, inevitable—the one certain thing you know concerning your future, and mine?"

"That we shall die."

"Yes. There's really only one question that can be answered, Genry, and we already know the answer. . . . the only thing that makes life possible is permanent, intolerable uncertainty: not knowing what comes next."

The fine irony, that this is the master Foreteller speaking, is almost irrelevant to Le Guin's profound narrative purpose. She herself is the master of a dialectical narrative mode in which nothing happens without involving its opposite. The shrewdly elliptical title *The Left Hand of Darkness* leaves out the crucial substantive in Le Guin's Taoist verse:

Light is the left hand of darkness
and darkness the right hand of light.
Two are one, life and death, lying
together like lovers in kemmer,
like hands joined together,
like the end and the way.

The way is the Tao, exquisitely fused by Le Guin into her essentially northern mythology. "Kemmer" is the active phase of the cycle of human sexuality on the planet Gethen or Winter, the site of *The Left Hand of Darkness*. Winter vision, even in the books widely separated in substance and tone from her masterpiece, best suits Le Guin's kind of storytelling. Mythology, from her childhood on, seems to have meant Norse rather than Classical stories. Like Blake's and Emily Brontë's, her imagination is at home with Odin and Yggdrasil. Yet she alters the cosmos of the Eddas so that it loses some, not all, of its masculine aggressiveness and stoic harshness. Her Taoism, rather than her equivocal Jungianism, has the quiet force that tempers the ferocity of the northern vision.

"Visibility without discrimination, solitude without privacy" is Le Guin's judgment upon the capital of the Shing, who in AD 4370 rule what had been the United States, in her novel, *City of Illusions* (1967). In an introduction to *The Left Hand of Darkness*, belatedly added to the book seven years after its publication in 1969, Le Guin sharply reminds us that "I write science fiction, and science fiction isn't about the future. I don't know any more about the future than you do, and very likely less." Like Faxe the Weaver, she prefers ignorance of the future, and yet, again like Faxe, she is a master of Foretelling, which both is and is not a mode of moral prophecy. It is, in that it offers a moral vision of the present; it is not, precisely because it refuses to say that "if you go on so, the result is so." The United States today still offers "visibility without discrimination, solitude without privacy." As for the United States in 4370, one can quote "Self," a lyric meditation from Le Guin's rather neglected *Hard Words and Other Poems* (1981):

> You cannot measure the circumference
> but there are centerpoints:
> stones, and a woman washing at a ford,
> the water runs red-brown from what she washes.
> The mouths of caves. The mouths of bells.
> The sky in winter under snowclouds
> to northward, green of jade.
> No star is farther from it than the glint
> of mica in a pebble in the hand,
> or nearer. Distance is my god.

Distance, circumference, the unmeasurable, goal, the actual future which can only be our dying: Le Guin evades these, and her narratives instead treasure wisdom or the center points. Yet the poem just before "Self" in *Hard Words*, cunningly titled "Amazed," tells us where wisdom is to be found, in the disavowal of "I" by "eye," a not un-Emersonian epiphany:

> The center is not where the center is
> but where I will be when I follow
> the lines of stones that wind about a center
> that is not there
> but there.
> The lines of stones lead inward, bringing
> the follower to the beginning
> where all I knew
> is flew.
> Stone is stone and more than stone;

the center opens like an eyelid opening.
Each rose a maze: the hollow hills:
I am not I
but eye.

One thinks of the shifting centers in every Le Guin narrative, and of her naming the mole as her totem in another poem. She is a maze maker or "shaper of darkness / into ways and hollows," who always likes the country on the other side. Or she is "beginning's daughter" who "sings of stones." Her Taoism celebrates the strength of water over stone, and yet stone is her characteristic trope. As her words are hard, so are most of her women and men, fit after all for northern or winter myth. One can say of her that she writes a hard-edged phantasmagoria, or that it is the Promethean rather than the Narcissistic element in her literary fantasy that provides her with her motive for metaphor.

In some sense, all of her writings call us forth to quest into stony places, where the object of the quest can never quite be located. Her most mature quester, the scientist Shevek in *The Dispossessed*, comes to apprehend that truly he is both subject and object in the quest, always already gone on, always already there. A Promethean anarchist, Shevek has surmounted self-consciousness and self-defense, but at the cost of a considerable loss in significance. He represents Le Guin's ideal Odonian society, where the isolated idealist like Shelley or Kropotkin has become the norm, yet normative anarchism cannot be represented except as permanent revolution, and permanent revolution defies aesthetic as well as political representation. Shevek is beyond these limits of representation and more than that, "his hands were empty, as they had always been." Deprived of the wounded self-regard that our primary narcissism converts into aggression, Shevek becomes nearly as colorless as the actual personality upon whom he is based, the physicist Robert Oppenheimer. Even Le Guin cannot have it both ways; the ideological anarchism of *The Dispossessed* divests her hero of his narcissistic ego, and so of much of his fictive interest. Jung is a better psychological guide in purely mythic realms, like Le Guin's Earthsea, than he is in psychic realms closer to our own, as in *The Dispossessed*.

Le Guin's greatest accomplishment, certainly reflecting the finest balance of her powers, is *The Left Hand of Darkness* (1969), though there are imaginative felicities in *The Beginning Place* (1980) that are subtler and bolder

than anything in *The Left Hand of Darkness*. But conceptually and stylistically, *Left Hand* is the strongest of her major narratives. It is a book that
sustains many rereadings, partly because its enigmas are unresolvable, and
partly because it has the crucial quality of a great representation, which
is that it yields up new perspectives upon what we call reality. Though
immensely popular, it seems to me critically undervalued, with rather too
much emphasis upon its supposed flaws. The best known negative critique
is by Stanisław Lem, who judged the sexual element in the book irrelevant to its story, and improbably treated in any case. This is clearly a weak
misreading on Lem's part. What the protagonist, Genly Ai, continuously
fails to understand about the inhabitants of the planet Winter is precisely
that their sexuality gives them a mode of consciousness profoundly alien
to his (and ours). Le Guin, with admirable irony, replied to feminist and
other critics that indeed she had "left out too much" and could "only be
very grateful to those readers, men and women, whose willingness to participate in the experiment led them to fill in that omission with the work
of their own imagination." Too courteous to say, with Blake, that her care
was not to make matters explicit to the idiot, Le Guin wisely relied upon
her extraordinary book to do its work of self-clarification.

The book's principal aesthetic strength is its representation of the character and personality of Estraven, the prime minister who sacrifices position, honor, freedom, and finally his life in order to hasten the future, by
aiding Genly Ai's difficult mission. As the ambassador of the Ekumen, a
benign federation of planets, Ai needs to surmount his own perspective
as a disinterested cultural anthropologist if he is to understand the androgynes who make up the entire population of the isolated planet alterna-
tively called Gethen or Winter. Without understanding, there is no hope
of persuading them, even for their own obvious good, to join with the rest
of the cosmos. What is most interesting about Ai (the name suggesting at
once the ego, the eye, and an outcry of pain) is his reluctance to go beyond
the limits of his own rationality, which would require seeing the causal link
between his sexuality and mode of consciousness.

The sexuality of the dwellers upon the planet Winter remains Le Guin's
subtlest and most surprising invention:

> A Gethenian in first-phase kemmer, if kept alone or with others
> not in kemmer, remains incapable of coitus. Yet the sexual impulse
> is tremendously strong in this phase, controlling the entire

personality, subjecting all other drives to its imperative. When the individual finds a partner in kemmer, hormonal secretion is further stimulated (most importantly by touch—secretion? scent?) until in one partner either a male or female hormonal dominance is established. The genitals engorge or shrink accordingly, foreplay intensifies, and the partner, triggered by the change, takes on the other sexual role (? without exception? If there are exceptions, resulting in kemmer-partners of the same sex, they are so rare as to be ignored).

The narrator here is neither Ai nor Le Guin but a field investigator of the Ekumen, wryly cataloging a weird matter. Her field notes add a number of sharper observations: these androgynes have no sexual drive at all for about twenty-one or twenty-two out of every twenty-six days. Anyone can and usually does bear children, "and the mother of several children may be the father of several more," descent being reckoned from the mother, known as "the parent in the flesh." There is no Oedipal ambivalence of children toward parents, no rape or unwilling sex, no dualistic division of humankind into active and passive. All Gethenians are natural monists, with no need to sublimate anything, and little inclination toward warfare.

Neither Le Guin nor any of her narrators gives us a clear sense of any casual relation between a world of nearly perpetual winter and the ambisexual nature of its inhabitants, yet an uncanny association between the context of coldness and the unforeseeable sexuality of each individual persists throughout. Though Lem insisted anxiety must attend the unpredictability of one's gender, Le Guin's book persuasively refuses any such anxiety. There is an imaginative intimation that entering upon any sexual identity for about one-fifth of the time is more than welcome to anyone who must battle perpetually just to stay warm! Le Guin's humor, here as elsewhere, filters in slyly, surprising us in a writer who is essentially both somber and serene.

The one Gethenian we get to know well is Estraven, certainly a more sympathetic figure than the slow-to-learn Ai. Estraven is Le Guin's greatest triumph in characterization, and yet remains enigmatic, as he must. How are we to understand the psychology of a man-woman, utterly free of emotional ambivalence, of which the masterpiece after all is the Oedipal conflict? And how are we to understand a fiercely competitive person, since the Gethenians are superbly agonistic, who yet lacks any component of sexual aggressiveness, let alone its cause in a sexually wounded narcissism? Most fundamentally we are dualists, and perhaps our involuntary and Universal Freudianism (present even in a professed Jungian, like Le Guin) is the result of that being the conceptualized dualism most easily available to us. But the people of Winter are Le Guin's shrewd way of showing us that all our dualisms—Platonic, Pauline, Cartesian, Freudian—not only have a sexual root but are permanent because we are bisexual rather than ambisexual beings. Freud obviously would not have disagreed, and evidently Le Guin is more Freudian than she acknowledges herself to be.

Winter, aside from its properly ghastly weather, is no Utopia. Karhide, Estraven's country, is ruled by a clinically mad king, and the rival power, Orgoreyn, is founded upon a barely hidden system of concentration camps. Androgyny is clearly neither a political nor a sexual ideal in *The Left Hand of Darkness*. And yet, mysteriously and beautifully, the book suggests that Winter's ambisexuality is a more imaginative condition than our bisexuality. Like the unfallen Miltonic angels, the Gethenians know more than either men or women can know. As with the angels, this does not make them better or wiser, but evidently they see more than we do, since each one of them is Tiresias, as it were. This, at last, is the difference between Estraven and Genly Ai. Knowing and seeing more, Estraven is better able to love, and freer therefore to sacrifice than his friend can be.

Yet that, though imaginative, is merely a generic difference. Le Guin's art is to give us also a more individual difference between Ai and Estraven. Ai is a kind of skeptical Horatio who arrives almost too late at a love for Estraven as a kind of ambisexual Hamlet, but who survives, like Horatio, to tell his friend's story:

> For it seemed to me, and I think to him, that it was from that sexual tension between us, admitted now and understood, but not assuaged, that the great and sudden assurance of friendship between us rose: a friendship so much needed by us both in our exile, and already so well proved in the days and nights of our bitter journey, that it might as well be called, now as later, love. But it was from the difference between us, not from the affinities and likenesses, but from the difference, that that love came.

The difference is more than sexual and so cannot be bridged by sexual love, which Ai and Estraven avoid. It is the difference between Horatio and Hamlet, between the audience's surrogate and the tragic hero, who is beyond both surrogate and audience. Estraven dies in Ai's arms, but uttering his own dead brother's name, that brother having been his incestuous lover, and father of Estraven's son. In a transference both curious and moving, Estraven has associated Ai with his lost brother-lover, to whom he had vowed faithfulness. It is another of Le Guin's strengths that, in context, this has intense pathos and nothing of the grotesque whatsoever. More than disbelief becomes suspended by the narrative art of *The Left Hand of Darkness*.

That Le Guin, more than Tolkien, has raised fantasy into high literature, for our time, seems evident to me because her questers never abandon the world where we have to live, the world of Freud's reality principle. Her praise of Tolkien does not convince me that *The Lord of the Rings* is not tendentious and moralizing, but her generosity does provide an authentic self-description:

> For like all great artists he escapes ideology by being too quick for
> its nets, too complex for its grand simplicities, too fantastic for its
> rationality, too real for its generalizations.

I could end there, but I would rather allow Le Guin to speak of herself directly:

> Words are my matter. I have chipped one stone
> for thirty years and still it is not done,
> that image of the thing I cannot see.
> I cannot finish it and set it free,
> transformed to energy.

There is a touch of Yeats here, Le Guin's voice being most her own in narrative prose, but the burden is authentic Le Guin: the sense of limit, the limits of the senses, the granite labor at hard words, and the ongoing image that is her characteristic trope, an unfinished stone. Like her Genly Ai, she is a far-fetcher, to use her own term for visionary metaphor. It was also the Elizabethan rhetorician George Puttenham's term for transumption or metalepsis, the trope that reverses time and makes lateness into an earliness. The late Ursula Le Guin was a grand far-fetcher or transumer of the true tradition of romance we call literary fantasy. No one now among us matches her at rendering freely "that image of the thing I cannot see."

Toni Morrison

(b. 1931)

TONI MORRISON, born in 1931, is best known for her lyrical fantasy novel *Beloved* (1987), but I continue to prefer *Song of Solomon* (1977) as her most permanent achievement, to date. Though she has not yet surpassed it, she remains at work, and so I will venture no prophecy as to her final eminence. Here I desire only to give a brief account of *Song of Solomon*, both for its own sake and because it shrewdly hints at a subtle critique of the tradition of Melville, Faulkner, and Ellison, which it joins, though warily and under protest, as befits the work of a self-proclaimed African American Marxist and feminist. And yet, literary tradition chooses an authentic writer, more than the other way around. Something also of Virginia Woolf's aestheticism lingers on in Morrison's style and vision, altogether (I think) to Morrison's benefit.

Milkman Dead, the protagonist of *Song of Solomon*, quests for visibility, in a clear reversal of Ellison's hero, and with the mingled gain and loss of coming a quarter century after *Invisible Man*. Morrison, commendably, is an immensely ambitious novelist, who takes large artistic risks. Milkman, her near-surrogate, is extraordinarily audacious, and becomes so incessant in his quest for his family's truth that pragmatically he must be judged doom-eager.

Dead is not Milkman's true name; it turns out to be Shalimar, pronounced *Shalleemone* or Solomon. Morrison, with her own visionary irony, uniquely gives us a hero who recovers his true name, at the cost of no less than everything, his life included. As parable, this is powerful; how can you be yourself until you void others' misnaming of you? Born Chloe Anthony Wofford, the novelist changed her name to Toni, modifying Anthony, while still an undergraduate. Milkman's best friend, or "enemy brother," is called Guitar, and the book ends with them engaged in a death struggle. Yet Milkman, unlike Guitar, is spiritually redeemed. He has recovered family history, personal truth, and a heroic myth, that of his ancestor Solomon/Shalimar, who flew back to Africa (without benefit of airplane) to escape bondage.

Morrison has an uncanny gift for fantasy; I find it becomes extravagant in *Beloved*, but aesthetically it is kept within limits in *Song of Solomon*. The reader (and this is Morrison's skill) never quite knows where reality and fantasy come into conflict in Milkman's story, which begins with a black insurance man's suicidal attempt at flight the day before the birth of baby Milkman (nursed at his mother's breast until he was four). Also at four, the child learned that unaided flight was impossible, and "he lost all interest in himself." Weaned into an exasperated dullness, Milkman suffers his impossible parents: Macon Dead, a slum landlord, and Ruth, who is deranged.

It is fair to say of the young man Milkman Dead that he combines his father's rapacity and his mother's solipsism. He emulates Hamlet by goading his Ophelia, Hagar, to madness, coldly rejecting her, and since Hagar cannot bring herself to kill Milkman, she dies instead. After a vain drive to go beyond his father in financial greed, Milkman starts out upon another quest, which is the primary strength of *Song of Solomon*. He goes south to the ancestral Shalimar, where an astonishingly aged crone, Circe, narrates his family's true history to him.

The return to Shalimar brings about a Circean metamorphosis in reverse, as Milkman painfully and slowly achieves his true inner form. Here Morrison brilliantly parodies Faulkner's famous saga "The Bear," where Ike McCaslin is initiated into the hunt. Milkman undergoes the same ritual with a black difference, taking on the living heart of a slain bobcat. Transformed, Morrison's hero recovers his true, Solomonic name, and leaps courageously to his final death-duel with Guitar.

It is remarkable that Morrison is able to sustain her symbolic parable with such a wealth of social realism that the fantastic seems only another version of the everyday. Refusing to continue as an Invisible Man, the refound Solomon learns to make a surrender to the air, and so to ride upon it as his ancestor did. What makes Milkman's apotheosis persuasive is Morrison's sheer brio, and her sure grasp of all her traditions.

Commenting upon *Song of Solomon* with the polemical fervor of her fused ideologies, Morrison insists that her reader must ask the questions of a community, and not of an individual:

> The reader as narrator asks the questions the community asks, and both reader and "voice" stand among the crowd, within it, with privileged intimacy and contact, but without any more privileged information than the crowd has. The egalitarianism which places us all (reader, the novel's population, the narrator's voice) on the

same footing reflected for me the force of flight and mercy, and the precious, imaginative yet realistic gaze of black people who (at one time, anyway) did not mythologize what or whom it mythologized. The "song" itself contains this unblinking evaluation of the miraculous flight of the legendary Solomon.

Morrison is certainly telling us why *Song of Solomon* should be read, but how can the solitary reader be true to herself if she does not ask her own questions, rather than the community's? You can argue (if you wish) that we ought to read to socialize ourselves, but who then will decide whether what or who is mythologized ought to have been? Morrison seems to argue that a black folk gaze could once mythologize and not mythologize simultaneously. I hear a totalizing ideology in that more-than-rational assertion, and I return to an ongoing contention: to read in the service of any ideology is not to read at all. Fortunately, the earlier Morrison had not yet incarnated the Spirit of the Age, and *Song of Solomon* remains a spur to the quest of how to read and why.

Philip Roth

(1933–2018)

P HILIP ROTH'S *Zuckerman Bound* (1985) binds together *The Ghost Writer* (1979), *Zuckerman Unbound* (1981), and *The Anatomy Lesson* (1983), adding to them as epilogue a wild short novel, *The Prague Orgy*. *Zuckerman Bound* is a classic *apologia*, an aggressive defense of Roth's moral stance as an author. Its cosmos derives candidly from the Freudian interpretation as being unbearable. Roth knows that Freud and Kafka mark the origins and limits of still-emerging literary culture, American and Jewish, which has an uneasy relationship to normative Judaism and its waning culture. I suspect that Roth knows and accepts also what his surrogate, Zuckerman, is sometimes too outraged to recognize: breaking a new road both causes outrage in others and demands payment in which the outrageous provoker punishes himself. Perhaps that is the Jewish version of Emerson's American Law of Compensation: nothing is got for nothing.

Zuckerman Bound merits something reasonably close to the highest level of aesthetic praise for tragicomedy, partly because as a formal totality it becomes much more than the sum of its parts. Those parts are surprisingly diverse: *The Ghost Writer* is a Jamesian parable of fictional influence, economical and shapely, beautifully modulated, while *Zuckerman Unbound* is more characteristically Rothian, being freer in form and more joyously expressionalistic in its diction. *The Anatomy Lesson* is a farce bordering on fantasy, closer in mode and spirit to Nathanael West than is anything else by Roth. *The Prague Orgy* is a disturbing eminence that rivals Thomas Pynchon's *The Crying of Lot 49* and episodes like the story of Byron the lightbulb in *Gravity's Rainbow*: obscenely outrageous and yet brilliantly reflective of a paranoid reality that has become universal. But the Rothian difference from Nathanael West and Pynchon should also be emphasized. Roth paradoxically is engaged in moral prophecy; he is outraged by the outrageous—in societies, others, and himself. There is in him nothing of West's Gnostic preference for the posture of the Satanic editor, Shrike, in *Miss Lonelyhearts*, or of Pynchon's Kabbalistic doctrine

of sado-anarchism. Roth's negative exuberance is not in the service of negative theology, but intimates instead a nostalgia for the morality once engendered by the Jewish normative tradition.

This is the harsh irony, obsessively exploited throughout *Zuckerman
Bound*, of the attack made upon Zuckerman's *Carnovsky* (Roth's *Portnoy's
Complaint*) by the literary critic Milton Appel (Irving Howe). Zuckerman
has received a mortal wound from Appel, and Roth endeavors to commem-
orate the wound and the wounder, in the spirit of James Joyce permanently
impaling the Irish poet, physician, and general roustabout, Oliver St. John
Gogarty, as the immortally egregious Malachi (Buck) Mulligan of *Ulysses*.
There is plenty of literary precedent for settling scores in this way; it is as
old as Hellenistic Alexandria, and as recent as Saul Bellow's portrait of Jack
Ludwig as Valentine Gersbach in *Herzog*. Roth, characteristically scru-
pulous, presents Appel as dignified, serious, and sincere, and Zuckerman
as dangerously lunatic in this matter, but since the results are endlessly
hilarious, the revenge is sharp nevertheless.

Zuckerman Unbound makes clear, at least to me, that Roth indeed is a
Jewish writer in the sense that Saul Bellow and Bernard Malamud were
not, and did not care to be. Bellow and Malamud, in their fiction, strive
to be North American Jewish only as Tolstoy was Russian, or Faulkner
was American Southern. Roth is certainly Jewish in his fiction, because
his absolute concern never ceases to be the pain of the relations between
children and parents, and between husband and wife, and in him this pain
invariably results from the incommensurability between rigorously moral
normative tradition whose expectations rarely can be satisfied and the reality of the way we live now. Zuckerman's insane resentment of the moralizing Milton Appel, and of even fiercer critics, is a deliberate self-parody of
Roth's more-than-ironic reaction to how badly he has been read. Against
both Appel and the covens of maenads, Roth defends Zuckerman (and so
himself) as a kind of Talmudic Orpheus, by defining any man as "clay with
aspirations."

What wins over the reader is that both defense and definition are conveyed by the highest humor. *The Anatomy Lesson* and *The Prague Orgy*,
in particular, provoke a cleansing and continuous laughter, sometimes so
intense that in itself it becomes astonishingly painful. One of the many
aesthetic gains of binding together the entire Zuckerman ordeal (it cannot
be called a saga) is to let the reader experience the gradual acceleration
of wit from the gentle Chekhovian wistfulness of *The Ghost Writer* on to
the Gogolian sense of the ridiculous in *Zuckerman Unbound*, and then to

the boisterous Westian farce of *The Anatomy Lesson*, only to end in the merciless Kafkan irrealism of *The Prague Orgy*.

Haunting *The Prague Orgy* necessarily is the spirit of Kafka, a dangerous influence upon any writer, and particularly dangerous for Roth. Witness his short novel *The Breast*, a major aesthetic disaster, surpassing such livelier failures as *Our Gang* and *The Great American Novel*. Against the error of *The Breast* can be set the funniest pages in *The Professor of Desire*, where the great dream concerning "Kafka's whore" is clearly the imaginative prelude to *The Prague Orgy*. David Kepesh, Roth's Professor of Desire, falls asleep in Prague and confronts "everything I ever hoped for," a guided visit with an official interpreter to an old woman, possibly once Kafka's whore. The heart of her revelation is Rothian rather than Kafkan, as she integrates the greatest modern Jewish writer with all the other ghosts of her Jewish clientele:

> "They were clean and they were gentlemen. As God is my witness, they never beat on my backside. Even in bed they had manners."
>
> "But is there anything about Kafka in particular that she remembers? I didn't come here, to her, to Prague, to talk about nice Jewish boys."
>
> She gives some thought to the question; or, more likely, no thought. Just sits there trying out being dead.
>
> "You see, he wasn't so special," she finally says. "I don't mean he wasn't a gentleman. They were all gentlemen."

This could be the quintessential Roth passage: the Jewish joke turned, not against itself, nor against the Jews, and certainly not against Kafka, but against history, against the way things were, and are, and yet will be. Unlike the humor of Nathanael West (particularly in his *The Dream Life of Balso Snell*) and of Woody Allen, there is no trace of Jewish anti-Semitism in Roth's pained laughter. Roth's wit uncannily follows the psychic pattern set out by Freud in his late paper on "Humor" (1928), which speculates that the superego allows jesting so as to speak some "kindly words of comfort to the intimidated ego." The ego of poor Zuckerman is certainly intimidated enough, and the reader rejoices at being allowed to share some hilarious words of comfort with him.

At the close of *The Anatomy Lesson*, Zuckerman had progressed (or regressed) from painfully lying back on his play-mat, *Roget's Thesaurus* propped beneath his head and four women serving his many needs, to wandering the corridors of a university hospital, a patient playing at being an intern. A few years later, a physically recovered Zuckerman is in Prague, as visiting literary lion, encountering so paranoid a social reality that New York seems, by contrast, the forest of Arden. Zuckerman, "the American authority on Jewish demons," quests for the unpublished Yiddish stories of the elder Sinovsky, perhaps murdered by the Nazis. The exiled younger Sinovsky's abandoned wife, Olga, guards the manuscripts in Prague. In a deliberate parody of James's "The Aspern Papers," Zuckerman needs somehow to seduce the alcoholic and insatiable Olga into releasing stories supposedly worthy of Sholem Aleichem or Isaac Babel, written in "the Yiddish of Flaubert."

Being Zuckerman, he seduces no one and secures the Yiddish manuscripts anyway, only to have them confiscated by the Czech Minister of Culture and his thugs, who proceed to expel "Zuckerman the Zionist agent" back to "the little world around the corner" in New York City. In a final scene subtler, sadder, and funnier than all previous Roth, the frustrated Zuckerman endures the moralizing of the Minister of Culture, who attacks America for having forgotten that "masterpiece," Betty MacDonald's *The Egg and I.* Associating himself with K., the hero of Kafka's *The Castle*, Zuckerman is furious at his expulsion, and utters a lament for the more overt paranoia he must abandon:

> [H]ere where there's no nonsense about purity and goodness, where the division is not that easy to discern between the heroic and the perverse, where every sort of repression foments a parody of freedom and the suffering of their historical misfortune engenders in its imaginative victims these clownish forms of human despair.

That farewell-to-Prague has as its undersong: here where Zuckerman is not an anomaly but indeed a model of decorum and restraint compared to anyone else who is at all interesting. Perhaps there is another undertone: a farewell-to-Zuckerman on Roth's part. The author of *Zuckerman Bound* at last may have exorcised the afterglow of *Portnoy's Complaint*. There is an eloquent plea for release in *The Anatomy Lesson*, where Zuckerman tries to renounce his fate as a writer:

> It may look to outsiders like the life of freedom—not on a schedule, in command of yourself, singled out for glory, the choice appar-

ently to write about anything. But once one's writing, it's *all* limits. Bound to a subject. Bound to make sense of it. Bound to make a book of it.

Zuckerman bound, indeed, but bound in particular to the most ancient of Covenants—that is Roth's particular election, or self-election. In his critical book *Reading Myself and Others* (1975), the last and best essay, "Looking at Kafka," comments on the change that is manifested in Kafka's later fiction, observing that it is

> touched by a spirit of personal reconciliation and sardonic self acceptance, by a tolerance of one's own brand of madness . . . The piercing masochistic irony . . . has given way here to a critique of the self and its preoccupations that, though bordering on mockery, no longer seeks to resolve itself in images of the uttermost humiliation and defeat. . . . Yet there is more here than a metaphor for the insanely defended ego, whose striving for invulnerability produces a defensive system that must in its turn become the object of perpetual concern—there is also a very unromantic and hardheaded fable about how and why art is made, a portrait of the artist in all his ingenuity, anxiety, isolation, dissatisfaction, relentlessness, obsessiveness, secretiveness, paranoia, and self-addiction, a portrait of the magical thinker at the end of his tether.

Roth intended this as commentary on Kafka's "The Burrow." Eloquent and poignant, it is far more accurate as a descriptive prophecy of *Zuckerman Bound*. Kafka resists nearly all interpretation, so that what most *needs* interpretation in him is his evasion of interpretation. That Roth reads himself into his precursor is a normal and healthy procedure in the literary struggle for self-identification. Unlike Kafka, Roth tries to evade, not interpretation, but guilt, partly because he lives the truth of Kafka's motto of the penal colony: "Guilt is never to be doubted." Roth has earned a permanent place in American literature by a comic genius that need never be doubted again.

Vitality, in the Shakespearean or Falstaffian sense, and its representation in personality and character, is Roth's greatest gift, which is why I would nominate *Sabbath's Theater* (1995) as his sublime achievement. It matters that we see how astonishing a creation *Sabbath's Theater* is. What are the authentic eminences of American fiction in the second half of the twentieth century? My experience as an obsessive reader would center first upon Thomas Pynchon's *The Crying of Lot 49, Gravity's Rainbow*, and *Mason & Dixon*, to which one adds Ursula K. Le Guin's *Left Hand of Darkness*, Cormac McCarthy's *Blood Meridian*, Don DeLillo's *Underworld*, and John Crowley's *Little, Big*. When I turn to Roth, I happily am deluged: the tetralogy *Zuckerman Bound, The Counterlife, Operation Shylock*, and then the American historical sequence that includes *Sabbath's Theater, American Pastoral, I Married a Communist*, and *The Human Stain*. The sheer drive and fecundity of this later Roth makes me think of Faulkner at his earlier splendor: *As I Lay Dying, The Sound and the Fury, Light in August, Absalom, Absalom!* Faulkner upon his heights is a frightening comparison to venture, but *Sabbath's Theater* and *American Pastoral* will sustain the contrast. Nothing even by Roth has the uncanny originality of *As I Lay Dying*, yet *Sabbath's Theater* and the terrible pathos of *American Pastoral* have their own uncanniness. The wildness and freedom of *Portnoy's Complaint* now seem very different when taken as a prelude to the advent of *Sabbath's Theater*, just over a quarter-century later.

The confrontation between Irving Howe and Roth over Roth's supposed self-hatred left some scars upon what ought to be called the novelist's aesthetic consciousness. In Shakespearean terms, Roth writes comedy or tragicomedy, in the mode of the Problem Plays: *Troilus and Cressida, All's Well That Ends Well, Measure for Measure*. The exquisite rancidities of this Shakespearean mode do not appear to be Roth's object. He seems to prefer Falstaff and Lear among Shakespeare's characters, and both of them get into Mickey Sabbath, who necessarily lacks the Falstaffian wit and Learian grandeur. Sabbath is a heroic vitalist, but in retrospect what else is Alex Portnoy? The comedy, painful to start with, hurts unbearably when you reread *Sabbath's Theater*. How hurtful is the hilarity of *Portnoy's Complaint*?

My favorite Yiddish apothegm, since my childhood, I translate as "Sleep faster, we need the pillows." Roth's inescapability is that he has usurped this mode, perhaps not forever, but certainly for the early twenty-first century. Sleeping faster is a cure for the anguish of contamination: by Jewish history, by Kafka, by one's audience after achieving celebrity with *Portnoy's Complaint*.

Alex Portnoy is not going to age into Mickey Sabbath: Roth's protagonists are neither Roth nor one another. But viewing Portnoy retrospectively, through Sabbath's outrageousness, allows readers to see what otherwise we may be too dazzled or too overcome by laughter to realize. Alex Portnoy, however mother-ridden, has an extraordinary potential for more life that he is unlikely to fulfill. Not that fulfillment would be glorious or redemptive; Sabbath's grinding vitalism carries him past the edge of madness. Portnoy, liberal and humane (except, of course, in regard to women he desires), calls himself "rich with rage," but his fiercest anger is light-years away from Sabbath's erotic fury.

Aside from Roth's complex aesthetic maturation, the difference between Portnoy and Sabbath is the shadow of Shakespeare, of King Lear's madness, and of Falstaff's refusal of embitterment and estrangement. Sabbath is fighting for his life, within the limits of what he understands life to be: the erotic, in all its ramifications. So intense is Sabbath that the denunciations directed at him are at once accurate and totally irrelevant, as here from his friend, Norman:

> "The walking panegyric for obscenity," Norman said. "The inverted saint whose message is desecration. Isn't it tiresome in 1994, this role of rebel-hero? What an odd time to be thinking of sex as rebellion. Are we back to Lawrence's gamekeeper? At this late hour? To be out with that beard of yours, upholding the virtues of fetishism and voyeurism. To be out with that belly of yours, championing pornography and flying the flag of your prick. What a pathetic, outmoded old crank you are, Mickey Sabbath. The discredited male polemic's last gasp. Even as the bloodiest of all centuries comes to an end, you're out working day and night to create an erotic scandal. You fucking relic, Mickey! You fifties antique! Linda Lovelace is already light-years behind us, but you persist in quarreling with society as though Eisenhower is president!" But then, almost apologetically, he added, "The immensity of your isolation is horrifying. That's all I really mean to say."
>
> "And there you'd be surprised," Sabbath replied. "I don't think you ever gave isolation a real shot. It's the best preparation I know of for death."

Roth has placed Sabbath near the outer limit of organized society: a beggar, vagrant, and courter of death. It does not matter: Sabbath is redeemed through sheer vitalism. Alex Portnoy now seems more a parody of that frenetic drive. *Portnoy's Complaint* is a marvelous comedy; *Sabbath's Theater* is a tragicomedy, and its Shakespearean reverberations are legitimate and persuasive.

Cormac McCarthy

(b. 1933)

BLOOD MERIDIAN (1985) seems to me the authentic American apocalyptic novel, more relevant now than when it was written. The fulfilled renown of *Moby-Dick* and of *As I Lay Dying* is augmented by *Blood Meridian*, since Cormac McCarthy is the worthy disciple both of Melville and of Faulkner. I venture that no other living American novelist, not even Pynchon, has given us a book as strong and memorable as *Blood Meridian*, much as I appreciate his *Crying of Lot 49*, *Gravity's Rainbow*, and *Mason & Dixon*. McCarthy himself has not matched *Blood Meridian*, but it is the ultimate Western, not to be surpassed.

My concern being the reader, I will begin by confessing that my first two attempts to read through *Blood Meridian* failed, because I flinched from the overwhelming carnage that McCarthy portrays. The violence begins on the novel's second page, when the fifteen-year-old Kid is shot in the back and just below the heart, and continues almost with no respite until the end, thirty years later, when Judge Holden, the most frightening figure in all of American literature, murders the Kid in an outhouse. So appalling are the continuous massacres and mutilations of *Blood Meridian* that one could be reading a United Nations report on the horrors of Syria in 2019.

Nevertheless, I urge the reader to persevere, because *Blood Meridian* is a canonical imaginative achievement, both an American and a universal tragedy of blood. Judge Holden is a villain worthy of Shakespeare, Iago-like and demoniac, a theoretician of war everlasting. And the book's magnificence—its language, landscape, persons, conceptions—at last transcends the violence, and converts goriness into terrifying art, an art comparable to Melville's and to Faulkner's. When I teach the book, many of my students resist it initially (as I did, and as some of my friends continue to do). Television saturates us with actual as well as imagined violence, and I turn away, either in shock or in disgust. But I cannot turn away from *Blood Meridian*, now that I know how to read it, and why it has to be read. None of its carnage is gratuitous or redundant; it belonged to the Mexico–Texas borderlands in 1849–50, which is where and when most of the novel is set. I suppose one could call *Blood Meridian* a "historical novel," since it chronicles the actual expedition of the Glanton gang, a murderous paramilitary force sent out by both Mexican and Texan authorities to murder and scalp as many Indians as possible. Yet it does not have the aura of historical fiction, since what it depicts seethes on, in the United States, and nearly everywhere else, in this third millennium. Judge Holden, the prophet of war, is unlikely to be without honor in our years to come.

Even as you learn to endure the slaughter McCarthy describes, you become accustomed to the book's high style, again as overtly Shakespearean as it is Faulknerian. There are passages of Melvillean-Faulknerian baroque richness and intensity in *The Crying of Lot 49*, and elsewhere in Pynchon, but we can never be sure that they are not parodistic. The prose of *Blood Meridian* soars, yet with its own economy, and its dialogue is always persuasive, particularly when the uncanny Judge Holden speaks:

> The judge placed his hands on the ground. He looked at his inquisitor. This is my claim, he said. And yet everywhere upon it are pockets of autonomous life. Autonomous. In order for it to be mine nothing must be permitted to occur upon it save by my dispensation.
>
> Toadvine sat with his boots crossed before the fire. No man can acquaint himself with everything on this earth, he said.
>
> The judge tilted his great head. The man who believes that the secrets of this world are forever hidden lives in mystery and fear. Superstition will drag him down. The rain will erode the deeds of his life. But that man who sets himself the task of singling out the thread of order from the tapestry will by the decision alone have taken charge of the world and it is only by such taking charge that he will effect a way to dictate the terms of his own fate.

Judge Holden is the spiritual leader of Glanton's filibusters, and McCarthy persuasively gives the self-styled judge a mythic status, appropriate for a deep Machiavelli whose "thread of order" recalls Iago's magic web, in which Othello, Desdemona, and Cassio are caught. Though all of the more colorful and murderous raiders are vividly characterized for us, the killing machine Glanton with the others, the novel turns always upon its two central figures, Judge Holden and the Kid. We first meet the Judge on page six:

an enormous man, bald as a stone, no trace of a beard, and eyes without either brows or lashes. A seven-foot-tall albino, he almost seems to have come from some other world, and we learn to wonder about the Judge, who never sleeps, dances and fiddles with extraordinary art and energy, rapes and murders little children of both sexes, and says that he will never die. By the book's close, I have come to believe that the Judge is immortal. And yet the Judge, while both more and less than human, is as individuated as Iago or Macbeth, and is quite at home in the Texan–Mexican borderlands where we watch him operate in 1849–50, and then find him again in 1878, not a day older after twenty-eight years, though the Kid, a sixteen-year-old at the start of Glanton's foray, is forty-five when murdered by the Judge at the end.

McCarthy subtly shows us the long, slow development of the Kid from another mindless scalper of Indians to the courageous confronter of the Judge in their final debate in a saloon. But though the Kid's moral maturation is heartening, his personality remains largely a cipher, as anonymous as his lack of a name. The three glories of the book are the Judge, the landscape, and (dreadful to say this) the slaughters, which are aesthetically distanced by McCarthy in a number of complex ways.

What is the reader to make of the Judge? He is immortal as principle, as War Everlasting, but is he a person, or something other? McCarthy will not tell us, which is all the better, since the ambiguity is most stimulating. Melville's Captain Ahab, though a Promethean demigod, is necessarily mortal, and perishes with the *Pequod* and all its crew, except for Ishmael. After he has killed the Kid, *Blood Meridian*'s Ishmael, Judge Holden is the last survivor of Glanton's scalping crusade. Destroying the Native American nations of the Southwest is hardly analogous to the hunt to slay Moby Dick, and yet McCarthy gives us some curious parallels between the two quests. The most striking is between Melville's chapter 19, where a ragged prophet who calls himself Elijah warns Ishmael and Queequeg against sailing on the *Pequod*, and McCarthy's chapter 4, where "an old disordered Mennonite" warns the Kid and his comrades not to join Captain Worth's filibuster, a disaster that preludes the greater catastrophe of Glanton's campaign.

McCarthy's invocation of *Moby-Dick*, while impressive and suggestive, in itself does not do much to illuminate Judge Holden for us. Ahab has his preternatural aspects, including his harpooner Fedallah and Parsee whaleboat crew, and the captain's conversion to their Zoroastrian faith. Elijah tells Ishmael touches of other Ahabian mysteries: a three-day trance off Cape Horn, slaying a Spaniard in front of a presumably Catholic altar in Santa Ysabel, and a wholly enigmatic spitting into a "silver calabash." Yet all these are transparencies compared to the enigmas of Judge Holden, who seems to judge the entire earth, and whose name suggests a holding, presumably of sway over all he encounters. And yet the Judge, unlike Ahab, is not wholly fictive; like Glanton, he is a historic filibuster or freebooter. McCarthy tells us most in the Kid's dream visions of Judge Holden, toward the close of the novel:

> In that sleep and in sleep to follow the judge did visit. Who would come other? A great shambling mutant, silent and serene. Whatever his antecedents, he was something wholly other than their sum, nor was there system by which to divide him back into his origins for he would not go. Whoever would seek out his history through what unraveling of loins and ledgerbooks must stand at last darkened and dumb at the shore of a void without terminus or origin and whatever science he might bring to bear upon the dusty primal matter blowing down out of the millennia will discover no trace of ultimate atavistic egg by which to reckon his commencing.

I think that McCarthy is warning his reader that the Judge is Moby Dick rather than Ahab. As another white enigma, the albino Judge, like the albino whale, cannot be slain. Melville, a professed Gnostic, who believed that some "anarch hand or cosmic blunder" had divided us into two fallen sexes, gives us a Manichaean quester in Ahab. McCarthy gives Judge Holden the powers and purposes of the bad angels or demiurges that the Gnostics called archons, but he tells us not to make such an identification (as the critic Leo Daugherty eloquently has). Any "system," including the Gnostic one, will not divide the Judge back into his origins. The "ultimate atavistic egg" will not be found. What can the reader do with the haunting and terrifying Judge?

Let us begin by saying that Judge Holden, though his gladsome prophecy of eternal war is authentically universal, is first and foremost a Western American, no matter how cosmopolitan his background (he speaks all languages, knows all arts and sciences, and can perform magical, shamanistic metamorphoses). The Texan–Mexican border is a superb place for a war-god like the Judge to be. He carries a rifle, mounted in silver, with its name inscribed under the checkpiece: *Et In Arcadia Ego.* In the American Arcadia, death is also always there, incarnated in the Judge's weapon, which never misses. If the American pastoral tradition essentially is the Western film, then the Judge incarnates that tradition, though he would require a director light-years beyond the late Sam Peckinpah, whose *The Wild Bunch* portrays mildness itself when compared to Glanton's paramilitaries. I resort though, as before, to Iago, who transfers war from the camp and the field to every other locale, and is a pyromaniac setting everything and everyone ablaze with the flame of battle. The Judge might be Iago before *Othello* begins, when the war-god Othello was still worshipped by his "honest" color officer, his ancient or ensign. The Judge speaks with an authority that chills me even as Iago leaves me terrified:

> This is the nature of war, whose stake is at once the game and the authority and the justification. Seen so, war is the truest form of divination. It is the testing of one's will and the will of another within that larger will which because it binds them is therefore forced to select. War is the ultimate game because war is at last a forcing of the unity of existence.

If McCarthy does not want us to regard the Judge as a Gnostic archon or supernatural being, the reader may still feel that it hardly seems sufficient to designate Holden as a nineteenth-century Western American Iago. Since *Blood Meridian*, like the much longer *Moby-Dick*, is more prose epic than novel, the Glanton foray can seem a post-Homeric quest, where the various heroes (or thugs) have a disguised god among them, which appears to be the Judge's Herculean role. The Glanton gang passes into a sinister aesthetic glory at the close of chapter 13, when they progress from murdering and scalping Indians to butchering the Mexicans who have hired them:

> They entered the city haggard and filthy and reeking with the blood of the citizenry for whose protection they had contracted. The scalps of the slain villagers were strung from the windows of the governor's house and the partisans were paid out of the all but exhausted coffers and the Sociedad was disbanded and the bounty rescinded. Within a week of their quitting the city there would be a price of eight thousand pesos posted for Glanton's head.

I break into this passage, partly to observe that from this point on, the filibusters pursue the way down and out to an apocalyptic conclusion, but also to urge the reader to hear, and admire, the sublime sentence that follows directly, because we are at the visionary center of *Blood Meridian*:

> They rode out on the north road as would parties bound for El Paso
> but before they were even quite out of sight of the city they had
> turned their tragic mounts to the west and they rode infatuate and
> half fond toward the red demise of that day, toward the evening
> lands and the distant pandemonium of the sun.

Since Cormac McCarthy's language, like Melville's and Faulkner's, frequently is deliberately archaic, the "meridian" of the title probably means the zenith or noon position of the sun in the sky. Glanton, the Judge, the Kid, and their fellows are not described as "tragic"—their long-suffering horses are—and they are "infatuate" and half-mad ("fond") because they have broken away from any semblance of order. McCarthy knows, as does the reader, that an "order" urging the destruction of the entire Native American population of the Southwest is an obscene idea of order, but he wants the reader to know also that the Glanton gang is now aware that they are unsponsored and free to run totally amok. The sentence I have just quoted has a morally ambiguous greatness to it, but that is the greatness of *Blood Meridian*, and indeed of Homer and of Shakespeare. McCarthy so contextualizes the sentence that the amazing contrast between its high gestures and the murderous thugs who evoke the splendor is not ironic but tragic. The tragedy is ours, as readers, and not the Glanton gang's, since we are not going to mourn their demise except for the Kid's, and even there our reaction will be equivocal.

My passion for *Blood Meridian* is so fierce that I want to go on expounding it, but the courageous reader should now be (I hope) pretty well into the main movement of the book. I will confine myself here to the final encounter between the preternatural Judge Holden and the Kid, who had broken with the insane crusade twenty-eight years before, and now at middle age must confront the ageless Judge. Their dialogue is the finest achievement in this book of augmenting wonders, and may move the reader as nothing else in *Blood Meridian* does. I reread it perpetually and cannot persuade myself that I have come to the end of it.

The Judge and the Kid drink together, after the avenging Judge tells the Kid that this night his soul will be demanded of him. Knowing he is no match for the Judge, the Kid nevertheless defies Holden, with laconic replies playing against the Judge's rolling grandiloquence. After demanding to know where their slain comrades are, the Judge asks: "And where is the fiddler and where the dance?"

> I guess you can tell me.
> I tell you this. As war becomes dishonored and its nobility called into question those honorable men who recognize the sanctity of blood will become excluded from the dance, which is the warrior's right, and thereby will the dance become a false dance and the dancers false dancers. And yet there will be one there always who is a true dancer and can you guess who that might be?
> You aint nothin.

To have known Judge Holden, to have seen him in full operation, and to tell him that he is nothing is heroic. "You speak truer than you know," the Judge replies, and two pages later murders the Kid, most horribly. *Blood Meridian*, except for a one-paragraph epilogue, ends with the Judge triumphantly dancing and fiddling at once, and proclaiming that he never sleeps and he will never die. But McCarthy does not let Judge Holden have the last word.

The strangest passage in *Blood Meridian*, the epilogue, is set at dawn, where a nameless man progresses over a plain by means of holes that he makes in the rocky ground. Employing a two-handled implement, the man strikes "the fire out of the rock which God has put there." Around the man are wanderers searching for bones, and he continues to strike fire in the holes, and then they move on. And that is all.

The subtitle of *Blood Meridian* is *The Evening Redness in the West*, which belongs to the Judge, last survivor of the Glanton gang. Perhaps all that the reader can surmise with some certainty is that the man striking fire in the rock at dawn is an opposing figure in regard to the evening redness in the West. The Judge never sleeps, and perhaps will never die, but a new Prometheus may be rising to go up against him.

If there is a pragmatic tradition of the American Sublime, then Cormac McCarthy's fictions are its culmination. *Moby-Dick* and Faulkner's major, early novels are McCarthy's prime precursors. Melville's Ahab fuses together Shakespeare's tragic protagonists—Hamlet, Lear, Macbeth— and crosses them with a quest both Promethean and American. Even as

Montaigne's Plato became Emerson's, so Melville's Shakespeare becomes Cormac McCarthy's. Though critics will go on associating McCarthy with Faulkner, who certainly affected McCarthy's style in *Suttree* (1979), the visionary of *Blood Meridian* (1985) and *The Border Trilogy* (1992, 1994, 1998) has much less in common with Faulkner, and shares more profoundly in Melville's debt to Shakespeare.

Melville, by giving us Ahab and Ishmael, took care to distance the reader from Ahab, if not from his quest. McCarthy's protagonists tend to be apostles of the will-to-identity, except for the Iago-like Judge Holden of *Blood Meridian*, who is the Will Incarnate. John Grady Cole, who survives in *All the Pretty Horses* only to be destroyed in *Cities of the Plain*, is replaced in *The Crossing* by Billy Parham, who is capable of learning what the heroic John Grady Cole evades, the knowledge that Jehovah (Yahweh) holds in his very name: "Where that is I am not." God will be present where and when he chooses to be present, and absent more often than present.

The aesthetic achievement of *All the Pretty Horses* surpasses that of *Cities of the Plain*, if only because McCarthy is too deeply invested in John Grady Cole to let the young man (really still a boy) die with the proper distancing of authorial concern. No one will compose a rival to *Blood Meridian*, not even McCarthy, but *All the Pretty Horses* and *The Crossing* are of the eminence of *Suttree*. If I had to choose a narrative by McCarthy that could stand on its own in relation to *Blood Meridian*, it probably would be *All the Pretty Horses*. John Grady Cole quests for freedom and discovers what neither Suttree nor Billy Parham needs to discover, which is that freedom in an American context is another name for solitude. The self's freedom, for Cormac McCarthy, has no social aspect whatsoever.

I speak of McCarthy as visionary novelist, and not necessarily as a citizen of El Paso, Texas. Emerson identified freedom with power, only available at the crossing, in the shooting of a gulf, a darting to an aim. Since we care for Hamlet, even though he cares for none, we have to assume that Shakespeare also had a considerable investment in Hamlet. The richest aspect of *All the Pretty Horses* is that we learn to care strongly about the development of John Grady Cole, and perhaps we can surmise that Cormac McCarthy is also moved by this most sympathetic of his protagonists.

All the Pretty Horses was published seven years after *Blood Meridian* and is set almost a full century later in history. John Grady Cole is about the same age as McCarthy would have been in 1948. There is no more an identification between McCarthy and the young Cole, who evidently will not live to see twenty, than there is between Shakespeare and Prince Hamlet. And yet the reverberation of a heroic poignance is clearly heard throughout *All the Pretty Horses*. It may be that McCarthy's hard-won authorial detachment toward the Kid in *Blood Meridian* had cost the novelist too much, in the emotional register. Whether my surmise is accurate or not, the reader shares with McCarthy an affectionate stance toward the heroic youth at the center of *All the Pretty Horses*.

Jay Wright
(b. 1934)

I RECALL PURCHASING *The Homecoming Singer* in 1971, at the suggestion of John Hollander. The poem that immediately captured me was the penultimate one, the extraordinary "Sketch for an Aesthetic Project," with its exuberant beginning:

> I stomp about these rooms in an old overcoat,
> never warm, but never very anxious
> to trot off to the thickly banked park,
> where the perpetual rain hangs in the trees,
> even on sunny days.

This wry origin indeed flowered into Jay Wright's ongoing aesthetic project, a mythic journey akin to that of Hart Crane, whose invocatory splendor hovers throughout *The Homecoming Singer*. Like Robert Stepto, I hear in Wright something of Robert Hayden, a touch of T. S. Eliot, and a few traces of other makers, but the undoubted precursor is Hart Crane, uncannily present as "Sketch for an Aesthetic Project" nears its conclusion:

> I have made a log for passage,
> out there, where some still live,
> and pluck my bones.
> There are parchments of blood,
> sunk where I cannot walk.
> But when there is silence here,
> I hear a mythic shriek.

If there is an aura of Eliot here, it remains *The Waste Land* as absorbed and countermanded by *The Bridge*. Wright, very early in his poetic career, seems to station himself on Crane's side in the agon with Eliot, choosing mythmaking, with all its hazards, over received faith:

This shriek in the coldness
is like music returning to me,
coming over the illusion of solitude,
swift and mad as I am,
dark in its act,
light
in the way it fills
my pitiless mind.

The directness of this lyricism has never left Wright, but his development after *The Homecoming Singer* has followed his precursor Crane's
trajectory, from an initial, heightened, rhetorical art of chant to a conceptually difficult mythmaking. Unlike Crane, Wright is a learned poet, and his
interweaving of a dense rhetoricity and an elaborate mythology, African yet
as personal as William Blake's, has kept his audience too sparse until now.
I do not wish to address myself to the complex matter of Jay Wright's place
in African American literary tradition, since I do not qualify as a scholarly
critic of that tradition. He seems to me a black poet only as May Swenson
was a woman poet or as John Hollander was a Jewish poet. The poems of
all these establish themselves as powerful utterances *within* the tradition
of utterance that is American poetry. Only later do I ponder the relation
of Swenson's riddles to Dickinson's, or of Hollander's plangent humor to
Moshe Leib Halpern's, or of Wright's rhapsodic liturgies to Hayden's prior
transformation of Hart Crane's symbolism in an African American context.

In Wright's powerful book *Soothsayers and Omens*, the final chant,
"The Dead," gives the central statement of his poetics, at least as I comprehend his vision. After admonishing his readers that our learning alone
cannot suffice, since "it is not enough / to sip the knowledge / of our failings," the poet chants an intricate rhapsody of the self's return from its
own achieved emptiness:

The masks dance
on this small point, and lead
this soul, these souls,
into the rhythm
of the eye stripped of sight,
the hand stripped of touch,
the heart stripped of love,

the body stripped of its own beginning,
into the rhythm
of emptiness and return,
into the self
moving against itself,
into the self
moving into itself,
the word, and the first design.

The *askesis* here is Wright's characteristic apotropaic gesture toward tradition, toward all his traditions. As an immensely learned poet, Wright tries to defend himself against incessant allusiveness by stripping his diction, sometimes to an astonishing sparseness. The same movement in W. S. Merwin damaged his art, but Wright's minimalism is fortunately not nearly so prevalent. His most characteristic art returns always to that commodious lyricism I associate with American poetry at its most celebratory, in Whitman, in Stevens, in Crane, in Ashbery. The ode "Desire's Persistence," which may be his strongest poem to date, opens out into a majestic epiphany of what the sage Emerson declared as the American Newness:

WINTER

Under the evergreens,
the grouse have gone under the snow.
Women who follow their fall flight
tell us that, if you listen, you can hear
their dove's voices ridge the air,
a singing that follows us to a bourne
                released from its heat sleep.
We have come to an imagined line,
                celestial,
that binds us to the burr of a sheltered thing
and rings us with a fire that will not dance,
in a horn that will not sound.
We have learned, like these birds,
to publish our decline,
when over knotted apples and straw-crisp leaves,

the slanted sun welcomes us once again
to the arrested music in the earth's divided embrace.

This intricate music, eloquently arrested and divided, conveys a north-ern New England ambiance, the poet's most persistent context in these mature years of his solitude. What matters most about this Winter chant is its astonishingly achieved high style, its hushed yet piercingly pitched voice altogether Wright's own. The birds' singing yields to the now soundless, stationary image of desire's flame, a desire paradoxically kept constant by its temporal awareness both of cyclic renewal and of cyclic decline.

It is not to be believed, by me, that a verbal art this absolute will continue to suffer neglect. A Pindaric sublimity that allies Hölderlin, Rilke, and Hart Crane with Jay Wright is not now much in fashion, but that mode of high song always returns to us again. As an authentic poet of the Sublime, Wright labors to make us forsake easier pleasures for more difficult plea-sures. Wright's reader is taught by him what Hölderlin and Rilke wished us to learn, which is that poetry compels us to answer the fearful triple question: More? Equal to? or Less than? Self is set against self, or an ear-lier version of the self against a later one, or culture against culture, or poem against poem. Jay Wright is a permanent American poet because he induces us to enter that agon—with past strength, our own or others'; with the desolations of culture; with the sorrows of history—and because he persuades us also that "it is not enough / to sip the knowledge / of our failings."

Don DeLillo

(b. 1936)

$\mathbf{D}$ON DELILLO'S masterwork is *Underworld* (1997), which is long, uneven, and wonderful. *White Noise* (1985) would appear to be his most popular novel: the paperback in which I have just reread it is the thirty-first printing. I doubt that it will prove as permanent as *Underworld*, but revisiting it demonstrates that the novel is much more than a period piece. Critics frequently associate DeLillo with William Gaddis and Robert Coover, as with the formidable Thomas Pynchon. *Underworld* is something different, and may have more affinities with Philip Roth than with Pynchon. DeLillo, in *White Noise*, is a High Romantic in the age of virtual reality and related irrealisms. Frank Lentricchia, DeLillo's canonical critic, is accurate in suggesting that Jack Gladney descends from Joyce's Poldy Bloom, and like Poldy, DeLillo's protagonist has a touch of the poet about him. One large difference is that Gladney is a first-person narrator; another is that Poldy has a benign immensity that Gladney cannot match. Though another cuckold, Poldy is a Romantic individualist, like Joyce himself. A century later, the amiable Gladney is trapped in a network of systems, another unit in the Age of Information.

DeLillo is a comedian of the spirit, haunted by omens of the end of our time. *White Noise* is very funny, and very disturbing: it is another of the American comic apocalypses that include Mark Twain's *The Mysterious Stranger*, Herman Melville's *The Confidence Man*, Nathanael West's *Miss Lonelyhearts*, and Pynchon's *The Crying of Lot 49*. That is a high order of company, and *White Noise* almost sustains it.

DeLillo is a master of deadpan outrageousness: Jack Gladney is chairman and professor of Hitler Studies at the College-on-the-Hill. Though he is the American inventor of his discipline, Gladney has no affective reaction to Hitler: it appears to be a subject like any other these days.

But all of *White Noise* is comic outrage; everything becomes funny, be it the fear of death, adultery, airborne toxic events, the struggles of the family romance, advanced supermarkets, or what you will. Simultaneously, everything becomes anxious, in a world where even the nuns only pretend to believe, and where the first three of Gladney's four wives each had some connection to the world of espionage.

Until *Underworld*, DeLillo's characters are curious blends of personalities and ideograms. Gladney is such a blend: we are persuaded by his love for Babette, his adulterous but well-meaning wife, and by his warm relations with his rather varied children. And yet he is just as much Fear-of-Death as he is a husband and a father.

Where is DeLillo in *White Noise*? Close to the end of the book, he gives us a long paragraph of astonishing power and distinction, one of the most memorable passages in American writing of the later twentieth century:

> We go to the overpass all the time. Babette, Wilder and I. We take a thermos of iced tea, park the car, watch the setting sun. Clouds are no deterrent. Clouds intensify the drama, trap the shape of light. Heavy overcasts have little effect. Light bursts through, tracers and smoky arcs. Overcasts enhance the mood. We find little to say to each other. More cars arrive, parking in a line that extends down to the residential zone. People walk up the incline and onto the overpass, carrying fruit and nuts, cool drinks, mainly the middle-aged, the elderly, some with webbed beach chairs which they set out on the sidewalk, but younger couples also, arm in arm at the rail, looking west. The sky takes on content, feeling, an exalted narrative life. The bands of color reach so high, seem at times to separate into their constituent parts. There are turreted skies, light storms, softly falling streamers. It is hard to know how we should feel about this. Some people are scared by the sunsets, some determined to be elated, but most of us don't know how to feel, are ready to go either way. Rain is no deterrent. Rain brings on graded displays, wonderful running hues. More cars arrive, people come trudging up the incline. The spirit of these warm evenings is hard to describe. There is anticipation in the air but it is not the expectant midsummer hum of a shirtsleeve crowd, a sandlot game, with coherent precedents, a history of secure response. The waiting is introverted, uneven, almost backward and shy, tending toward silence. What else do we feel? Certainly there is awe, it is all awe, it transcends previous categories of awe, but we don't know whether we are watching in wonder or dread, we don't know

what we are watching or what it means, we don't know whether it is permanent, a level of experience to which we will gradually adjust, into which our uncertainty will eventually be absorbed, or just some atmospheric weirdness, soon to pass. The collapsible chairs are yanked open, the old people sit. What is there to say? The sunsets linger and so do we. The sky is under a spell, power-ful and storied. Now and then a car actually crosses the overpass, moving slowly, deferentially. People keep coming up the incline, some in wheelchairs, twisted by disease, those who attend them bending low to push against the grade. I didn't know how many handicapped and helpless people there were in town until the warm nights brought crowds to the overpass. Cars speed beneath us, coming from the west, from out of the towering light, and we watch them as if for a sign, as if they carry on their painted surfaces some residue of the sunset, a barely detectable luster or film of telltale dust. No one plays a radio or speaks in a voice that is much above a whisper. Something golden falls, a softness delivered to the air. There are people walking dogs, there are kids on bikes, a man with a camera and long lens, waiting for his moment. It is not until some time after dark has fallen, the insects screaming in the heat, that we slowly begin to disperse, shyly, politely, car after car, restored to our separate and defensible selves.

It is a major American prose poem, marked by the aura of the airborne toxic event, and yet balanced upon the edge of a transcendental revela-tion. DeLillo, who is so easily mistaken for a Postmodernist End-Gamer, is rather clearly a visionary, a late Emersonian American Romantic, like the Wallace Stevens who turns blankly on the sand in "The Auroras of Autumn." Light bursts through, and the sky, as in Stevens, takes on an exalted narrative life. Awe transcends fear, transcends the past of awe. Is it wonder or dread, an epiphany or mere reductive pollution? What matters is that brightness falls from the air, before all the viewers return to their separate selves.

This is more than Transcendentalism in the last ditch, or Romanticism on the wane. Nothing is affirmed, not even illusion. We turn to DeLillo for woe and wonder alike, accurately persuaded of his high artistry, of some-thing well beyond a study of the nostalgias.

With the passing of Philip Roth, one can venture that the major American novelists now at work are Thomas Pynchon, Don DeLillo, and Cormac McCarthy, while Nell Freudenberger, Joshua Cohen, and William Giraldi lead a generation of younger writers. For DeLillo, I would name these as *White Noise, Libra,* and *Underworld,* certainly his principal book up to this time. Roth, immensely prolific, wrote his masterpiece in the scabrous *Sabbath's Theater,* while his tetralogy, *Zuckerman Bound,* and *American Pastoral* are equally likely to survive our era. McCarthy's *Blood Meridian* continues to overwhelm me: *Suttree* before it, *All the Pretty Horses* later, also should be permanent. Pynchon, named by Tony Tanner as DeLillo's precursor, is central to our narrative fiction. *The Crying of Lot 49* and *Gravity's Rainbow* have defined our culture—to call it that—and *Mason & Dixon* is even more remarkable, a work of amazing geniality and a kind of hopeless hope.

If just four recent fictions are to be selected for the United States in the early years of the twenty-first century, then name them as *Blood Meridian, Sabbath's Theater, Mason & Dixon,* and *Underworld.* All of DeLillo is in *Underworld,* and so is New York City 1951–96. He has not written the epic of the city; perhaps Hart Crane did that forever, with *The Bridge* (1930). But DeLillo's sense of America, in the second half of the twentieth century, is achieved perfectly in *Underworld.*

DeLillo, a wisdom writer, makes no Hemingwayesque attempt to challenge Shakespeare and Tolstoy. Nor does he desire any contest with Pynchon, though Tony Tanner shrewdly implies that this was unavoidable. Pynchon's cosmos of paranoia, indispensable waste, plastic consumerism is the literary context of *Underworld.* DeLillo is highly aware of his own belatedness, yet his resources are extraordinary, and he so subsumes Pynchon so as to achieve a distinguished triumph over any anguish of contamination that might have impeded *Underworld.* By the time the vast book concludes, DeLillo's relation to Pynchon is like Pynchon's own relation to *The Recognitions* of William Gaddis and to Borges. The Pynchon–DeLillo implicit contest becomes akin to *Blood Meridian*'s struggle with Melville and Faulkner or Roth's permanent status as Franz Kafka's grandnephew (as it were).

Tanner, disappointed with *Underworld,* argued otherwise, and sometimes cannot be refuted. I wince when Tanner observes: "And, crucially, *Underworld* has no Tristero." Tristero remains the greatest of Pynchonian inventions: *The Crying of Lot 49*'s sublimely mad, subversive alternative to the United States Postal Service is not matched by *Gravity's Rainbow*'s interplay between the System and the Zone. Nor, as Tanner insists, does *Underworld* have so persuasive a universal connection to justify its declarations that everything is linked and connected. But again, DeLillo knows this and makes of his supposed weakness a radical strength.

Tanner is again accurate when he observes that Nick Shay, DeLillo's surrogate, as a character is just not there at all, nor does Shay want to be. The only character with a consciousness before Mason and Dixon, anywhere in Pynchon, is Oedipa Maas, and she is there only in the closing moments of the novella. The only consciousness in DeLillo is DeLillo; despite his supposed Postmodernism, he is a High Romantic Transcendentalist determined not to be out of his time. If there is religiosity in *Underworld*, it is not DeLillo's and is portrayed as part of the waste. And yet there is something more profound than mere nostalgia in DeLillo's Romanticism. His authentic masters are Emerson, Thoreau, Whitman, and his visions, flashing out against the noise and the waste, are enduring illuminations.

At the opening of "Self-Reliance," Emerson gave us a superb irony:

> In every work of genius we recognize our own rejected thoughts: they come back to us with a certain alienated majesty.

DeLillo lovingly parodies this in Nick Shay's final meditation:

> Maybe we feel a reverence for waste, for the redemptive qualities of the things we use and discard. Look how they come back to us, alight with a kind of brave aging.

Tanner was anxious about the epiphanies of DeLillo's urban transcendentalism, and wondered if they were only evidences of a decayed Catholicism. And yet, DeLillo's vibrant Emersonianism seems to me clear enough. *Underworld*, which Tanner says is totally reliant on history, actually is self-reliant and like Emerson is adversarial to history. Old Bronx boy and baseball fan that I am (like DeLillo, addicted to the Yankees), I thrill to the Prologue of *Underworld*, which I wish had kept its title of "Pafko at the Wall." Though you *could* say that DeLillo is following baseball history in his vision of Bobby Thomson's "Shot Heard Round the World" in October 1951, I myself have strong memories of that moment at the old Polo

Grounds, and what I recall is mere history, and "it is all falling indelibly into the past." Romantic vision of the high mode, whether in "Song of Myself" or *Underworld*, is precisely what does not fall.

Thomas Pynchon
(b. 1937)

W E ALL CARRY about with us our personal catalog of the experiences that matter most—our own versions of what they used to call the Sublime. So far as aesthetic experience in twentieth-century America is concerned, I myself have a short list for the American Sublime: the war that concludes the Marx Brothers' *Duck Soup*; Faulkner's *As I Lay Dying*; Wallace Stevens's "The Auroras of Autumn"; nearly all of Hart Crane; Charlie Parker playing "Parker's Mood" and "I Remember You"; Bud Powell performing "Un Poco Loco"; Nathanael West's *Miss Lonelyhearts*; and the story of Byron the lightbulb in Pynchon's *Gravity's Rainbow*.

I am not suggesting that there is not much more of the Sublime in *Gravity's Rainbow* than the not quite eight pages that make up the story of Byron the Bulb. Pynchon is the greatest master of the negative Sublime at least since Faulkner and West, and if nothing besides Byron the Bulb in *Gravity's Rainbow* seems to me quite as perfect as all of *The Crying of Lot 49*, that may be because no one could hope to write the first authentic post-Holocaust novel and achieve a total vision without fearful cost. Yet the story of Byron the Bulb, for me, touches one of the limits of art, and I want to read it very closely here, so as to suggest what is most vital and least problematic about Pynchon's achievement as a writer, indeed as the crucial American writer of prose fiction at the present time.

For Pynchon, ours is the age of plastics and paranoia, corporations and capitalists dominated by the System. No one is going to dispute such a conviction; reading *The New York Times* first thing every morning is sufficient to convince one that not even Pynchon's imagination can match journalistic irreality. What is more startling about Pynchon is that he has found ways of representing the impulse to defy the System, even though both the impulse and its representations always are defeated. In the Zone (which is our cosmos as the Gnostics saw it, the *kenoma* or Great Emptiness) the force of the System, of They (whom the Gnostics called the Archons), is in some sense irresistible, as all overdetermination must be irresistible. Yet there is a Counterforce, hardly distinguished in its efficacy, but it never does (or can) give up. Unfortunately, its hero is the extraordinarily ordinary Tyrone Slothrop, who is a perpetual disaster, and whose ultimate fate, being "scattered" (rather in the biblical sense), is accomplished by Pynchon with dismaying literalness. And yet, Slothrop, who has not inspired much affection even in Pynchon's best critics, remains more hero than antihero, despite the critics, and despite Pynchon himself.

There are more than four hundred named characters in *Gravity's Rainbow*, and perhaps twenty of these have something we might want to call personality, but only Tyrone Slothrop (however negatively) could be judged a self-representation (however involuntary) on the author's part. Slothrop is a Kabbalistic version of Pynchon himself, rather in the way that Scythrop the poet in Thomas Love Peacock's *Nightmare Abbey* is intentionally a loving satire upon Peacock's friend the poet Shelley, but Kabbalistically is a representation of Peacock himself. I am not interested in adding *Nightmare Abbey* to the maddening catalog of "sources" for *Gravity's Rainbow* (though Slothrop's very name probably alludes to Scythrop's, with the image of a giant sloth replacing the acuity of the Shelleyan scythe). What does concern me is the Kabbalistic winding path that is Pynchon's authentic and Gnostic image for the route through the *kelipot* or evil husks that the light must take if it is to survive in the ultimate breaking of the vessels, the Holocaust brought about by the System at its most evil, yet hardly at its most prevalent.

The not unimpressive polemic of Norman Mailer—that fascism always lurks where plastic dominates—is in Pynchon not a polemic but a total vision. Mailer, for all his legitimate status as Representative Man, lacks invention except in *Ancient Evenings*, and there he cannot discipline his inventiveness. Pynchon surpasses every American writer since Faulkner at invention, which Dr. Samuel Johnson, greatest of Western literary critics, rightly considered to be the essence of poetry or fiction. What can be judged Pynchon's greatest talent is his vast control, a preternatural ability to order so immense an exuberance at invention. Pynchon's supreme aesthetic quality is what Hazlitt called "gusto," or what Blake intended in his Infernal proverb: "Exuberance is Beauty."

Sadly, that is precisely what the Counterforce lacks: gusto. Slothrop never gives up; always defeated, he goes on, bloody and bowed, but has to yield to entropy, to a dread scattering. Yet he lacks all exuberance; he is the American as conditioned reflex, colorless and hapless.

Nothing holds or could hold *Gravity's Rainbow* together—except Slothrop. When he is finally scattered, the book stops, and the apocalyptic rocket blasts off. Still, Slothrop is more than a Derridaean dissemination, if only because he does enable Pynchon to gather together 760 pages. Nor is *Gravity's Rainbow* what is now called "a text." It is a novel, with a beginning, an end, and a monstrous conglomerate of middles. This could not be if the *schlemiel* Slothrop were wholly antipathetic. Instead, he does enlist something crucial in the elitest reader, a something that is scattered when the hero, poor Plasticman or Rocketman, is apocalyptically scattered.

Pynchon, as Richard Poirier said, is a weird blend of the esoteric and insanely learned with the popular or the supposedly popular. Or, to follow Pynchon's own lead, he is a Kabbalistic writer, esoteric not only in his theosophical allusiveness (like Yeats) but actually in his deeper patterns (like Malcolm Lowry in *Under the Volcano*). A Kabbalistic novel is something beyond an oxymoron not because the Kabbalah does not tell stories (it does) but because its stories are all exegetical, however wild and mythical. That does give a useful clue for reading Pynchon, who always seems not so much to be telling his bewildering, labyrinthine story as to be writing a wistful commentary upon it as a story already twice told, though it hasn't been, and truly can't be told at all.

That returns us to Byron the Bulb, whose story can't be told because poor Byron the indomitable really is immortal. He can never burn out, which at least is an annoyance for the whole paranoid System, and at most is an embarrassment for them. They cannot compel Byron to submit to the law of entropy, or the death drive, and yet they can deny him any context in which his immortality will at last be anything but a provocation to his own madness. A living reminder that the System can never quite win, poor Byron the Bulb becomes a death-in-life reminder that the System also can never quite lose. Byron, unlike Slothrop, cannot be scattered, but his high consciousness represents the dark fate of the Gnosis in Pynchon's vision. For all its negativity, Gnosticism remains a mode of transcendental belief. Pynchon's is a Gnosis without transcendence. There is a Counterforce, but there is no fathering and mothering abyss to which it can return.

And yet the lightbulb is named Byron, and is a source of light and cannot burn out. Why Byron? Well, he could hardly be Goethe the Bulb or Wordsworth the Bulb or even Joyce the Bulb. There must be the insouciance of personal myth in his name. Probably he could have been Oscar the Bulb, after the author of *The Importance of Being Earnest* or of that marvelous fairy tale "The Remarkable Rocket." Or perhaps he might have been Groucho the Bulb. But Byron the Bulb is best, and not merely for ironic purposes. Humiliated but immortal, this Byron, too, might proclaim:

> But there is that within me which shall tire
> Torture and Time, and breathe when I expire;
> Something unearthly, which they deem not of,
> Like the remembered tone of a mute lyre.

Byron the Bulb is essentially Childe Harold in the Zone:

> He would not yield dominion of his mind
> To spirits against whom his own rebell'd.

Like Childe Harold, Byron the Bulb is condemned to the fate of all High-Romantic Prometheans:

> there is a fire
> And motion of the soul which will not dwell
> In its own narrow being, but aspire
> Beyond the fitting medium of desire;
> And, but once kindled, quenchless evermore,
> Preys upon high adventure, nor can tire
> Of aught but rest; a fever at the core,
> Fatal to him who bears, to all who ever bore.

There are, alas, no high adventures for Byron the Bulb. We see him first in the Bulb Baby Heaven, maintained by the System or Company as part of its business of fostering demiurgic illusions:

> One way or another, these Bulb folks are in the business of pro-
> viding the appearance of power, power against the night, without
> the reality.

From the start, Byron is an anomaly, attempting to recruit the other Baby Bulbs in his great crusade against the Company. His is already a voice in the Zone, since he is as old as time.

Trouble with Byron's he's an old, old soul, trapped inside the glass prison of a Baby Bulb.

Like the noble Lord Byron plotting to lead the Greeks in their revolution against the Turks, Byron the Bulb has his High-Romantic vision:

> When M-Day finally does roll around, you can bet Byron's elated. He has passed the time hatching some really insane grandiose plans— he's gonna organize all the Bulbs, see, get him a power base in Berlin, he's already hep to the Strobing Tactic, all you do is develop the knack (Yogic, almost) of shutting off and on at a rate close to the human brain's alpha rhythm, and you can actually trigger an *epileptic fit*! True. Byron has had a vision against the rafters of his ward, of 20 million Bulbs, all over Europe, at a given synchronizing pulse arranged by one of his many agents in the Grid, all these Bulbs beginning to strobe *together*, humans thrashing around the 20 million rooms like fish on the beaches of Perfect Energy—Attention, humans, this has been a warning to you. Next time, a few of us will *explode*. Ha-ha. Yes we'll unleash our *Kamikaze squads*! You've heard of the Kirghiz Light? well that's the ass end of a firefly compared to what we're gonna—oh, you haven't heard of the—oh, well, too bad. Cause a few Bulbs, say a million, a mere 5% of our number, are more than willing to flame out in one grand burst instead of patiently waiting out their design hours. . . . So Byron dreams of his Guerrilla Strike Force, gonna get Herbert Hoover, Stanley Baldwin, all of them, right in the face with one coordinated blast.

The rhetoric of bravado here is tempered and defeated by a rhetoric of desperation. A rude awakening awaits Byron, because the System has in place already its branch, "Phoebus," the international lightbulb cartel, headquartered of course in Switzerland. Phoebus, god of light and of pestilence, "determines the operational lives of all the bulbs in the world," and yet does not as yet know that Byron, rebel against the cartel's repression, is immortal. As an immortal, bearer of the Gnostic Spark or *pneuma*, Byron must acquire knowledge, initially the sadness of the knowledge of love:

> One by one, over the months, the other bulbs burn out, and are gone. The first few of these hit Byron hard. He's still a new arrival,

still hasn't accepted his immortality. But on through the burning hours he starts to learn about the transience of others: learns that loving them while they're here becomes easier, and also more intense—to love as if each design-hour will be the last. Byron soon enough becomes a Permanent Old-Timer. Others can recognize his immortality on sight, but it's never discussed except in a general way, when folklore comes flickering in from other parts of the Grid, tales of the Immortals, one in a kabbalist's study in Lyons who's supposed to know magic, another in Norway outside a warehouse facing arctic whiteness with a stoicism more southerly bulbs begin strobing faintly just at the thought of. If other Immortals *are* out there, they remain silent. But it is a silence with much, perhaps, everything, in it.

A silence that may have everything in it is a Gnostic concept but falls away into the silence of impotence, on the part of the other bulbs, when the System eventually sends its agent to unscrew Byron:

At 800 hours—another routine precaution—a Berlin agent is sent out to the opium den to transfer Byron. She is wearing asbestos-lined kid gloves and seven-inch spike heels, no not so she can fit in with the crowd, but so that she can reach that sconce to unscrew Byron. The other bulbs watch, in barely subdued terror. The word goes out along the Grid. At something close to the speed of light, every bulb, Azos looking down the empty black Bakelite streets, Nitralampen and Wotan Gs at night soccer matches, Just-Wolframs, Monowatts and Siriuses, every bulb in Europe knows what's happened. They are silent with impotence, with surrender in the face of struggles they thought were all myth. *We can't help*, this common thought humming through pastures of sleeping sheep, down Autobahns and to the bitter ends of coaling piers in the North, *there's never been anything we could do.* . . . Anyone shows us the meanest hope of transcending and the Committee on Incandescent Anomalies comes in and takes him away. Some do protest, maybe, here and there, but it's only information, glow-modulated, harmless, nothing close to the explosions in the faces of the powerful that Byron once envisioned, back there in his Baby ward, in his innocence.

Romantics are Incandescent Anomalies, a phrase wholly appropriate to John Ashbery's belated self-illuminations also, defeated epiphanies that always ask the question: Was it information? The information that Pynchon gives us has Byron taken to a "control point," where he burns on until the committee on Incandescent Anomalies sends a hit man after him. Like the noble Lord Byron, who was more than half in love with easeful death before he went off to die in Greece, Byron the Bulb is now content to be recycled also, but he is bound upon his own wheel of fire, and so must continue as a now involuntary prophet and hero:

> But here something odd happens. Yes, damned odd. The plan is to smash up Byron and send him back right there in the shop to cullet and batch—salvage the tungsten, of course—and let him be reincarnated in the glassblower's next project (a balloon setting out on a journey from the top of a white skyscraper). This wouldn't be too bad a deal for Byron—he knows as well as Phoebus does how many hours he has on him. Here in the shop he's watched enough glass being melted back into the structureless pool from which all glass forms spring and re-spring, and wouldn't mind going through it himself. But he is trapped on the Karmic wheel. The glowing orange batch is a taunt, a cruelty. There's no escape for Byron, he's doomed to an infinite regress of sockets and bulbsnatchers. In zips young Hansel Geschwindig, a Weimar street urchin—twirls Byron out of the ceiling into a careful pocket and Gesssschhhhwindig! out the door again. Darkness invades the dreams of the glassblower. Of all the unpleasantries his dreams grab in out of the night air, an extinguished light is the worst. Light, in his dreams, was always hope: the basic, mortal hope. As the contacts break helically away, hope turns to darkness, and the glassblower wakes sharply tonight crying, "Who? *Who?*"

Byron the Bulb's Promethean fire is now a taunt and a cruelty. A mad comedy, "an infinite regress of sockets and bulbsnatchers," will be the poor Bulb's destiny, a repetition-compulsion akin to the entropic flight and scattering of the heroic *schlemiel* Slothrop. The stone-faced search parties of the Phoebus combine move out into the streets of Berlin. But Byron is off upon his unwilling travels: Berlin to Hamburg to Helgoland to Nürnberg, until (after many narrow escapes):

He is scavenged next day (the field now deathempty, columned, pale, streaked with long mudpuddles, morning clouds lengthening behind the gilded swastika and wreath) by a poor Jewish ragpicker, and taken on, on into another 15 years of preservation against chance and against Phoebus. He will be screwed into mother (*Mutter*) after mother, as the female threads of German light-bulb sockets are known, for some reason that escapes everybody.

Can we surmise the reason? The cartel gives up, and decides to declare Byron legally burned out, a declaration that deceives nobody:

Through his years of survival, all these various rescues of Byron happen as if by accident. Whenever he can, he tries to instruct any bulbs nearby in the evil nature of Phoebus, and in the need for solidarity against the cartel. He has come to see how Bulb must move beyond its role as conveyor of light-energy alone. Phoebus has restricted Bulb to this one identity. "But there are other frequencies, above and below the visible band. Bulb can give heat. Bulb can provide energy for plants to grow, illegal plants, inside closets, for example. Bulb can penetrate the sleeping eye, and operate among the dreams of men." Some bulbs listened attentively—others thought of ways to fink to Phoebus. Some of the older anti-Byronists were able to fool with their parameters in systematic ways that would show up on the ebonite meters under the Swiss mountain: there were even a few self-immolations, hoping to draw the hit men down.

This darkness of vain treachery helps to flesh out the reason for Byron's survival. Call it the necessity of myth, or of gossip aging productively into myth. Not that Phoebus loses any part of its profit; rather, it establishes a subtler and more intricate international cartel pattern:

Byron, as he burns on, sees more and more of this pattern. He learns how to make contact with other kinds of electric appliances, in homes, in factories and out in the streets. Each has something to tell him. The pattern gathers in his soul (*Seele*, as the core of the earlier carbon filament was known in Germany), and the grander and clearer it grows, the more desperate Byron gets. Someday he will know everything, and still be as impotent as before. His youthful dreams of organizing all the bulbs in the world seem impossible now—the Grid is wide open, all messages can be overheard, and there are more than enough traitors out on the line. Prophets traditionally don't last long—they are either killed outright, or given an accident serious enough to make them stop and think, and most often they do pull back. But on Byron has been visited an even better fate. He is condemned to go on forever, knowing the truth and powerless to change anything. No longer will he seek to get off the wheel. His anger and frustration will grow without limit, and he will find himself, poor perverse bulb, enjoying it.

This seems to me the saddest paragraph in all of Pynchon; at least, it hurts me the most. In it is Pynchon's despair of his own Gnostic Kabbalah, since Byron the Bulb does achieve the Gnosis, complete knowledge, but purchases that knowledge by impotence, the loss of power. Byron can neither be martyred nor betray his own prophetic vocation. What remains is madness: limitless rage and frustration, which at last he learns to enjoy.

That ends the story of Byron the Bulb, and ends something in Pynchon also. What is left is the studying of new modalities of post-Apocalyptic silence. Pynchon seems now to be where his precursor Emerson prophesied the American visionary must be:

There may be two or three or four steps, according to the genius of each, but for every seeing soul there are two absorbing facts,—*I and the Abyss*.

If at best the *I* is an immortal but hapless lightbulb and the *Abyss*, our Gnostic foremother and forefather, is the socket into which that poor *I* of a bulb is screwed, then the two absorbing facts themselves have ceased to absorb.

Sources and Acknowledgments

The text in this book is set in 10 point New Caledonia, originally designed in 1939 under the name Cornelia for the Mergenthaler factory in Berlin by American designer William A. Dwiggins. Diagnosed with diabetes in 1922 (the year he apparently coined the term "graphic designer"), Dwiggins changed the focus of his career, scorning advertising and focusing on book design, illustration, and calligraphy: "I will produce art on paper and wood after my own heart with no heed to any market." When he created Cornelia he was inspired by a new version of the popular nineteenth-century font Scotch Roman that had been created for the Mergenthaler foundry in New York. In 1982 Alex Kaczun reworked Dwiggins's typeface for Linotype and released it as New Caledonia. The chapter titles are set in Chronicle Display by Hoefler Type; other display elements are in Idlewild (Hoefler) and Trade Gothic Next (Linotype).

The paper is an acid-free Forest Stewardship Council–certified stock that exceeds the requirements for permanence of the American National Standards Institute. The binding material is Arrestox, a cotton-based cloth with an aqueous acrylic coating manufactured by Holliston, Church Hill, Tennessee. Text design and composition by Gopa & Ted2, Inc., Albuquerque, New Mexico. Printing by McNaughton & Gunn, Saline, Michigan; binding by Dekker Bookbinding, Grand Rapids.